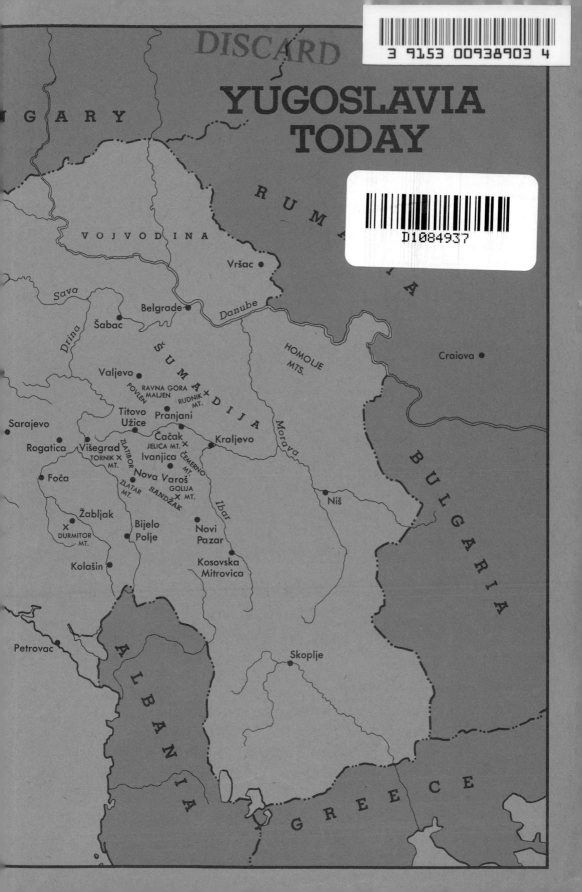

YUGOSLAVIA TODAY

HUNGARY

RUMANIA

VOJVODINA

Vršac •

Sava

Belgrade •

Danube

Craiova •

Drina

Šabac •

HOMOLJE
MTS.

Š
U
M
A
D
I
J
A

Valjevo •

RAVNA GORA
POVLEN MALJEN
RUDNIK
MT.

Morava

BULGARIA

Sarajevo •

Titovo
Užice

Pranjani •

Kraljevo •

Čačak
JELICA MT. ✕

Rogatica •

Višegrad •
ZLATIBOR
TORNIK ✕
MT.

Ivanjica •
ČEMERNO
MT. ✕

Foča •

Nova Varoš •
ZLATAR
MT.
SANDŽAK
GOLIJA
✕ MT.

Ibar

Niš •

Žabljak •
✕
DURMITOR
MT.

Bijelo
Polje •

Novi
Pazar •

Kolašin •

Kosovska
Mitrovica •

Petrovac •

A
L
B
A
N
I
A

Skoplje •

G R E E C E

TITO,
MIHAILOVIĆ
AND
THE ALLIES,
1941-1945

TITO, MIHAILOVIĆ AND THE ALLIES, 1941-1945

Walter R. Roberts

RUTGERS UNIVERSITY PRESS
New Brunswick, New Jersey

Library of Congress Cataloging in Publication Data

Roberts, Walter R   1916–
    Tito, Mihailović and the Allies, 1941–1945.
    Bibliography: p.
    1. World War, 1939–1945—Yugoslavia.   2. Tito,
Josip Broz, Pres. Yugoslavia, 1892–   3. Mihailović,
Draža, 1893–1946.   4. World War, 1939–1945—Diplomatic
history.   I. Title.
D754.Y9R6   940.53′497   72–4197
ISBN 0–8135–0740–5

Manufactured in the United States of America
by Quinn & Boden Company, Inc., Rahway, New Jersey

To GISA

Contents

Maps

Photographs

Preface

In 1960, the United States Government assigned me to the American Embassy in Belgrade as Counselor for Press and Cultural Affairs. It was my first real connection with Yugoslavia. In preparation for the assignment, I read avidly, especially on the country's history. But as my reading brought me up to Yugoslavia's role in World War II and the relations between the Allies and the different Yugoslav factions inside and outside the country, I found that the literature disintegrated into confusion and contradiction. Writers who espoused the cause of the Communist Partisans gave a version of the facts most often completely at variance with accounts by supporters of the Royalist Četniks.

There are many books and monographs printed in Yugoslavia since 1945 which eulogize the Partisans. In this category falls Vladimir Dedijer's *Josip Broz Tito,* which in an abridged English version has received wide distribution in Britain and America. It is a complete endorsement of the Communist case. Books written by emigrant Yugoslavs, such as Constantin Fotić's *The War We Lost,* depict the Royalist Četniks as if they could have done no wrong. Even the British-American literature covering the period of 1941–45 emanates almost invariably from protagonists of one side or the other and mostly from participants in Yugoslav events; for instance, a number of them were liaison officers with either the Partisans or the Četniks. Fitzroy Maclean's *Disputed Barricade* is something of a classic, but it is a highly sympathetic biography of Tito and thus heavily weighted on the Partisan side. Conversely, Albert Seitz's *Mihailović, Hoax or Hero* subscribes uncritically to the Četnik cause.

Soon after I arrived in Yugoslavia, I set about uncovering the facts for myself. I rapidly discovered not only that the literature was often full of inaccuracies—wrong dates, wrong names, wrong places—but that the documents and the persons constituting the primary sources of information on this subject were either not available or not responsive to the question at issue. Yugoslav archives were incomplete, the British files were still closed, American sources were only partially available because the archives of the Office of Strategic Services (OSS) were inaccessible, and the captured German documents were of limited use for this kind of study.

Despite these limitations, I nevertheless began patient research into such material as was available, and I initiated correspondence or interviews with more than one hundred participants in wartime events—British, American, Yugoslav and German. Facts began to separate from fiction, and I succeeded in pinpointing dates, places and names of individuals.

It soon became clear that the story of the relations between the Allies and the different Yugoslav factions during World War II could not be told without examining the origins and development of the two resistance movements in Yugoslavia and their relationship to the Yugoslav Government-in-Exile. What were the true aims and aspirations of the Četniks and the Partisans, and did these change during the course of the war? Who was Draža Mihailović and what was his actual role? Was he hero, traitor or neither? Did he and his Četniks fight the enemy or collaborate? And who was Tito and what were his goals? Was he a Soviet agent or a Yugoslav revolutionary?

The Allied attitudes toward Yugoslavia were influenced, moreover, not only by events inside Axis-occupied Yugoslavia, but also by the development of the European war and the importance which the Big Three ascribed to the Yugoslav area of operations. Churchill's interest in action in the Balkans contrasts with Roosevelt's profound aversion to any large-scale commitment of American forces there. Stalin was curiously late in developing any interest in Southern Europe.

In the early war years only Britain exhibited any interest in Yugoslavia. Was Churchill's concern for Yugoslav affairs based solely on military or also on political considerations?

What was the attitude of the Soviet Union toward events inside Yugoslavia? Did it deliberately set about creating another satellite for Soviet Communism in Eastern Europe, or was this an unexpected benefit?

Finally, the United States: What did Roosevelt think of the Balkans? He was known to have had strong pro-Serb feelings, but were these translated into pro-Mihailović policies?

In short, this book sets down the heretofore untold story of what in fact happened in the relations between the Allies and the different Yugoslav factions during World War II. It presents verified information from primary sources, much of it unavailable in the published literature.

I have concentrated principally on describing Yugoslav-American relations during this period, tracing them from the moment when, after the

Axis occupation of Yugoslavia, the American Minister, Arthur Bliss Lane, left Belgrade on May 16, 1941, to the arrival of the American Ambassador to Yugoslavia, Richard C. Patterson, in Belgrade on March 31, 1945. During that period of almost four years, Yugoslav-American relations were conducted in two channels. The first was the diplomatic channel—relations between the U.S. Government and the Yugoslav Government-in-Exile through the Yugoslav mission in Washington and the American mission to that Government in London and Cairo. Second, there was the military channel—the relations established between American military (including OSS) officers and the resistance forces operating within Yugoslavia.

I am grateful to all those participants in war-time events whom I have been able to find and who answered my letters or met with me personally: C. D. Armstrong, S. W. Bailey, Melvin O. Benson, Arthur M. Cox, F. W. Deakin, Vladimir Dedijer, B. N. Deranian, Edward Glavin, Edward Green, Kenneth Greenlees, K. F. Heinz, John Henniker-Major, Ellery Huntington, Louis Huot, Robert Joyce, V. Lada-Mocarski, L. L. Lemnitzer, Franklin Lindsay, Robert McDowell, Fitzroy Maclean, Sergije Makiedo, Walter Mansfield, Josef Matl, Turner McBaine, Robert Murphy, George Musulin, L. A. Neveleff, Carl Norden, Timothy Pfeiffer, Stoyan Pribichevich, Jaša Rajter, Karl Rankin, Walter Ross, George Selvig, Mike Stoyanovich, C. L. Sulzberger, Charles Thayer, Robert Thompson, Hans Tofte, John Toulmin, Vladimir Velebit, Zvonimir Vuckovic and George Wuchinich. Also, Colonel Zvonimir Kljaković of the Military History Institute in Belgrade and Sir Llewellyn Woodward of Oxford, England, have been most helpful.

My thanks also go to Professor George F. Kennan, who was Ambassador to Yugoslavia during part of my tour of duty there; to Professor Lyman Kirkpatrick, Jr., of Brown University, where I spent a year as Diplomat-in-Residence; to Professor Alex N. Dragnich of Vanderbilt University; to John C. Campbell of the Council on Foreign Relations; to Andrew Berding, former Assistant Secretary of State; and to my colleagues, James Bradshaw, F. Gunther Eyck, Robert Haney, Murray Lawson, Roth Newpher, Michael O'Mara, Lazar Pistrak, Slavko Todorovich and George Wynne, as well as to Inge Dierolf, Mary Quirk and Kathy Skovran, for their valuable assistance.

Walter R. Roberts

Washington, D.C.
March 1973

AUSTRIA
(Annexed by Germany
March 11, 1938)

HUNG
(Joined Tripartite
Pact Nov. 20, 1940)

Ljubljana

Zagreb

Sarajevo

A d r i a t i c   S e a

ITALY
(Formed Axis with
Germany in 1936)

YUGOSLAVIA in 1941

R Y

RUMANIA
(Joined Tripartite Pact
November 23, 1940)

Belgrade

BULGARIA
(Joined Tripartite Pact
March 1, 1941)

Cetinje

Skoplje

ALBANIA
(Invaded by Italy
April 7, 1939)

G R E E C E
(Invaded by Italy
October 28, 1940)

TITO,
MIHAÍLOVIĆ
AND
THE ALLIES,
1941-1945

Historical Introduction

There is a saying that Yugoslavia is a country with seven frontiers, six republics, five nationalities, four languages, three religions, two alphabets and one boss.*

It has not always been that way. Yugoslavia (the land of the South Slavs —*jug* meaning south) did not exist even as a country before 1918. It was created as a result of World War I.

As late as the nineteenth century the area which makes up most of Yugoslavia today was divided between the Habsburg Empire and the Ottoman Empire. (Only Montenegro, which was originally part of Serbia, never completely succumbed to the Turks.)

In 1804, a Serb named Djordje Petrović—also known as "Black" Djordje or Kara Djordje because of his dark complexion (*kara* means black in Turkish)—organized a revolt against the Turks, to whom Serbia had lost its independence in 1389. Kara Djordje's revolt, at first successful, ended, however, in failure. In 1815, Miloš Obrenović launched another revolt against the Turks which had some measure of success in that Serbia, while not free, became an autonomous principality. By 1830 complete internal autonomy was achieved. Serbia's independence was internationally recognized in 1878, and its territory was considerably increased. Following the Balkan Wars of 1912–13, Serbia acquired large portions of Macedonia and became a next-door neighbor of Montenegro.

On June 28, 1914, Archduke Franz Ferdinand, heir-apparent to the Habsburg throne, while visiting Sarajevo, capital of the then Austrian province of Bosnia-Hercegovina, was assassinated by Gavrilo Princip, a Serbian nationalist. This act touched off World War I.

---

* Frontiers: Italy, Austria, Hungary, Rumania, Bulgaria, Greece, Albania.
  Republics: Slovenia, Croatia, Serbia, Macedonia, Montenegro, Bosnia-Hercegovina.
  Nationalities: Slovenian, Croatian, Serbian, Macedonian, Montenegrin.
  Languages: Slovenian, Croatian, Serbian, Macedonian.
  Religions: Serbian-Orthodox, Catholic, Moslem.
  Alphabets: Latin, Cyrillic.
  Boss: Tito.

After the war, those portions of present-day Yugoslavia that were part of the defeated Austro-Hungarian Empire (Slovenia, Croatia and Bosnia-Hercegovina) joined Serbia in a united kingdom, called the Kingdom of the Serbs, Croats and Slovenes. The Montenegrins deposed their own king and joined the new country. The King of Serbia, Peter Karadjordjević, a descendent of Kara Djordje, became king of the new state. For the next twenty-three years the country experienced great difficulties both domestically and internationally.

It proved impossible to reconcile the several national groups having different historical and cultural backgrounds. Particularly intense was the conflict between the federal-minded Croats, who had been part of a defeated nation in World War I, and the Serbs, who had been on the victorious side and a majority of whom preferred a unitary organization of the state. The Croats had been a favored minority in the Austro-Hungarian Empire, where they served in important military and civilian positions, and they prided themselves on being better educated and more "civilized" than the rustic Serbs, who had lived under Turkish domination for almost five centuries. The Croats were in the great majority Roman Catholic, whereas the Serbs belonged to the Orthodox Church.

In 1929, Peter's son, Alexander, who had succeeded to the throne in 1921, dismissed the parliament and set up a personal dictatorship which, instead of achieving national unity, had a devastating effect on Yugoslavia's political life. Later in the year, the country's name was changed from Kingdom of the Serbs, Croats and Slovenes to *Yugoslavia*.

On the international scene, Bulgaria, Hungary and Italy, all covetous of Yugoslav territory, attempted to exploit the internal dissension in the country by appealing to its different unhappy national minorities. Yugoslavia, in response, relied on the Little Entente (with Rumania and Czechoslovakia, created in 1921 to counter Hungarian irredentism), on the Balkan Entente (with Rumania, Greece and Turkey, created in 1934 to stave off Bulgarian territorial aspirations) and on its ties with France and the League of Nations (against the predatory aims of Italy).

After Hitler's assumption of power in Germany in 1933, Yugoslavia followed with deep anxiety the gradual collapse of this entire treaty system. On October 9, 1934, King Alexander was assassinated in Marseilles by Croatian nationalists. His son, Peter, was then only eleven years old, hence three regents were appointed to govern the country in his name. Prince Paul, Alexander's cousin and one of the regents, became the real ruler. The League of Nations refused to condemn the murder of the King. Similarly, it did not act against Mussolini's aggression in Ethiopia, Hitler's occupation of the Rhineland and the annexation of

Austria on March 11, 1938. Suddenly, Yugoslavia found itself a neighbor of Nazi Germany.

Seeing France and Britain standing idly by as Hitler and Mussolini (who had formed an alliance in 1936 later to be known as the Axis) marched forward, Yugoslavia concluded that the system of treaties and the League of Nations offered no protection against threats to its territorial integrity. Since Germany, in addition, had become most interested in Yugoslav raw materials for its growing war machine while Yugoslavia's traditional friends showed no concern for the economy, Yugoslavia became economically more and more dependent on Hitler's Reich.

On April 7, 1939, Italy invaded Albania. Although Yugoslavia was not immediately and directly affected by Germany's attack on Poland on September 1, 1939, which resulted in the declaration of war on Germany by Britain and France, the vise tightened on October 28, 1940, when Italy—which had declared war on Britain and France on June 10, 1940—invaded Greece from Albania. Yugoslavia's apprehensions increased rather than diminished when Italy found itself in great military difficulties, for the Yugoslav leaders knew that Hitler would have to come to Mussolini's help, particularly if the British were considering a landing in Greece.

Meanwhile, two of the other three neighbors of Yugoslavia were forced by Germany to join the tripartite Berlin-Rome-Tokyo Pact signed on September 27, 1940. Hungary acceded on November 20, and Rumania on November 23, 1940.

With this, the stage was set for Germany's further moves into the Balkans, which form the point of departure for the ensuing narrative.

PART I: 1941

The Beginnings of Resistance

NINETEEN FORTY-ONE was the year in which the British-Axis war became a global confrontation. Germany attacked the Soviet Union in June and Japan the United States in December. In April, Germany launched a lightning attack on Yugoslavia which resulted in a quick victory, but by autumn the world heard of epic resistance there to the Axis occupation. Of the major Allies only Britain, however, showed an interest in the struggle inside Yugoslavia and sent in supplies and a British liaison officer. Yet those resistance forces which professed an active role proved to be far less committed than others who were then unknown to the Western Allies.

1

YUGOSLAVIA JOINS THE TRIPARTITE PACT

Early in 1941, with France defeated and almost all of Western Europe under German occupation, Great Britain stood practically alone against Germany and Italy. At home it faced the invasion threat and the continuing German air attacks, and on the high seas the war against the U-boats; in the Middle East it conducted a campaign aimed at the destruction of the Italian armed forces in North Africa; and in the Balkans it attempted to shore up the Greeks against the Italians and to rally Yugoslavia and Turkey against the Axis. But it was precisely because of British victories against the Italians in North Africa and particularly Greek victories against Mussolini's armies in Greece that the Germans cast their eyes in the direction of the Balkans. For having decided at the end of 1940 to attack the Soviet Union on May 15,[1] the Germans were eager to secure their southern flank.

At the beginning of the year, their attention was directed more toward Bulgaria than Yugoslavia. After succeeding in aligning Hungary and Rumania at the end of 1940, the German aim was also to have Bulgaria accede to the Tripartite Pact in order to complete the arc and be able to move troops into Greece to aid the hard-pressed Italians. Yugoslavia was to be kept neutral, with the possibility of a German-Yugoslav nonaggression pact playing a role in the German calculation.

The British, on the other hand, were most concerned lest the Germans succeed in getting to Greece through Bulgaria and were quite prepared to slow down their victorious drive in North Africa against the Italians in order to help the Greeks. Turkey and Yugoslavia played an important role in their considerations. For if a combined Greek-British force were to hold up a German-Italian advance in Greece, then Turkey and Yugo-

11

slavia, the British hoped, might be drawn in on the Allied side and a new "Balkan League" created.

To this end, Prime Minister Winston Churchill sent Foreign Secretary Anthony Eden and General Sir John Dill, Chief of the Imperial General Staff, to the Middle East and also to Athens, where they arrived on February 22, 1941. The discussions with the Greek Government persuaded the British officials that the Greeks would fight on even if the Germans were to join the Italians. Plans were worked out for British forces from the Middle East to land in Greece.

Meanwhile, as the Italian military situation in Greece deteriorated, the Germans decided that not only Bulgaria but also Yugoslavia must join the Tripartite Pact. With this in mind, the Yugoslav Prime Minister, Dragiša Cvetković, and the Foreign Minister, Aleksandar Cincar-Marković, were invited to meet the German leaders. They saw Foreign Minister Joachim von Ribbentrop on the morning of February 14 near Salzburg and in the afternoon proceeded to meet Adolf Hitler in Berchtesgaden. On that occasion, Hitler told the Yugoslav statesmen that the best way to keep peace in the Balkans was for the Yugoslavs to join the Tripartite Pact.[2] At the end of the conference, a possible meeting between Hitler and the Regent, Prince Paul, was discussed. Such a meeting took place in Berchtesgaden on March 4, at which time Hitler once again urged Yugoslavia's accession to the Tripartite Pact while Prince Paul reserved his position. A few days before, on March 1, Bulgaria had succumbed to German pressures and joined the Pact. On March 2, the German Army began to move from Rumania into Bulgaria.

The United States, not yet at war, watched these developments with great concern. As early as January 1941, Colonel William J. Donovan, who later headed the Office of Strategic Services, went on a special mission to Greece, Turkey, Bulgaria and Yugoslavia to ascertain for President Franklin D. Roosevelt the situation in those countries. He was in Belgrade from January 23 to 25 and visited the Regent, the Prime Minister, and several other Yugoslav officials. He explained to them the established United States policy of giving every possible assistance short of war to countries willing to fight for their independence.

The Soviet Union—which was of course intensely interested in Balkan affairs—had one overriding aim: to stay out of the war. Having signed a nonaggression pact with Germany in Moscow on August 23, 1939, the Soviets watched the struggle for the Balkans between Britain and Germany with deep apprehension. Only on June 24, 1940, had Yugoslavia and the USSR established diplomatic relations—until late 1939 a Czarist representative appeared on the Belgrade diplomatic list. Dr. Milan Gavrilović was the Yugoslav Minister in Moscow and V. A. Plotnikov the Soviet Minister in Belgrade. When Gavrilović in early February 1941 attempted to ascertain the Soviet Government's attitude toward German policy in the Balkans, he gathered that the Soviets were guided above all by a desire not to get involved in the war. Nevertheless, the Yugoslav Prime Minister asked Plotnikov for material help to shore up the weak Yugoslav Army, and when the Soviet Minister returned to Moscow late in February he took with him an extensive Yugoslav shopping list.

The British, German, Italian, Soviet and American Legations in Belgrade, particularly those three representing countries at war, were immensely active in the first weeks of 1941. Within the British Legation a small group was reporting to the highly secret Special Operations Executive (SOE) in London. The SOE had been created by Prime Minister Churchill on July 16, 1940, under the Minister of Economic Warfare, Hugh Dalton, whom Churchill had instructed to "set Europe ablaze." A number of British officials who had known the Balkans well were in Belgrade during those early months of 1941. They included Tom Masterson, Hugh Seton-Watson, Julian Amery and others who were to play important roles in the SOE during the war.

From Athens, Eden and General Dill went to Turkey, where their discussions with the Turkish leaders were not encouraging from the British point of view. Turkey did not wish to be drawn into the war.[3] Upon their return to the Greek capital, the British officials talked on March 2 with Ronald Ian Campbell, the British Minister in Belgrade, who had come to Athens. He returned to Yugoslavia with a letter from Eden to the Regent in which the latter was urged to join Britain and Greece in the defense of the Balkan peninsula. On March 7, the first British troops landed in Greece. How important the British regarded their return to the European continent can be seen by the fact that they were not deterred by the disturbing news which reached them just at that time that the Germans had started reinforcing the sagging Italians in North Africa.

On March 10, Churchill sent a telegram to Roosevelt informing him of the British decision to send troops to Greece. He added: "At this juncture the action of Yugoslavia is cardinal. No country ever had such a military chance. If they will fall on the Italian rear in Albania there is no measuring what might happen in a few weeks." [4]

Far from falling on the Italian rear, the Yugoslav Government was slowly but inexorably moving in an opposite direction, toward following Bulgaria's example of joining the Tripartite Pact.

On March 21, 1941, the American Minister in Belgrade, Arthur Bliss

Lane, was instructed to advise the Yugoslav Government that the U.S. was prepared to offer Yugoslavia all facilities under the recently enacted Lend-Lease Act and that the Yugoslav assets on deposit in the United States would continue at Yugoslavia's disposal as long as the country remained free and independent.[5] The latter point was emphasized because U.S. authorities had inquired a few days earlier about the reasons for certain transfers of Yugoslav assets from the U.S. to neutral countries. The only possible interpretation was that these assets were being transferred in order to avoid their becoming blocked by the U.S. Government should Yugoslavia adhere to the Tripartite Pact.

On March 25, the Yugoslav Government, having succumbed to German pressure, signed the Pact in Vienna. On the next day, Churchill sent a telegram to the British Minister in Belgrade:

Do not let any gap grow up between you and Prince Paul or Ministers. Continue to pester, nag and bite. Demand audiences. Don't take No for an answer. . . . This is no time for reproaches or dignified farewells. Meanwhile . . . do not neglect any alternative to which we may have to resort if we find present Government have gone beyond recall. . . .[6]

COUP D'ÉTAT AND AXIS ATTACK

On March 27, Serbian officers of the Yugoslav General Staff led a coup d'état against Prince Paul and the Cvetković Government. While the uprising had been in preparation for several months, the adherence to the Tripartite Pact provided the leaders of the coup with the final impetus. Indeed, the British SOE in Belgrade has claimed some small credit for persuading the initiators of the uprising to act fast. Prince Paul was relieved of his regency functions and sent into exile. The son of King Alexander was elevated to the throne as King Peter II a few months before his eighteenth birthday. He in turn appointed General Dušan Simović, commander of the Yugoslav Air Force, as Prime Minister.

Immediately following the coup d'état, the United States Government informed the new Yugoslav Government that lend-lease assistance was now available to Yugoslavia, and President Roosevelt, from a Carribean cruise, cabled King Peter his best wishes. Upon his return to Washington, the President received the Yugoslav Minister to the United States, Constantin Fotić, at which time, according to Fotić, Roosevelt called in the Lend-Lease Administrator, Harry Hopkins, to go over the list of Yugoslav requests which had arrived in the meantime.

Fotić writes that the President asked whether it would not be better for

Serbia to become a homogeneous state by divorcing itself from its western provinces, and he quotes him as saying: "You will again be strong and won't waste your efforts in those endless domestic problems and discussions." [7]

The news of the coup d'état in Belgrade was received with great satisfaction in England. Churchill was about to address the Conservative Central Council when the first telegram reached him, and he inserted a reference to the event in his speech, saying: "Here at this moment I have great news for you and the whole country. Early this morning the Yugoslav nation found its soul. A revolution has taken place in Belgrade. . . ." [8] Eden and Dill had reached Malta on their way back to London, but Churchill asked them to return to Athens. On April 1, General Dill actually went to Belgrade (in civilian clothes), where he found only confusion and the Yugoslav Government unwilling to receive Eden for fear of provoking Germany. The Yugoslavs were not prepared to sign any agreement with the British.

But they were interested in signing an agreement with the Soviet Union, and this suited the Soviet Government. On April 5, a pact of friendship and nonaggression was signed in Moscow by the Soviet Premier-Foreign Commissar, V. M. Molotov, and the Yugoslav Minister, Gavrilović. It bound the two countries for five years to pursue a policy of neutrality and "strictest friendship" in the event one of them was attacked. In announcing the pact at 5 A.M. on April 6, Moscow radio said that the treaty had been signed the night before "after negotiations which had been taking place during the past few days." Pictures in the Soviet press showed that I. V. Stalin, the General Secretary of the Communist Party of the USSR, who was to take over also as Premier a month later, attended the signing. On April 4, Molotov had informed the German Ambassador in Moscow that the Yugoslav Government had proposed a treaty of friendship and nonaggression and that the Soviet Government had accepted the proposal. When the German Ambassador requested reconsideration of the treaty, Molotov replied that Yugoslavia had signed a treaty with Germany (the Tripartite Pact) and therefore the Soviet Government thought it could conclude an agreement with Yugoslavia that was not as far-reaching as the German-Yugoslav treaty. [9]

As soon as Hitler heard of the coup d'état in Belgrade he issued a directive (No. 25) which said that the "military Putsch in Yugoslavia has changed the political situation in the Balkans." It added: "Even if Yugoslavia at first should give declarations of loyalty, she must be considered as a foe and therefore must be destroyed as quickly as possible." [10]

On April 6, 1941, Germany launched its attack with a ferocious air assault on undefended Belgrade, killing more than 5,000 civilians, and on the same day it invaded Greece from Bulgarian bases. Even though the Yugoslav Government had not renounced its adherence to the Tripartite Pact, German infantry and tanks crossed the Yugoslav borders from Austria, Hungary, Rumania and Bulgaria. Italian planes joined in the attack. The United States took an immediate and forceful position, calling the invasion "barbaric." Secretary of State Cordell Hull said that the American people had the greatest sympathy for Yugoslavia, which had been so outrageously attacked. Hull's statement concluded: "This Government with its policy of helping those who are defending themselves against would-be conquerors is now proceeding as speedily as possible to send military and other supplies to Yugoslavia." [11] President Roosevelt confirmed these sentiments with another personal message to King Peter dated April 8, 1941.[12]

The British Government sent a similar message to the Yugoslav Government, calling the German invasion a "savage outrage" and welcoming Yugoslavia "as a resolute and powerful ally." The statement also said that "we will conduct the war in common and make peace only when right has been vindicated and law and justice are again enthroned."

On April 9, Churchill spoke in the House of Commons and deplored Yugoslavia's inaction when Greece was attacked by Italy and her refusal to enter, in January and February, into effective staff conversations with Greece, Turkey or Britain. He then recalled the slow encirclement of Yugoslavia and how the Yugoslav leaders were called "to Hitler's footstool." He hailed the change of government in Belgrade and said this of the Nazi leadership: "A boa constrictor who had already covered his prey with his foul saliva and then had it suddenly wrested from his coils would be in an amiable mood compared with Hitler, Göring, Ribbentrop and the rest of the Nazi gang." He concluded his statement by declaring that the Axis forces were encountering resistance in Yugoslavia and Greece and that "British and Imperial troops have not up to the present been engaged."

The Soviet Government remained silent even though, according to Minister Gavrilović, it showed privately "utmost sympathy," for which the Yugoslav envoy expressed deep gratitude to Stalin. The Soviet media, at first, even refrained from mentioning the outbreak of hostilities. On April 9, *Red Star* spoke for the first time of fighting in Yugoslavia, adding that Germany was facing a serious enemy inasmuch as the Yugoslav Army's high morale and fighting spirit had been manifested repeatedly in action. On April 12, the Soviet Government officially rebuked Hungary for having moved troops into Yugoslavia and declared that this had created "a particularly bad impression in the Soviet Union." On April 16, in one of the last references to the fighting in Yugoslavia, *Red Star* said that the first stage of the operations in Yugoslavia could be considered completed with the fall of Belgrade, but "the German command in the southeast now faces a new task of advance into the interior of the country."

YUGOSLAVIA CAPITULATES

Yugoslavia, which in the face of the Axis aggression had declared war on Germany and Italy on April 7, immediately found itself in the deepest difficulties, not only due to the speed and power of the German attack but also because of the lamentable unpreparedness of the Yugoslav Army and the obvious unwillingness of a large part of the non-Serb, particularly Croat, elements to offer resistance. As early as April 10, the "Independent State of Croatia" was created by the German occupation authorities. On April 11, Italian and Hungarian troops crossed the Yugoslav borders.

Meanwhile, King Peter and the Simović Government had fled to Montenegro with the intention of leaving Yugoslav soil. This hasty disposition to abandon the country brought to the British Government its first doubts about the adequacy of the Royal Yugoslav Government's will to fight. On April 13, Churchill sent a telegram to the British Minister in Belgrade:

We do not see why the King or Government should leave the country, which is vast, mountainous, and full of armed men. German tanks can no doubt move along the roads and tracks, but to conquer the Serbian armies they must bring up infantry. Then will be the chance to kill them. Surely the young King and the Ministers should play their part in this.[13]

But by that time Campbell had lost all contact with the King and the Yugoslav Government, who went by air from Nikšić to Athens on April 14 and 16 respectively. On April 17, two representatives of the Yugoslav General Staff and of the absent Royal Government capitulated to the Germans in Belgrade.

The American Minister, Lane, who had tried vainly to communicate with the outside world to obtain instructions, left the Yugoslav capital by car for Budapest on April 29 from whence he telephoned Washington. He then returned to Belgrade to close the Legation. On May 16, he and other Legation officials departed by Danube steamer for Budapest. A skeleton staff, including Karl Rankin and Peter Constan, remained in a consular capacity. When the U.S. requested that Germany close all consular offices in America by July 10, Germany retaliated by asking the United States to withdraw all its consular officials in Germany and the occupied areas by July 15. The American officers left Belgrade on that day, and the doors of the American Legation were not to reopen until almost four years later. The American Consulate in Zagreb, the only other U.S. consular establishment in Yugoslavia, ceased to operate at the same time.

Bulgarian troops crossed into Yugoslavia on April 19, two days after the Yugoslav capitulation. Meanwhile, the German war machine, abetted by Bulgarian and Italian troops, had rolled on in Greece, occupying the country, including the Greek islands. On April 21, the British Army decided to evacuate Greece, and the Greek Government moved to Crete on April 23. (On May 20, Germany began its assault on Crete, which resulted in the quick capture of the island.)

Shortly before the British evacuation, King Peter and his Government, having stayed in Greece for a few days, continued on to Alexandria and then to Jerusalem, where they arrived on April 21 for a stay of about two months. James Roosevelt, son of the President, was traveling in the Middle East and visited King Peter in Jerusalem, bringing him a personal message of sympathy and friendship from the President.

From Jerusalem the Yugoslav Government announced that Yugoslavia would continue the war against Germany and Italy and that it had declared war on Hungary and Bulgaria on May 4. Previously, Roosevelt, having been informed by Minister Fotić that Hungary and Bulgaria had joined in the aggression of the Axis against Yugoslavia, issued two proclamations, on April 15 and 24, invoking the Neutrality Act against those two countries since they had attacked Yugoslavia without provocation. On April 25, Secretary Hull made a statement in which he said:

"The United States Government continues to recognize the Government of King Peter II as the Government of Yugoslavia and the position of Mr. Constantin Fotić as Yugoslav Minister here is not affected by the exile of his Government." The United States Government also released to the Government-in-Exile the Yugoslav assets which were frozen when Yugoslavia joined the Tripartite Pact.

Within a short time Yugoslavia, at German initiative but with the eager collaboration of its neighbors, was totally dismembered. It began with the creation of the "Independent State of Croatia," under the Croatian Fascist Ante Pavelić, who had organized the assassination of King Alexander in Marseilles in 1934 and had lived in Italy prior to April 1941.

He incorporated the province of Bosnia-Hercegovina into this "state" and offered the "crown" of Croatia to the House of Savoy. King Victor Emmanuel of Italy named his second cousin, the Duke of Spoleto, to the "throne." The Duke took the name of Tomislav II (a Tomislav had once ruled independent Croatia before the Magyars conquered it), but he never even visited his "kingdom."

Italy took western Slovenia, a large section of the Adriatic coast, the Adriatic islands and Montenegro. Germany annexed the eastern part of Slovenia. Serbia was carved up—parts going to Hungary, such as the Vojvodina, parts to Bulgaria, such as Macedonia, and a section of the southwest even going to Italy's puppet, Albania. That part of Serbia which was not annexed, and which had essentially the old pre-1912 borders, remained under German-Bulgarian occupation. On May 12, Minister Fotić formally protested the unlawful creation by the German Reich of the "Independent State of Croatia" and declared that his Government considered null and void all acts relating to the establishment of that so-called state.[14]

On instructions from his Government, he followed this up on May 24 with another note of protest in which he drew the attention of the United States Government to agreements signed in Rome on May 18 between the "Independent State of Croatia" and Italy, ceding certain portions of Yugoslavia to Italy.[15] Secretary Hull took note on May 28 of the Yugoslav Government's statements of May 12 and 24 and reiterated the indignation of the U.S. Government and the American people at the invasion and mutilation of Yugoslavia by various member states of the Tripartite Pact.[16]

On June 5, Fotić informed the United States Government of the further dismemberment of Yugoslavia by the Axis powers—the partition of Slovenia between Italy and Germany. On June 8, King Peter sent an open telegram from Jerusalem direct to President Roosevelt in which he listed a long series of massacres of Serbs by the Germans, Bulgarians, Hungarians and Croats. "In the name of my imperilled people I make appeal to you that the raising of your voice and the voice of your great nation may end these crimes," he said. Roosevelt asked the Secretary of State whether King Peter's telegram should be made public. The State Department thought that since King Peter was just then moving to London, publicity was not necessary. Instead, he proposed that the American Ambassador in Britain call on the King, stating that his message had received the President's most careful and sympathetic attention; that the Government and people of the U.S. felt the utmost indignation at the invasion and mutilation of Yugoslavia; and that the President had repeatedly made known the sentiment of the American people with regard to this act of aggression.

On June 21, King Peter and his Government arrived in London to take up residence in the British capital, and Prime Minister Simović and Foreign Minister Momčilo Ninčić were received by Churchill on June 26. Several members of the Yugoslav Government then came to the United States. Fotić learned that since America was still neutral it wanted to avoid giving the impression of establishing part of the Yugoslav Government-in-Exile on American soil. Hence it was decided that the members of the Government should establish residence in Canada, whence they could come on visits to the United States.[17] Minister Fotić saw Roosevelt on July 10, 1941, and reports that the President spoke of King Peter almost as though he were expressing a paternal interest. "The President asked me to assure the King of his sincere friendship, and expressed his admiration for the sacrifices the Serbs had made to defend their country," Fotić adds.[18]

MIHAILOVIĆ REACHES THE SERBIAN MOUNTAINS

In Yugoslavia, meanwhile, the German and other Axis armed forces were consolidating their hold on the country, but they were not successful in establishing it completely. Immediately upon the capitulation of the Yugoslav armed forces, a colonel of the General Staff, Dragoljub (Draža) Mihailović, who was then in Bosnia, vowed that he would continue to fight "in the Četnik way." The name Četnik derives from *četa* or armed band.

The Četnik organization had its origin in the Serbian battles of liberation from the Turks in the nineteenth century. It had played an important role during the two Balkan Wars of 1912 and 1913 and also during the First World War. It had a central organization with a chief (*vojvoda*) and local organizations in a large number of places throughout the country, principally in Serbia. The most important posts were held by Royal Yugoslav (mostly Serb) officers, for whom Četnik work was a full-time activity, even in peacetime. Thus when the Germans invaded Yugoslavia they met an organization specifically trained and adapted for guerrilla warfare.

Mihailović decided to make his way from Bosnia to the Western mountains of Serbia, where—as a Serb—he expected to feel more at home and where the terrain would be more suitable for guerrilla operations. He avoided capture by the Germans, who took 200,000 prisoners of war—all

Serbs. (Croat prisoners were released or impressed into the Croatian Home Guard.) On the night of May 12, 1941, he reached the plateau of Ravna Gora south of Valjevo with seven officers and twenty-four non-commissioned officers and men.

A native of Ivanjica, Serbia, Mihailović was forty-eight years old. In 1910 he had entered the Military Academy. He participated in the Balkan Wars and the First World War, was wounded and decorated several times and in 1922, as a major, became a member of the General Staff. In 1934, he was sent to Sofia and in 1936 to Prague as military attaché. In 1937, Mihailović returned to Yugoslavia, but his outspokenness brought him in conflict with General Milan Nedić, Minister of the Army and Navy. He was even court-martialed and sentenced to ten days' imprisonment for refusing to withdraw a report in which he accused politicians of diverting funds intended for defense. During his assignment in Belgrade immediately before the German attack, he was favorably known to members of the British Legation.[19]

The leader of the Četnik organization at the time war broke out was Kosta Pećanac. He did not share Mihailović's interest in resisting the occupying powers, and thus the Četnik organization was split in two. Indeed, when on August 29, 1941, the German military commander in Serbia appointed General Nedić as puppet Prime Minister of Serbia, Pećanac made a personal deal with Nedić.

The situation in Četnik territory was further complicated by different groups of irregulars in Serbia. In addition to the Pećanac Četniks and the Mihailović Četniks there were local commanders who fought against both as well as against one another. And of course there were those who openly collaborated with the occupying forces. They were the followers of Nedić, who also called themselves Četniks, and the adherents of the Serbian Fascist, Dimitrije Ljotić.

Christie Lawrence, a British officer who was captured by the Germans on Crete in June 1941 and who escaped from a prisoner-of-war train while it headed north through Yugoslavia, was able to observe the utter confusion, backbiting, antagonism and bloody hostility that prevailed between the divergent groups in Serbia. During his year there, he talked to Pećanac and also to Mihailović.[20] In June 1942, he was turned over to the Germans by a Četnik officer who originally belonged to the Pećanac organization but later changed allegiance to Nedić and finally operated independently under the Germans.

In order to dissociate himself from the Četniks who collaborated with the Germans, Mihailović at first called his movement the "Ravna Gora Movement." However, as the other Četniks became mere adjuncts of the occupying forces, the name Četnik was once again associated with Mihailović.

As early as August 1941, Mihailović established a civilian advisory body, the Central National Committee, which was composed of Serbian political leaders, some of whom, like Dragiša Vasić and Stevan Moljević, were known for their strong nationalist views.

Soon after he reached the Ravna Gora area, Mihailović set about informing his Government of his activity. On June 19, a clandestine Četnik courier reached Istanbul, whence royalist Yugoslavs relayed the information to their principals that a Colonel Mihailović seemed to be organizing resistance against the Axis.

Cairo soon emerged as the focal point of all information regarding activities within Yugoslavia. The Government-in-Exile's representative in Cairo was Jovan Djonović, and the SOE office there was under the direction of the last SOE chief in Belgrade, Tom Masterson.

Mihailović established radio contact with the British early in September 1941, when one of his radio operators succeeded in getting through to a British ship in the Mediterranean. He used standard Yugoslav Army equipment—a set powered by about five hundred pocket batteries and not designed for long-range contact. The first radio message addressed by Mihailović to his own Government was received on September 13, 1941. It was picked up in Malta and relayed to London.[21] It announced that he had gathered the remnants of the Yugoslav Army around him in the mountains of Serbia to continue resistance.

TITO ORGANIZES RESISTANCE

After Germany attacked the Soviet Union early on June 22, 1941, another movement sprang into action—the Communist Party of Yugoslavia (CPY). Its General Secretary was Josip Broz, an identity known only to the top echelons in the Party, since the CPY was illegal in prewar Yugoslavia.

Born in Kumrovec near Klanjec in the district of Zagorje in Croatia in 1892—he was thus one year older than Mihailović—Broz grew up in that part of Yugoslavia that was then in the Austro-Hungarian Empire. He served in the Austrian Army in World War I, was wounded on the Carpathian front in March 1915, spent over a year in a prisoner-of-war hospital in Russia and later in a POW camp, from which he escaped just before the Bolshevik revolution in 1917. He stayed on in Russia and became there a Communist Party member in 1919, returned to Yugoslavia with a Russian wife in 1920, and in 1924 was elected to a local position of the illegal CPY. Thereafter in the interwar period he was in and out of Yugoslavia and indeed in and out of Yugoslav jails because of Communist activities. He became General Secretary in 1939.

During his career as Communist agent and functionary, Josip Broz assumed many aliases. The one that became permanent was Tito. He had used it for the first time in 1934 during a meeting of the Central Committee of the Communist Party of Yugoslavia held in Vienna. There are many speculations and hypotheses about the origin of this name, but Tito's own explanation is that it had literary significance in his native Zagorje.[22]

The role of the Communist Party in Yugoslavia between March 25, the day Yugoslavia joined the Tripartite Pact, and the German attack on the Soviet Union on June 22 has been the subject of many contentions from those who say that the Communists sat on their hands, continuing to subscribe to the Communist theory that this was a struggle between the British "imperialists" and the Axis, to those who declare that the Communists rose against the occupiers long before June 22, 1941. The truth lies somewhere in between. The CPY did not rise against the occupying forces, but knowing from various sources and indications that Germany intended to attack the Soviet Union, it made preparations to go into action when the day came. It is interesting that Tito believed these reports more than Stalin, who belittled them and regarded them as British maneuvers to spread discord between Germany and the USSR. Tito himself described this period in his Report to the Fifth Party Congress in July 1948 as having been used by the CPY "for final preparations for an uprising." Obviously, there is great sensitivity in Yugoslav Party circles to the charge that a German attack on Yugoslavia meant less to them than a German attack on the Soviet Union.

Tito was in Zagreb, the capital of Croatia, when the German attack on Yugoslavia came. With forged papers, he went to Belgrade on May 8, 1941, by train. There, in a villa in the fashionable suburb of Dedinje, he began organizing the Party's Central Committee. On the day of the German attack on the Soviet Union, instructions were sent out by the Comintern [23] to all Communist parties to come to Russia's aid. The message which the CPY received from the Comintern concluded with a sentence the significance of which was to haunt Partisan-Soviet relations in the months and years to come: "Take into consideration that at this stage your task is the liberation from Fascist oppression and not Socialist revolution." [24] This, obviously, could only mean that the task of the preservation of Communist power in Russia was to be given precedence, even by Yugoslav Communists, over the prospects for the establishment of Communist power in Yugoslavia—that the Yugoslav Revolution, in other words, was to be sacrificed to the defense of the Soviet regime.

On the same day, June 22, the Politburo of the Central Committee of the CPY met in secret in Belgrade under the chairmanship of Tito and examined measures which the Party would take in view of the German attack on the Soviet Union. It issued a proclamation in which it pledged unconditional support of the Soviet Union. On June 27, the Central Committee of the CPY appointed Tito Commander in Chief of all projected national liberation military forces.[25] On July 1, the Comintern sent precise instructions calling for immediate action.[26]

On July 4, 1941, the Politburo met again in Belgrade and resolved to call on the approximately 10,000 members of the CPY—quite a few of whom were veterans of the Spanish Civil War—to rise against the invaders. And so the Communist Party took up the fight under Tito's leadership. (July 4 is still celebrated in Yugoslavia as the Day of the Fighter—*Dan Borca*.) It concentrated on Serbia, Bosnia and Montenegro.

The first major success of the Partisans, as Tito's guerrilla followers were henceforth to be called, was in Montenegro. There, the Italians had connived with Montenegrin separatists, known as the *Zelenaši*, or "Greens," who had been opposed to Montenegro's fusion with Yugoslavia in 1918.[27] They announced the setting up on July 12 of a "Kingdom of Montenegro." A general uprising, strongly abetted by the Communists, began on the following morning, however. Within two days, two Italian divisions were disarmed and large quantities of arms and equipment fell into the hands of the Montenegrins.

With the exception of three towns, the whole of Montenegro was for a short time free of Italian troops, but in the succeeding weeks the Italians were able to reoccupy most of the lost territory. They had intended to put Prince Mirko, nephew of the Queen of Italy and grandson of Nikola, the last Montenegrin King, on the throne, but he refused. So Montenegro was run by an Italian military governor.

In Serbia, Communist sabotage became immediately so widespread that as early as July 22 a telegram from the German authorities in Belgrade to Berlin regarding Communist activity in Serbia requested the dispatch to the Yugoslav capital of a Nazi specialist in these matters.[28] Telegrams of August 1, reporting Communist terroristic acts, and of August 8, proposing ways of dealing with the Communist insurrection in Serbia, were followed by one on August 12 indicating a further deterioration of the situation. That telegram [29] said that "collaboration between the Četnik leadership and the Communists has not yet been encountered, but the Communists are seeking to influence the Četnik rank and file with false slogans and in some instances by coercive measures, as the Military Commander [30] has learned." In a telegram of August 27, Felix Benzler, Plenipotentiary of the German Foreign Ministry with the military commander in Serbia, reported that since his telegram of August 12,

. . . the situation has become more acute. The Communist movement is spreading and is operating with nationalist slogans which begin to meet with a response . . . attacks on transportation installations, municipal offices and mining installations are increasing. German troops can move about in the country either by car or by train practically only in convoys.[31]

The appointment of Nedić as puppet Prime Minister on August 29 was an attempt by the Germans to have the Serbs themselves crush Communist insurrection, but by September 11, Benzler had to report that the Nedić Government

does not seem to be able to master the insurrectionary movement with its own forces because the newly organized formations thus far employed are evidently proving to be unreliable. . . . Under the influence of nationalistically camouflaged Communist slogans, individual Četnik groups are now also taking up positions against the German occupation troops, although so far there has been no fighting involving them. . . . We must now prepare, however, for having to crush the insurrectionary movement alone.[32]

On September 16, Hitler assigned to Field Marshal Wilhelm List, Wehrmacht Commander, Southeast, the task of crushing the insurrectionary movement in the southeastern area, and General Franz Böhme, the commanding general in Serbia, in turn, was given authority in the area of insurrection.[33] By the end of the month an offensive was under way against the rebels—principally the Communists but also those Četniks who did not subordinate themselves to the Germans and Nedić. At that time, the Partisans had established a liberated area in and around Užice, where an armament factory was in full operation.

It was not until September 18 that Tito personally joined the Communist-led resistance forces in the hills of Serbia, at Robaje near Valjevo. He had come south with the help of an Orthodox priest, *Pop* (Father) Milutinović, and an ethnic German member of the Communist Party of Yugoslavia, Jaša Rajter, with whom he chatted in the train in perfect German in order not to arouse German suspicions. (Among the ethnic Germans in Yugoslavia, very few belonged to the CPY.) Tito knew German from his childhood days, from his service in the Austrian Army and from extended stays in Vienna after the First World War. His fellow travelers included two girls, one of whom was Tito's personal secretary. Traveling more than forty-eight hours by train, horse-cart and on foot, the five of them had some narrow escapes before they reached Partisan territory.

Within a few days after his arrival in liberated territory, Tito held a military conference in Stolice, near Krupanj, with Partisan commanders from all parts of the country; some members of the Politburo of the Central Committee of the CPY also participated. It was decided to establish Partisan headquarters in each province of Yugoslavia and to transform the present Partisan headquarters into a Supreme Command of the Partisan forces. The conference further resolved to set up in the liberated areas "national liberation committees" which would be the bearers of the people's authority.[34]

TWO DIFFERENT CONCEPTS OF RESISTANCE

The two movements—the Ravna Gora (Četnik) Movement and the Partisans—found themselves side by side in the same part of Serbia and at first even collaborated to some extent.

It is now clear, however, that Mihailović and Tito had entirely different concepts of resistance. Although there were some clashes between the Germans and the Četniks as early as May 1941, Mihailović thought of resistance in terms of setting up an organization which, when the time was ripe, would rise against the occupying forces. Such a time would come, in his opinion, when Allied victory was assured and the liberation of Yugoslavia imminent.

Mihailović followed the policy laid down by the Yugoslav Government-in-Exile on July 22, 1941, when it issued a declaration explaining the impossibility of continuing resistance. It asked the population to bear calmly the hardships of occupation and to believe in an Allied victory which would bring freedom to Yugoslavia. The declaration, which was read over the British Broadcasting Corporation (BBC), admonished the Yugoslav people to avoid battles and to await the signal from London. Tito, on the other hand, in accordance with Comintern directives, was determined to strike immediately in order to relieve pressure on the Russian front.

As a result, such sabotage, particularly on communication lines, as was carried out in that initial period was undertaken largely by the Partisans. Mihailović followed suit now and then against his better judgment in order not to leave the resistance entirely to the Communist-led guerrillas. On occasions, some of Mihailović's commanders even made common cause with the Partisans on their own responsibility and against Mihailović's orders. In this way he lost several commanders to the Partisans—among them *Pop* (Father) Vlada Zečević, who later became a high Partisan official—and with them a number of his followers who were eager to fight the Germans.

THE BRITISH GOVERNMENT TAKES AN INTEREST

The Yugoslav Prime Minister, who had received indirect reports from Istanbul and Cairo about Mihailović's activities, mentioned the subject, though probably not Mihailović's name, to Churchill, and on August 28, the latter sent a memorandum to Hugh Dalton, under whose direction SOE fell:

> I understand from General Simović that there is widespread guerrilla activity in Yugoslavia. It needs cohesion, support, and direction from outside. Please report briefly what contacts you have with these bands and what you can do to help them.[35]

Dalton replied forthwith that a mission was being dispatched to Yugoslavia to investigate the situation.

British policy with regard to European resistance movements was to restrain them from activities which would lead to their premature destruction. With regard to Yugoslavia, Dalton formulated this policy in August 1941:

The Yugoslavs [the exiled Royal Yugoslav Government], the War Office, and we are all agreed that the guerrilla and sabotage bands now active in Yugoslavia should show sufficient active resistance to cause constant embarrassment to the occupying forces, and prevent any reduction in their numbers. But they should keep their main organization underground and avoid any attempt at large scale risings or ambitious military operations, which could only result at present in severe repression and the loss of our key men. They should now do all they can to prepare a widespread underground organization ready to strike hard later on, when we give the signal.[36]

This British policy coincided initially with the concepts on the basis of which Mihailović's movement was being operated.

The mission which Dalton mentioned to Churchill was to be a purely Yugoslav one. Two Royal Yugoslav officers, Major Zaharije Ostojić, who had accompanied Prince Paul to Greece and thence went to Cairo, and Major Mirko Lalatović, who had taken a Yugoslav airplane from

Montenegro to Greece and had also gone to Cairo, were selected by the Yugoslav chief representative in Cairo, Djonović, to undertake this task. It was only at the last minute, and probably as a result of Churchill's inquiry to Dalton, that a British officer was added to the mission. He was Captain D. T. Hudson, who had worked for SOE in Yugoslavia before the coup while he was a mining engineer in the Zajača mines in Serbia. A British submarine landed him, the two Yugoslav officers and a Yugoslav radio operator, Veljko Dragičević, on the coast of Montenegro near Petrovac on September 20, 1941.[37]

The Yugoslav-British party carried two radio sets, one a Mark III set which weighed fifty-five pounds, needed regular current and could not run on storage batteries. The other was a small "J" set which could not operate more than thirty minutes—otherwise it would burn out, as indeed it soon did. Its range was only 300 miles, which meant that it could barely reach Malta from Montenegro. It could not reach it at all from Serbia.

It is clear that the instructions which Ostojić and Lalatović had received from Djonović were not the same as those which Hudson had been given by Masterson. The former were told to go to Mihailović's headquarters while the latter was asked to report on the guerrilla situation in general. This led to serious dissension between the Yugoslav officers and Hudson. Upon landing in Yugoslavia, Hudson radioed that the British-Yugoslav mission, called "Bullseye," found guerrilla groups which were Communist-oriented and well-organized, and he suggested that aid be sent them. While Ostojić and Lalatović were eager to reach Mihailović, Hudson had no such instructions until October 9, when SOE Cairo ordered him to go to Četnik headquarters. It will be recalled that the first direct radio message from Mihailović had reached the British just as Hudson was leaving for Yugoslavia. Since then other uncoded radiograms had arrived in Cairo, and the British wanted Hudson to give Mihailović a code. (He apparently had at least two codes with him, so he was able to retain one for his exclusive use.)

What happened on the way from Montenegro to Ravna Gora is not completely clear and, regrettably, Hudson, the only survivor of the group, refuses to talk about his mission. On October 19, Hudson sent his last message on his own transmitter to Cairo in which, as in previous radiograms, he referred to guerrilla actions on the part of Communists and patriots against the Italians in Montenegro in contradistinction to "national" elements, which were standing aside. After that, he and Ostojić apparently went ahead, while Lalatović and Dragičević (the latter hauling the fifty-five-pound radio set) followed. Hudson and Ostojić were escorted by several Montenegrin Partisans (Milovan Djilas, Arso Jovanović and Mitar Bakić) to Užice, where Tito had his headquarters.

The official Yugoslav diary, *Hronologija,* does not mention a meeting between Tito and Hudson in Užice, but it appears that the two met, probably on October 24. Tito refers to such a meeting,[38] and Deakin seems to have further details.[39] Tito recalls that he asked Hudson why London had proclaimed Mihailović a national hero when he was in fact not fighting, to which, according to Tito, Hudson replied that the British Government had not the slightest idea about Mihailović. Deakin reports that Hudson allegedly offered Tito technical data, including a code, to establish contact with Cairo, but that Tito indicated that he would prefer Allied help via the Soviets.

Ostojić had gone on to Ravna Gora while Hudson stayed in Užice, and he had briefed Mihailović on Hudson's rather positive views about the Partisans. Nevertheless, Ostojić went back to Užice with the task of bringing Hudson to Ravna Gora, since the code which Hudson carried was vital to the Četniks. Lalatović and Dragičević had not yet reached Užice when Hudson and Ostojić set out for Ravna Gora on October 25.[40]

Shortly thereafter, Lalatović and Dragičević arrived in Užice, but while Lalatović went on to Ravna Gora, Dragičević refused to join him and instead stayed, with Hudson's radio set, at Partisan headquarters.

In view of what Ostojić had reported to Mihailović about Hudson's attitude toward the Partisans, the Četnik leader did not receive the first British liaison officer as warmly as might have been expected, even though Hudson gave Mihailović a code for communicating with Cairo. It is, however, important to note that this was a British code and that henceforth all Mihailović messages, code-named "Villa Resta," even those to his own Government, were known to the British. Conversely, all Hudson's messages, even though he used his own code, had to go over the Mihailović transmitter, since his set had remained in Užice.

Not only did the British send a liaison officer to Mihailović, but in line with their policy laid down in August 1941 regarding guerrilla operations in Yugoslavia, they also discussed with the Government-in-Exile the question of supplies to the Četniks. Marjanović,[41] citing Royal Yugoslav Government files, mentions a discussion on this subject between King Peter and Churchill on October 13, and Kljaković[42] speaks of three *aide-mémoire* from Prime Minister Simović to the British Government, a letter dated October 20, an affirmative response six days later, Simović's talk with Eden on October 29 and finally a letter by Dill to Simović of

October 31 to the effect that "in a few days" Mihailović would receive guns, rifles, revolvers, bandages and gold and that other supplies would follow.

Actually, the British Chiefs of Staff had felt that the revolt in Yugoslavia was premature, "but the patriots have thrown their caps over the fence and must be supported by all possible means." On November 7, 1941, Middle East Command was instructed by London to get in supplies by submarine, aircraft or local craft.[43]

2

EARLY ČETNIK-PARTISAN RELATIONS

Meanwhile, on September 19, 1941, the day after Tito reached his Partisan units, Mihailović and Tito met for the first time, at Tito's initiative, at Struganik, between Robaje and Ravna Gora. (Mihailović had met in August with Partisan representatives, at their initiative.) The talks went well enough, but no real agreement to cooperate was reached because the different concepts of resistance were irreconcilable.

There was some correspondence between Tito and Mihailović after the Struganik talks regarding closer collaboration, and a new meeting between the two was arranged. It took place on October 27, 1941, at Brajići, between Užice and Ravna Gora. Mihailović took Hudson along, but did not wish him to attend the actual meetings although Tito had suggested that Hudson participate.[1] Mihailović apparently was anxious to avoid Hudson's witnessing the clash of mutually unacceptable concepts held by the two organizations.

Mihailović's policy, which at that time conformed with instructions from the Government-in-Exile and indeed with British thinking, became even firmer when news reached his headquarters of terrible reprisals meted out by the Germans during the preceding few weeks.

In line with an order by Hitler, the Chief of the High Command of the German Armed Forces, Field Marshal Wilhelm Keitel, had issued a directive on September 16, 1941, which declared that all uprisings in occupied territories must be regarded as Communist-inspired and that fifty to one hundred hostages should be executed for every German killed.[2] On October 10, the German commanding general in Serbia, Franz Böhme, decreed that the directive of the Chief of the German High Command be carried out in the most draconic manner—that without ex-

31

AGREED PARTITION OF YUGOSLAVIA, 1941

— — — — — Partition boundary, 1941

— · — · — · — International boundary, 1937

BANAT

RUMANIA

elgrade

ANNEXED
BY BULGARIA

S E R B I A

Danube

UNDER GERMAN
MILITARY COMMAND

Morava

Novi Pazar

BULGARIA

CEDED TO
ALBANIA

Skoplje

OCCUPIED
BY GERMANY

ANNEXED
BY BULGARIA

UNDER
BULGARIAN ADMINISTRATION

G R E E C E

TURKEY

OCCUPIED
BY GERMANY

ception one hundred hostages be executed for every German killed.[3] This directive was the basis for a bloodbath which took place in the Serbian town of Kragujevac on October 21. A large number of males, including high-school boys, were executed, 2,300 in all, according to German estimates.[4] This made a deep impression on Mihailović, and he vowed not to allow himself to be pushed into operations against the Germans unless he was sure that it would result in total liberation of the country.

Tito recalls [5] that during the meeting at Brajići he offered Mihailović the supreme command but adds that had he accepted it, he would not have served under the Četnik leader. This second conference between Tito and Mihailović ended with some measure of agreement. Mihailović was to obtain half of the production of the Partisan-held Užice ammunition and rifle factory. In return, Mihailović promised Tito a share of whatever parachute drops he might obtain from the British.

This agreement, however, was very short-lived. Clashes between the Partisans and the Četniks broke out almost immediately. Each side subsequently blamed the other for initiating the incidents. The Četniks say that on October 28, the day after the Tito-Mihailović meeting, the Partisans attacked the smelting works at Zajača (south of Loznica) held by the Četniks. But evidence supports the now widely recognized view that the civil war started when, on the night of November 1–2, the Četniks, according to a message by Captain Hudson to Cairo, "grossly underestimating the Partisans' hold on their followers, unsuccessfully attacked Užice." Shortly before, Mihailović had sent a telegram to his Government in London in which he said that he had reached a reconciliation with the "communists" but that the peace could not long endure since the Partisans did not want to turn over Čačak and Užice to the Četniks. Mihailović told his Government that he "feared" his Četniks would have to occupy Užice in order to prevent the strengthening of the Communist movement. When it became apparent that the Četnik attack on Užice went badly, Mihailović sent a series of radio messages to his Government in which he asked it to intervene with the British to speed up the delivery of aid. "British promise of support," Hudson reported later, "had the effect of worsening Četnik-Partisan relations. When I first arrived at Ravna Gora . . . before Četnik-Partisan hostilities, Mihailović already knew by telegram that he would get British support. He felt rightly that no one outside the country knew about Partisans. . . ." [6]

The Yugoslav Government-in-Exile relayed the pleas of Mihailović to the British. However, when Captain Hudson became aware of the seriousness of the clashes between the Četniks and the Partisans, he advised Cairo to stop sending arms to Mihailović because he wanted to prevent British arms' being used for civil warfare. Actually, only one consignment—on November 9—had by then been received. But the Četniks expected a second one and waited a whole night in bitter cold for the drop. Next day, Hudson told Mihailović of his radiogram to Cairo. Mihailović was furious, and relations between Hudson and the Četniks, which had started poorly in view of Hudson's disagreements with his travel companions, Ostojić and Lalatović, thus went from bad to worse.

Meanwhile, the German offensive, begun late in September against what the Germans called Communist bands, which, however, included also those Četniks who did not collaborate with the Germans and Nedić, was in full swing in Serbia. Kraljevo had fallen on October 16 and Valjevo on October 25, and the Germans were driving toward Partisan and also Četnik headquarters.

Assuming that he would not receive further supplies from the British, seeing his forces unsuccessful in their battles with the Partisans and deeply perturbed by the German offensive into Serbia with its attendant massacres, Mihailović allowed himself to be persuaded by the German Intelligence Service to meet with representatives of the German commanding general. The initiative came from the German captain, Josef Matl, with a Četnik colonel, Branislav Pantić, acting as a go-between. The German Intelligence Service had become aware of the deep split between the Četniks and the Communist-led guerrillas and was anxious to exploit it. Believing that if the enemy is divided, one tries to neutralize at least one of the enemy factions, Captain Matl, who had already established contacts with some of the supporters of Mihailović, made his move. His idea was to establish a *modus vivendi* between the German occupation authorities and Mihailović's resistance forces. At the meeting, which took place on November 11 in the small village of Divci on the Kolubara River, the German negotiators, however, demanded Mihailović's complete surrender. This he rejected. He was ready to leave German communication lines and economically important towns alone provided the Germans would leave him in peace in the mountains, but he was not prepared to surrender unconditionally. The meeting failed, and the state of belligerency continued.[7] It should be added that Mihailović did not report to his Government that he had met with German representatives and, of course, the news about the meeting was tightly held from Hudson.

On November 14, Tito sent a message to Mihailović in which a third meeting was proposed to resolve the problems that had arisen between

King Peter and President Roosevelt at the White House, June 1942. From
A King's Heritage. Courtesy of Mrs. Frank Lowe

the two factions. The meeting took place on November 18 and 20 at
Čačak. This time Mihailović and Tito did not participate themselves.
Tito's delegates were Aleksandar Ranković, Ivo Lola Ribar and Petar
Stambolić; Mihailović was represented by Major Lalatović, who had
come with Hudson to Yugoslavia, and Major Radoslav Djurić. A tenuous
agreement was finally reached on eight points, including a joint court of
inquiry to investigate the responsibilities for the breaking of the last
agreement, with the culprits to be tried by court martial; joint operational staff and coordinated action against the Germans; prisoners on
both sides to be returned; neither side to let the Germans into the other's
territory.

On November 27, representatives of the Partisans and the Četniks
met again in Čačak, and on the following day, in view of the German
offensive, moved to Pranjani to discuss questions resulting from the
agreement of November 20. Hudson participated in the meetings and
reported later (May 1943): "In the peace parleys which followed and

which I attended, the Partisans refused to consider peace, unless Mihailović agreed to the closest cooperation, including a joint headquarters, with the Partisans retaining their identity, political commissars, propaganda, etc." [8]

The agreement of November 20, however, was never implemented. It came at the height of the German offensive, later called by the Partisans the First Offensive. Appeals by telephone from Tito to Mihailović on November 27 and 28 did not move the Četnik leader to take joint action. By the end of November the Partisans had been forced to retreat south into Italian-occupied territory.[9] The Četniks went into the hills of Ravna Gora, but remnants of their forces were under German attack throughout December.

After the last Partisan-Četnik meeting in Pranjani on November 28, Captain Hudson accompanied the Partisan representatives to Užice to look for his radio transmitter.[10] He had arrived in Yugoslavia, it will be recalled, with two sets. One was too weak to reach Malta from Serbia and anyway had burned out. The other heavier set had stayed in Užice when his radio operator decided to join the Partisans. Thus, since arriving in Ravna Gora, Hudson had been dependent on the Četnik transmitter, and in view of his poor relations with Mihailović and the Četniks, he was most eager to recover his own transmitter.

However, as soon as Hudson arrived in Užice, the Germans overran the city, and Hudson had no choice but to retreat south with the Partisans. During the retreat, he found Dragičević with his radio transmitter and, according to Dedijer's *Diary*, on December 1, having reached the Uvac River at Radojinja, decided to return to Mihailović. He was a British officer whose assignment was to Mihailović's headquarters, and he was determined to abide by his orders, although his departure for Ravna Gora undoubtedly heightened already strong Partisan suspicions of British motives.

Over a hundred Partisans, though for different reasons, were also going north, and he joined them. However, only a few were with him when an independent Četnik unit led by Boža Javorski attacked them, took Hudson and the Partisans prisoner and confiscated the radio transmitter, which he had recovered on the retreat to the Sandžak. During the night, Hudson escaped and made his way back to Ravna Gora alone and, of course, without his radio transmitter.[11]

MIHAILOVIĆ INACTIVE

When Mihailović realized the impact of the German offensive, he decided to disband most of his forces temporarily and to keep only a small staff. On December 5, he closed down his radio transmitter in order not to give the Germans hints about his whereabouts. (He did not resume radio transmissions until January 1942.) But the Germans were nevertheless closing in on him. On the morning of December 6, he was almost captured, and only by jumping out of a window in the nick of time was he able to save himself. During the whole day he lay in a small trench covered with leaves and shrubbery while the Germans looked for him, occasionally even jumping over him.[12]

Having finally thrown off his pursuers and re-established communication with his staff, Mihailović went into hiding. Only three guards (Blagoje Kovačević, Nikola Mandić and Franja Seničar), one radio operator (Slobodan Likić) and a personal aide (Zvonimir Vučković) were with him as they moved about in the area of Rudnik Mountain for the next three months, until Mihailović went south and eventually to Montenegro.[13] At the same time, Četnik headquarters was divided into two parts. The larger one, under the direction of Lieutenant Colonel Dragoslav Pavlović, stayed close to Ravna Gora, while the smaller one (mainly G-2) under Major Ostojić kept near Mihailović.

After Hudson returned to Ravna Gora on December 7, he remained close to Pavlović and since nobody could go to Mihailović without Ostojić's approval, Hudson was unable to see the Četnik leader throughout this period. On December 1, Mihailović had radioed that Hudson had not returned from Užice, and that was the last the British heard of their liaison officer for four months.

On December 3, the Yugoslav Middle East Command in Cairo issued the first communiqué on the fighting in Yugoslavia, announcing that three German divisions had launched a major offensive against Yugoslav positions in the valley of the Western Morava River. A United Press report on the communiqué said that military experts in Cairo referred to the campaign as the opening of a "third front" which forced the Germans to fight again in the Balkans at a time when they were hard pressed in Russia and North Africa. The communiqué asserted that Serbian troops under Colonel Draža Mihailović "are resisting successfully in the face of furious onslaughts," though in the vicinity of Užice "enemy tank attacks have obliged one of our units to withdraw." Unwittingly using the word "partisan," the communiqué added that "partisans have carried out several successful operations in the enemy's rear."

Even earlier, the Government-in-Exile, supported by the western press, had been successfully pursuing a propaganda campaign to build up Mihailović, the Četniks and their supposed exploits against the Germans. These feats of arms were considerably exaggerated. The British and the American Governments, however, believed in and furthered this propaganda. The mass media, most of the time innocently, followed suit. In the autumn of 1941, *The New York Times,* for instance, carried frequent reports from its former Belgrade correspondent, Ray Brock, then stationed in Istanbul, regarding the battles which Mihailović's Četniks were supposed to be waging against the Germans. On February 1, 1942, *The New York Times Magazine* also featured an article by Brock which spoke of "one vast battlefield." This was at a time when Mihailović was completely inactive.

It was an understandable error. Heroic resistance was legendary in Serbian history. From a morale point of view, after the many setbacks suffered thus far in the war, this fiction of a gallant and active center of resistance in the heartland of Europe was also a most rewarding subject.

Almost nobody knew the facts, and those few who wondered did not really want to know. Reading the reports which Benzler, Plenipotentiary of the German Foreign Ministry with the military commander in Serbia, sent to Berlin during the autumn of 1941, one is struck by the fact that he mentioned solely Communist activities. In a telegram of December 3, 1941, he reported the successful conclusion of the operations against the Communist bands.

. . . Furthermore there exists in the person of Col. Draža Mihailović a rallying point for all insurgents with nationalist leanings. This person who is said to have his headquarters in the mountains between Čačak and Valjevo in the village of Ravna Gora has not many followers any longer but should nevertheless not be underestimated . . . at the present moment he does not present any acute danger, particularly as he has become an enemy of the Communists, with whom he had first cooperated, and is indeed fighting them.[14]

There have been charges that the internecine warfare between Četniks and Partisans was due to collusion between the Germans and the Četniks. This contention is not substantiated by the evidence. On the other hand, it is undoubtedly true that Mihailović was not unhappy with the expulsion of the Partisans from Serbia. The Četniks may even, here and there, have "helped along." But there was at that time no understanding between him, or any commanders acting under his orders, and the Germans.[15]

EARLY MYSTERY REGARDING TITO'S IDENTITY

For a long time, no one in the West knew the name of the man who led the Partisans. There is no record that Hudson ever mentioned Tito's name in his early telegrams, and Mihailović apparently referred to Tito only once, on November 5, 1941, when he called him the "Communist leader in Serbia, under the false name 'Tito.' " The British, who deciphered Mihailović's telegram of November 5, obviously failed to note Tito's name, and the Yugoslav Government, too, appeared not to have appreciated the news imparted by Mihailović.

It is reported [16] that during the first Tito-Mihailović meeting in September, 1941, the Partisan leader's entire introduction was: "I am Tito." Questioned why he did not give his full name, Tito supposedly declared, "It will be known one day." Later on, he is quoted as having said in the same conversation: "I come from up there." The Mihailović group took this to mean that he was a Russian who had parachuted into Yugoslavia. They were fortified in this belief by what they regarded as a somewhat strange accent and intonation in Tito's Serbo-Croatian. Tito recalled later [17] that he knew that Mihailović had taken him for a Russian and that his explanation that he was a Croatian Communist was apparently not persuasive. The Soviet Government knew, of course, who Tito was but for a long time never referred to him by name.

Tito himself, who had signed the first six communiqués from Partisan headquarters with the initials "T. T.," began with communiqué No. 7, issued on October 1, 1941, to use the signature "Tito." The first six communiqués were still printed in Belgrade by the illegal press of the CPY, but beginning with the seventh communiqué the situation had changed: Tito had arrived in liberated territory, a printing press was in operation in Užice, and Partisan headquarters had become Supreme Headquarters.

The Germans had learned of the existence of a man called Tito as early as August, 1941. By October, German Military Intelligence correctly connected Tito not only with the resistance movement but also with the Communist Party without, however, knowing yet that he was Josip Broz.

ČETNIK-ITALIAN RELATIONS IN MONTENEGRO

After the successful uprising of Montenegrin "Whites" and Communists against the Italian occupiers in July 1941, the Communists had taken charge of the situation. There is no doubt that their rule was bloody and antagonized many. When the Italians counterattacked in the summer, they discovered that determined opposition came only from the Communists and that the other elements of the population simply stood aside.

The Italian military governor, General A. Pirzio Biroli, soon became aware of this cleavage between Communist and non-Communist Montenegrins and had already in the autumn of 1941 put out secret feelers to local nationalist (Četnik) leaders to the effect that the Italian occupation forces would leave them and their men undisturbed in the countryside provided they would in turn leave the Italian garrisons and communications in peace. The Montenegrin Četnik leaders accepted, and this was the beginning of Italian-Četnik collaboration. However, it should be pointed out that this cooperation started at a time when Mihailović was still in Serbia and had no control over events in Montenegro, where local Četnik leaders like Bajo Stanišić and Pavle Djurišić decided matters without reference to Mihailović, even though there was some courier contact, and Djurišić himself actually came to Ravna Gora in December 1941.

By late autumn, the Partisans, attacked by the Italians and cold-shouldered by the Četniks, had practically lost every toehold in Montenegro. Tito himself, coming from Užice, considered the climate in Montenegro too unfriendly and proceeded through the Italian-occupied Sandžak directly to Bosnia. On the way, he almost lost his life on December 14 when the house where he stayed in Nova Varoš was discovered by Italian troops. But like Mihailović exactly a week earlier he escaped in the nick of time. By December 24, he was in Rogatica in eastern Bosnia. There he linked up with Svetozar Vukmanović-Tempo, whom he had sent to Bosnia in July 1941 to organize the Partisans. Tempo had succeeded quite well in his mission, so that when Tito arrived a comparatively large area of Bosnia was in Partisan hands.

On December 21, an important step was taken in the military field when the Partisans announced the formation of the First Proletarian Brigade under Koča Popović, the model for twenty-nine such brigades which, a year later, were merged into the Yugoslav Army of National Liberation organized into army corps and divisions. The Germans, who realized that both resistance movements, the Communists and the Četniks, had somehow escaped destruction early in December, learned of one group's arrival in eastern Bosnia but thought that it was led by Mihailović.[18]

APPEALS TO THE SOVIET UNION

As the news of Mihailović's problems with the Partisans reached the Government-in-Exile, it decided to approach the Soviet Government both indirectly through the British Government and directly to persuade the Russians to put pressure on the Partisans to submit to Mihailović's command. Soviet-Yugoslav relations had undergone a series of fluctuations since April 5, 1941, when, only a few hours before the Luftwaffe began its bombardment of Belgrade, the two countries signed in Moscow a pact of friendship and nonaggression.

When the attack occurred, the Soviets remained silent. After Yugoslavia's capitulation, Nazi Germany put pressure on the Soviet Government to sever relations with Yugoslavia and other occupied countries. The Soviets succumbed, and having previously withdrawn their Chargé, V. Z. Lebedev, from Belgrade, on May 9 asked the Yugoslav Minister, Gavrilović, to leave Moscow, which he did on May 19, going to Ankara.

After the German attack on the USSR, the Soviets reconsidered their action, and on July 8, the Russian Ambassador in London, Ivan Maisky, on instructions from his Government, told the Yugoslav Minister in London, Dr. Ivan Subbotić, that the USSR was prepared to conclude an agreement regarding the restoration of diplomatic relations.[19] The Yugoslav Government-in-Exile thereupon instructed Subbotić to tell Maisky that it wanted the restoration not only of diplomatic relations but also of the friendship treaty signed on the day of the German attack on Yugoslavia. The Soviets, however, were apparently only interested in the restoration of diplomatic relations, and on July 11 Maisky informed Simović and Ninčić: "Our diplomatic relations were temporarily suspended and now they are fully restored." On July 19, the Yugoslav Legation in Moscow reopened, and Gavrilović returned from Ankara to his post. On September 3, 1941, the Soviet Government designated Alexander E. Bogomolov as Soviet Minister to the Yugoslav Government-in-Exile in London.

The Soviet Government was aware of the situation inside Yugoslavia through the information which the CPY was continuously forwarding to the Comintern. A secret radio transmitter in the house of a Zagreb lawyer, Dr. Vladimir Velebit, was the main relay point. The Soviet Legation in Sofia also served as a go-between. Yugoslav archives hold a radiogram dated August 17, 1941, in which the Comintern was advised of Partisan military activities.[20] But the Soviets, who, in the summer and autumn of 1941, were reeling back toward Moscow as a result of ferocious German onslaughts, had no time to spend on details regarding events in Yugoslavia. All they were interested in was resistance to the Germans, and to that end the Soviet Ambassador in Britain, Maisky, actually proposed, in October 1941, to "coordinate" British and Russian policy in Yugoslavia.[21]

The Yugoslav Government-in-Exile approached the Soviet Government on November 17 to seek Partisan acceptance of Mihailović as resistance commander. (Earlier in November, the Government-in-Exile had upgraded Mihailović's title from "Commander of the Četnik Forces" to "Commander of the Yugoslav Army in the Homeland.") The démarche was made in Kuibyshev (temporary seat of the Soviet Government) by the Yugoslav Chargé d'Affaires, Dragomir Bogić, who called on Andrey Vyshinsky, the Assistant Foreign Minister.

At the same time, the Yugoslav Government-in-Exile asked the British Government to intervene with the Soviets. Foreign Secretary Eden, whose only direct information about the situation in Yugoslavia came from the reports of Captain Hudson, was visited by Prime Minister Simović early in November. Simović requested that the British Government ask the Soviet Government to urge the Partisans to place themselves under Mihailović. On November 15, Sir Alexander Cadogan, the Permanent Under Secretary in the Foreign Office, talked to Ambassador Maisky about the situation in Yugoslavia, and Maisky promised to ask Moscow to stop the Communists from fighting Mihailović.

On November 16, the British Government informed its Ambassador in Moscow, Sir Stafford Cripps, that the British policy toward the revolt in Yugoslavia was to do its utmost to provide the forces under Mihailović with the supplies necessary to maintain the movement. Cripps was instructed to take the matter up with the Soviet Government and ask that it urge the Communist elements to put themselves at the disposal of Mihailović as the national leader. On November 18, Cripps called on Vyshinsky, who said that the Soviet Government had no communication with the Yugoslavs and no control over the Communist elements in that country.

A few days later, on November 24, the British military mission in Moscow asked the Soviet Defense Ministry "to intervene promptly with the rebels in Yugoslavia." The British memorandum declared:

At the particular request of the Soviet Government the British Government has encouraged the uprising in Yugoslavia, and therefore it is in the interest of the Soviet Government to help bring about unity of the insurgents in Yugoslavia . . . the British Government regards Col. Mihailović as the only possible leader and . . . all parties should obey his orders or should at least work with him.[22]

These requests from the Yugoslav Government-in-Exile and the British Government to support Mihailović and the Četniks put the Soviets in a difficult position. For at the same time they not only were receiving through the Comintern appeals from the Partisans for arms, medicines, shoes, coats, and other supplies, but moreover, beginning with the Četnik attack on Užice, the Partisans were complaining to the Comintern that Mihailović and the Četniks were collaborating with the German forces.

While these *démarches* of the Governments of Britain and Yugoslavia remained unanswered, the Soviet Government took an important and, from the Yugoslav Government's point of view, positive step, in that it began to give all credit for Yugoslav resistance to Mihailović. The Parti-

sans who listened to Moscow radio were deeply disturbed. Dedijer reports
that Tito immediately saw great significance in the switch by Moscow
radio, assuming that the Russians had been forced into it. He halted all
anti-Četnik operations, saying: "We must be careful not to cause difficulties in the foreign relations of the Soviet Union." [23] On November 25,
however, Tito sent a telegram to the Comintern in which he reiterated
his views of Mihailović and the Četniks ". . . because Moscow radio is
reporting a horrible stupidity about D. Mihailović. . . . Tell your superiors to stop reporting stupidities which are spread by Radio London." [24]
But Moscow radio continued well into 1942 to praise Mihailović as the
leader of the Yugoslav resistance forces.

Meanwhile, the British Government, having put pressure on the Soviet
Government, decided to urge the Yugoslav Government-in-Exile to
persuade Mihailović to come to terms with the Partisans. On November
18 Cadogan wrote Simović that his Government desired to do everything
in its power to reconcile the Četniks and the Partisans. He recalled the
British initiative in Moscow and urged that Mihailović avoid reprisal
measures against the Communists. He suggested that the Yugoslav Government direct Mihailović in this respect, thus acting in the same manner
as the Russians vis-à-vis the Partisans. Cadogan even thought that King
Peter might be advised to send messages to both Mihailović and the
Partisans. [25]

While the Soviets refrained from instructing the Partisans to stop
their feud with the Četniks, Simović sent a radiogram next day to
Mihailović in which he told him of the initiatives in Moscow "so that
Partisans will discontinue actions and submit to your command." He
added: "Continue your attempt to smooth over differences and to prevent
any action of reprisal." The telegram arrived at the time of the meeting
at Čačak and coincided with Moscow radio's praise for Mihailović. Undoubtedly, these two events stimulated the Četnik-Partisan agreement
of November 20, even though it turned out to be inoperative.

Mihailović replied to Simović on November 22 that he had done everything in his power to halt the fratricidal fighting, which he said was
started by the other side. He added that he had made the greatest effort
to unite all forces and to complete the organization for the decisive fight
against the Germans. [26]

In a letter which Eden sent Simović on November 28, the Foreign
Secretary expressed his happiness at the news that Mihailović had settled
his differences with the Partisans. Eden informed Simović that the British
Government would now resume sending matériel and money to Mihailović, but that these deliveries would be dependent upon the maintenance
of a united front under his leadership. (The next British supply drop did

not arrive until the end of March 1942.) He urged Simović to send a message in this sense to Mihailović, and he added that he had asked the British Ambassador in Moscow to urge the Soviets to send a similar request to the Partisans to maintain a united front under Mihailović.

Also on November 28, Churchill sent a memorandum to General Sir Hastings Ismay for the Chiefs of Staff Committee and the Chief of the Air Staff: "Everything in human power should be done [to help the guerrilla fighters in Yugoslavia]. Please report what is possible." [27]

Meanwhile Mihailović informed Simović that the Partisans had left Serbia and disappeared as an organized force. At a time when he was disbanding his own forces he told Simović that he was working on the unification of all national forces in the Balkans.

Obviously not questioning the radiograms from Yugoslavia, Simović replied on December 3, congratulating Mihailović on the unification of all resistance forces. Also on December 3, he thanked Eden for the understanding shown by the British Government and assured him of the success of the actions undertaken by Mihailović.[28]

On December 7, while Mihailović was in hiding and no longer in radio contact, the Yugoslav Government-in-Exile promoted him to the rank of brigadier general.

When Eden went to Moscow in December 1941 to discuss with the Soviet leaders the prosecution of the war and a possible future peace, the question of Yugoslavia was raised by Stalin, who proposed, among other points, that the country be re-established and be given the Italian islands and certain coastal towns on the Adriatic. Eden replied that Britain had assured the U.S. that it would make no commitments regarding postwar boundaries. He added, however, that before Yugoslavia was attacked in April 1941, Britain had told the Yugoslav Government that it was prepared to reconsider the Italian frontier of Yugoslavia at the expense of Italy.

THE U.S. IS UNINFORMED

Up to the autumn of 1941, the only channel between the U.S. Government and the Yugoslav Government-in-Exile existed in Washington, where the Yugoslav Minister, Fotić, continued to exercise his functions. On September 5, however, President Roosevelt informed King Peter that he had named Anthony J. Drexel Biddle, Jr., as American Minister to the Yugoslav Government. Biddle was already serving in London as U.S. Ambassador to the Polish and Belgian Governments-in-Exile and as Minister to the Norwegian and Netherlands Governments-in-Exile.

There is no evidence that the Yugoslav Government-in-Exile, either through Fotić in Washington or through Biddle in London, approached the U.S. Government regarding the Četnik-Partisan problem. Apparently unaware of the problem, the U.S. Government did not raise it with the Yugoslavs either.

Other matters were of course transacted between the two Governments. Earlier in the year Fotić had called to the attention of the State Department various dismemberment measures in Yugoslavia by the Axis powers. He launched a new protest on November 4, this time against the incorporation of Yugoslav territory by Bulgaria. Secretary Hull assured Fotić on December 3 that the United States Government viewed with the same indignation the acts of the Bulgarian Government in extending its control over those parts of Yugoslavia occupied by Bulgarian forces as was expressed previously regarding the invasion and partitioning of Yugoslavia by other neighboring states.[29]

When Fotić saw Roosevelt on December 20, the U.S. was already at war with all the Axis powers following the Japanese attack on Pearl Harbor on December 7. Fotić informed the President of the massacres which had been perpetrated in Yugoslavia. He had sent a memorandum to the President on December 5 requesting an opportunity to submit personally more information on the subject of atrocities committed by Pavelić's regime against the Serbs living in Croatia. Fotić says that as early as August 19, the chief of the Balkan desk in the State Department had given him a report that Pavelić and his *Ustaše* (meaning rebels) were engaged "in a comprehensive policy of extermination of the Serbian race in the Independent State of Croatia." Literally hundreds of thousands of Serbs living in Croatia were annihilated by the *Ustaše*. Fotić writes that the President was deeply shocked by the atrocities perpetrated against the Serbs and assured Fotić of his great sympathy for them. He adds that the President "spoke with admiration of the resistance, reports of which are coming in daily," and he quotes the President as expressing his conviction that after the war "the Serbs will rise again as a great people."[30] Without implying that he may have reported his talks with the President from his own point of view, it should be stressed here that Fotić was a Serb. As will be seen later, President Roosevelt spoke in similar terms to Eden on the occasion of the latter's visit to Washington in March 1943.

THE SITUATION AT THE END OF 1941

The military and political situation had changed dramatically in 1941. The Soviet Union and the United States, both neutral at the beginning of this narrative, had entered the war, successive victims of premeditated aggression. At year's end, the German Army stood deep in Russia even though it already felt the strength of the first major counteroffensives of the Red Army. The United States, having in the last month of the year lost the major part of its battle fleet in the air attack on Pearl Harbor, was in no position to halt the relentless drive of the Japanese in the Far East. In Africa, the British had put to rout the Italian occupiers and had returned Emperor Haile Selassie, the first victim of Axis aggression, to his throne in Addis Ababa. Farther north, the German Afrika Korps had taken over the main burden from the Italians; nevertheless the British forces were again advancing westward, having recaptured Benghazi in Libya on Christmas Eve.

In this over-all military picture, events in Yugoslavia were necessarily remote to the major powers, particularly the United States. Britain and the Soviet Union had some strategic interest there, for any problems the Germans might encounter in the Balkans could delay the arrival of troops and matériel in North Africa and also indirectly relieve the pressure on the Russian front. It was for that reason that the British established liaison with Mihailović and the Comintern intensified its radio contact with the Partisans. But the information that reached the British and Soviet Governments, as well as the Yugoslav Government-in-Exile, was often only fragmentary and almost always one-sided, either Četnik or Partisan.

We now know that the development of the resistance movement in Yugoslavia in 1941 can be explained only by the political situation in the country at the time of the Axis attack. Yugoslavia was divided internally, and most of the nationalities of which the country was composed resented the Serbian hegemony. There were no "all-Yugoslav" political parties except one: the illegal Communist Party. The military collapse of Yugoslavia would have occurred even if Yugoslavia had been a closely knit nation, for the German and other Axis armies had thrown an overwhelming force into the battle, and the Yugoslavs were woefully ill prepared. But the end would not have come so fast, and it would not have been so easy for the Axis powers to dismember the country had there been a greater degree of unity.

In this situation, there were only two groups who could be expected to have a stake in resistance: the Serbs and the Communists. But a problem arose for the latter. Inasmuch as, at the time of the Axis attack, the Soviet Union and Germany were bound by a nonaggression pact, the Communists of Yugoslavia, as loyal members of the Comintern, did not initiate action until the Germans attacked the Soviet Union. When they did rise

up, they followed Comintern admonishments not to pursue, as might be
expected of a Communist Party, the objective of Socialist revolution, but
solely that of liberation from enemy occupation.

It soon became apparent that the Četniks' appeal was only to the Serbs
(and to those Montenegrins and others who regarded themselves as Serbs),
while the CPY attracted Yugoslavs from all national groups, including
the Serbs. Indeed, the CPY exploited the internal dissatisfaction in the
country by de-emphasizing the Communist character of the Partisan
movement and by appealing to all groups, irrespective of their political,
national and religious affiliations, to rise against the occupiers. By the end
of 1941, it became evident, even though it was not perceived outside
Yugoslavia, that this "popular front" approach was succeeding, certainly
in the non-Serbian part of the country. The brutal occupation and the
cruelty and repression of the Croatian Fascist regime helped the Partisans
in attracting non-Communists to their ranks. Where could a non-Serb
who wanted to fight have turned except to the Partisans?

Even though the Partisans outwardly stressed the popular front idea,
the strictest Communist discipline was applied organizationally, and all
leading positions in the Partisan movement were in Party hands.

In virtually every respect, the Četniks were the direct opposite of the
Partisans. Whereas the Partisans, following Comintern directives, looked
upon the resistance movement as an organization actively engaged against
the occupier, the Četniks, in line with the policy of the Yugoslav and
British Governments, remained more or less passive in the face of the
enemy.

The Communists were ready to risk much, the Četniks little. Two
hundred thousand Serbian officers and men were prisoners of war in
Germany, hundreds of thousands of Serbs were being slaughtered by the
Croatian Fascist regime, and the German reprisals in Serbia cost additional thousands of lives. The danger existed that the Serbs, the most
numerous nationality, might become a minority in a Yugoslavia of the
future.

The Partisans were revolutionaries, the Četniks were for the restoration
of the *status quo ante*. The Partisans appealed to the broad masses of all
Yugoslavia, but the Četniks restricted their appeal, with minor excep-
tions, to the Serbs. The Partisan movement was an organization of young
people—Tito in his late forties was "old" and called then (as he still is
today) *Stari*—"old man"—by his immediate followers. The Partisans were
clean-shaven—Tito never missed a day shaving even during the most
difficult battles. While the Četniks were an older group, they looked much
more so because they—and Mihailović—let their beards grow in old
Serbian tradition. Mihailović, too, was addressed by his adherents as "old

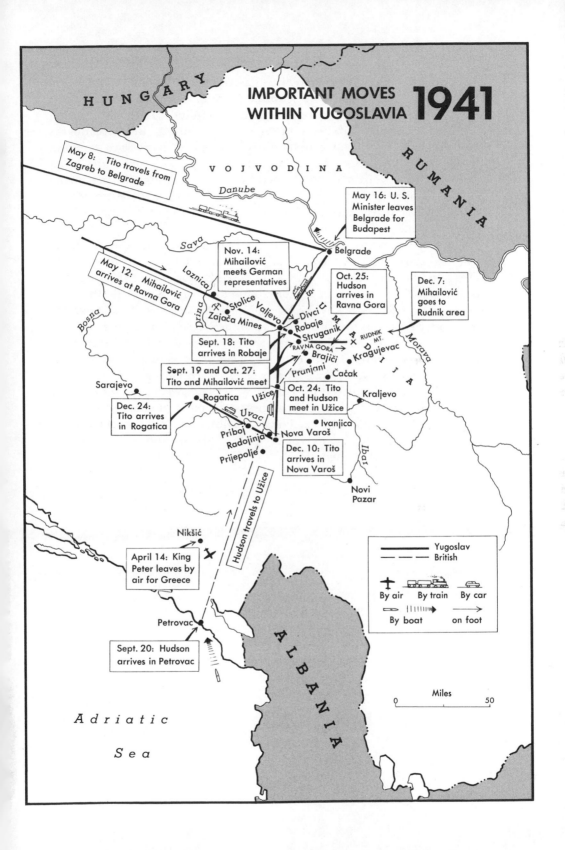

IMPORTANT MOVES WITHIN YUGOSLAVIA 1941

HUNGARY

RUMANIA

VOJVODINA

Danube

May 8: Tito travels from Zagreb to Belgrade

May 16: U. S. Minister leaves Belgrade for Budapest

Sava

Belgrade

May 12: Mihailović arrives at Ravna Gora

Loznica

Nov. 14: Mihailović meets German representatives

Oct. 25: Hudson arrives in Ravna Gora

Dec. 7: Mihailović goes to Rudnik area

Bosna

Drina

Stolice

Valjevo

Zajača Mines

Divci

Robaje

Struganik

RAVNA GORA

RUDNIK MT.

Kragujevac

Morava

Sept. 18: Tito arrives in Robaje

Brajiči

Prunjani

Čačak

Sept. 19 and Oct. 27: Tito and Mihailović meet

Oct. 24: Tito and Hudson meet in Užice

Kraljevo

Sarajevo

Rogatica

Užice

Dec. 24: Tito arrives in Rogatica

Uvac

Ivanjica

Priboj

Radojinja

Nova Varoš

Ibar

Prijepolje

Dec. 10: Tito arrives in Nova Varoš

Novi Pazar

Hudson travels to Užice

Nikšić

April 14: King Peter leaves by air for Greece

Petrovac

ALBANIA

Sept. 20: Hudson arrives in Petrovac

— Yugoslav
--- British

By air   By train   By car

By boat   on foot

Adriatic

Sea

Miles
0   50

man," but they used the more familiar, typically Serbian word, *čiča*. Women played an important role in the Partisan movement, none among the Četniks. The Partisans were a highly disciplined, centrally directed organization, the Četniks were much less coordinated, and Mihailović's influence over Četnik units beyond his immediate control was tenuous.

While the Partisans were led by a political leader and the Četniks by an expertly trained officer of the General Staff, it is significant that many Partisan leaders other than Tito had had fighting experience in the Spanish Civil War, while the Četnik leaders, as Yugoslav Army officers, had practically no battle experience at all.

It is not surprising, therefore, that at the end of 1941, the Partisans, who had started out as a comparatively small group of members of the CPY, had become a sizable and still-growing movement which encompassed significant numbers of non-Communists. Even though they had been ejected from Serbia by the German First Offensive and had retreated into eastern Bosnia, they had become an active resistance force of some influence. At year's end, the Četniks were static and had been disbanded in Serbia (though not in Montenegro, where some sort of collaboration with the Italians had begun). The two resistance movements which had more or less collaborated until October 1941 had become bitter enemies.

What little news appeared in the western press mentioned only the exploits of Mihailović. The Partisans were unknown to the world at large, and among the Allies, only the Yugoslav, British and Soviet Governments were aware of them.

PART II: 1942

Mihailović–Allied Hero

NINETEEN FORTY-TWO was the year in which the German war machine experienced its first major setbacks, administered by the Red Army at Stalingrad and by the British in North Africa. In Yugoslavia, resistance to the Axis occupation mounted, and the world became aware of two resistance forces inside the country which, however, bitterly opposed each other. This placed the major European Allies—Britain and the USSR, more so than the United States—in a quandary; but only Britain continued to insert itself into Yugoslav affairs. Supply drops to Mihailović were resumed, and a senior liaison officer reinforced the British representation at Četnik headquarters. Doubts about Mihailović's activities began to be raised by some British officials who were wondering whether the "other" resistance movement was not really more important militarily.

3

MIHAILOVIĆ INACTIVE—THE PARTISANS UNDER ATTACK

Early in 1942, the Yugoslav Government-in-Exile, which was badly split among its Serb, Croat and Slovene members, had to be reconstituted by King Peter. The crisis was in fact inherent. Prime Minister Simović was hardly on speaking terms with his colleagues, Professor Slobodan Jovanović (a Serb), Dr. Juraj Krnjević (a Croat) and Dr. Miha Krek (a Slovene). King Peter had his own group of advisers led by Professor Radoje Knezević, who with his brother, Živan, had played a major role in the coup d'état of March 27, 1941.

The British Minister, G. W. Rendel, relates how he was told by Jovanović, Krnjević and Krek that they had asked King Peter to dismiss Simović.[1] The King assented, appointing Jovanović as Prime Minister on January 11, 1942. At the same time, Mihailović, who since December 7 had the rank of brigadier general, was named Minister of the Army, Navy and Air Force (a new ministry), succeeding General Bogoljub Ilić, who had been Minister of the Army, and Simović, who had held the post of Minister of the Navy and Air Force.

This appointment came at a time when Mihailović was in hiding in the Rudnik Mountain area. He had resumed his radio transmissions on January 6 but shortly thereafter closed them down again because the Germans intensified their search for him. Mihailović did not come back on the air until March 22. Hudson was with, or more accurately near, him, but Mihailović was deeply annoyed not only because Hudson had, in November, recommended the suspension of British supply flights but also because he had "defected" to the Partisans, albeit for a short time only. Until April 1942, contact between the two was nonexistent. Hudson was denied access to Mihailović's headquarters and often had to subsist on near-starvation rations. He had no radio transmitter, and for this reason, no Hudson communications were received in Cairo in the early months of 1942. The British Government, having had no word from Hudson and unwilling to rely solely on the information supplied by the Yugoslav Government-in-Exile, made several attempts to send missions to Yugoslavia.

Two missions actually reached their destination early in 1942. One, code-named "Disclaim," parachuted on February 5 onto Romanija Mountain (east of Sarajevo) and the other, code-named "Hydra," came on February 4 by submarine to Petrovac—almost exactly where Hudson had landed.[2] Both groups had orders to get in touch with Mihailović and Captain Hudson. The former group, however, was captured by Croatian troops.[3] The second group was headed by Major Terence Atherton, who before the war had been a newspaperman in Belgrade and was a member of SOE. He was accompanied by an Irish radio operator and a Yugoslav officer.

There was a third mission, code-named "Henna," consisting of two Yugoslav officers. The same submarine that carried Atherton had put this mission ashore on the island of Mljet on January 27. After a long journey through Yugoslavia, the leader of that mission, Lieutenant Rapotec, arrived in Istanbul in July 1942 with reports that added to the confusion of the British about the situation inside Yugoslavia.[4]

The Atherton mission landed in Partisan-held territory, and it aroused immediate suspicion among the Partisans, who remembered Hudson, Ostojić and Lalatović. Tito's headquarters was then in Foča, in southeastern Bosnia, and a letter from the Montenegrin Partisans, dated February 13, 1942, apprised him of the arrival of Atherton in Montenegro.[5] Tito replied that the mission should be sent to Foča, where Atherton and his two associates arrived on March 19.[6]

Tito, who was in regular contact with the Comintern and who hoped to receive a Soviet mission, had grave doubts about the intentions of his British guests. In a letter to Moše Pijade, Tito wrote on April 6 that there was something "not right" about the English mission.[7] Two days later he allegedly wrote a letter to the CP of Croatia in which he charged the British with intensifying the Yugoslav civil war and warned the Croatian Party not to allow itself to be "used" by the British missions.[8] His suspicion was reinforced when on the night of April 15 all three members of the Atherton group departed without saying good-bye and leaving behind their radio set, which they had never used because of technical problems. Nobody knew where they had gone. At Tito's headquarters it was first thought that they were heading toward the Sandžak or Montenegro.[9]

More likely, they were looking for Mihailović and Hudson, who at that time were still in Serbia, although Mihailović had already decided to join the Montenegrin Četniks.

The first news of Atherton was received in London on May 15, when Mihailović, while on his way to Montenegro, informed his Government of the existence of a British mission—the Yugoslav member of the mission had apparently been found, but Atherton and the radio operator were missing—and inquired why neither the British nor the Yugoslav Government had apprised him of that mission. A few days later, Mihailović received a letter from Atherton, whereupon, on May 24, Mihailović radioed London that Atherton had written him "after his escape from Communist detention" and that he was trying to find Atherton. On May 30, Mihailović was advised by London that "Atherton is our man. He was sent in January. Help him and take his advice." [10]

Atherton and Patrick O'Donovan, the Irish radio operator, were never heard from again. The assumption of those who have looked into the case, particularly Deakin,[11] is that both were murdered and that the large sums of gold sovereigns which Atherton had carried with him were stolen. As early as April 17, two days after Atherton left Partisan headquarters, Dedijer predicted his murder by the Četniks,[12] and on May 27, Mihailović accused the Partisans of murdering him. Even today the Četnik proponents and the Partisan defenders heatedly ascribe to each other the responsibility for Atherton's death.

Earlier in the year, while Mihailović was in hiding in Serbia and Tito's headquarters was in eastern Bosnia, the Germans launched an attack against the Partisans, called by the latter the Second Offensive. It began in the middle of January 1942 and lasted for several weeks but was unsuccessful from the German point of view, for the Partisans retained control of a relatively large territory in eastern Bosnia. After they settled down at their new headquarters in Foča, the Partisans abandoned the old method of getting in touch with the Comintern through their secret transmitter in Zagreb and set up a direct radio link. The Partisans also took a major step in the political field by issuing, in February, directives on the organization of local national liberation committees, which acted as government organs in Partisan territory.

In Montenegro, the Partisans, after having lost ground to the Italians and Četniks in the autumn of 1941, had regained some initiative. On February 8 they had even proclaimed such territory of Montenegro as they held to be an integral part of the USSR.[13] Their wrath against the Četniks, with whom they had cooperated in July 1941 but who turned away from them later in the year, was applied with typical Montenegrin fury. The Montenegrin Četniks, or "Nationalists" as they called themselves, reacted to all this by formalizing their tacit cooperation with the Italians, and on March 6, Colonel Stanišić, one of their leaders, actually concluded an agreement with the Italians.[14] In a directive from Tito dated March 10, the Montenegrin Partisans were instructed to put the civil war ahead of the fight against the occupier—to liquidate the Četniks even if that meant avoiding battles with the Italians.[15] By the end of March, however, the Italians launched an offensive against the Partisans in which the Montenegrin Četniks joined and which succeeded in clearing Montenegrin territory of practically all Partisan forces. German and Croatian *Ustaše* troops joined in this Third Offensive, which lasted until June, attacking Partisan forces in eastern Bosnia.

THE BRITISH RESUME HELP TO MIHAILOVIĆ

On May 9, 1942, Prime Minister Jovanović sent a letter to Eden in which he requested the dispatch of a large quantity of arms and ammunition to the Četniks. A few days later, King Peter addressed a similar letter to King George VI. Eden replied to Jovanović on May 15, saying that between March 30 and April 24, 1942, six operations comprising thirteen overflights had been undertaken during which gold pieces, arms, ammunition, a radio transmitter and personnel were parachuted. On May 22, King George answered King Peter's letter in the same vein.

At that time, Mihailović was on his way from German-occupied Serbia to Italian-occupied Montenegro. In February he had made the decision to move south not only to escape constant German harassment but also to be nearer those Četnik forces which were strong and obviously unmolested by the enemy. The Montenegrin Četnik leaders, particularly Djurišić, welcomed his decision.

Mihailović had left the Rudnik Mountain area at the beginning of March and met Major Lalatović, Captain M. Uzelac and Captain Nikola Kalabić in Preljina near Čačak. His escort group of fifty to sixty men under Lieutenant Perović joined him there. Mihailović and his party crossed the Western Morava River near the village of Zablaće and then went over Jelica Mountain on to Čemerno Mountain. It was at that time (March 22) that he resumed his radio transmissions, and one of the first inquiries he received from Cairo concerned the whereabouts of Captain Hudson. On March 29, he replied that Hudson was with him, which was not quite true inasmuch as Hudson, while in the general area, was kept away from the general. On March 30, the British attempted an airdrop for the first time since the only previous one on November 9, 1941. However, several of the parachute drops went astray and eventually ended up in German hands. Others were damaged because the bundles came apart.[16]

With the Germans on his trail, Mihailović sent a radio message on April 5 (No. 133) warning that the area of Čemerno Mountain was no longer safe, and he went on south to Golija Mountain, arriving on April 9. While on Golija, Christie Lawrence, the escaped British prisoner of war, had a talk with Mihailović but was unable to see Hudson, who, he was told by another escaped British POW, "lives in a village a few miles from here and does nothing. You never saw a man more browned off. He is virtually a prisoner." [17] Whether or not this was an exaggeration, it is a fact that at that time Mihailović, undoubtedly in view of the concern expressed by Cairo, reestablished contact with Hudson by sending a message inviting him to the Četnik headquarters. The reunion took place on Mt. Zlatar, where Mihailović and his party had moved after having left Golija early in May. On Zlatar they were joined by other members of Mihailović's staff (including Hudson) who had gone there separately. The whole of the staff, which had split up in December in Serbia, was reunited.[18] Also at that time, Hudson finally resumed his radio transmissions to Cairo although, without a set of his own, he had to use Mihailović's transmitter.

In the second half of May, Mihailović left for Montenegro, where he arrived on June 1, just at the tail end of the Third Offensive. Tito, too, had crossed into Montenegro from his headquarters in Foča only a couple of weeks earlier to command his battered Partisans but could not prevent their and his expulsion from Montenegro by Italian and Četnik troops.

While Mihailović and his party went on foot to the general's new headquarters near Mt. Durmitor, Ostojić, Lalatović and Hudson passed themselves off as Nedić followers and went by truck through the Italian-held towns of Nova Varoš, Prijepolje and Bijelo Polje.[19] At Šahovići in northern Montenegro, Ostojić left the group and went on foot to Mihailović's headquarters, reaching it on June 16; Lalatović and Hudson arrived there on June 23. On his way to the general's headquarters, Captain Hudson wrote Mihailović a letter dated June 11, 1942, in which he asked the general's permission to talk to the leaders of the Montenegrin Četniks to assure them that "Great Britain is resolved to support one hundred per cent your efforts to unify all the National forces in the country and your preparations for the action against the occupiers at the opportune moment when chances for success can be expected." [20]

THE SOVIETS STAY ALOOF

In early February, the Comintern finally answered the Partisans' repeated requests for arms and supplies. A telegram from Moscow said: "There is a possibility that we shall be sending people to you in the near future . . . let us know exactly where our plane could land. . . ." [21] Tito replied on February 17 that what he needed were medicines, munitions, automatic arms, boots and material for uniforms. [22]

The Partisans cleared an airfield of snow every night for weeks and waited in the bitter cold for the arrival of a Soviet plane. It never came. An earlier thought of helping the Partisans must have been vetoed by the highest Soviet authorities, and on March 29, the Comintern began to intimate in a radiogram that aid would not be sent: "The technical difficulties are enormous." This Tito-Comintern radio exchange regarding the possible dispatch of a Soviet mission occurred at a time when Atherton was in Partisan-held territory. Indeed, Tito had apprised the Comintern of Atherton's arrival, and the possibility cannot be excluded that the Soviets, once informed of the arrival of a British mission, decided not to interfere in the situation and to leave the ground to the British, at least for the time being.

The Comintern also replied to the messages in which the Partisans had castigated Mihailović and the Četniks. On March 5, a radiogram from the Comintern rebuked the Partisans for "acquiring a Communist character." It asked: "Why . . . did you need to form a special proletarian brigade?" and added: "It is difficult to agree that London and the Yugoslav Government are siding with the invaders. There must be some great misunderstanding here."

Later in March, the Comintern cabled: ". . . it is not opportune . . . to emphasize that the struggle is mainly against the Četniks. World opinion must first and foremost be mobilized against the invaders; mentioning or unmasking the Četniks is secondary." [23]

The Partisans persisted, however. They demanded of the Comintern that the Soviet Government publicly condemn Mihailović and the Četniks for their collaboration. Before Foreign Minister Molotov visited London in May 1942, the Partisans sent Moscow a detailed report on the situation in Yugoslavia and particularly on the "treason" of the Četniks. Molotov, however, did not bring up this subject when he talked to Foreign Minister Ninčić.

In March 1942, the Yugoslav Government-in-Exile had suggested to the Soviet Government the ratification of the treaty of friendship signed on April 5, 1941, a few hours before the Germans attacked Yugoslavia.

The Soviets countered by proposing a new treaty of mutual assistance. Negotiations proceeded, but Fotić says [24] that the British Government counseled against signing such a treaty. Ninčić told Molotov while the latter was in London that, in view of the British doubts, the Yugoslav Government wished to postpone the signature.

In April and in May 1942, the Yugoslav Government-in-Exile renewed its appeals to the Soviet Government to persuade the Partisans to place themselves under Mihailović's command. On April 20, Stanoje Simić, who succeeded Gavrilović in January 1942 as Yugoslav Minister to the USSR, was instructed to make representation at the Soviet Foreign Ministry. He cabled back to London that the Soviets took the view that the activities of all Communist parties abroad were outside their competence. On April 29, the Yugoslav Prime Minister asked the British Foreign Office again to persuade the Soviet Government to take measures which would result in the Partisans' placing themselves under Mihailović.

On May 16, 1942, Prime Minister Jovanović invited Soviet Minister Bogomolov to see him. He told him that the Yugoslav Government-in-Exile insisted that the Soviets persuade the Partisans to join forces with Mihailović. Bogomolov answered that the relations between Mihailović and the Partisans were a purely domestic problem in which the Soviets did not wish to interfere. He reportedly added that the Soviet Government considered everyone a Partisan who was fighting the Germans and consequently so considered General Mihailović.[25]

During the negotiations in London between the British Government and Molotov resulting in the Anglo-Soviet treaty of May 26, 1942, the question of the future of Yugoslavia, which had been raised during Eden's visit in Moscow five months earlier, was not pursued.

KING PETER VISITS THE UNITED STATES

Early in 1942, after the United States had entered the war, the question of aiding the resistance forces in Yugoslavia was discussed between Minister Fotić and U.S. authorities. Fotić says that Colonel Donovan, who was then Director of the Office of Coordinator of Information, sent Frank Mauran (Fotić calls him "Morand") to Cairo to determine how aid could be sent into Yugoslavia. There was no question as to who would be the recipient of such aid. Mihailović alone figured at that time in the calculations of the U.S. Government. It is reported by Fotić that Mauran reached an agreement with General Borivoje Mirković, Commander of the Yugoslav Air Force, who was the principal organizer of the coup d'état of March 27, 1941, and whose headquarters was then in Cairo.

According to Fotić, the agreement provided for American matériel and supplies to be flown in four bombers to the Middle East, the bombers to be allocated to the then practically nonexistent Yugoslav Air Force. It also called for closer cooperation with Mihailović's guerrillas to be achieved by parachuting Yugoslav officers and men as well as some American observers into Yugoslavia to be attached to Mihailović's headquarters.

There are no American records confirming this agreement reached by Mauran and reported by him to Fotić on March 11, 1942.[26] However, there are records showing that in May 1942, Mauran wrote a memorandum to Donovan [27] regarding the possibility of sending food to the Mihailović units, and in June 1942, Mauran reported that he had discussions with the commander in chief and executive officer of the Yugoslav forces in the Near East.

Fotić says that on May 16, 1942, Donovan informed him of Roosevelt's decision to send 400 tons of concentrated food as a gift to Mihailović in recognition of the services he was rendering to the Allies. According to Fotić, the food was packed in special containers each holding ten packages of five pounds and wrapped in the tricolor of the Yugoslav flag. On the white field of this tricolor wrapping there was printed—and Fotić says in "Serbian"—a message from Roosevelt greeting Mihailović and his brave warriors and wishing them good luck in their difficult struggle. Each package also contained detailed instructions for the preparation of the food and bore the facsimile of the President's signature. Fotić says that he was informed that the President had given personal instructions for the dispatch of this food to the Middle East without delay, to be flown from there as speedily as possible to "Serbia" and dropped in the mountains. Fotić writes that the food had arrived in Egypt by the end of the summer of 1942, but nearly one year later it was discovered that, "despite the personal and formal order of the President of the United States," it had never reached its destination. "It was established in May 1943, that part of the food had been used in the winter of 1942–43 to supply the civilian population of the island of Malta," Fotić adds.[28]

In March 1942, the State Department suggested to the President that he might wish to send King Peter a telegram on the occasion of the anniversary of the coup d'état in Belgrade a year earlier. Roosevelt agreed, and on March 27, 1942, a cable was sent by the President to King Peter in London:

On this anniversary of the memorable day when the Yugoslav people boldly resolved to face the dangers threatening their liberty and honor, and entrusted their destiny to your leadership, I send this message of friendship. The people of the United States join with me in this greeting to the people of Yugoslavia. We are sure of their victory in the valiant struggle for the restoration of their freedom.

This telegram was sent at a time when the Yugoslav Government was pressing for some reply regarding the scheduling of a visit of King Peter to the U.S., which had been suggested by the Yugoslavs for almost a year. On April 8, 1942, the State Department recommended to the President that the visit not be delayed further and proposed it take place in June. The President concurred, and on June 22, 1942, King Peter, accompanied by Foreign Minister Ninčić, arrived in the United States from England.

It appears to have been a very successful trip. On June 24, the President gave a dinner for the King which was attended by the highest U.S. officials, including the Vice-President, the Speaker, the Secretary of State and several members of the Cabinet, Senators and Representatives, the Chief of Staff and the Chief of Naval Operations, and on the Yugoslav side by the Foreign Minister and other members of his party, by the Yugoslav Minister in Washington and by Dr. Ivan Šubašić, the Ban (Governor) of Croatia, who was then living in the U.S. In a toast, Roosevelt paid tribute to Mihailović and promised that the Allies would send him help. The President asked King Peter to discuss with Colonel Donovan the problem of sending supplies and establishing closer liaison between Mihailović and the United States. The President also suggested a lend-lease agreement with Yugoslavia, which was subsequently signed on July 24, 1942, by Secretary of State Hull and the Yugoslav Foreign Minister.[29] One other matter discussed during the visit was the training in the United States of airmen who had escaped from Yugoslavia.

While in Washington, King Peter addressed a joint session of the United States Congress, and in view of subsequent events it is of significance that during his visit in the United States, he was cordially received by a number of Yugoslavs or former Yugoslavs who were known to have had leftist tendencies.

The White House issued a statement on July 24, after the King's departure, concerning the President's discussions with King Peter in which "the fine achievements of General Mihailović and his daring men" were described as "an example of spontaneous and unselfish will to victory." How little was known in Washington about events in Yugoslavia can be seen by the fact that this statement was issued at a time when Mihailović's forces were inactive against the Germans and collaborating with the Italians. On August 3, in reply to a wire from King Peter, Roosevelt sent the King a telegram expressing his personal pleasure at the King's visit to Washington: "It gave also to the American people an opportunity to do honor to the valiant Yugoslav people in their noble and unceasing fight for the liberation of their country," the President said.[30] There is no evidence that the Partisan-Mihailović problem was discussed on a bilateral basis between the American and Yugoslav statesmen, although Fotić reports that he had discussions regarding this matter with Foreign Minister Ninčić.

King Peter's visit to Washington coincided with Churchill's, and on June 24 Roosevelt had a meeting with King Peter and Ninčić in which Churchill joined. While there is no record of that meeting available, Ninčić told Assistant Secretary of State Adolf A. Berle, Jr., on June 30 that Churchill had made a remark on that occasion that discouraged both him and King Peter. "You are beginning to tire out your friends," Ninčić quoted Churchill as having observed—a clear indication of impatience on the part of Churchill with the Yugoslav Government-in-Exile.[31]

THE PARTISANS LABEL MIHAILOVIĆ A TRAITOR

On July 28, 1942, a few days after King Peter's departure from the United States, the Communist Party newspaper in New York, *The Daily Worker,* carried a report that Mihailović had been labeled a Fascist and a traitor by Radio Free Yugoslavia. Minister Fotić visited Under Secretary of State Sumner Welles on August 5, 1942, and called attention to this report. He added that up to ten days before, *The Daily Worker* had almost daily published a photograph of Mihailović under headlines proclaiming him the great leader of the southern Slav forces of resistance against Hitler. Fotić denied that there was a Radio Free Yugoslavia station.[32] As it turned out, Fotić was wrong. Such a station existed. It had been broadcasting since November 2, 1941, and was first located at Ufa in the Urals, but in April 1942, moved into the Comintern building in Moscow. Its director was Veljko Vlahović, one of the leaders of the CPY.

What had happened was that on July 6, 1942, Radio Free Yugoslavia broadcast a resolution of the "patriots" of Montenegro, Sandžak and Bosnia which accused the Četniks and Mihailović of being collaborators and also condemned the attitude of the Government-in-Exile. Radio Free Yugoslavia could not have broadcast the Partisan resolution, which Tito had forwarded to the Comintern on June 21, without the consent of the Soviet authorities. It thus appears that the persistent radiograms sent by Tito finally achieved their purpose: The Soviet Government was moving away from all-out support of the Yugoslav Government-in-Exile, the Četniks and Mihailović. Whether by coincidence or because the broadcast of July 6 over Radio Free Yugoslavia had come to his attention, Mihailović sent a telegram (No. 310) to his Government on July 15 in which he asked that it publicly denounce Pećanac, Ljotić and Nedić as traitors. The Yugoslav Government, using BBC facilities, proceeded to do so.

Concerned by the transmissions of Radio Free Yugoslavia (and also by the content of the bulletins published by the Soviet Embassy in London), the Yugoslav Government protested vehemently to the Soviets. This *démarche* was made on August 3, 1942, in Kuibyshev by Yugoslav Minister Simić to the Soviet Assistant Foreign Minister, S. A. Lozovsky. Two days later, the Soviet Foreign Ministry presented to the Yugoslav Legation in Kuibyshev a detailed memorandum charging that Mihailović and his Četniks were cooperating with the Italians against the Partisans. On August 7, Soviet Ambassador Maisky gave the British Foreign Office a copy of the memorandum. On August 19, the Yugoslav Legation delivered a memorandum to the Soviet Foreign Ministry repudiating these charges. On the following day, Eden wrote to Maisky that the British could not regard the charges as based on accurate and objective information and proposed discussing the matter with the Soviets. The Soviets never replied.[33]

On September 2, Prime Minister Jovanović sent Bogomolov another note in connection with the accusations made against Mihailović. Minister Biddle reported to the State Department on September 11 that he had talked to Bogomolov, who wished to make clear his Government's views regarding resistance activities: Under conditions such as then existed in Yugoslavia, it was useless to attempt to appoint heroes. They created themselves; they came to the fore by the sheer weight of their own qualities of leadership. Hence, if Mihailović failed to rally the forces of resistance behind his own banners, attempts from the outside to build him up as a leader would hardly be effectual. The very fact that he was not able to consolidate the various factions behind him would seem to be ample proof that he did not enjoy the full support of the Yugoslav people. Consequently, other leaders were coming to the fore to direct the energies of those who were reluctant to follow his leadership. Bogomolov told Biddle that he wanted him to know these views, since the Yugoslav Government had adopted the position that Moscow should take steps to urge all the forces to get behind Mihailović. While there was little doubt as to the wisdom and advantages of consolidated action on the part of the resistance forces, attempts from the outside to influence people on the question as to who should or who should not lead them could hardly be expected to prove effective.[34]

On the other hand, at the same time (September 14, 1942), the Soviets and the Yugoslav Government-in-Exile raised their missions to Embassies, much to the annoyance of the Partisans when they learned about it. Tito even sent a strongly worded communication to Moscow protesting this action.[35] Later in the autumn, the Soviets proposed to send a Russian military mission and aid to Mihailović as well as to establish joint broadcasting. Jovanović sent Mihailović a telegram on November 30, 1942, apprising him of this latest Soviet offer and explaining why the Yugoslav Government had rejected the proposal:

We are insisting first on immediate cessation of radio and press campaign against Yugoslav Army under your command; second, on the Partisans' being told not to attack our armed forces; third, for Partisans to be placed under your command. Only when this is done can there be talk of further cooperation.[36]

This ambivalence on the part of the Soviet Government—propaganda support for the Partisans but correct relations with the Yugoslav Government-in-Exile and indeed attempts to establish liaison with Mihailović—continued into early 1944.

4

THE STATE DEPARTMENT BECOMES CONCERNED

In October 1942, the State Department seemed for the first time to become concerned about possible international repercussions of the Četnik-Partisan problem.

On October 5 and 6, Acting Secretary Welles discussed the Yugoslav situation with the Soviet Ambassador in Washington, Maxim Litvinov, who repeated to Welles some of the Soviet allegations of Četnik collaboration with the Italians previously presented to the Yugoslav Government. Welles told Litvinov that it seemed to him "in the highest interest of our two governments that Yugoslav forces should not be fighting each other nor assisting the enemy against the other but should be united in fighting the enemy and that it was to be hoped that some way might be found in which this result could be obtained." [1]

At the same time, the State Department sent a message to Biddle, who now had the rank of Ambassador after the U.S. and Yugoslavia raised their missions to embassies on September 29, 1942. The telegram asked him to inquire whether "as had been confidentially reported, certain British circles have become mistrustful of Mihailović and tolerant of the partisan faction." [2] Biddle replied that he knew of no such developments. He pointed out that on the occasion of the opening of the Yugoslav House in London, on September 24, 1942, Eden had praised Mihailović for the fight against the occupation forces. Biddle also mentioned that in September 1942, Eden expressed to the Soviet Ambassador in London, Maisky, his hope that the Soviet and Yugoslav Governments could reach an early agreement in connection with the conflict between Mihailović and the Partisans.

Previously, on August 16, the British Army, Navy and Air commanders in the Middle East—General Sir Claude Auchinleck, Admiral Sir Henry Harwood and Air Marshal Sir Arthur Tedder—had sent a telegram to Mihailović: "With admiration we are following your operations which are of inestimable value to our Allied cause."

But there were other signs pointing in a different direction. Biddle himself reported that Fotić had informed the Yugoslav Government in London that the British censor in Washington had received instructions from London to permit as little mention as possible of Mihailović's name. Also, by October 1942, a new attitude had begun to develop at the BBC. Not only was Mihailović's name used less frequently but, more significantly, the BBC Yugoslav transmissions began to mention Partisan military activities. This occurred at a time when only Radio Free Yugoslavia (though not Soviet media) and *The Daily Worker* in London and New York made reference to Partisan operations, while the Western press still spoke solely of Mihailović and his Četniks. On October 19, 1942, Mihailović sent a radiogram (No. 828) to his Government complaining about the BBC Yugoslav transmissions and their editor, H. D. Harrison.[3]

DOUBTS ABOUT MIHAILOVIĆ

In the late autumn of 1942, the Yugoslav Government-in-Exile became very concerned about the increasing number of rumors in London that Mihailović was not only inactive against the enemy but even collaborating with the Italians. It therefore decided to ask the general whether he or his commanders had in fact collaborated. Mihailović replied on December 22, 1942 (No. 1181):

I do not permit any collaboration with the Italians. . . . Have confidence in us. We shall never do anything that could harm the Allied cause. Because of the large number of the enemy, we strive to beat one after the other. A fight against all of them at the same time would be useless and unsuccessful. In the course of the winter I shall reach Karlovac and Zagreb with my units. By annihilating Pavelić's Croatia, I shall strike at the nerve center of our greatest enemies, the Germans.[4]

In analyzing this message, one must first dismiss Mihailović's statement that he would reach Karlovac and Zagreb in the winter. He did not have the wherewithal for such an operation and in all probability had not the intention either. On the other hand, he made it perfectly plain that the fight against his internal enemies had priority over the battle against the occupation forces.

We know now that after Mihailović had established headquarters in Montenegro in June and after his command had been raised by royal decree to Supreme Command of the Yugoslav Army in the Homeland, of which he was appointed Chief of Staff on June 10, he became so absorbed by his domestic foes that he concentrated almost his entire attention on them. Mihailović appeared convinced that the Germans and Italians were passing phenomena which the Allies would take care of, but he wanted his forces to be in control of Yugoslavia when the day of liberation came. His primary attention was, of course, directed at the Partisans, but he also fought the Croatian *Ustaše* and the followers of the Serbian Fascist Ljotić, allies of the Germans and Italians. Early in September 1942, he began to take on Nedić, too.

On September 9, Mihailović called through leaflets and clandestine radio transmitters for civil disobedience to the Nedić regime. Bloody fighting broke out between Četniks and Nedić followers and as a result, the German High Command became actively involved in the persecution of Četniks, many of whom were captured and executed.[5] There is evidence that particularly during November and December 1942, German troops were fighting Četniks if for no other reason than to bolster the Nedić regime.

On January 3, 1943, Nedić issued an order in which he referred to

some kind of command of the Army of the Homeland [which] began on September 9, 1942 to give orders throughout Serbia to the mayors of towns to leave their posts and to go to the mountains and to all others to refuse to accept the abandoned posts, recommending disobedience to our Serbian as well as to the occupational authorities. . . . The command of the Yugoslav Army of the Homeland is nothing but a small band of outlaws and desperados who, like bloodthirsty communists, and often together with them, endeavor to defame completely the Serbian people by means of plundering and acts of common sabotage unworthy of officers and honest men.[6]

On January 19, 1943, the German commanding general in Serbia, Paul Bader, issued the following order:

A small group of rebels under the leadership of former Col. Draža Mihailović is fighting against the legal Serbian Government of Prime Minister General Nedić. These rebels consider themselves regulars of the Yugoslav Army and are inspired by a criminal thirst for glory. . . . These ambitious and blind fanatics will not take into consideration reality. . . . I call upon all Serbs to cooperate in destroying this nest of trouble-makers.

Thus there were hostilities between the Četniks and the Germans in this period even though the vital issue was less the Četnik-German relationship than the fact that the Germans supported Nedić

The relationship of the Četniks with the Italian occupation troops was, however, a different matter. There is, as we have seen, convincing evidence that "cooperation" between the Italians and the Montenegrin Četniks started as early as the autumn of 1941 when Mihailović was still in Serbia. In 1942, this "cooperation" had grown to such an extent that Italian and Četnik troops joined forces during the Third Offensive against the Partisans in Montenegro.

Also in other parts of Yugoslavia occupied by the Italians, particularly in Dalmatia and Hercegovina, which were part of the Independent State of Croatia, accommodations were reached between local Četnik commanders and the Italian Army. (Croatia was divided into a northern German and a southern Italian occupation zone, although it had its own troops.) The two Četniks who played a particular role were Dobrosav Jevdjević in Hercegovina and *Pop* (Father) Momčilo Djujić farther to the north. How much control Mihailović actually had over them is not clear. That their agreements with Italian commanders in 1942 were reached without Mihaliović's prior knowledge is very likely.

Actually, these agreements,[7] which provided for Italian arms, clothing and food for the local Četnik units on condition that the Italians not be attacked, were denounced by Mihailović later. He was particularly incensed when he learned that Jevdjević participated in early January 1943 in an Axis military conference prior to the Fourth Offensive against the Partisans. Indeed, when the Yugoslav Government in early 1943 awarded Jevdjević the Karadjordje Star for his services during the *Ustaše* massacres in 1941, Mihailović prevented the actual announcement of the award because of Jevdjević's too-far-reaching agreement with the Italians.[8]

Another reason why Mihailović may have opposed the award was his knowledge that, in Jevdjević's Hercegovina territory, the Četniks took terrible revenge against the population for the *Ustaše* atrocities committed in Croatia. Moslems and Croats were killed in large numbers. Dr. Živko Topalović, one of Mihailović's advisers, wrote about "the catastrophic consequences of the policy of Serbian Četnici" in the Western parts of Yugoslavia. "To them there was no difference between the *Ustaše* and the Croats. The commanders, especially Jevdjević and Djujić, were destroying the Croatian and Moslem population at every opportunity. . . ."[9]

In pursuing his fight against his internal enemies, Mihailović was in short quite prepared to accept arms for this purpose from the Italians;

but he opposed actual agreements with them as compromising his position as a fighter on the Allied side.

Demonstrating that he was in the Allied camp, he sent a radiogram on November 11, 1942, to the British commanders in the Middle East, Admiral Harwood, General Sir Harold Alexander and Air Marshal Tedder, congratulating them on their victory over Field Marshal Erwin Rommel at El Alamein:

The complete victory brought about by destroying the joint German and Italian forces means the beginning of one of the most glorious periods in history. The Yugoslav Army of King Peter the Second is enraptured with this victory and follows your every move with intense interest awaiting the moment for full and final victory.[10]

On January 25, 1943, Mihailović sent yet another telegram to Harwood, Alexander and Tedder congratulating them on the defeat of the Italians, hoping for early victory in North Africa and a "victorious march on Europe." He added: "The Yugoslav Army in the Homeland will once again show the entire world who the Yugoslavs are and that they know how to fight for liberty." [11]

By December 1942, the number of news items implying that General Mihailović was not only inactive against the occupation forces but was even cooperating with them had reached such proportions that the Yugoslav Government-in-Exile felt it necessary to issue a statement, on December 16, summarizing the actions which it said Mihailović had recently undertaken.[12] No specific claims of operations or of acts of sabotage were made, but the statement was full of exaggerations. For instance, the assertion that "the activities of the forces of General Mihailović alone are tying up 30 to 40 Axis divisions in Yugoslavia" would have been grossly inflated, even if all the resistance forces in Yugoslavia had been under his command.

THE BRITISH SEND A SENIOR
OFFICER TO MIHAILOVIĆ

The British Government was not happy with the contradictory news coming out of Yugoslavia. On the one hand, the Yugoslav Government-in-Exile claimed a wide variety of anti-Axis actions by Mihailović and his Četniks; on the other, the Soviet Government appeared to have information which seemed to belie these claims. The messages from Captain Hudson, after he resumed communications with Cairo in June 1942, appeared to lack consistency. While he reported that the Montenegrin Četnik leaders were collaborating with the Italians and that Mihailović was not undertaking military or sabotage operations, he proposed, at the same time, large arms drops.

As a first step, the British decided to strengthen the communications channel with both Mihailović and Hudson, and to that end a British officer, Lieutenant P. H. A. Lofts, and two British radio operators were dropped to Mihailović's headquarters on September 26, 1942.[13] While this put the radio link on a more secure basis and indeed allowed Hudson to report adequately on the situation in Mihailović-held territory, SOE nevertheless decided that the time had come to send a new man, and a senior one, to Yugoslavia. Clearly, the British had some doubts about Hudson's analyses, although a perusal of his messages indicates that he appears to have had a good perception of the situation. Thus, in September 1942 he told SOE that the Partisan organization was miles ahead of Mihailović's and, "after chasing each other around Yugoslavia, the final scene will probably take place in Belgrade." On November 15, Hudson sent a long radiogram to Cairo in which he reported that Mihailović had agreed "to adopt the policy of collaboration with the Italians pursued by the Montenegrin Četniks." With regard to Serbia, Hudson cabled that the opportunities for sabotage were not exploited because of Mihailović's unwillingness:

When I press for continuous large-scale sabotage, the General and his entourage reply that half a million Serbs have already been killed in the fight against the Axis and that they cannot risk reprisals; they emphasize they will not depart from this standpoint for the sake of any outside interest. I consider him perfectly capable of coming to any sound understanding with either Italians or Germans which he believes might serve his purposes without compromising him. Any such understanding would be based on his conviction of an Allied victory and would be directed to the purpose of smashing the hold of the Communists on the people.

On Christmas Day 1942, Colonel S. W. Bailey arrived by parachute at Mihailović's headquarters, which had been near Kolašin in Montenegro since early October. He was accompanied by a British radio operator. Like Hudson, he had been a mining engineer before the war and a staff member of the British-owned Trepča mines near Kosovska Mitrovica in Serbia. Bailey knew the country and the language well. Also, like Hudson, he belonged to the SOE, for whom he had worked in Belgrade before 1941. He had spent some months in the United States in 1942.

A desire for better information was, however, not the only reason for sending Bailey to Mihailović's headquarters. The war in North Africa was moving into a decisive phase. In September 1942, General Alexander, the new commander in chief of British Forces in the Middle East, had called for widespread attacks on the key German rail communications through Yugoslavia and Greece, and the Yugoslav Government had been so informed. It in turn had sent Mihailović an order dated September 20 in which, referring to General Alexander's request, it said: "The enemy communication lines are extremely overloaded and with continuous attack you could do our Allies a new favor." [14] One of Bailey's tasks was to find out what Mihailović had done about sabotaging the railroads running down the Sava and Morava valleys. (He was to learn, actually, that Mihailović had done little, if anything.)

On December 1, 1942, the Chief of the British Imperial General Staff sent a message to Mihailović on the occasion of Yugoslavia's Unity Day:

I cannot let the 24th anniversary of the unification of the Serbs, Croats and Slovenes into one Kingdom pass without expressing my felicitations for the wonderful undertaking of the Yugoslav Army. I am not only thinking of the forces which have joined the ranks of our Army in the Near East in the triumphant hour, but also of your undefeatable Četniks under your command who are fighting night and day under the most difficult war conditions. I am convinced, Your Excellency, that the day will soon come when all your forces will be able to be united in a free and victorious Yugoslavia; the day when the enemy against whom we are jointly fighting, shoulder to shoulder, will be crushed forever.[15]

This message was sent because it was felt that inasmuch as a year before a congratulatory note had been dispatched to the then Yugoslav Minister of the Army, the failure to convey a message in 1942 might have been misinterpreted by the Yugoslavs. The matter was, however, complicated by the fact that the new Minister was Mihailović. Accordingly, it was decided to transmit the message to the military attaché at the Yugoslav Embassy in London with the request that it be forwarded to Mihailović. The British had not intended to publish the message, but the Government-in-Exile seized the opportunity to exploit the text. This came at a time when the situation in Yugoslavia had become the subject of intense deliberation within the British Foreign Office, where the passivity of Mihailović against the Axis was contrasted with the resistance of the Partisans to the Germans and Italians. On December 17, 1942, Eden sent a memorandum to Churchill in which he said that it might be argued that it would be in Britain's short-term interest to break with Mihailović, "who is at present contributing little to the general war effort, and to transfer our support and assistance to the Partisans who are offering active resistance to the occupying forces." Eden rejected this alternative and recommended continued support of Mihailović "in order to prevent anarchy and Communist chaos after the war." [16]

Within a few days, on December 22, Vladimir Milanović, the Yugoslav Assistant Foreign Minister, was told by Sir Orme Sargent, the Deputy Under Secretary of State, that the Communists were much more active than Mihailović, who, Sargent added, had not fought the Germans and Italians since October 1941.[17] This statement created consternation within the Yugoslav Government-in-Exile, but worse was yet to come.

One week later, on December 29, Major Živan Knežević, Secretary of the Yugoslav War Cabinet, had a conversation with Major Peter Boughey, whom he described as "an expert for Yugoslav military affairs," [18] but who in reality was a member of SOE's London staff. According to Knežević's report, Boughey declared that Mihailović openly collaborated with the Italians—that he was a Quisling, like Nedić; the one collaborated with the Italians, the other with the Germans. Therefore, no British arms could be sent to Mihailović.

On December 31, the Yugoslav Prime Minister told the British Ambassador [19] to the Government-in-Exile, Rendel, of the Sargent-Milanović and Boughey-Knežević talks. What had happened? he asked. Since the question of Mihailović's reappointment as Minister was under consideration, he wanted to know whether there was any change in the British attitude. Rendel notes: "As I was aware that the question of transferring our support from Mihailović had been under serious consideration, I was a little guarded in my reply. . . . I said that Major Boughey was not entitled to discuss political questions but that I would immediately get into touch with the Foreign Office. . . . " [20]

The Foreign Office was exercised over Boughey's "blundering," although his superiors in SOE denied Boughey's having made such a statement. On the next day, January 1, 1943, the British Ambassador called on the Yugoslav Prime Minister and assured him that the British Government had not changed its position regarding Mihailović and in fact had only a few days previously sent Colonel Bailey as liaison officer to Mihailović in order to establish even closer relations with him.

Questions have been posed as to whether the British did not have one resistance policy in Western Europe and another for Yugoslavia, asking the Norwegians, Danes, and French to lie low and the Yugoslavs to rise. This is a charge that cannot be lightly dismissed. However, a thorough study of the evolution of the Yugoslav resistance situation shows that it was by Yugoslav choice that it developed entirely differently there. As early as 1941, when the world knew nothing yet about the Partisans, the Yugoslav Government-in-Exile decided to claim that the Četniks had risen against the occupier. It asked the British for arms and supply drops to Mihailović. When the British found out that the arms were not used for sabotage but for civil war purposes, a crisis of confidence developed which was to plague British-Četnik relations for the rest of the war.

THE YUGOSLAV PROBLEM IN THE U.S.— LOUIS ADAMIC'S ARTICLE

In the United States, the friction between American citizens of Serbian and those of Croatian descent reached a new level of bitterness upon publication of *The Daily Worker* article accusing Mihailović of collaboration.

The Serbian-Croatian problem was an old one of course, exacerbated by the resistance of Mihailović, a Serb, and the lack of resistance in Croatia and heightened further by the enormous crimes committed by Croatian *Ustaše* against the Serbian inhabitants of Croatia. Generalizations were the order of the day: Americans of Serbian descent considered themselves to be the "good guys" and accused all those of Croatian extraction of being evil. What a boon for the Croats, when suddenly Mihailović was charged with collaboration.

The situation deteriorated to such an extent that the Director of the Office of War Information, Elmer Davis, had to call a meeting on September 18, 1942, of all editors of the Serbian, Croatian and other Yugoslav papers in the United States to urge them to forget differences and get together as Americans or Americans-to-be, fight the war and leave European quarrels alone.

The personality of the Yugoslav envoy in Washington also played a part. Being an outspoken Serb, he was violently opposed by the Croat minority in the country, and as early as January 2, 1942, the State Department asked Biddle in London to let the Yugoslav Government know of intrigues against Fotić and of the U.S. Government's confidence in and respect for him. When the Legations were raised to Embassies, the Croat elements in the Yugoslav Government attempted to hold up Fotić's promotion to Ambassador.

On October 16, 1942, Dr. Šubašić, former Governor of Croatia, sent a letter to Roosevelt in which he informed him that a month earlier he had protested the Ambassadorial appointment to King Peter and to the Croatian Vice Premier of the Yugoslav Government because of Fotić's "anti-Yugoslav, anti-Croat and Greater Serbia" activities. Šubašić thereupon severed all connection with the Yugoslav Government.

During the summer of 1942, the Yugoslav Information Center in New York, which was of course under the control of the Embassy in Washington but was staffed mostly by Croats, had changed its line and began putting out material at variance with the policy of the Embassy.

On September 3, 1942, Roosevelt addressed the International Students Assembly in Washington [21] and, among other things, talked of the fighting spirit in Norway, Holland, Belgium, France, Czechoslovakia, Poland, Serbia and Greece. The fact that the President spoke of Serbia rather than Yugoslavia and did not mention Croatia distressed the Croatian Vice Premier of the Yugoslav Government-in-Exile to such an extent that he mentioned his sorrow to the American Minister.[22]

Early in August 1942, the Yugoslav Government inquired "confidentially and unofficially" whether the U.S. Government would be willing to raise the rank of the respective missions to that of Embassy. Since the British Government had already taken that step in May and the U.S. had raised the rank of its missions to Norway and the Netherlands, the President agreed, and on October 5 Fotić presented his credentials as Ambassador of Yugoslavia. Fotić reports on his talk with the President on that occasion and quotes him as saying that Churchill, during his stay in Washington the preceding June, had proposed an Anglo-American declaration about the reconstruction of Yugoslavia. "You may be surprised," Fotić quotes Roosevelt as having said, "that I did not agree with the Prime Minister, but I consider that questions concerning the reconstruction of Yugoslavia must be decided primarily by the Serbian people"— yet another instance of the President's pro-Serbian views.[23]

Fotić also reports that in the same talk with Roosevelt, he asked for the President's assistance "in carrying out the plan to assure help to General Mihailović which had been presented by the King during his visit, and which the President had approved." The President, Fotić says, expressed surprise that no effective progress had been made, and asked him to see Colonel Donovan again "to make sure that no further delay should occur." [24] Fotić then reports that, following the President's suggestion, he had several meetings with Donovan "who seemed eager to proceed with the plans which the President and the King had agreed upon in principle." But Fotić adds that all his efforts met "with very little success," and "despite the willingness and good will of General Donovan [he was still a colonel at that time] and his assistants, the plan as a whole was never carried out." Only one part was realized, namely, some fifty Yugoslav airmen were brought from the Middle East to the U.S. to undergo training which would enable them to fly modern aircraft. The part of the plan which Fotić says was not realized concerned the shipment of short-wave sets, armaments, food and equipment.

The problems of delivering U.S. supplies to Mihailović were of course almost insurmountable at that time. U.S. troops had not yet landed on the African continent—the first Americans were to arrive in North Africa on November 8. No OSS mission had yet been established in Cairo. All supplies intended for Mihailović would have had to be transferred to the British or the Yugoslavs in Cairo. The latter had no planes to ferry supplies to Mihailović, and the British only a very few. No wonder that despite Donovan's "good will," the plans for supplying Mihailović could not be fulfilled.

On December 19, 1942, *The Saturday Evening Post* published an article by Louis Adamic which represented to all intents and purposes the beginning of the propaganda war in the American press between the supporters of Mihailović and the adherents of the Partisans.

Adamic, an American writer of Slovenian birth who had not been involved in the Serbian-Croatian antagonism, explains the background of this article.[25] He describes how, in the summer of 1942, his attention had been drawn to dispatches in *The Daily Worker* about "Partisan-Liberation" operations in Yugoslavia. He says that he had known Louis Budenz, the editor of *The Daily Worker,* since the early thirties—years before Budenz joined the Communist Party. Adamic got in touch with him, and Budenz produced long cables to his paper from Moscow which quoted reports of Partisan operations. Communiqués issued in London by the Yugoslav Government-in-Exile covering the same battles, often giving the same dates, attributed these actions to Mihailović, Adamic adds, and appeared in *The New York Times* and other papers. He began to wonder. Before writing his article, Adamic says that he talked to many people who were familiar with Yugoslav affairs.

The Saturday Evening Post article was a sober piece of journalism, devoid of emotional accusations, and, considering the lack of information at the time, an amazingly accurate, objective and well-informed analysis. The article discussed Mihailović and the Četniks on the one hand and the Partisans on the other. Tito's name was never mentioned.

Five days before, *Time* carried an article entitled "Mihailović Eclipsed" which also spoke of the emergence of the Partisans as the main antagonists of the Germans in Yugoslavia and described the actions of the "Army of National Liberation" without mentioning Tito's name. The article charged Mihailović not only with inactivity but also with collaboration with the Italians.

The U.S. Government, however, which had no observers yet in the area and apparently relied completely on information from the Yugoslav Government-in-Exile, dismissed all these charges and continued to credit Mihailović with all resistance in Yugoslavia. It therefore looked for a way to express continued American support for him. Inasmuch as the United States had at no time been directly in touch with Mihailović and in view of the fact that two messages, one from the British General Staff and one from General Alexander, had been addressed to Mihailović, the Department of State suggested to the Secretary of War, Henry L. Stimson, that General Dwight D. Eisenhower, as commander of the American forces in the European area, send a personal telegram of greeting to the Yugoslav general. In a letter dated December 30, 1942, Secretary of State Hull suggested to Stimson the following as a suitable text:

General Draža Mihailović, Commanding General of the Yugoslav Forces in Yugoslavia. The American forces in Europe and Africa send greetings to their comrades in arms, the resourceful and gallant Yugoslav military units under your splendid leadership. These brave men banded together on their native soil to drive the invader from their country are serving with full devotion the cause of the United Nations. May the New Year bring them full success.[26]

On January 1, 1943, the War Department dispatched a message to Eisenhower suggesting that he send such a congratulatory telegram to Mihailović, which Eisenhower proceeded to do.

On December 31, 1942, Under Secretary Welles wrote a letter to Fotić in which he assured him that

. . . the Government of the United States has complete confidence in the patriotism of General Mihailović, and full admiration for the skill, endurance, and valor with which he and the Yugoslav patriots associated with him have continued their noble struggle for the liberation of their country. We consider that the military actions in Yugoslavia to which you refer [27] constitute an important element in the general conduct of the war of the United Nations against the Axis powers.[28]

THE PARTISAN ASSEMBLY AT BIHAĆ

Although the Partisans had since early 1942 planned their return to Serbia, they had to shelve this idea because they realized how weak they were there. The Partisan command in Serbia reported to Tito in June 1942 that there were but 852 Partisans in all of Serbia.[29] On the other hand, Partisan strength had been reported from Croatia and west and central Bosnia. Accordingly, on June 24, 1942, the Partisans, having disengaged themselves from the latest enemy attack—the Third Offensive—started the long trek which began near Foča and ended at the Bosnian town of Bihać, close to the Croatian border.

During their march through Bosnia in the summer and autumn of 1942, the Partisans cleared large areas of enemy troops. New recruits from the liberated areas actually increased the Partisans' fighting power, and the five Proletarian Brigades comprising approximately 1,000 fighters each had grown, according to Partisan claims, to an army of 150,000 men,[30] undoubtedly a considerably inflated figure.

It is now clear that during 1942 the CPY, despite Moscow's known opposition, changed its priorities. Originally, in line with Comintern instructions, it had gone into action to help the Soviet Union in its fight against the Nazis. Even though the Communists intensely desired that the CPY take over the country at the end of the war, these revolutionary aims were relegated to the background in view of the Comintern mandate. But as the Soviet Union stopped the German advance and the Partisan movement gained strength in Yugoslavia, the Communist leaders began to look upon their battles more and more as steps toward the eventual assumption of political power.

As soon as the Partisan command reached Bihać, the Politburo of the Central Committee of the CPY decided to make a major move in the political field by calling a meeting of all local liberation committees. Tito informed the Comintern on November 12 that the Partisans hoped to set up "something like a government which is to be called the National Liberation Committee of Yugoslavia." Moscow, however, while calling the creation of such a committee very necessary and important, urged caution: "Do not look upon the Committee as a sort of government. . . . Do not put it in opposition to the Yugoslav Government in London. At the present stage do not raise the question of abolition of the monarchy." [31]

Tito, who had personally invited, over the signature of "Commandant Tito," [32] seventy-one "prominent fighters and patriots" to the Bihać meeting, gave the opening speech on November 26—a remarkable address in that his faith in the Soviet Union was unshaken despite the disappointments he had experienced during 1942 at the hands of the USSR. Although he had wanted to set up "something like a government," in view of the advice he had received from Moscow, he told the delegates: "Comrades, we have no possibility of setting up a legal government, because international relations and conditions do not permit it as yet." [33] He did not spell out the reasons. And despite the fact that the Partisans had obtained no help from the USSR, he ended his speech by saying that "all we have achieved so far in our struggle is in some measure due to our great Slav brothers the Russians and all the peoples of the Soviet Union. . . . Long live our great Ally the Soviet Union! Long live the heroic Red Army!" And after that he added: "Long live our Allies—Britain and America! Death to Fascism—Freedom to the People!"

The fifty-four delegates who had reached Bihać elected the Anti-Fascist Council of National Liberation of Yugoslavia (AVNOJ),[34] which in turn issued a six-point program.[35] But following Comintern advice, echoed by Tito in his opening speech, the Bihać Assembly did not create a government. It did not even elect Tito to head AVNOJ but instead appointed to that post Dr. Ivan Ribar, an old non-Communist politician whose two sons, Ivo Lola and Jurica, were in the Party and who had joined the Partisans only recently.

The Bihać program called for liberation from the invaders, independence and true democratic rights; for inviolability of private property and individual initiative in industry, trade and agriculture; for no radical changes in the social life and free elections after the war; for the renunciation of coercion and lawlessness; and for equal national rights to all peoples of Yugoslavia, mentioning specifically Serbs, Croats, Slovenes, Macedonians and Montenegrins.

While AVNOJ was not a government, it laid the foundation for a regime radically different from the one that had fled the country a year and a half before, one of whose Ministers was now General Mihailović.

THE SITUATION AT THE END OF 1942

As the year 1942 drew to a close, the Germans were no longer the invincible warriors. On the eastern front they were suffering a crushing defeat at the gates of Stalingrad. In North Africa, Rommel's Afrika Korps was on the run westward pursued by General Alexander's army. American troops under General Eisenhower had arrived in North Africa.

In this context, resistance in Yugoslavia continued to interest the Russians and British (far more than the Americans) because more German manpower tied down in Yugoslavia meant fewer troops on the eastern front, and more sabotage of the north-south communication lines in the Balkans meant greater supply problems for the Germans in Africa. However, it was only the British who actually had sent liaison officers and some arms, matériel and money into Yugoslavia—to the Četniks, the only resistance movement with which they had any contact. Conversely, the Russians sent neither liaison officers nor arms nor matériel to the

Partisans with whom they were, through the Comintern, in regular radio communication.

It seems evident that neither the British nor the Russians were at that stage of the war highly interested in the political problems in Yugoslavia. The Četnik-Partisan struggle was an annoyance to both the British and the Soviet Governments in that it weakened Yugoslav resistance potential. Precisely because the British Government had solely military considerations in mind, it began, at lower levels, to have doubts about Mihailović's inactivity and to take an interest in the actions of the Communists. The Soviets found it politically easier to raise questions about Mihailović and show sympathy for the Communists. Yet they were most careful in their relations with the Yugoslav Government-in-Exile. For the United States, Yugoslavia was at that time a distant country, the geography of which had only a limited significance in the pursuit of the war. America regretted the existence of a civil war, and since it recognized the Yugoslav Government-in-Exile as the only legal government, it felt duty-bound to support it and its commander in Yugoslavia, General Mihailović.

Inside Yugoslavia, the resistance movement had assumed ever larger political aspects. Whereas a year before, the Četniks had sprung into action to preserve Yugoslavia (or at least Serbia) as an Allied citadel, and the Partisans had risen to support the Red Army, Mihailović's and even more Tito's tactics had changed in 1942. Now Tito's primary goal was to introduce a new political order into the country, while Mihailović's main aim was to foil that attempt. To achieve their objectives, both Tito and Mihailović had taken some extraordinary measures.

The most important step on the Partisan side was the decision to hold a congress at Bihać. There, a basis was laid for a federally oriented state in which all nationalities of Yugoslavia would have equal rights. The Bihać resolution, however, did not advocate a Communist regime. In order to achieve the broadest possible support in the country, a document was drafted which could have been accepted by practically every Yugoslav.

In the military field, the Proletarian Brigades were converted into a National Liberation Army. Three enemy offensives had been overcome, and while Partisan losses had been grievous, the strength of the movement, the effectiveness of the army and the size of territory under its command had actually increased. And so had their hatred of their internal adversaries.

The Četniks, in turn, had become fully aware of the enormous dangers which the Partisan movement posed for them. During the second half of 1942, Mihailović rallied his forces and achieved somewhat better cohe-

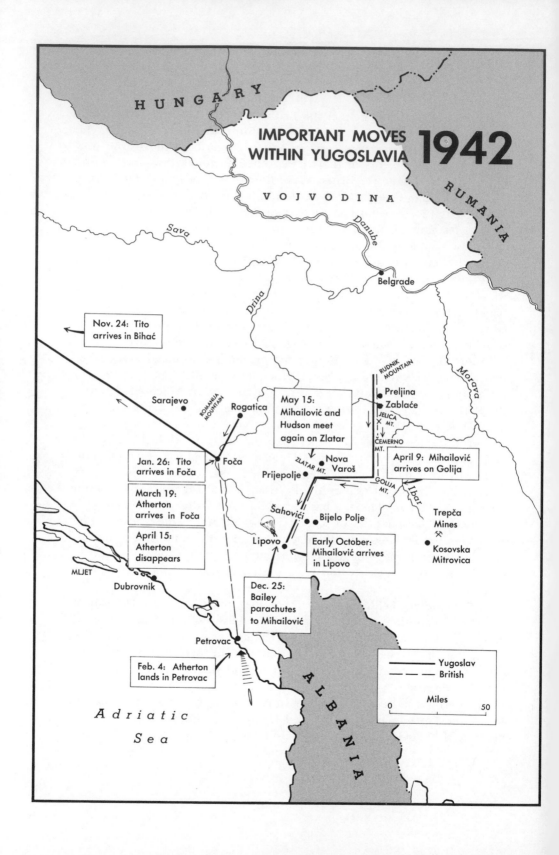

IMPORTANT MOVES WITHIN YUGOSLAVIA **1942**

HUNGARY

RUMANIA

VOJVODINA

Sava

Danube

Drina

Belgrade

Nov. 24: Tito
arrives in Bihać

RUDNIK MOUNTAIN

Morava

Sarajevo

ROMANIJA MOUNTAIN

Rogatica

May 15:
Mihailović and
Hudson meet
again on Zlatar

Preljina
Zablaće

JELICA MT.

ČEMERNO MT.

April 9: Mihailović
arrives on Golija

Jan. 26: Tito
arrives in Foča

Foča

ZLATAR MT.

Nova
Varoš

Prijepolje

GOLIJA MT.

Ibar

March 19:
Atherton
arrives in Foča

Šahovići

Bijelo Polje

Trepča
Mines

April 15:
Atherton
disappears

Lipovo

Early October:
Mihailović arrives
in Lipovo

Kosovska
Mitrovica

MLJET

Dubrovnik

Dec. 25:
Bailey
parachutes
to Mihailović

Petrovac

Feb. 4: Atherton
lands in Petrovac

ALBANIA

Yugoslav
British

Miles
0   50

Adriatic

Sea

sion of his movement, but his control over his commanders continued to be spotty, and collaboration of some of them with the Italians continued.

Both the Partisans and Četniks, despite their different aims and aspirations, desperately wanted to see the Allies win, but the primary aim of their fighting, at the end of 1942, was to determine the future political structure of Yugoslavia.

PART III: 1943

Civil War

NINETEEN FORTY-THREE was the year in which the Allied squeeze against the Axis in Europe began to show significant results. The Red Army was moving westward, and the British and American forces, having cleared North Africa, landed in Sicily and in September knocked Italy out of the war. This had important consequences for Yugoslavia since large portions of the country were Italian-occupied. The two resistance movements were fighting each other, and for purely military reasons the British began to support the Partisans with supplies and a military mission because they were fighting the enemy. The U.S. for the first time sent liaison officers to both resistance movements, while the Soviet Union continued to remain aloof.

5

THE BRITISH GOVERNMENT TRIES AGAIN TO ACHIEVE COORDINATION OF YUGOSLAV RESISTANCE

At the beginning of 1943, the American Chargé in London, H. Freeman Matthews, reported to the State Department that the British Foreign Office was becoming more concerned about the Mihailović-Partisan problem. However, Matthews' telegram of January 5 demonstrated that the British did not have a clear idea of who the Partisans were and by whom they were led.

These partisans are mostly located along the Dalmatian coast and in Croatia [Matthews reported] . . . they appear to be small bands with local leadership who at first confined themselves to attacks on General Mihailović. Lately, however, they have also been sabotaging and attacking the Nazis and the Italians. . . . There seems to be no really prominent leader of these groups, but they are numerous enough to warrant the attention and concern of the Yugoslav, British and Soviet Governments.[1]

In the same telegram, Matthews also said that the British Government was in touch with the Soviet Government regarding a coordination of the two resistance movements in Yugoslavia. Ambassador Biddle reported at the same time that the Yugoslav Prime Minister had informed him of these British efforts, saying that he was hopeful of constructive results.

The Soviet Government, however, told the British that it had "no direct influence or communication with the Partisans," which the British did not believe. Literally, of course, the Soviets were correct in that all communications passed between the Comintern and the Partisans. At the same time, the Soviet Ambassador to the Yugoslav Government-in-

Exile, Bogomolov, assured Prime Minister Jovanović that his Government's relations with the Yugoslav Government continued to be normal. He said that the Russian note of August 1942, which had charged the Četniks with collaboration with the Italians, should be treated more in the light of an observation than as a matter bearing on the relations between the two Governments.[2]

The Yugoslav Prime Minister—who was now also Foreign Minister, Ninčić having been dropped from the Cabinet on December 30—remarked to Biddle that the Soviet Ambassador was always friendlier when he knew that British-Yugoslav relations were more strained.

Eden and Jovanović met on January 11, at which time the Yugoslav Prime Minister handed an *aide-mémoire* to Eden. It dealt with three questions: help for Mihailović; the publicity given to Partisan activities by the BBC; and the British failure to transmit Mihailović's telegrams to the Yugoslav Government.

On February 8, Eden wrote Jovanović with regard to the shipment of supplies that "Col. Bailey has been authorized to discuss these matters personally with General Mihailović and as a result of these discussions we hope to receive a full list of his requirements." Eden added: "I can assure you that when this list has been received every effort will be made to supply the arms mentioned with the least possible delay."[3]

As far as the other two items in Jovanović's *aide-mémoire* were concerned—the tone of BBC broadcasts and the nondelivery of Mihailović's messages to his Government—they continued to plague the Foreign Office in the months to come. Repeatedly, it had to intervene with the BBC. In one of his telegrams in February 1943, Bailey said that his position with Mihailović was being prejudiced by the BBC's apparent support of the Partisans. A BBC item of February 21, 1943, declared: "The Yugoslav Partisans represent the only organized military force now fighting in occupied Europe." The Foreign Office protested and the BBC apologized, saying that an error had been committed. Yet the line did not really change.

With regard to the Mihailović telegrams, it must be emphasized that they went first to SOE Cairo, where they were translated into English and only then forwarded to SOE London. SOE London then transmitted them mostly in batches to the Foreign Office, which passed them on to the British Ambassador to the Yugoslav Government and he, in turn, sent them to the Yugoslav Prime Minister. That was a long process, and it has been established that some telegrams were not forwarded by SOE Cairo because of "military considerations." Others were held up inordinately either by SOE Cairo or SOE London. No wonder that such an

Colonel Bailey and General Mihailović, 1943. From *Mihailović—Hoax or Hero*

arrangement created mistrust on the part of the Yugoslavs. They thought up several devices to circumvent the British, for instance, communication via the Yugoslav Legation in Ankara. At one point, in June 1943, the British Government discovered much to its distress that the Yugoslav Government knew of telegrams sent to it by Mihailović before the British in London had seen them. It turned out that a Yugoslav colonel in Cairo who somehow had learned of them had sent them on directly to the Yugoslav Government.

It should be added that the Yugoslav Government's messages to Mihailović were also transmitted through the British. The Yugoslav Prime Minister would hand over a telegram in French to the British Ambassador, who in turn would transmit it to the Foreign Office, which then gave it to SOE London for referral to SOE Cairo. Thence it was sent to Mihailović, with the British mission fully apprised. Not until the summer of 1943 did Mihailović succeed in establishing a direct radio link with his Government, but the British, of course, were able to decipher his messages; it was their code.

One other problem that arose between the Yugoslav Government-in-Exile and the British concerned the Yugoslav request of February 20, 1943, that the British drop about twenty-five Yugoslav officers to Mihailović since he was short of trained staff. The British Ambassador replied that air sorties were far too few to undertake such an expedition.

During the Casablanca Conference between Roosevelt and Churchill in January 1943—at which the term "unconditional surrender" was first used—Yugoslavia was apparently not discussed, although Churchill reports [4] that after the conference he met the President of Turkey and handed him a document regarding the conference which contained the following paragraph: "The breaking down of Italy would lead to contact with the Western Balkans and with the highly hopeful resistance maintained both by General Mihailovitch in Serbia and the Partisans in Croatia and Slovenia."

THE BRITISH IN CAIRO TAKE AN INITIATIVE

On January 8, 1943, the Foreign Office received a summary of the first reports from Colonel Bailey. Mihailović's headquarters, he radioed, was in the village of Gornje (Upper) Lipovo, twelve kilometers northwest of Kolašin. British headquarters was one kilometer south in the same village. The British mission was living in peasant houses, but Bailey hoped to secure adequate quarters shortly. "For benefit of curious fortunates in Cairo, food and drink is rough but there is no female society here." Bailey reported that Mihailović's reaction to his credentials was good, and since he was living as the general's guest he would not "send appreciation of political situation and other ticklish subjects" until he returned to his headquarters in about ten days. "Our doubts regarding the authorship of Hudson's telegrams were unfounded," Bailey radioed and added that Hudson's "standing with General Mihailović is much better than I anticipated." Bailey ended his initial messages by pointing out that the upkeep of Hudson's headquarters before Bailey's arrival, including a bodyguard of ten men supplied by Mihailović had cost an average of 50,000 lire monthly. "Please send a quarter million lire . . . gold is losing its value."

By February, Bailey's radiograms became more substantive. On February 19 he cabled: "Mihailović's organization, outlook and aims are essentially military. The propaganda and political aspects of his activities

are handled inadequately, superficially and shortsightedly . . . Mihailović refuses to delegate authority and is surrounded by inept and lazy
staff officers. . . . Mihailović is stubborn and conceited regarding his
diplomatic powers of deceiving us."

These and other telegrams from Bailey were carefully read by British
SOE officers in Cairo concerned with the situation in Yugoslavia. They
were struck by the fact that Bailey seemed to assess Mihailović's strength
as confined to Serbia. Bailey suggested that it might be worth while for
the British to find out what the situation in other parts of Yugoslavia
was really like. He was the first, as far as is known, to recommend that
Yugoslavia be divided into Partisan and Četnik areas with an armistice
line between them.

Simultaneously, 240 backlogged messages arrived from Hudson (who
had meanwhile been promoted to major) in which he analyzed the Četnik
movement since his arrival at Ravna Gora in October 1941.[5] These telegrams clarified the basic origins of the civil war. Hudson criticized the
British decision to renew the dispatch of supplies to Mihailović (after it
was stopped at Hudson's urging in November 1941) without awaiting
Hudson's report on the Četnik-Partisan negotiations in the second half
of November 1941. Hudson's recommendation was that Mihailović be
forced to declare his policy and to dissociate himself from those Četniks
who were nominally under his command, but in effect acted as auxiliary
Italian troops.

At the same time, information reached the British in Cairo which
was only later made available to the top command of SOE in Cairo and
in London, regarding the military effectiveness of the Partisans.[6] This
highly classified information concerned German and Italian troop movements, and clearly showed that the Partisans were the enemy of the
Axis. In areas where Mihailović was in control, Axis troop activities
were either light or nonexistent. One of the SOE officers who studied
the situation closely was a former Fellow of Wadham College in Oxford,
F. W. Deakin, who had helped Churchill for five years before the war
in his literary work.[7] He had been with SOE for some time, served with
it in the United States and arrived in Cairo in December 1942. He was
to join Bailey at Mihailović's headquarters early in 1943.

It has been charged that SOE in Cairo was infiltrated by known Communists. The name of James Klugman is mentioned in this connection.
It is correct that Klugman was on the SOE staff in Cairo, but he was
never in a policy-making position, let alone "the wartime chief of Balkan
intelligence." [8] On the other hand, there were important persons in both
SOE Cairo and SOE London who had strong pro-Mihailović feelings.

On January 17, 1943, Radio Free Yugoslavia broadcast the text of a note of protest which the Supreme Command of the Army of National Liberation and the Executive Committee of AVNOJ had sent to the Governments of the United States, Great Britain and the Soviet Union. It charged the Četnik movement with collaboration with the occupying forces and the Government-in-Exile with treason and with conducting a war against the liberation movement through its Minister, Draža Mihailović. The note requested the three Governments to send an Allied commission to Yugoslavia "to establish . . . the actual state of affairs and once and for all to put an end to the frightful deception and error of public opinion." [9]

Churchill, who stopped off in Cairo early in February 1943 after the Adana Conference with the President of Turkey, discussed the Yugoslav situation with the British authorities there. At his request, he was given an SOE paper which was about to be presented to the commanders in chief in the Middle East for their consideration. It was dated January 30, 1943, and made these points:

1. Only four aircraft [Liberators] were at SOE's disposal for Yugoslavia, Greece and Crete. There were only 25 sorties between March 1942 and January 1943.

2. Mihailović undoubtedly represents resistance groups in Serbia. They tie down 3 German and 6 Bulgarian divisions. In the face of savage reprisals, acts of sabotage against Axis communications and economic enterprises have been carried out successfully. In addition to the 9 above-mentioned divisions there are 3 more German, 19 Italian, 6 Croat and 3 Hungarian divisions, i.e., over half a million Axis troops in Yugoslavia. Mihailović's subordinate commanders in Montenegro have made local arrangements with the Italian authorities which amounted to mutual non-aggression pacts including cooperation against Partisan elements. There has never been any evidence to suggest that Mihailović has made any compromise whatever with the Germans. Aid to Mihailović is as necessary as ever but developments outside Serbia render it necessary to consider the value of strengthening resistance in other areas.

3. There is abundant evidence from enemy, Russian and internal sources of organized fighting against the occupying forces in Slovenia and Croatia. It is not accurate to adopt the German technique of branding the whole movement in those areas as Communist. Aid must be organized for these groups by the British because otherwise either Americans or Russians will, for different reasons, take a practical interest which would lead to a weakening of the British position. The prospect of two members of the United Nations backing mutually antagonistic groups within Yugoslavia could only have lamentable consequences. The same organization which supports Mihailović should extend assistance to

other resisting elements and attempt to reunite Mihailović and the Partisans. SOE is ready to act but does not have enough aircraft.[10]

This balanced and objective paper made a great impression upon Churchill, and on his way home he discussed it with General Eisenhower in Algiers with a view to enlisting his interest and possibly to securing American help toward the provision of more Liberators. The paper was thereupon discussed in London, and immediately a question arose as to whether its implementation would mean a change of policy. SOE felt that its policy had always been:

1. To support Mihailović;
2. To infiltrate British officers to other resistance elements;
3. If information from these officers justifies it, to send them all possible support.

The Foreign Office, however, believed that this would mean a change of policy, and it was decided first to approach the Soviet Government. A message was therefore sent to Moscow in which it was suggested that it might be of interest and advantage to the Russians if Soviet agents were sent to the Partisans simultaneously with British officers and for the same purpose. The Foreign Office felt that it might thus avoid any subsequent suspicions that the British were doing something behind the Soviets' back. When the Soviets showed no interest, the British Government decided on March 3 to accept the SOE proposal. The authorizing telegram to Cairo did not deviate from the established British policy of supporting Mihailović, but it permitted the infiltration to other resistance movements. Should the reports from infiltrating officers justify it, the telegram said, all possible support should then be given to these other resistance forces, although the British Chiefs of Staff felt that the aircraft available to SOE were not sufficient to support both the Četniks and the Partisans. At a meeting on March 4, the Chiefs of Staff declared that "it seems sounder on military grounds to back Mihailović since he could provide some organization and control whereas under the Partisans chaos would probably ensue when the Axis forces were defeated." [11] Deakin reports that on March 23 a formal decision was taken in Cairo "to authorize SOE to proceed with its plan to make contacts in Partisan territory."

On February 24, 1943, the American Chargé in London, Matthews, reported on a conversation at the Foreign Office, which for the first time indicated "that the time has come to get in contact with the Partisans." [12] The Foreign Office stressed that it would continue to support Mihailović, but said that unfortunately the amount of practical aid furnished him by the British had not been great because of the difficulties of getting supplies in by air and the uncertainty of the identity of their eventual recipients. The Foreign Office told Matthews that the British had furnished money to Mihailović, "and I was told in confidence that there are two British liaison officers with him at the present time." In other words, the American Government heard in February 1943, probably for the first time, of Major Hudson and Colonel Bailey, though not by name, and quite obviously U.S. authorities were never given their telegrams to read.

At the same time, the Foreign Office told Matthews that the British liaison officers had found that Mihailović "has at no time been in touch with the Germans, though apparently in one instance his forces and Italians were simultaneously attacking the Partisans." (The reference was undoubtedly to the Third Offensive.)

Matthews' telegram to the State Department made two other points: The Foreign Office had asked its Ambassador in Moscow, Sir Archibald Clark Kerr, to inform the Soviet Government that the British, in pursuit of their "policy of supporting any group which is willing to fight the Axis," would like to establish contact with the Partisans. He was to make clear that the British had no ideological motive. (Matthews was not told of the British offer to the Russians to join them in a mission.) Matthews was asked to keep all this in strictest confidence, inasmuch as the Yugoslav Government in London had not yet been told of these British intentions. The other point made to Matthews was that there was no thought of withdrawing British support from Mihailović and his "gallant" army. Indeed several more British officers were parachuted into Mihailović's territory in the course of 1943, including a brigadier.

Just at that time (February 26), Bailey notified SOE in Cairo that unless Mihailović obtained more supplies from the British he could not push him into undertaking more sabotage operations. Bailey pointed out that Mihailović had received only two supply drops in the past five months. "I can no longer convince him that our interest is serious," Bailey cabled. To which SOE replied on February 28 that it simply did not have sufficient aircraft for operations in both Yugoslavia and Greece.

On March 23 the American Chargé in London followed up his talk of February 24 at the Foreign Office and found the situation evolving in several respects: [13] First, the Soviets had replied to the British initiative regarding helping the Partisans by saying that they did not wish in any way to cooperate. The Soviets, in other words, continued their policy of aloofness to the Partisans and of correct relations with the Government-in-Exile. Second, the Foreign Office had decided to go ahead and establish contact with the Partisans. Third, the Foreign Office was now convinced that "such recent fighting against the Axis as has gone on in Yugoslavia has been entirely the work of the Partisans, both the Communist group and the Croat group." (The British were apparently under the impression that there was a distinction between the "Communists" and the "Croats"—a difference that never existed.) Finally, the Foreign Office was persuaded of Mihailović's collaboration, at least with the Italians. Mihailović, Sargent told Matthews, "has frankly admitted that he has maintained contact with the Italians and . . . that he is getting supplies from them." What Sargent apparently referred to was a speech which Mihailović delivered in the presence of Colonel Bailey.

MIHAILOVIĆ'S SPEECH

On February 28, 1943, in the village of Donje (Lower) Lipovo in Montenegro, General Mihailović addressed his troops, and this speech represented, to all intents and purposes, the beginning of the end of British-Mihailović collaboration, although the end did not come until about a year later.

Bailey reported that Mihailović said:

(a) That the Serbs were now completely friendless; that the British to suit their own strategic purposes, were pressing them to engage in operations without any intention of helping them, either now or in the future; that the British were trying to purchase Serb blood at the cost of a trivial supply of munitions, that he needed no further contact with the western democracies, whose sole aim was to win the war at the expense of others; (b) that King Peter and his Government were not guests, but virtually prisoners of the British, who were shamelessly violating Yugoslav sovereignty by conducting negotiations on internal Yugoslav problems directly with Moscow; (c) that the hypocritical and anti-Yugoslav activities of the Partisans was a satisfaction for the Allies' lust for fraud; however, nothing the Allies could do or threaten, could divert the Serbs from their vowed and sacred duty of annihilating the Partisans; (d) that as long as the Italians comprised his only adequate source of help generally, nothing the Allies could do would force him to alter his attitude towards them . . . ; (e) that his enemies were the Ustashi [Ustaše], the Partisans, the Croats and the Moslems; that when he had dealt with these, he would turn to the Germans and the Italians.[14]

Bailey's report hit the British Government like a bombshell. On March 30, 1943, Ambassador Rendel handed Prime Minister Jovanović a note signed by Churchill as Acting Foreign Secretary (in Eden's absence) which said:

His Majesty's Government cannot ignore this outburst nor accept without explanation and without protest a policy so totally at variance with their own. They could never justify to the British people nor to their own Allies their continued support of a movement, the leader of which does not scruple publicly to declare that their enemies are his Allies—whether temporarily or permanently is immaterial—and that his enemies are not the Germans and Italians, invaders of his country, but his fellow Yugoslavs and chief among them men who at this very moment are fighting and giving their lives to free his country from the foreigners' yoke. . . .

. . . unless General Mihailović is prepared to change his policy both toward the Italian enemy and toward his Yugoslav compatriots who are resisting the enemies, it may well prove necessary for His Majesty's Government to revise their present policy of favouring General Mihailović to the exclusion of the other resistance movements in Yugoslavia.[15]

Fotić argues [16] that Bailey did not correctly report Mihailović's speech and that he gave some passages "an entirely different significance," but he has to admit that the speech was unfortunate, adding that it was given only after repeated pressure from the British to help the war effort without receiving from them the wherewithal for such an effort. Be that as it may, the British Government was deeply perturbed. While it had no intention of abandoning Mihailović, it was nevertheless persuaded that the general should be brought to a sense of reality.[17]

The Yugoslav Government, which had not known of Mihailović's speech until the receipt of the British note, was equally shocked. On April 6 it sent a letter to the Foreign Office in which it assured the latter that it shared its concern. It also immediately sent a directive to Mihailović, the text of which was coordinated with the British Foreign Office. In it, Mihailović was told of British reaction to his speech, of the possibility that Britain might revise its policy "of favoring the general to the exclusion of the other resistance movements in Yugoslavia" and of the hope that the improvement of the military situation in the Middle East might result in increased supplies to Mihailović. The general was given an order to conduct his policy vis-à-vis the Italians and other Yugoslav resistance forces in such a manner as not to subject himself to reproach either from the British or the Yugoslav Government.[18] The British were satisfied with the tone and substance of the Yugoslav Government's letter and directive to Mihailović.

As the pot began boiling, the American Ambassador to the Yugoslav Government learned that several weeks earlier the Yugoslav Government on its own had inquired of the general whether he had visited the Italian General Negri and whether the Četnik leader, Jevdjević, had concluded some form of agreement with the Italians.

Actually, there had been three inquiries—one in December 1942 and the other two in February 1943.

On February 4, Prime Minister Jovanović sent the following message to Mihailović:

For the American press it is necessary to have a statement from you (1) that you have never ceased fighting (2) that you have done everything to put an end to the fratricidal fighting and that this ideological battle has been imposed on us by the other side and (3) that you do not collaborate with any aggressor or individual traitor.

On February 26, the Yugoslav Prime Minister sent yet another message to Mihailović:

We have heard last September that Jevdjević concluded a pact with the Italians and afterwards you visited General Negri in Mostar. For these reasons, the Soviet Government has told us that it considers you to be collaborating with the Italians. The British and American press started a campaign in this sense. We have up to now refuted these allegations but since the campaign continues and becomes detrimental to our cause and you, I beg you to inform us exactly.

In his answer to this last inquiry, Mihailović declared that Jevdjević had no command and, with regard to his alleged visit to General Negri, Mihailović stated:

I did not go to Mostar at the time mentioned nor at any time during the war. I have had no meetings with Italians, nor with Italian generals. The Italians as well as the Germans have, on several occasions, attempted to arrange such meetings but they never took place for I always refused them with supreme contempt. The Germans made another attempt a few days ago. . . .[19]

Ambassador Biddle, in analyzing Mihailović's reply, wondered whether the general, by denying the allegations in the first person, "might not conceivably have naively hoped thus to sweep aside the question of cooperation by his 'lieutenants' with the Italians."

Fotić states [20] that Mihailović's answer to his Government's directive of early April "seemed to have given entire satisfaction to His Majesty's

Government." However, this was not the case. The Foreign Office considered Mihailović's reply "vague" and felt that he "had given no indication either of closer cooperation with the Allies and severance of his relations with the Italians or of his willingness to try to come to terms with Partisans and other Yugoslav groups at present engaged in fighting the Axis." [21] Furthermore, the Foreign Office was annoyed that it was often difficult for Bailey to see the general.

On May 7, 1943, the British forwarded yet another note to the Yugoslav Government, asking it to transmit to Mihailović a detailed communication which expressed the British hope of sending him "material support on a more considerable scale than in the past," provided a complete understanding was reached with him regarding the following points: The primary objective of his movement must be resistance to the Axis; there must be the closest and most constant collaboration between Mihailović and the British Commander in Chief, Middle East, through Colonel Bailey; all collaboration must now cease with the Italians; nor must there be any contact or collaboration with Nedić, the Serbian puppet Premier. (Surprisingly, the British directive added: "Any derogation from this principle could only be agreed to after consultation with the British Commander in Chief through Colonel Bailey and with the approval of the British and Yugoslav Governments.")

The directive again made a distinction between guerrilla groups in Croatia and Slovenia and the Partisans. It asked Mihailović to cooperate with the former and to reach a peaceful settlement with the latter. The general was then requested to work out with Bailey a program of resistance and the planning of the number and locations of other British missions under Bailey. The Yugoslav Government forwarded this British directive to Mihailović on May 12.

All this was reported to the State Department by the American Ambassador to Britain, John G. Winant, on May 14.[22] In the same telegram Winant said that "the British feel the time has come when some British officers, and American officers if we so desire, should be sent to Yugoslavia to endeavor to organize resistance on a more effective scale."

What the British had in mind, and what Winant did not spell out, was of course the dispatch of British and possibly also American officers to the Partisans. Actually, as we shall see presently, preparatory drops into Partisan territory by two teams of Canadians of Yugoslav origin had already been made.

On June 1, 1943, Mihailović replied (No. 1597), essentially accepting the British proposals of May 7 and insisting:

It is not in the least necessary to emphasize continuously that my only enemy is the Axis. I avoid battle with the communists in the country, and fight only when attacked. I am ready to establish the closest and most sincere cooperation with the British Supreme Command in the Middle East, and it is through no fault of mine that this cooperation has not already been established. Colonel Bailey has been with my staff for many months now, but the British Command has taken no special steps in regard to this, even though Colonel Bailey has stressed a number of times that he was waiting for instructions on this matter. . . . I consider all inference that cooperation with the Italians must cease, and that there should be no contact or cooperation with former General Nedić to be superfluous, since I have repudiated with contempt all attempts at such cooperation.[23]

A new dispute arose immediately, however, when Bailey handed Mihailović an instruction from the British Middle East Command to remove himself east of the Ibar River, where Četnik commanders had cooperated with British missions, leaving to the Partisans the rest of the country, where he was "weak" or his commanders "cooperated with the Axis." The British telegram said that the Partisans "represent a good and effective fighting force in all parts where only the Quislings represent General Mihailović." [24]

This instruction was sent by the SOE chief in Cairo at the behest of the Commander in Chief, Middle East, but without referring it to SOE London and the Foreign Office. Mihailović reacted strongly on June 1 (No. 1598), and the Yugoslav Government-in-Exile backed the general in his refusal to comply. Thereupon the British Government, upset by this "bad muddle," informed the Yugoslav Government that this order by British Middle East Headquarters had been a mistake. The SOE chief in Cairo was told in the future not to forward to Bailey important messages which had not been cleared by London.

THE OSS ENTERS THE SCENE—
EDEN VISITS WASHINGTON

The Office of Strategic Services (OSS) was created by President Roosevelt in June 1942 when he divided the Office of Coordinator of Information (COI) into two agencies: the OSS and the Office of War Information (OWI).

Colonel William Donovan, who had been chief of the COI, became director of OSS. (The OWI directorship went to newsman Elmer Davis.) This reorganization took place in order to separate intelligence from information functions and "black" (covert) from "white" (overt) operations. Within OSS, one branch was devoted to special operations (SO) and was to a large extent equivalent to the British SOE.[25] The officer in charge of OSS (SO) was Colonel Preston Goodfellow.

The British SOE and the American OSS (SO) soon began to establish liaison, and one of the first SOE officers who arrived in Washington was Tom Masterson, who had been head of SOE in Belgrade at the time of the German attack and who was later in charge of SOE Balkan operations in Cairo. It was his function to advise OSS on Balkan and Middle East affairs.

SOE-OSS (SO) relationships, which started out with the best of intentions, never really flourished. As the older organization SOE tried to keep OSS (SO) out of some theaters and if this was not practicable, to put the American organization under its preponderant influence. The OSS reacted to such an attitude by keeping certain ideas and projects to itself. There were also a number of other misunderstandings.[26]

Early in March 1943, the United States Government proceeded with plans to set up an OSS mission in Cairo with the purpose, among others, of establishing liaison with the resistance forces inside Yugoslavia. Colonel Ellery C. Huntington, Jr., a high OSS official in Washington, along with Colonel Gustav Guenther and Major Louis Huot, flew from London to Algiers and thence to Cairo to set up the mission. It was to be headed by Colonel Guenther, with Major Huot assuming responsibility for the mission's special operations section and Lieutenant Commander Turner H. McBaine for the secret intelligence section.

Thereafter, Huntington flew back to Washington to take charge of all special operations in OSS (succeeding Colonel Goodfellow), and Colonel Guenther and Major Huot returned to London. Both of them went back to Cairo in April 1943. There, Huot, as the officer whose section corresponded to the British SOE, established liaison with his British counterparts. The head of SOE Cairo was Lord Glenconner, an ex-naval officer working as a civilian. Brigadier Keeble was chief of staff, and Basil Davidson headed the Yugoslav section.

By the time the OSS became interested in Balkan operations in the spring of 1943, SOE Cairo had been involved in Yugoslav affairs for two years. Actually, in March 1943, SOE had received from the British Chiefs of Staff a new order of priority for its operations. After the victories in North Africa and in view of the contemplated landings in Italy, operations in the Balkans ranked second only after the Italian islands and Corsica and Crete.[27] Accordingly, an airfield was constructed at Derna in Libya for the aircraft which were at SOE's disposal. These included at that time not only the previously available four Liberators but also six Halifaxes which were added at Churchill's specific order after his visit to Cairo in February 1943 [28] and four more Halifaxes which were assigned by the British Chiefs of Staff on March 4, 1943.

In Washington, President Roosevelt expressed some thoughts regarding Yugoslavia when he had dinner with British Foreign Secretary Eden and Presidential aide Harry Hopkins on March 14. According to Hopkins,

. . . the President expressed his oft repeated opinion that the Croats and Serbs had nothing in common and that it is ridiculous to try to force two such antagonistic peoples to live together under one government. He, the President, thought that Serbia . . . should be established by itself and the Croats put under a trusteeship. At this point Eden indicated his first obvious objection to the Trustee method which the President is going to propose for many states. Eden did not push it but it was clear to me [Hopkins] that the British Government have made up their minds that they are going to oppose this. Eden thought the President's opinion about the inability of the Croats and the Serbs to live together a little pessimistic and he, Eden, believed it could be done.[29]

On March 24, the Yugoslav Chargé in Washington, Dr. Vladimir Rybar, in the absence of Ambassador Fotić, who was on consultation in London, called on Assistant Secretary Berle and inquired about Eden's visit as it affected Yugoslavia. Berle told Rybar that to the best of his knowledge Yugoslavia had not been discussed. At the same time Rybar expressed concern that "there seemed to be a growing desire to favor the Partisans on the part of this Government." [30] Berle answered by assuring Rybar that the United States Government had not changed its policy. Indeed, on March 26, President Roosevelt sent King Peter a "message of friendship" on the occasion of the second anniversary of the coup d'état in Belgrade: "With defiant courage the Yugoslav people cast back the challenge of a powerful aggressor and chose, under your inspiring leadership, valiantly to maintain their right to live as a free nation. This act still stands as a noble example of the principles our united arms are now defending."

During his conversation with Rybar, Berle seemed to have expressed a desire to have more facts about the activities of Mihailović and his army as well as the position of the Partisans. Rybar thereupon, under date of April 14, sent to the State Department a long account of the nature and extent of guerrilla activities in Yugoslavia which was of course highly pro-Četnik and derogatory of the Partisans.[31]

In this connection it is noteworthy that on March 30, 1943, SOE London sent a report to the Foreign Office commenting on the sabotage operations claimed by Mihailović: "Our opinion is that on the whole there is no reason to suppose that he has been exaggerating wildly." To which Sir Orme Sargent replied: "It is certainly more encouraging than I had thought." [32]

On April 5, Churchill sent Roosevelt a cable in which he commented on Eden's discussions in Washington and the general war situation. With regard to Yugoslavia, Churchill considered it an important objective to get a "footing" on the Dalmatian coast so that the "insurgents can be fomented by weapons, supplies and possibly commandos." Only Mihailović's Četniks figured at that time in Churchill's thinking, despite the general's speech of February 28 and the fact that British liaison with other resistance groups had already been authorized. "I believe," he cabled, "that, in spite of his present naturally foxy attitude, Mihailović will throw his whole weight against the Italians the moment we are able to give him any effective help." [33]

THE FOURTH OFFENSIVE

With the Axis military situation in North Africa deteriorating visibly, the Germans became more concerned than ever with the possibility that the Allies might land troops in the Balkans. In such circumstances, strong resistance forces could make the defense of the Balkan peninsula more difficult for the Germans. The likelihood of losing the supply of the raw materials of Yugoslavia, such as timber, copper and particularly bauxite, was an additional reason for German concern. Hence a decision was taken by Hitler to crush the resistance in Yugoslavia, and a directive to that effect was issued on December 16 to the German Commander Southeast. Accordingly, on January 20, 1943, the Germans and Italians launched their Fourth Offensive against the Partisans, called "Operation *Weiss* (White)."

The German aim (not the Italian, however, as will be seen presently) was the destruction of both resistance movements, the Partisans first and the Četniks later. Operation White was to be divided into three parts—White 1, White 2 and White 3—the last an Italian operation directed entirely against the approximately 20,000 Četniks in the Montenegro-Hercegovina area.

Even before the Germans and Italians began their offensive, the Partisans had been considering moving south into Montenegro and Hercegovina in order to be closer to Serbia. They knew they had to get back into Serbia, because only by controlling Serbia would they ever be able to control Yugoslavia. In Bihać in November 1942, the Partisans had officially

and openly announced what had been on their minds for some time—
that this fight was no longer solely a battle against the Axis; at stake was
future political power in the whole country. They were therefore deeply
troubled by the fact that their internal adversaries, the Četniks, more or
less controlled this southern part of Yugoslavia. In fact, Tito's plans included an attack across the Neretva River in Hercegovina, the southern
side of which was held by Italian and Četnik units. He calculated that he
would gain militarily (the Italians would be an easier enemy than the
Germans) and politically by wresting territory from Četnik control.

When the Germans and Italians attacked, the Partisans were ready.
So were the Četniks, who were determined to prevent the Partisans from
entering their domain. On February 17, 1943, Mihailović sent this order
to Stanišić, one of the Četnik field commanders: "Expelled from their
Soviet Republic in Western Bosnia, they . . . have come to rally the
proletariat of Hercegovina, Montenegro and Serbia and to set up a new
Republic. . . . Now is the time to beat the Communists to their knees,
if we act wisely. . . ." [34]

White 1 was terminated by the Axis forces on February 18 and succeeded exactly a week later by White 2, which, in turn, was completed on
March 20. By that time the Partisans, after grim and bloody battles, had
broken through the encirclement, saving thousands of wounded and sick.

The Partisans say that there was collaboration between the Četniks
and the Axis forces during the Fourth Offensive. That there was a mutually advantageous Četnik-Italian relationship is beyond doubt. But it
was not the kind of collaboration characteristic of the relationship between the Germans and the Croatian *Ustaše*. There was never any doubt
as to who was the master in German-occupied Croatia, but in Italian-
occupied Četnik territory, the occupier-occupied relationship became
occasionally very fuzzy. Colonel Bailey has told the author that often the
Četniks protected the Italians from the Partisans rather than the other
way around.

Četnik collaboration with the Germans, however, was another matter.
What the Četniks were doing was to attempt to prevent the Partisans
from entering "their" territory, and in that respect their and the Germans' aims coincided. But any direct collaboration between the Četniks
and the Germans must be excluded, simply because the objective of the
German High Command was the destruction of the Četniks.

Actually, a most peculiar situation arose during the Fourth Offensive:
The Germans and Italians attacked the Partisans, and in that undertaking, the Italians used Četnik troops as allied forces. Yet the Germans,
allies of the Italians, told the latter repeatedly that if they discovered

Četnik forces fighting alongside them they would not hesitate to attack the Četniks, whom they regarded as Germany's enemies.[35]

The Italians, on the other hand, refused to abide by the German wishes and in the end failed to carry out their assignment during the third phase of Operation *Weiss*—to disarm and annihilate the Četnik forces. The Germans were convinced that the Četniks could not be allowed to remain an operating resistance force since they would immediately come to the aid of an Allied invasion.

Mihailović's radio messages to his commanders, which the Germans said they deciphered, convinced them that Mihailović was as anti-Italian as he was anti-German. Accordingly, the Germans told the Italians during the Fourth Offensive that they were being used by the Četniks as arms suppliers but that the ultimate Četnik aim was to throw the Italians into the sea when the proper time came.

Just before the Fourth Offensive ended, Mihailović somewhat mysteriously left his headquarters at 2 A.M. on March 16, and Bailey cabled to Cairo, "Destination not revealed to me." Bailey advanced several possibilities but leaned toward the following: "He may be assuming personal command of operations against the Partisans."

Having extricated themselves from the Axis offensive, the Partisans were, as Tito himself explained,[36] not going after the Germans but pursuing their original objective of ousting from Montenegro the Četniks, whom, in an order to his troops on March 30, 1943,[37] Tito called "the greatest threat." On the day before, Tito wrote a letter to a commander in Bosnia in which he gave him certain military instructions, including the admonition: "On your way . . . do not fight Germans. . . ."[38] This standstill took place at a time when highly sensitive Partisan-German negotiations were taking place in Zagreb. The same letter continued: "Your most important task at this moment is to annihilate the Četniks of Draža Mihailović and to destroy their command apparatus which represents the greatest danger to the development of the National Liberation Struggle. . . ."

It soon turned out that the Četniks were no match for the Partisans, even though the latter had just been hit hard by the Axis Fourth Offensive. On March 23, Bailey had reported to Cairo that the fighting was going against the Četniks, and he added: "It is not impossible that Mihailović and Company will flee without worrying unduly about the fate of this mission and abandon us as they did Major Hudson last year." As it turned out, this did not happen. On April 12, Mihailović was ordered by his Government to rejoin Bailey at Lipovo, which he did.

On April 19, Mihailović was forced by the Partisan advances to move his headquarters, and he and Bailey left Lipovo for an encampment high up on the hills some twenty kilometers north of Berane. The Partisans were occupying large sections of Montenegro and in some measure doing the job which the Germans had assigned to the Italians during the Fourth Offensive but which the Italians had refused to carry out. The defeat which the Partisans administered to the Četniks was in fact a military blow from which the latter never recovered.

Meanwhile, the Germans were preparing a new offensive, the Fifth, to be directed mainly against the Partisans in Montenegro but also against the Četniks who had escaped the Partisan attacks in the aftermath of the Fourth Offensive. As German troops took new positions, several German-Četnik encounters occurred, such as a Četnik attack upon German positions near Berane.[39] On the morning of May 13, the Germans actually reached Mihailović's headquarters which the general, tipped off, had evacuated only two hours before, leaving northward for Serbia.

THE GERMANS OPPOSE ITALIAN-
ČETNIK COLLABORATION

From December 18 to 20, 1942, an Italian-German conference took place at Hitler's field headquarters in the Görlitz Forest in East Prussia. It was attended on the German side by Hitler, Foreign Minister von Ribbentrop and Field Marshal Keitel, and on the Italian side by Foreign Minister Galeazzo Ciano and the Chief of the General Staff, General Ugo Cavallero. During that conference, Hitler brought up the Balkan situation and told the Italians that the enemy must be prevented from continuing guerrilla attacks against Axis communications. In a separate meeting on December 19, among Ribbentrop, Keitel, Ciano and Cavallero, Keitel told the Italians that the Fuehrer had decided that the remaining resistance in Yugoslavia would have to be crushed before the winter was over (Hitler directive of December 16, which launched the Fourth Offensive). Keitel referred to the fact that General Mario Roatta, who commanded the Italian 2nd Army in Yugoslavia, had favored political action, but Hitler now absolutely forbade this. Cavallero tried to intervene in favor of the Četniks, but Ribbentrop said they were conspirators and must be liquidated.[40]

On January 3, 1943, just before the Fourth Offensive, a conference took place in Rome between German and Italian military leaders. It was attended by the German commander in the Balkans, General Alexander Löhr,[41] General Cavallero, General Roatta, one of Pavelić's generals, and also by Jevdjević, one of the Četnik leaders (who, however, had gone to the Rome conference without Mihailović's knowledge). Hitler's demand had apparently not yet penetrated. The Italians continued to press for Četnik participation in anti-Partisan moves, and Jevdjević was most eager to assist.

Ribbentrop visited Rome between February 24 and 28—while the Fourth Offensive was in progress—and carried a long letter from Hitler to Mussolini dated February 16. In this letter, a part of which dealt with Yugoslavia, Hitler said:

The situation in the Balkans, Duce, preoccupies me greatly. However useful it might seem to play opposing factions off against one another, I hold it to be extremely perilous as long as the parties involved . . . agree unconditionally on one point: their limitless hatred of Italy and Germany. . . . I detect a special danger, Duce . . . in the way the Mihailović movement has been developing. The great mass of the coordinated and trustworthy data in my possession reveals clearly that this movement, which is ably organized and energetically directed from the political point of view, awaits only the moment in which it can turn against us. . . . Mihailović seeks to obtain the arms and supplies for the execution of these plans by pretending to assist your troops. . . . My conscience bids me, Duce, to put you on your guard against the further prosecution of such a policy. . . .

In the interests of our common aims I consider it desirable that your Second Army regard Mihailović and his movement as uncompromising enemies of the Axis powers and I ask you, Duce, to give orders to this end to your higher commanders . . . it is essential that the furnishing of arms and supplies to his forces stop immediately . . . it will be necessary to disarm his units . . . to eliminate resistance . . . through determined concentric attacks. . . . If this is not done, Duce, if the Communists and Četniks are not disarmed . . . a revolt will certainly break out in the case of an [Anglo-American] invasion. . . . I believe, Duce, that there are obligations of which one cannot relieve oneself through political shrewdness but only through the full commitment of one's forces. . . . The correctness of my views is amply confirmed by the incontrovertible evidence resulting from our surveillance of telegraphic and radio traffic.[42]

Ribbentrop saw Mussolini on February 25 (Ciano was no longer Foreign Minister) and during their discussion (as well as subsequent ones on the following three days) the Balkan situation figured prominently. Clearly, there was a basic divergence of views between the Italian and the German side, with regard not only to the resistance movements but also concerning how to deal with them.[43]

Mussolini replied on March 9 to Hitler's letter of February 16, which Ribbentrop had delivered and again the Balkan situation took up a large part.[44] He commented on his recent Rome talks with Ribbentrop and he began his references to the Balkans by complaining that Operation *Weiss* (the Fourth Offensive) was not successful. He blamed the Germans, while the Italians, he added, reached their objectives. He then referred to his discussions with Ribbentrop in Rome in February and said:

We are fully in agreement that both Četniks and Partisans are enemies of the Axis and that tomorrow in the case of a landing [of the Allies] would make common front against us. . . . In view of the fact that for reasons of guerrilla tactics several thousand Četniks have previously been armed locally by Italian commands—like all Balkan peoples the Četniks are very skilled in guerrilla warfare and they have fought well against the Partisans at least until now—I have called General [Mario] Robotti [who in January 1943 had succeeded General Roatta[45] as commander of the 2nd Army in Croatia] and Pirzio Biroli [Governor of Montenegro and commander of the 9th Army] to Rome and have given them the following orders: a) no further arms to be furnished to the Četniks; b) they are to be disarmed as soon as the Partisans no longer constitute a dangerous armed movement . . . ; c) General of the Army Pirzio Biroli has been charged with working out a coordinated agreement with the German High Command concerning future actions to be taken in respect to the movement of Gen. Mihailović who, irrespective of whether he is treated as a traitor in the transmissions of the Partisan radio, is in any case our enemy by reason of his being the Minister of War of the Yugoslav Government in London. . . ."

On May 19, Hitler sent Mussolini a teletype message in which he said that he was determined to destroy the Yugoslav fighting groups, "while your General Pirzio Biroli is working for their preservation—indeed the Italians have actually created some of these formations." And: "I have tried with really angelic patience to arrive at cooperation in the Balkan area, but my efforts have failed thanks to repeated—I am forced to use this hard word—sabotage and lack of will to restore order." [46]

Mussolini reacted promptly. On May 22 he answered[47] by recalling first the gist of the Rome conversations with Ribbentrop and then stating:

In consequence of these accords, the Italian side immediately suspended all further distribution of arms; the resupply of munitions was reduced to the minimum and elements of the formations were purged to reduce their cohesion gradually. Thus, without delay, measures were taken to weaken and reduce these

formations. . . . The proof of the above is furnished by the fact that, unlike
in the past, the Četnik formations are besieged by Partisan attacks. Though
fighting resolutely, they have not been able to carry out an effective resistance
and have been in the process of rapid dissolution.

Mussolini then pointed out that, in view of the failure of Operation
Weiss, the Partisans had succeeded in fleeing to Montenegro, and thus
"the necessary precondition for the disarming of the Četnik formations
as established by the Rome accords did not supervene." Mussolini
complained that the German commander in chief, Löhr, and General
Robotti met on May 5 in Zagreb, but Löhr failed to mention anything
about a new German offensive (the Fifth Offensive, code-named *Schwarz*
[Black] which started on May 15 and was directed against both Partisans
and Četniks). "On the contrary," he wrote, "the German action against
the Četniks and the Montenegrin nationalists [48] was initiated without the
slightest prior notice to the Italian side. Obviously, the German High
Command adopted a new assessment, according to which it was considered indispensable to move up the timetable for the elimination of
the Četnik danger. But of this, the Italian Supreme Command was not
informed. . . ." (This was quite true. The Germans, in view of their
experience during the Fourth Offensive, distrusted Italian motives, particularly their collaboration with the Četniks.)

Mussolini then urged an accord on the modalities of action. "By now
Mihailović's bands know perfectly well our aims," he wrote, ending his
message by citing a telegram which he had sent to General Biroli urging
him to arrive at agreements with the Germans "to provide a radical
solution of the situation as regards all who were, are or would be our
enemies." Thus Mussolini succumbed to Hitler's pressures, but by May
1943 his power and authority had considerably diminished, and his commanders in the field no longer carried out his instructions to the letter.
Two months later, on July 25, he was ousted.

THE GERMANS AND THE PARTISANS HOLD DISCUSSIONS

There were forces in the German hierarchy, too, which were interested in
accommodations with the Četniks. The attempt of Capain Matl to persuade the German authorities to come to an agreement with Mihailović
in the autumn of 1941 has been mentioned. Another attempt was to
take place in May 1943. There were even efforts to achieve an accommodation with the Partisans.

Early in August 1942, the Partisans captured a German engineer by the name of Hans Ott and seven other Germans in the area of Livno in Bosnia. The task of the Germans was ostensibly to seek new sources of metal and timber for the German war machine, but at the same time, Ott was working for the German Intelligence Service with the aim of establishing contact with the Partisans.

Ott asked to be brought to Partisan headquarters to deliver an important message. This was arranged, and upon arrival there, Ott proposed that he and his group be exchanged for Partisans in Zagreb jails. His proposal was accepted. Ott was freed on his word of honor and he informed General Edmund Glaise von Horstenau, the German Plenipotentiary General in Zagreb,[49] that Tito was prepared to exchange the eight Germans for ten Partisans who were in German, Italian or Croatian hands. Since most of the ten Partisans were in Italian custody, Glaise von Horstenau turned to General Roatta. The German Minister in Zagreb, Siegfried Kasche, sent the German Foreign Office a telegram dated August 14, 1942, in which he informed Ribbentrop of this development and suggested that the Foreign Office intervene with the Italians to free these Partisans.

There was nothing basically new in Partisan-Axis prisoner exchanges. Partisans and Italians exchanged prisoners in Montenegro as early as the winter of 1941–1942.[50] As far as the Germans were concerned, the German High Command, regarding the Partisans as rebels and not as combatants, rejected prisoner exchanges, but local German commanders sometimes departed from the rule and occasional prisoner exchanges took place. (The first exchange of captured German soldiers and arrested Partisan followers had been effected in the autumn of 1941 in the Čačak area.)[51]

There is reason to believe that when the German Intelligence Service commissioned Ott to get in touch with the Partisans more was intended than mere prisoner exchanges. In any case, his capture and the fact that more and more Germans had fallen into Partisan hands during the summer and autumn of 1942 spurred the conclusion of German-Partisan agreements on the exchange of prisoners. These agreements were negotiated on the Partisan side by the representative of the Supreme Command, Marijan Stilinović. On September 5, 1942, one of these agreements was carried out in an area between Duvno and Livno in Bosnia. Thirty-eight captured Partisans and members of their families, including Dedijer's wife, were turned over by the Germans in exchange for one higher German officer captured by the Partisans in the battle of Livno.[52]

In the autumn of 1942, the Partisans decided to reassess their situation. Clearly, the Soviets were not sending them help. At the same time, the

Partisans had proof that the British were supporting Mihailović. The Italians were not in an aggressive mood, and there were hints from German sources that some kind of accommodation might be possible. Should this not be probed further so that the Partisans could be free to pursue the civil war and finish off the Četniks?

Within the framework of negotiating further prisoner exchanges, a meeting was arranged while the Fourth Offensive was still in progress between the commanding general of the German 717th Infantry Division, Lieutenant General Benignus Dippold, and three high-ranking representatives of the Yugoslav Army of National Liberation: Miloš Marković, Vladimir Petrović and Koča Popović. Only Popović, an army commander, used his real name. Marković was in reality Milovan Djilas, a member of the Politburo of the Central Committee of the CPY, and Petrović was an alias for Vladimir Velebit, in whose house in Zagreb the radio transmitter was hidden through which the CPY and the Comintern had exchanged messages in 1941.

A German memorandum [53] states that the German-Partisan conversation took place in Gornji Vakuf (west of Sarajevo) on March 11, 1943, from 9:30 to 11 A.M. It records that on the occasion of a previous prisoner exchange a German-Partisan discussion had taken place in Livno on November 17, 1942, at a lower level, with Ott participating on the German side, and that on that date a letter had been dispatched to General Glaise von Horstenau which dealt with political questions. During the March discussions, the Partisan delegation stressed that the Partisans saw no reason for fighting the German Army—they added that they fought against German troops only in self-defense—but wished solely to fight the Četniks; that they were oriented toward the propaganda of the Soviet Union only because they rejected any connection with the British; that they would fight the British should the latter land in Yugoslavia; that they did not intend to capitulate, but inasmuch as they wanted to concentrate on fighting the Četniks, they wished to suggest respective territories of interest.

The content of this German memorandum of conversation is confirmed by a document which the Partisan delegation left behind and which bears the signatures of the three Partisan emissaries. In it Djilas, Velebit and Popović proposed not only further prisoner exchanges and German recognition of the right of the Partisans as combatants but, what was more important, the cessation of hostilities between German forces and the Partisans. The three delegates confirmed in writing that the Partisans "regard the Četniks as their main enemy." Eleven days earlier, on February 28, Mihailović had said precisely the same thing, namely that his internal foes, the Partisans, were his main enemy, but he said it in the presence of Colonel Bailey, who reported the speech to London. The written Partisan proposals, however, have remained generally unknown.

A few days later, on March 17, the German Minister in Zagreb, Kasche, sent a telegram to Berlin in which, clearly referring to the German-Partisan talks, he reported the possibility "that Tito and supporters will cease to fight against Germany, Italy and Croatia and retire to the Sandžak in order to settle matters with Mihailović's Četniks. . . .

Under circumstances possibility exists that Tito will demonstratively turn his back on Moscow and London who left him in the lurch. The wishes of the Partisans are: Fight against the Četniks in the Sandžak, thereafter return to their villages and pacification in Croatian and Serbian areas; return of camp-followers to their villages after they are disarmed; no executions of leading Partisans on our part. . . . It is my opinion that this possibility should be pursued since secession from the enemy of this fighting force highly regarded in world opinion would be very important. In fact, the Tito Partisans are, in their masses, not Communists and in general have not committed extraordinary excesses in their battles and in the treatment of prisoners and the population. I refer to previous written reports and also to my conversation with State Secretary von Weizsäcker. Request instructions. In talks with Casertano [Italian Minister in Zagreb] and Lorković [Croatian Foreign Minister] I found that the above development would be treated positively.[54]

Meanwhile, in the wake of the discussions between the three high Partisan representatives and Lieutenant General Dippold, further talks were arranged at Zagreb. Clearly, the discussions in Zagreb were intended to go beyond prisoner exchanges. Otherwise Stilinović, the Partisan prisoner of war negotiator, would have participated. But instead Velebit and Djilas passed again through the German lines and were brought by a German military plane from Sarajevo to Zagreb on March 25, 1943. There they had talks with Glaise von Horstenau and his staff.

Not having received a reply from Ribbentrop to his message of March 17, Kasche sent another telegram to his Foreign Minister on March 26, 1943, in which he reported that two duly authorized representatives of Tito had arrived in Zagreb for the purpose of discussions with German, Italian and Croatian military representatives. One of them, Kasche said, was Dr. Petrović, a Croat, and the other a Montenegrin by the name of Marković. These people, he added, again offered to stop fighting if they could be left in peace in the Sandžak. Kasche emphasized that the newest discussions had uncovered an increasingly strong desire on the part of the Partisans to end hostilities. He completed his estimate of the situation with these words: "I see the possibility of saving our manpower and blood and thus of succeeding more quickly. This could be of real significance far beyond this area."

On March 29, Ribbentrop sent Kasche a telegram in which he prohibited all contact with the Partisans and asked on what Kasche based his optimism.

Kasche replied on March 31 that neither he nor the German Legation had any contact with Tito. Such contacts as had taken place with the Partisans were conducted by German military authorities and solely in connection with prisoner exchanges. (Kasche quickly forgot that only five days earlier he had reported more substantive talks with Tito's emissaries.) He confirmed that "the German, Ott," who was in Livno as head of the German coal and bauxite drilling operations, had worked for him before being captured by the Partisans in the summer of 1942. Ott's "personal knowledge of the Partisans" had made possible negotiations concerning the exchange of important prisoners and allowed "an insight into the domestic and military situation of the Partisans to an extent otherwise impossible up to then." Kasche added that during all negotiations so far "the reliability of Tito's promises has been confirmed." He continued:

I think the Partisan question is misjudged by us. Our fight therefore has been practically without success anywhere. It should be based more on political and less on military means. Complete victory over the Partisans is unattainable militarily or through police measures. Military measures can destroy clearly defined areas of revolt, security measures can discover communications and serve to finish off Partisans and their helpers. The extent of success depends on troops and time available. If both are scarce the possibility of political solutions should not be rejected out of hand.

Militarily, Kasche said, it would be useful if the Partisans were given a free hand in their battles with the Četniks. On the other hand, a simultaneous German attack against both Tito and the Četniks would only serve to bring the two enemies together in a common front against the German occupation.

The discussions between the Partisan representatives and the Germans in Zagreb regarding a possible cessation of hostilities got nowhere, not only because the Partisan proposals were unacceptable to the Germans [55] but, above all, because Berlin utterly opposed any accommodation with the Partisans. When apprised of the Zagreb contacts, Hitler reportedly said: "One does not negotiate with rebels—rebels must be shot." [56]

While the substantive negotiations ended in failure, new prisoner exchanges were agreed upon. Djilas returned to Partisan headquarters on March 30 with twelve Partisans who had been held in the ill-famed concentration camp of Jasenovac.

Dedijer, who talked to Djilas upon his return, does not report whether Djilas told him anything about the negotiations with the Germans but he quotes Djilas as having given him various impressions of life in Zagreb, such as that women were wearing shorter skirts than at the time of the outbreak of the war and that he had gone to a movie.[57]

Velebit stayed on longer. His aim was to obtain the release and to bring out of occupied territory a Slovenian Communist named Herta Has. She was the mother of Tito's then two-year-old son, Aleksandar. Back in 1929, while Tito was in jail, Polka, his Russian wife, returned to the Soviet Union with their son, Žarko. After his release, Tito went to Moscow but found his wife no longer interested in marriage with him. He obtained a divorce and after his return to Yugoslavia in 1939 met Herta, with whom he lived in Zagreb until he went to Belgrade early in May 1941.[58] When Velebit left Zagreb for Partisan territory accompanied by Herta Has, neither the Croatians nor the Germans had any idea that they had released the mother of Tito's second son.[59]

In the middle of April, as news reached Zagreb of battles between Partisans and Četniks in Montenegro (during the Fourth Offensive), Minister Kasche sent a new telegram to Ribbentrop in which he recommended that the Germans not attack the Partisans but rather sit back and let Tito and Mihailović fight it out and wear each other down. Ribbentrop's reply, dated April 21, was clear:

Your telegram 1607 of April 17 requires my statement that it is not our purpose through clever tactics to play off the Četniks and the Partisans against each other but to annihilate them both. After we have succeeded in rallying the Duce to our view, namely that both the Četniks and the Partisans must be annihilated, we cannot on our part propose a tactic which is not dissimilar from the Italian method of using the Četniks against the Partisans.

This telegram sounded the death knell to any possible accommodation between the Germans and the Partisans. (Glaise von Horstenau committed suicide after the war, and Kasche was hanged by the Tito regime.)

The fact remains, however, that the Partisans, who labeled Mihailović and the Četniks traitors for their accommodation with the enemy, sent two high-ranking officers to the German general in Zagreb with the purpose of arranging a cease-fire, after having declared in writing that their main enemies were the Četniks and not the occupying Axis forces. No wonder that there is great sensitivity in Yugoslav Communist circles about that chapter in history. None of the official Yugoslav documents mentions the Velebit-Djilas trip to Zagreb, while every possible Četnik-Axis meeting is duly recorded. Djilas himself refers to a Partisan-German parley but limits it to the Partisan aim of obtaining German recognition of the Partisans as combatants and does not mention his own participation in the talks.[60] It must of course be said that the accommodations reached between the Četniks and the Italians (though not the Germans) went beyond a cease-fire; yet this episode nevertheless shows that nothing in a civil war situation is ever black or white—there is only an infinite variety of shades of grey. Add to this the methods of guerrilla warfare—hit-and-run attacks one day, avoiding battles the next, temporary accommodations with the enemy the day after—and one describes the situation as it then existed in Yugoslavia. This situation is not unique, as events in recent years have shown repeatedly.

6

WHO IS TITO?

In a telegram to the State Department on September 9, 1942, the American Minister to the Yugoslav Government-in-Exile identified for the first time the leader of the Partisans by name.[1] But the name was not Tito. He reported that the Yugoslav Foreign Minister, Ninčić, had called him Lebedev. It seems that this information had reached the Yugoslavs in London from inside Yugoslavia—though not from Mihailović—and since the Government-in-Exile was convinced that the Partisans were Soviet agents, it accepted the identification of Lebedev as the Partisan leader, particularly since Lebedev had been the Soviet Chargé in Belgrade at the time of the German attack.

The British at first had no idea who the Partisan leader was. They later heard that Radio Free Yugoslavia had mentioned Tito by name in November 1942, and Hudson's long series of telegrams in early 1943 for the first time also referred to Tito as the Partisan leader without, however, further identifying him. Late in 1942 the name Tito began to appear in the Western press. On November 20, 1942, Hanson W. Baldwin, military editor of *The New York Times,* referred to "Nagy and Tito, Hungarian Communists." When the news of the Bihać Assembly reached the Western press, articles appeared which gave Tito the military and Ribar the civilian command of the Partisans. *The New York Times* of January 30, 1943, identified Tito as Lebedev, although Soviet Ambassador Bogomolov was quoted as saying that Lebedev was in Moscow and would soon be in London.

In the wake of the Bihać Assembly, the Yugoslav Communist Party organ *Borba* [2] published a photograph of Tito in its issue No. 29 of

113

December 6, 1942, and this photo led the German and Croatian authorities in Zagreb to the file of Josip Broz.

On February 13, 1943, the Croatian regime sent a memorandum to the German Legation in Zagreb confirming that Tito was Josip Broz, a Croatian Communist who had been convicted of illegal political activities in Zagreb in 1928 and sentenced to five years' imprisonment.[3] While the dossier indicated that Broz had been a high official in the CPY before the war, it did not refer to him as the General Secretary. Mihailović, who had been intensely interested in Tito's background ever since they met in 1941, sent a telegram (No. 1397) to his Government on March 8, 1943, in which he wrote: "After a year and a half of destruction in our country no one yet knows the true name of the Partisan Chief of Staff." [4]

Less than three weeks later, on March 27 (No. 1446), Mihailović asked:

Can a convict like Josip Broz who is listed with the Zagreb police under No. 10434, alias leader of the Communists under the name of Tito, be compared with the Yugoslav army as a national fighter . . . ? . . . the plunderer of churches and convict, Josip Broz, a locksmith's assistant from the county of Klanjec in Croatia . . . hiding internationally under the false and mysterious name of Tito. . . .[5]

Thus, between March 8 and March 27, Mihailović became aware of the discovery made earlier in the year by the Croatian regime. The source of his information was undoubtedly an article in the Belgrade paper, *Novo Vreme,* of March 5 entitled "Who is Tito, Leader of the Communists in Bosnia?" which was based on a similar story in the German-language paper in Zagreb, *Neue Ordnung,* of February 28, 1943. On March 20, the Nazi Party paper, *Völkischer Beobachter,* carried an article with Tito's picture from the Zagreb police files and the number 10434. The Western press, however, never picked up these revelations. Only after Allied liaison officers reached the Partisans a few months later was the name Tito linked with Josip Broz.

A memorandum which the Yugoslav Embassy in Washington sent to the State Department on April 14, 1943, stated: [6] "The names of the principal Partisan leaders were unknown in pre-war Yugoslavia. Tito and Nagy [probably Kosta Nadj, one of the Partisan field commanders], two names frequently mentioned, are from all appearances partly or completely foreign." In other words, the Yugoslav Embassy in Washington had not yet been apprised that Mihailović had reported the identity of Tito to his Government a month earlier.

In early May, Tito received a telegram from Moscow informing him that the Comintern was to be disbanded as the leading center of the international workers' movement because ". . . the centralized form of international organization no longer corresponds to the needs of the further development of the Communist Parties of the different countries . . . [and] has even become an obstacle to this development."

Tito did not comment immediately. Three weeks later, after he had been prompted to reply and after the Comintern had ceased to exist, he responded: "Under the banner of Marx, Engels, Lenin, Stalin, our Party will continue to do its duty to its people." This statement was signed by Tito as General Secretary and by Aleksandar Ranković, Milovan Djilas, Edvard Kardelj, Ivan Milutinović and Franc Leskošek as members of the Politburo.[7]

Even though the Comintern was officially disbanded, it continued for several months—until a Soviet military mission arrived in Partisan territory in February 1944—to function as transmission center for Partisan-Soviet messages. This suited the Soviet Government well. Throughout 1943, it thus maintained its correct relationship with the Yugoslav Government-in-Exile. Its sole link, however, was through the Soviet Ambassador to the Yugoslav Government. The Yugoslav Ambassador in Moscow, Stanoje Simić, began to side with the Partisans rather than with his principals in London and thus lost all contact with his Government, although he declared that he was not in touch with the Partisans.[8]

THE BRITISH ESTABLISH LIAISON WITH THE PARTISANS AND STRENGTHEN THEIR MISSION WITH THE ČETNIKS

After the decision was taken by SOE in Cairo to send probing missions into Partisan territory, a number of Canadian volunteers of Yugoslav origin left Derna airport in Libya for Yugoslavia. Code-named "Hoathley I," the first group, consisting of Steven Serdar, George Diklić and Milan Družić, parachuted on April 21 near Zvornik in Bosnia. The second, code-named "Fungus," with Pavle Pavlović, Petar Erdeljac and Alexander Simić, came down on the same day in the Lika area in Croatia.[9] Both groups were landed "blind" because it was not known where the main headquarters of the Partisan movement was situated. As it was, the second group landed not far from Partisan headquarters in Croatia, which was then in Brinje near Ogulin. They were immediately taken to headquarters, which informed Tito's Supreme Headquarters of the arrival of the mission. Tito, in turn, sent a directive on April 23 to Croatian

Captain Deakin and Tito in Jajce, 1943. *Courtesy of F. W. Deakin*

headquarters to hold the parachutists until it was established who they were, and not allow themselves to be provoked as in the case of Atherton a year earlier.[10] Croatian headquarters thereupon did not let the Fungus mission make contact with Cairo, but five days later, Tito instructed Croatian headquarters to allow the mission to begin using its transmitter.[11] Only then did the mission radio its arrival to SOE Cairo. On May 7 SOE Cairo asked Fungus whether Croatian headquarters would receive a British mission, and on May 17 Cairo received an affirmative response.

Thereupon, Cairo dispatched the first British mission to the Partisans. On May 18, Major William D. Jones, Captain A. D. N. Hunter, and radio operator Ronald Jephson found themselves "slowly and comfortably drifting to the moonlit turfs of Croatia."[12]

The British in Cairo had at that time no idea whether Croatian Partisan headquarters was *the* Partisan headquarters, but they knew that there were Partisan forces farther south in Montenegro. Hence the Fungus mission was advised by Cairo to propose the dispatch of another British mission to the southern headquarters. This proposal was duly forwarded by Croatian headquarters to Tito on May 12. He replied on May 17 that a British liaison officer should be sent to Partisan headquarters in Montenegro.[13] The Fungus mission relayed this invitation to Cairo forthwith.[14] The Commander in Chief, Middle East, General Sir Henry Maitland Wilson,[15] promptly accepted the invitation, and a mission was readied. Even before it took off, Cairo had learned from the British mission in Croatia that the headquarters in Montenegro was indeed the top command of the Partisans and that it was there that a man called Tito was in command.

The Partisans, who only a few weeks earlier had told the Germans that they wished to have no connection with London, were thus now disposed to receive a British mission. The German Fifth Offensive had just begun on May 15, which convinced the Partisans that the German leadership not only rejected any kind of accommodation but on the contrary was determined to annihilate them.

On May 28, 1943, Captain F. W. Deakin, then thirty-one years old, and Captain W. F. Stuart, a tough forty-two-year-old Canadian who had spent the greater part of his life in the Balkans and knew its languages and peoples as well as his own, parachuted into an agreed landing zone near Durmitor Mountain in Montenegro. It was a joint SOE-Military Intelligence mission, code-named "Typical," with Deakin heading the SOE and Stuart the M.I. side. On Deakin's staff were a radio operator, Corporal Walter Wroughton, and Ivan Starčević, a Canadian of Croatian origin. With Stuart came Sergeant John Campbell and a radio operator who called himself "Rose," later identified by Deakin as a Palestinian Jew named Peretz Rosenberg.[16] The joint mission of six was met by a Partisan officer and taken to Tito's headquarters.

Deakin was selected to head this mission after an earlier proposal that he follow Colonel Bailey as second-in-command of the British mission to the Četniks failed to materialize. Prime Minister Churchill, who knew Deakin well, had nothing to do with his assignment to Yugoslavia. As a matter of fact, he learned of Deakin's inclusion in the mission only after it had landed safely.

Deakin reports [17] that his directive was to bring the good wishes of the British headquarters in Cairo; to attempt to synchronize Partisan efforts with the Allied offensive in the Mediterranean, particularly in regard to attacks on the main lines of communication running through Yugoslavia; not to get involved in civil war; to point out to the Partisan command the British attitude in regard to Mihailović; and to use any influence to avoid local clashes.

The British arrived during the Fifth Offensive and within a few days found themselves in the thick of battle. On June 9, Stuart was killed by a German bomb which also wounded Deakin and Tito. This shattered all doubts: Deakin could inform SOE Cairo that Germans and Partisans were locked in mortal battle. More than 100,000 German and other Axis troops were engaged with about 20,000 Partisans, who, while sustaining heavy losses, were inflicting equal if not heavier casualties on the Germans and their allies.

On June 10, the German commander of the operation, General Rudolf Lüters, announced that "the last phase of the battle, the hour of the final liquidation of the Tito Army, has come."

To the chagrin of the German High Command, the main Partisan forces had succeeded by the second half of June in forcing their way out of the Axis vise, in an action known in Partisan annals as the Battle on the Sutjeska, and reaching the relative safety of the mountains of eastern Bosnia.[18] Even before all this happened, those Četniks who had survived the battles of the Fourth Offensive and whom the Germans had hoped to annihilate during the Fifth Offensive had escaped to Serbia. The Germans accused the Italians of facilitating this Četnik retreat.

Soon after Deakin arrived at Tito's headquarters, he recommended to Cairo the dispatch of medical supplies, arms, food and explosives to the Partisans, and on June 8, the most difficult day for the Partisans during the Fifth Offensive, the Middle East Defense Committee in Cairo (a joint military and political command) reported to London its plan to send material aid to the Partisans west of the Ibar River and to the Četniks east of that river. This division of territory had been proposed on June 1 to Mihailović, who reacted negatively. He was supported by his Government, and the British Government on June 16 ordered Cairo to drop the idea as operationally unworkable and politically unwise, but only after the Middle East Defense Committee message had been dispatched to London.

The clear implication of the Middle East Defense Committee's proposal, which judged that "the Partisans are now the most formidable anti-Axis element in Yugoslavia and our support of them is therefore logical and necessary," was that the Partisans would receive more help than the Četniks. This was far different from merely establishing contact with the Partisans, and, naturally it aroused a great deal of controversy in London. The British Chiefs of Staff, in a reversal of their preference for exclusive support of Mihailović only three months before, generally favored the proposal. On June 6, even before the arrival of the telegram from Cairo, the Chiefs had declared in a memorandum:

It is clear from information available to the War Office that the Četniks are hopelessly compromised in their relations with the Axis in Hercegovina and Montenegro. During the recent fighting in the latter area, it has been the well organized Partisans, rather than the Četniks, who have been holding down the Axis forces.[19]

On June 17, the Chiefs of Staff recommended to the Foreign Office that "we should supply Croatian guerrillas and Communist partisans with war material inasmuch as these groups represent the most formidable anti-Axis elements existing outside Serbia." [20] However, the Foreign Office and Lord Selborne, the new Minister of Economic Warfare, who was responsible for SOE affairs, had their doubts—the latter saying that "my sympathy is definitely with Mihailović who has kept the flag flying since 1941"; the former arguing that to write off Mihailović as ineffectual was politically undesirable and militarily premature.

Meanwhile, Churchill involved himself in the controversy. He writes that after Deakin and others had dropped into Partisan territory, "much evidence had accumulated." He continues:

Toward the end of the month my attention was drawn to the question of obtaining the best results from local resistance to the Axis in Yugoslavia. Having called for full information, I presided at a Chiefs of Staff Conference at Downing Street on June 23. In the course of the discussion, I emphasized the very great importance of giving all possible support to the Yugoslav anti-Axis movement which was containing about 33 Axis divisions in that area. This matter was of such importance that I directed that the small number of additional aircraft required to increase our aid must be provided, if necessary, at the expense of the bombing of Germany and of the U-boat war.

Up to that time, few British supplies had reached Yugoslavia. Twenty-three tons of material had been dropped to the Četniks,[21] and the first air drop to the Partisans was to take place on June 25. The paucity of supplies to the Četniks was due not only to the small number of aircraft available to SOE but also to the fear on the part of some British officials that the arms might be used largely against the Partisans. That no supplies had been dropped to the Partisans was of course due to the fact that liaison with them had been established only shortly before.

As a result of the Chiefs of Staff conference of June 23, 1943, thirty-two bombers were placed at SOE's disposal in the Mediterranean.[22]

On June 27, the Chiefs of Staff replied to Cairo's proposal of June 8. They accepted the idea of supplying the Partisans with war material, but insisted that Partisans operating in close proximity to the Četniks should first be required to give assurances to British liaison officers "that no operation will be carried out against Mihailović except in self-defense." The Chiefs reiterated London's opposition to the demarcation of two different territories, for Partisans and Četniks. The telegram added that support for Mihailović should be continued so long as he accepted the British directive of May 7 which, it will be recalled, contained four demands and which Mihailović had generally agreed to on June 1.

Even before the Chiefs of Staff's reply reached Cairo, parachute drops to the Partisans began, on June 25, mainly intended for use in the destruction of the north-south rail line through Bosnia.

By the end of June, the British had three missions with the Partisans: Deakin with Supreme Headquarters, Hunter in Croatia and Jones in Slovenia, where this Canadian veteran of World War I became a legendary figure.

Deakin's messages to Cairo had mentioned Tito's background, but not until September was Tito identified in the Western press as Josip Broz. C. L. Sulzberger reported in *The New York Times* of September 14 that the Partisans were led by Josip Broz, but he did not make the connection with Tito. A UP dispatch from London carried in *The New York Times* of October 1 finally mentioned "General Josip (Tito) Broz." Tito's full background became known only after Vladimir Dedijer reached Cairo later in the year.

Not long after his arrival at Partisan headquarters, Deakin became persuaded that the Partisans were justified in charging the Četniks with collaboration, not only with the Italians but also with the Germans. He so informed Cairo in a series of telegrams. This was the first time that Cairo had heard from a British source of Četnik collaboration with the Germans. While Hudson and Bailey had said many negative things about Mihailović, the question of collaboration with the Germans was never raised by them, and Deakin's radiograms therefore made a deep impression upon those in Cairo and London who were concerned with British policy regarding Yugoslav affairs. Deakin did not report, because he did not know and of course was not told by the Partisans, that the latter themselves had negotiated with the Germans at a very high level only two months before his own arrival in Yugoslavia. He believed that what he himself had witnessed [23] proved Četnik-German collaboration, even though the Bosnian Četniks whom the Partisans had caught were in all probability not Četniks in the real sense of the word, *i.e.*, not Mihailović-controlled. Moreover, the German aim, at the time of Deakin's radiograms to Cairo, was the annihilation of both Partisans and Četniks; only a few months later, in November, did the Germans permit nonaggression pacts with local Četnik commanders.

At the start of the Fifth Offensive, Mihailović, having narrowly escaped German capture on May 13, was on his way north to Serbia accompanied by the British mission. His route back was almost the same one he had taken a year earlier when he went south to Montenegro. At the end of May he recrossed the Western Morava River, about ten kilometers west of Čačak. During the next fifteen months, until he went to Bosnia in September 1944, he spent most of his time near Maljen and Povljen Mountains, south of Valjevo. His headquarters was never permanent, and he moved within that region as dictated by security, staying in one place a few days or weeks and then moving thirty to forty kilometers in another direction. In August he was near Ivanjica, in September on Mt. Tornik close to Zlatibor. In October he moved back north to the area between Valjevo and the Drina, and during the winter of 1943–1944 he spent at least three months near the village of Makovište on the Pašina Ravna plateau on Povljen Mountain.

At the time Mihailović returned to Serbia in May 1943, the British mission was strengthened by the dispatch of liaison officers who were dropped to several Četnik commanders with instructions to prod them into action against railroads and mines. But instead of successes similar to the wrecking of the north-south rail line in Bosnia by the Partisans they could report only the great reluctance of Mihailović and his commanders to undertake sabotage operations.

One of the British liaison officers with the Četniks was Major Jasper Rootham, who parachuted into Yugoslavia in the area of the Homolje Mountains near the Danube on May 21, 1943, and stayed until the British mission left at the end of May 1944. He writes that the reason the Četniks gave him for their attitude was the lack of supplies, and adds that the four Liberator aircraft at the disposal of SOE in Derna made only a few drops into Četnik territory. The Četniks refused to believe that it was the shortage of aircraft that was responsible. "Major, you tell me that the whole of the British Empire can only spare four airplanes for this work of supplying the Yugoslav Army of the Fatherland?" one of the Četnik commanders said to Rootham.[24] Nevertheless, Rootham was constantly assured that sabotage was going on. "The trouble was that . . . it was never anything about which we could send first-hand information to our Headquarters," he writes.[25]

As far as German-Četnik armed encounters were concerned, Rootham says that they definitely occurred but originated invariably with the Germans. The Četniks gave as reason for not attacking the Germans the continued reprisals against the Yugoslav population. These actions hit the Serbs particularly hard, for they were already being victimized by the *Ustaše* killers. The Četniks' fear increased that, in any future Yugoslav state, the Serbian majority might have been turned by mass slaughters into a minority. Rootham writes that Mihailović's policy was to avoid clashes with the Germans, to wait for an Allied victory and then to rise against the occupying forces, but his deceptiveness proved his undoing. Had he stated plainly his intentions, he might have obtained British understanding. He tried, however, to make the Allies believe that he was fighting the Germans when in fact his policy was to avoid engagements. When there were German attacks on the Četniks, British liaison officers were often misled regarding the extent of Četnik and German casualties. Rootham writes that on one occasion he was asked by a Četnik leader to tell the BBC that 153 civilians in a certain village had been killed by the Germans; it was established later that the figure was five.[26]

At the time of Rootham's arrival and until late in 1943 the Germans regarded the Partisans and Četniks as practically equal foes. "Communists" and "Mihailović supporters" were continually arrested and executed, according to entries in the German War Dairy.

A price of 100,000 gold marks was placed equally on the heads of Tito and Mihailović. This offer, which was published and broadcast by the Germans and their allies all over Yugoslavia on July 21, 1943, was later the subject of recriminations, particularly by the followers of Mihailović. They have charged that Tito's supporters suppressed the fact that the same reward was offered for Mihailović as for Tito.[27] It is a fact that in both Britain and the United States, the news media reported only that the Germans had offered 100,000 gold marks for the capture of Tito. On September 21, 1943, for instance, a reproduction of the poster offering a reward for Tito, but omitting Mihailović, accompanied an article by Louis Adamic in the New York afternoon paper, *PM*.

While liaison officer in Serbia, Rootham saw clear evidence of civil war and said that it would be wrong to generalize about who was the aggressor. Apart from anything else, it is very difficult to say who is the aggressor and who is not in warfare between guerrilla units. Moreover, Rootham writes, the country is large, and the forces were small and mobile. One party's territory today may be the other party's tomorrow. On one occasion, Rootham had to remind one of the Četnik commanders that he and other British officers had been sent to organize the fight against the Germans and not to take part in private wars.

There is a German report that on July 7, 1943, Mihailović sent an order to his commanders, in view of the Allied landings in Sicily, to prepare uprisings but not to rise until he gave the signal.[28] On July 16, 1943, Mihailović called on his Četniks—the Germans say they deciphered his message—to dislodge the Partisans from the Adriatic coast so that in the event of a landing there the Allies would find his forces and not the Communists.[29] While Mihailović hoped for such landings, the Communists opposed them and therefore were determined to make certain that no Četnik forces would be along the Adriatic to pave the way for the Allies.

It was not until a year later that the British and American officers with the Partisans became aware that the Partisan effort, too, had assumed more and more the character of a civil war. But since the Partisans found themselves continuously the object of German attacks, they could not concentrate as much as they wanted on fighting their internal enemies. To drive the Četniks out of Montenegro, and particularly Serbia, had been their major aim since 1942, however.

Rootham writes that in eastern Serbia, where he operated, the Partisans had little following because of events in 1941. At that time they had spurred the people to rise, telling them the Russians would soon come. The uprising was cruelly put down by the Germans, the Russians did not come, and the Partisans fled. On the other hand, according to Rootham, the fact that Mihailović's actions were vastly exaggerated by the Yugoslav Government-in-Exile did not help him with the people either.

THE GERMAN INTELLIGENCE SERVICE TRIES
TO ESTABLISH CONTACT WITH MIHAILOVIĆ

In May of 1943, there was yet another attempt on the part of the German Intelligence Service to get in touch with Mihailović. It was a bizarre affair involving the commander of the 4th Regiment of the Brandenburg Division, Lieutenant Colonel Friedrich W. Heinz.[30] That division was to have played a role in a conspiracy aimed at killing Hitler by planting a bomb in his airplane on March 13, 1943. The bomb did not explode, and thereupon the regiments of the Brandenburg Division were dispersed immediately to various battlefields, the 4th Regiment to Yugoslavia. Lieutenant Colonel Heinz received the order to capture Mihailović alive.

Having heard from Italian officers that collaboration with Mihailović was possible, Heinz went directly to the German command for the Balkans in Salonika and proposed not to capture Mihailović, but to attempt to collaborate with him. He obtained concurrence for his plan from the chief of staff, Major General Hermann Förtsch. From Italian officers Heinz had learned that Mihailović's headquarters, then still in Montenegro, was somewhere around Kolašin and Berane, and he proceeded to put this information to the test.

On May 7, 1943, accompanied by Lieutenant Eucker and his driver, Sergeant Karbeutz (both spoke Serbo-Croatian), Heinz drove unarmed to Kolašin. After passing Četnik guards, Heinz and his companions were brought to a house where they began negotiating with Mihailović's emissaries, Djurišić (undoubtedly Pavle Djurišić) and Popović, his chief of staff.

After several hours, a man entered the room who Heinz thought was Mihailović, but who did not identify himself as the general. (It was probably not Mihailović, whom Bailey places at that time north of Berane, an area he did not leave until he went to Serbia a week later.) This officer agreed to a proposal which contained the following three points:

1. The leader of the Četniks regards Tito and the Communist Partisan movement as the main enemy of Serbia and is prepared to collaborate actively and unconditionally with Germany in the battle with and defeat of that enemy.

2. To prove that General Mihailović and the Četnik leaders are prepared to conduct this battle sincerely and without hidden motives, they are ready to make available a Yugoslav legion which, under Mihailović's command, would fight on the German side.

3. This agreement, which is intended to lead to an immediate collaboration between the German Army and the Četniks, will be valid only until such time as either American or British troops land on the Adriatic coast. Thereafter, the Četnik leaders would be unable to guarantee the reliability of the Četnik troops.

Heinz sent this draft immediately to Berlin to Admiral Wilhelm Canaris, head of the German Intelligence Service, and to the Commander in Chief Southeast in Salonika. Such a fundamental step required a decision by Hitler. The answer came quickly. Hitler's headquarters relieved Heinz of his command and indicted him for "negotiating with the enemy," but Admiral Canaris arranged to have the indictment dropped.

The German 1st Mountain Division thereupon received orders to capture Mihailović, Djurišić and Popović, and they succeeded in taking the latter two on May 14 at Kolašin by deceiving the Italian troops who guarded their headquarters. Mihailović had already left for Serbia.

Djurišić and Popović were driven away in a car carrying Red Cross markings and sent to Germany. In the summer of 1944, Djurišić escaped from a German POW camp, made his way back to Yugoslavia, rejoined Mihailović, and lost his life in the spring of 1945 while trying to lead some Četnik units toward Italy.

The established pattern thus persisted: first, a local Axis initiative for an accommodation exploiting the Četnik hatred for the Partisans or the Partisan hatred for the Četniks; then a readiness by either the Četniks or the Partisans to engage in discussions; and finally, either an accommodation, as in the case of Italians with Četniks, or a rejection by the Nazi leadership of any proposed arrangement between local German authorities and Četniks or Partisans.

Six months later, however, the Nazi leadership was persuaded to change its position, and local nonaggression pacts were concluded with several regional Četnik commanders.

FOTIĆ TALKS TO ROOSEVELT

Upon his return from consultation in London, Ambassador Fotić called on Under Secretary of State Welles on April 29, 1943. During the conversation, Fotić mentioned that Yugoslav Prime Minister Jovanović and Churchill had never met and that Yugoslavia was not represented at the Court of St. James's, because of the inability of the Serb and Croat elements in the Yugoslav Government to agree on an ambassador. (When the Legations were raised to Embassies in May 1942, the Yugoslav Minister, Ivan Subbotić, was not elevated and the post of Ambassador remained vacant until September 17, 1943, when, after the departure of the Government-in-Exile for Cairo, Bogoljub Jeftić was appointed by King Peter as Ambassador to Britain.)

Fotić requested an appointment with Roosevelt and told Welles he wished to take up with the President the matter of the food packages which the President had sent to Mihailović. They had arrived in Cairo but had not been forwarded by "the British authorities." He also desired to put forward a request that American officers be attached to Mihailović "both in order that we might know through them the true state of affairs in Serbia and in order that the sole contact of General Mihailović with the outside world should not be only through the group of British officers attached to him." [31]

A meeting was arranged, and the President saw Fotić on May 5, 1943.[32] Fotić reports that the President "manifested considerable interest in the Yugoslav situation." With all of North Africa about to be cleared of

German and Italian forces and an invasion of Italy imminent, Roosevelt told Fotić that he "was convinced that the position of Yugoslavia would become increasingly important." The President predicted Italy's surrender and said that "the guerrillas in Yugoslavia might become of much greater importance than they had been in the general plan of military operations." He "was grieved by Yugoslavia's internal dissensions, but expressed the hope that some arrangement might be made under which each group would operate in a separate section of the country, thus avoiding further fratricidal fighting."

Fotić says that he told the President of Mihailović's efforts to come to an agreement for united resistance and of the campaign against Mihailović in Britain and the United States, which "had made the Communists even more uncompromising in their attitude."

The President remarked, according to Fotić, that ". . . the policy of the American Government had not been influenced by anti-Mihailović propaganda, and that he personally had confidence in General Mihailović and had decided to proceed with the shipment of arms and supplies to him." Fotić reports that the President was "shocked" when he told him that the 400 tons of food sent in the autumn of 1942 as FDR's gift had never been delivered to Mihailović and that 112 tons of it had been "appropriated for uses entirely different from those intended." The President promised Fotić "that he would issue personal instructions that the remaining 288 tons be sent without delay to the General." Fotic adds: "Unfortunately, even the President's personal instructions did not ensure the shipment of the remainder of this food to Mihailović."

Fotić then reports that the President asked him what could be done to "allay the fighting between the Partisans and the Četniks," to which Fotić replied that "the assignment of American officers to both groups and, eventually, the allotment to each group of a specific area of operations could probably bring about a certain narrowing of the rift between them." American liaison officers "in each group would enable the President to appraise the whole Yugoslav military and political situation on the basis of reliable and direct American reports."

This is at variance with Fotić's preceding talk with Welles, in which he had mentioned sending liaison officers only to Mihailović. Indeed, in a subsequent meeting with Welles on May 11, Fotić again referred only to liaison with Mihailović.

This question of sending American liaison officers to Yugoslavia had been discussed in the State Department after Fotić proposed the idea to the Under Secretary on April 29, 1943. Believing that Fotić's proposal concerned only the dispatch of officers to Mihailović, the State Department's reaction was negative. Its reasoning was that it would be unwise to involve American officers in the dispute between Mihailović and the British and to expose the U.S. "to charges of complicity in Mihailović's alleged traffic with the Axis and in his civil strife with other factions in Yugoslavia." [33]

On May 11, Fotić told Welles that when he had called on Roosevelt on May 5, he had, in the name of the King, urgently submitted a request "that American Army officers be detailed as attachés to General Mihailović." [34] According to Welles' account, Fotić did not mention, as he does in his book, that he also spoke of liaison officers to the Partisans, and it must therefore be doubted that he actually made such a suggestion to the President. He told the Under Secretary that the President had asked him whether he had discussed this problem with the British Ambassador, Lord Halifax. Fotić had replied that he had not, whereupon the President had said that he himself would take it up with Lord Halifax.

THE OSS INDEPENDENTLY DECIDES ON LIAISON

Meanwhile, the OSS had decided to send American liaison officers to Yugoslavia. On May 11, Donovan (now a general) informed the President that "two OSS representatives left yesterday for Cairo, one to establish liaison with Mihailović in Serbia and the other to be attached to the Partisans." [35] Donovan wrote the memorandum on the day Fotić called on Welles, who obviously did not yet know about the OSS decision. However, he seems to have heard about it after his talk with Fotić and informed the Yugoslav Ambassador the following day. Fotić says that he was told by Welles that two American officers were to go to the Četniks and two to the Partisans.[36] Since the OSS plan provided for only one officer each, it must be assumed that either Welles misinformed Fotić or Fotić misunderstood Welles' message.

The State Department office responsible for Yugoslav affairs knew nothing about the decision to send liaison officers to Yugoslavia. As a matter of fact, an interoffice memorandum of May 17 urged continued caution regarding the dispatch of liaison officers. It added, however, that since the British had just proposed it, the State Department opposition to sending American liaison officers to Mihailović need no longer be quite so firm. Clearly, whoever wrote the memorandum misunderstood the British proposal, which involved the sending of liaison officers to the Partisans, not to Mihailović. Opposition to sending American liaison officers to Mihailović stemmed not only from the British-Mihailović conflict and the fear of involvement in that controversy; it was also felt that the Russians would not favor the dispatch of American liaison officers to Mihailović. This was certainly a misreading of Soviet policy. For these reasons, the memorandum suggested that a decision be deferred. The author of the memorandum obviously did not know that two officers were already on their way to establish liaison with both Yugoslav factions. The American decision was taken before the British had proposed the dispatch of American liaison officers, and it can only be assumed that it was directly related to the establishment of an OSS mission in Cairo.

The two OSS representatives who left Washington for Cairo were George Musulin and George Wuchinich. According to Donovan's memorandum to the President, they left on May 10, but other records and the statements of Musulin and Wuchinich seem to indicate that they actually left about a month earlier. Musulin was slated to go to the Četniks, Wuchinich to the Partisans. While both reached Yugoslavia eventually, they were not the ones who first established liaison with Četnik and Partisan headquarters, in August 1943.

Between May 12 and May 25, a conference code-named "Trident" took place in Washington between Roosevelt and Churchill and their staffs. Organized resistance in North Africa ceased on the second day of the conference, and the invasion of Italy was at hand. The conference concerned itself with grand strategy; the Balkan situation was hardly discussed. There apparently was no mention of the political and military problems in Yugoslavia.

7

BRITISH POLICY CHANGES

On June 17, Jovanović resigned as Prime Minister of the Yugoslav Government-in-Exile. He had been in office for almost a year and a half. Throughout, his Government was plagued by the perennial Serb-Croat problem. It had, for instance, been impossible to agree on a simple declaration of war aims, and when King Peter made known his intention to marry, a Cabinet crisis broke out, which the Croat members of the Government exploited in order to have Jovanović replaced.

Jovanović told the British Foreign Secretary on June 17 of his decision to resign. Eden is quoted as having suggested on that occasion that a future government should take account of the political situation inside the country where, Eden thought, the Partisans had succeeded in rallying many to their side.[1]

Before the Government resigned it finally agreed on a declaration of war aims, which the Yugoslav Embassy in Washington transmitted to the State Department on June 21.[2] This declaration was an attempt not only to resolve differences of opinion among the Serb and Croat elements in the Government but also to appear to be amenable to the British, in that the "activity of our guerrillas" was mentioned without naming Mihailović. Privately, Jovanović sent a message to Mihailović on June 20 in which he expressed the hope that, after an Italian capitulation, the Četniks would gain militarily over the Partisans by the acquisition of Italian fighting men and their arms.[3]

On June 26 the Cabinet crisis was resolved when another Serbian politician, Miša Trifunović, took over the Premiership. Two days later King Peter broadcast an appeal to the people of Yugoslavia to have faith in their Allies and to close ranks. The King expressed his admira-

129

tion for all those national fighters, without regard to "what temporary name they may be fighting under," who had recently "so successfully" thrown back a fresh German offensive. Clearly implied were the Partisans and the German Fifth Offensive.

Ambassador Biddle reported a conversation which he had with the Soviet Ambassador to the Yugoslav Government, who said he was "favorably impressed" by the speech. Biddle added that the London *Daily Worker* considered it "a welcome change." [4]

On June 30, 1943, the American Ambassador to Britain, Winant, reported to the State Department that the Embassy had "orally but officially" been informed by the Foreign Office that "after careful and thorough consideration on the part of the Prime Minister and the War Cabinet a modification in British policy with respect to Yugoslavia has been decided upon." [5] Winant stated that the British found Mihailović's reply to the latest British communication regarding his policies and activities "generally satisfactory." Winant's telegram continued:

On the other hand, reports received from British officers in contact with various Partisan groups have convinced the British that the latter are sufficiently important, active and well organized to furnish effective resistance to the Axis and that they are in fact fighting. The British have consequently now decided to give them material aid on a fairly substantial scale. They will continue also to help Mihailović on the specific understanding that no arms or supplies furnished him shall be employed for any other purpose than fighting the Axis. Through their representatives on the spot the British feel that they will be in a position soon to know whether this condition is violated and whether Mihailović continues to play with the Italians and fight the Partisans.

The telegram then pointed out that the number of British liaison officers at that time stationed with both groups was only eleven, and that even those who were sent in "blind" had received an enthusiastic welcome from the Partisans. The telegram ended by saying that the new policy of giving military aid to the Partisans and of increasing the monthly total of help given all Yugoslav groups would be communicated to the Soviet Government through the British Embassy in Moscow. It would also be made known to the Yugoslav Government-in-Exile, "some elements of which . . . will not be enthusiastic over the decision to help the Partisans."

The British Embassy in Washington sent an *aide-mémoire* to the State Department on July 6 which contained essentially these same points: that the British would support both Mihailović and the Partisans; that they would continue efforts to unify all resistance movements and that to that end British liaison officers had been instructed to arrange if possible a nonaggression agreement between Mihailović and the Partisans; that the British proposed to bring their "radio propaganda into line with this new policy and to extend publicity to all groups fighting the Axis as soon as General Mihailović and the Partisans have given the assurances for which they have been asked." (The *aide-mémoire* still made a false distinction between Croatian guerrillas and Communist Partisans.)

On July 7 and 22, 1943, Churchill sent telegrams to General Alexander (then commander of the 15th Army Group, consisting of the U.S. 7th Army and the British 8th Army, which landed in Sicily on July 10) referring to the situation in the Balkans and the opportunities that might arise in connection with the Allied Italian campaign.[6]

The second telegram indicated that the Prime Minister had his forthcoming meeting with Roosevelt in Quebec in August very much on his mind. Sicily was about to be "cleaned up" and "great prizes lie in the Balkan direction," Churchill said. He told Alexander that there were now thirty-nine Axis divisions in Yugoslavia—seventeen Italian, nine German, five Bulgarian and eight Croat divisions. Each figure was an overestimate; in Yugoslavia there were then in fact fourteen Italian, five German, three Bulgarian and three Croat divisions, practically all of them under strength.[7] Even before Churchill sent Alexander his first telegram, the latter, on July 3, had sent a message to Tito in which he wished him success in his battle against the Axis, congratulated him on his victory during the recent German offensive and told him of the forthcoming invasion of Europe, *i.e.,* Sicily.[8] It is interesting to note that while Yugoslavia fell under General Wilson's jurisdiction as Commander in Chief, Middle East, it was General Alexander who communicated with Tito, and Churchill wrote to Alexander, not to Wilson. It can only be assumed that at that time Churchill and Alexander looked at Yugoslavia from the point of view of the Italian campaign rather than as a separate problem.

Before leaving for Quebec, Churchill "decided to pave the way for further action in the Balkans by appointing a senior officer to lead a larger mission to the partisans in the field, and with the authority to make direct recommendations" to him about future moves.[9]

He wrote Eden on July 28, 1943:

Mr. Fitzroy Maclean, M.P., is a man of daring character, with Parliamentary status and Foreign Office training. He is to go to Yugoslavia and work with Tito largely for SOE. The idea is that a Brigadier should be sent out to take command later on. In my view we should plump for Maclean and make him the Head of any mission now contemplated, and give him a good military staff officer under his authority. What we want is a daring Ambassador-leader with these hardy and hunted guerrillas. If you agree, please act in this sense with the War Office and SOE and use my influence for what it is worth.

King Peter reports [10] that before Churchill's departure for Quebec he had a talk with him during which Churchill told the King of the dispatch to Tito's headquarters of a personal friend, Captain Deakin, and said that Deakin had been in touch with the Prime Minister by radio for several weeks. Churchill said that Deakin had reported that the Partisans were a very effective and brave fighting force, though at the moment extremely harassed by a German offensive. Through Deakin, Churchill had heard that Mihailović's forces had attacked the Partisans in the rear when they were fighting the Germans. King Peter told Churchill that he had heard just the opposite from Mihailović.

While the Prime Minister was on his way to Canada, the Trifunović Government fell because of Serb-Croat antagonism and was replaced by King Peter on August 10 with a government composed of nonpolitical appointees headed by a career diplomat, Dr. Božidar Purić. Fotić says [11] that when Purić sought Eden's reaction to the proposal to reappoint Mihailović as Minister, "he was assured by Eden that there would be no objections whatever."

On July 25, the King of Italy dismissed Mussolini and designated Marshal Pietro Badoglio as head of a new Italian Government. Both Germany and the Allies immediately perceived the likely consequences of this step—negative for Germany and positive opportunities for the Allies. True, for several months Italy had been at the end of its military strength and thus of questionable utility to Germany and an easier enemy of the Allies. Nevertheless, its departure from the war would change the military situation drastically for both Germany and the Allies.

Therefore, neither side lost time in preparing for this eventuality. Germany undertook detailed measures in or close to all Italian-held areas in order to be ready to take over in case of Italy's exit from the war. Thus, on August 8, 1943, a new and enlarged High Command Southeast was set up in Belgrade with responsibilities for the entire Balkan area; Field Marshal Maximilian von Weichs was appointed chief of that command. (General Löhr, who had up to then commanded the Balkans from Salonika, continued under Weichs to be responsible for Greece until March 1945, when he replaced Weichs.) The Italian occupation forces in the Balkans, inactive since the end of the Fourth Offensive in March 1943, assumed an even more passive role after Mussolini's fall.

General Glaise von Horstenau reported on August 2 that officers of the Italian 2nd Army appeared to have opened negotiations with both Četniks and Partisans with the aim of leaving the latter in control of important places like Split, thus helping to build a revolutionary army which would welcome the British. An earlier report made reference to rumors that Italian troops had sold their arms to the population in Karlovac and Ogulin.[12]

As soon as Churchill heard of Mussolini's fall, he saw opportunities for an intensified campaign against Germany, for the anticipated surrender of the Italian armies in the Balkans would allow commandos and supplies to be sent into Yugoslavia, Albania and Greece. The Germans apparently monitored a telephone call on July 29 between Churchill and Roosevelt which confirmed their fears of an imminent Italian surrender. But the long surrender negotiations gave them time to prepare for Italy's "treason."

During these negotiations, Badoglio offered information about the cooperation which the Italians could give to Mihailović. However, in view of the quality and morale of the Italian troops and the bad impression this might create among the resistance forces, this offer was not accepted by Roosevelt and Churchill, who were then meeting in Quebec.[13]

On September 8, Italy surrendered unconditionally, and on October 13 even declared war on Germany. Mussolini, who had been a prisoner of the new Italian authorities, was freed by the Germans in a daring raid on September 12, brought to Vienna, and thereafter established a Republican-Fascist government in the German-occupied part of Italy.

THE QUEBEC CONFERENCE

In anticipation of the Quebec Conference, code-named "Quadrant," the American Joint Chiefs of Staff met to discuss strategy on August 10, 1943, before conferring with Roosevelt. During that session the question of operations in the Balkans was also touched upon.[14] General George C. Marshall, the Army Chief of Staff, felt that the President was opposed to operations in the Balkans, and particularly to U.S. troop participation in them, on the ground that they represented an uneconomical use of shipping and also because of the political implications. Roosevelt's reluctance to employ American forces in the Balkans was probably related—at least subconsciously—to the defeat suffered by Allied troops on the Gallipoli peninsula in Turkey in 1915, for which Churchill, then First Lord of the Admiralty, was blamed.

Also on August 10, the Secretary of War, Henry L. Stimson, who had recently returned from England, conferred with the President at the White House, handing him a letter in which he said:

> . . . the British theory . . . is that Germany can be beaten by a series of attritions in northern Italy, in the eastern Mediterranean, in Greece, in the Balkans, in Rumania and other satellite countries. . . . To me . . . that attitude . . . seems terribly dangerous. . . . None of the methods of pinprick warfare can be counted on by us to fool Stalin into the belief that we have kept that pledge [the opening of the second front].[15]

The Joints Chiefs of Staff met with the President and Stimson later the same day. Roosevelt said that he had learned from Stimson that Churchill currently favored operations in the Balkans. Stimson qualified this statement, pointing out that Churchill had disclaimed any wish to land troops in the Balkans but had indicated that the Allies could make notable gains in the area if the Balkan peoples were given more supplies. The Secretary of War said, however, that Eden wished the Allies to invade the Balkans. To this the President added that the British Foreign Office did not want the Balkans to come under Soviet influence, and therefore the British desired "to get to the Balkans first." He himself did not wish to follow the logic of the British thinking on the Balkans. He did not believe, he stated, that the USSR desired to take over the Balkan states but rather that it wanted to "establish kinship with other Slavic peoples." He assured the U.S. military leaders that he himself was opposed to Balkan operations, believing it undesirable to base hopes for victory on political imponderables. He declared that it was "unwise to plan military strategy based on a gamble as to political results." [16]

Churchill's position was set forth in a paper dated August 17 in which he spoke of "minor descents across the Adriatic," suggesting that "we could act across the Adriatic to stimulate the Patriot activities in the Balkan peninsula." [17]

At the Quebec Conference, which took place from August 17 to 24, Roosevelt indicated his desire to have the Balkan divisions which the Allies had trained, particularly the Greeks and Yugoslavs, operate in their own countries. He expressed the belief that it would be advantageous if these Balkan divisions were to follow and harass the Germans should the latter decide to withdraw from the Balkans to the line of the Danube.[18] Churchill suggested that commando forces could also operate in support of the guerrillas on the Dalmatian coast.

Since neither the British nor the American head of government expressed an interest in offensive land operations by the U.S. and Britain in the Balkans, such a possibility was not pursued. The final decision was that operations in that area were to be limited to supplying Balkan guerrillas by air and sea, minor commando raids, and bombing of strategic objectives.[19] There is no record that the Partisan-Četnik problem was raised, let alone discussed, at the Quebec Conference.

In view of the Quebec decision, Wilson put before the Middle East Defense Committee a proposal to keep the resistance movement alive throughout the winter and to maintain pressure on the Germans "with the object of bringing off a culminating effort of all groups in the spring of 1944, timed to coincide with such major operations as would be taking place in Europe." [20] He writes that to achieve this end, it would have been necessary to encourage and keep supplied those leaders who were prepared to produce results regardless of their political opinions and "in short not to prejudice the immediate military objective to longer term political conceptions." But Wilson also makes the point that in this he differed with the British Ambassador to the Yugoslav Government-in-Exile, who felt that assistance should be given only to those who might be favorable to a return of King Peter after the liberation of the country, i.e., only to Mihailović.

The continued influence of those British officials who felt as the Ambassador did was illustrated by an event shortly thereafter. When Churchill proposed to raise the rank of the head of the mission to the Partisans to brigadier, the proponents of Mihailović succeeded in having the head of the British mission to the Četniks raised to the same rank, much to the annoyance of Tito when he later heard about it.

The British Middle East command in conjunction with SOE at first envisaged the appointment of two brigadiers to head the respective missions to the Partisans and the Četniks, with an SOE officer having mainly political responsibility to be second in command. Maclean's assignment as deputy of the mission to the Partisans had not been received with enthusiasm by SOE. The objection only increased when Churchill proposed that Lieutenant Colonel Maclean head the mission instead of a brigadier already selected. Thus Bailey, a full colonel, was to be second in command of the mission to the Četniks, while a lieutenant colonel would head the mission to the Partisans. But Churchill was determined, and on August 3, 1943, he sent the following telegram to Wilson: "I attach importance to his [Maclean's] having full command both military and civil and being furnished with a suitable military staff officer." It was so decided and Maclean was raised to brigadier.

It is therefore not surprising that Maclean did not look forward to working for SOE. When he arrived in Cairo at the end of August, before his departure for Yugoslavia, he told Wilson that "he did not feel . . . he could go into the Balkans dependent on an organization in which he had no confidence." [21] Wilson shared some of these opinions regarding SOE and so did British diplomats in Cairo. Both resented the fact that SOE was responsible neither to the War Office nor the Foreign Office, but to a separate organization in London. Wilson's answer to this problem was to propose placing SOE under military control. In this he succeeded to a large extent in the months to follow.

YUGOSLAV AIRMEN TRAIN IN THE U.S.

In the United States at that time, Yugoslav-American relations were dominated by a trifling issue compared to the intractable problems which occupied the British and Yugoslav Governments. This issue was the arrangement for service of a group of Yugoslav airmen as a unit with the U.S. Army Air Force. As mentioned earlier, during King Peter's visit in Washington in July 1942, initial discussions took place regarding the possible training of Yugoslav airmen in the U.S. Several subsequent conversations led to the training of forty-two Yugoslavs brought from the Middle East to Salinas, California. The Yugoslav Government-in-Exile had assumed that these airmen would serve as a Yugoslav unit integrated into the U.S. Army Air Force in the Middle East. On June 28, 1943, the Yugoslav Ambassador, Fotić, called on the Under Secretary of State and expressed his unhappiness at the plan to give these men commissions in the U.S. Army. He said it was in the highest degree important from the standpoint of morale in Yugoslavia that they serve as a Yugoslav unit.[22]

Fotić continued his representations on July 28, 1943, when he called on Assistant Secretary Berle. He followed this up with a memorandum on August 3, with yet another call on Welles on August 11, and submitted a further memorandum to the Department of State on August 14. The matter involved not only the State Department but also the OSS, to which the formation of a Yugoslav aviation unit was originally referred by the President. It involved also General Henry H. Arnold, Commanding General, Army Air Forces; General Marshall, Chief of Staff of the U.S. Army; Admiral William D. Leahy, Chief of Staff to Roosevelt, and finally the President himself. In the end, the OSS (General Donovan and Colonel Goodfellow) prevailed over General Arnold, and the forty-two airmen (twenty-four officers and eighteen noncommissioned officers) were not only activated as a Yugoslav detachment but were assigned four B-24 Liberator bombers.[23]

On September 7, the Yugoslav Ambassador called on Roosevelt and asked him to make the presentation of the four Liberators "personally, with an appropriate ceremony, instead of sending the Yugoslav airmen in a routine way to their new assignment." [24] Fotić reports that the President was "greatly interested." Next, the Ambassador visited Harry Hopkins at the Naval Hospital in Bethesda. He says he found Hopkins "quite enthusiastic about my proposal. [He] stressed the importance of demonstrating American interest in Yugoslavia and in Central Europe, because of the British tendency to consider problems in that part of Europe as of interest only to Great Britain and the Soviet Union." On September 29, Roosevelt outlined to Fotić the arrangements under which the four B-24s would be flown to the North African Theater and informed him of a dedication ceremony to be held at Bolling Field on October 6 in which the President hoped to participate.[25]

Fotić gave a speech on that occasion, in which he told the Yugoslav airmen that in addition to their regular missions with the U.S. Air Force "they would have the privilege of carrying supplies to Mihailović and his courageous fighters." Fotić says he had felt that "in loyalty to the President," his draft should be cleared by the State Department in view of the anti-Mihailović campaign. He adds that this was done and that he was informed that the White House had no objection to it.[26]

The President did attend and in his speech said:

May these planes fulfill their mission under your guidance. They are built with two great objectives. The first is to drop bombs on our common enemy success-fully and at the right points. The second is to deliver to your compatriots in Yugoslavia the much-needed supplies for which they have waited so long—food, medicine—yes, arms and ammunition. . . . I am sure you will have every success in this great mission that you are undertaking. Remember always that we are comrades in arms.[27]

Fotić remarks that this was the last time he saw President Roosevelt.

The planes were flown by their Yugoslav crews to Cairo, where they were officially accepted by King Peter, who had meanwhile moved with his Government from London to Cairo.

On November 2 the King sent a cable to Roosevelt saying that the Liberators "are truly magnificent machines" and adding: "I take this opportunity to renew my personal and my people's warmest thanks to you Mr. President and to the American nation for this generous gift." [28]

The detachment was under the command of the United States Army Air Force. It was attached to a B-24 squadron of the 15th American Air

Force, where it operated as an integral part of the squadron, living and flying together with the American crews. The squadron participated in air raids over Greece, Germany, Austria, Italy and Bulgaria.[29] Three of the bombers had been shot down by January of 1944. The crew of the remaining Liberator had carried out more than fifty long-range missions by the end of the war. In August 1945, eleven of the fourteen remaining members of the detachment were either commissioned or enlisted in the Army of the United States by directive of President Harry S. Truman.

THE GOVERNMENT-IN-EXILE MOVES TO CAIRO

King Peter and the Government-in-Exile now headed by Purić arrived in Cairo on September 28, 1943. Rumors of their possible move had circulated in London early in the year. On March 23 the American Chargé d'Affaires, Matthews, had asked Sir Orme Sargent whether there was any likelihood of the Yugoslav Government's being "transplanted" to Cairo, as has been done with the Greek Government. Sargent replied that it war far too fragile: "It would probably fall to pieces en route." [30] On June 30 the American Ambassador, Winant, reported to the Department of State that the possibility of transferring the Yugoslav Government to the Near East was under discussion in London.[31]

The reason for the move to Cairo, which was proposed by King Peter in a letter to Churchill on March 31 [32] and supported by the British after their change of policy, was that neither the British nor the Yugoslav Government was happy with the other's proximity. The Yugoslavs preferred to be farther away, and the British frankly wished them to go. Cairo was the logical place because it was close to Yugoslavia, the Greek Government was there, too, and General Wilson, Commander in Chief, British Forces, Middle East, who had responsibility for all matters east of a theoretical line running down the middle of the Adriatic, had his headquarters in Cairo. American diplomatic representation to the Yugoslav Government-in-Exile shifted from Ambassador Biddle to Ambassador Lincoln MacVeagh, who was already Ambassador to the Greek Government-in-Exile. His nomination was confirmed by the Senate on November 12, 1943.[33]

THE FIRST AMERICAN LIAISON OFFICERS
ARRIVE IN YUGOSLAVIA

After Washington reached the decision to send American liaison officers to both Četnik and Partisan headquarters, OSS Cairo proceeded to implement it. Several plans were drawn up, involving not only officers who had been in Cairo for some time but also the two OSS representatives —Musulin and Wuchinich—who had come from Washington headquarters, the former with the specific task of establishing liaison with the Četniks and the latter with the Partisans. Their missions were, however, scratched. Thereafter Captain C. George Selvig and Captain Melvin O. Benson were named to join Colonel Bailey's mission with Mihailović. On July 7, 1943, Colonel Guenther, the OSS chief in Cairo, wrote Colonel Bailey:

This letter will introduce to you Captain George Selvig and Captain M. O. Benson. Both leave here [Cairo] early tomorrow morning to join you and be attached to your mission. During the past few days there have been conferences here regarding their assignment and the services they have before them. We believe that the exigencies of their assignment have all been considered and that they go to you with orders which should ensure harmonious relations with you and your colleagues. I feel certain they will prove a valuable addition to

Captain Mansfield in Yugoslavia, 1943. *Courtesy of W. R. Mansfield*

Captain Benson on the island of Vis, December 1943. *Courtesy of M. O. Benson*

your staff, and thank you for the opportunity you have afforded them to share with you in some degree the great honor of your mission.[34]

This mission, as well as one to the Partisans, was cancelled at the last minute, and it was decided to send Selvig, accompanied by Musulin, to the Četniks and Benson, accompanied by Wuchinich, to the Partisans. These drops were scrapped because of bad weather over the target areas in Yugoslavia.

Meanwhile, Major Huot, head of the special operations section in OSS Cairo, went to London in July for a meeting with Donovan. There he met Walter R. Mansfield, a Marine Corps captain and member of Donovan's law firm who was assigned to OSS. Mansfield joined Huot on the latter's return trip to Cairo. After Mansfield's arrival in Egypt, he was ordered to go on a one-man mission to the Četniks. On August 18, he parachuted onto Čemerno Mountain not far from Ivanjica in Serbia and proceeded from there to Mihailović's headquarters.

At the same time, it was decided to send a one-man mission also to the Partisans. Benson, who had been in Cairo for some time, was selected, and he dropped in the early morning hours of August 22 on Petrovo Polje near Travnik in Bosnia not far from Tito's headquarters, which was about to be moved to Jajce. Mansfield and Benson thus became the first official Americans to set foot in Yugoslavia since the U.S. Legation closed its doors in Belgrade in July 1941.

In October, Musulin went to Četnik-held Yugoslavia. In November, Wuchinich joined Slovenian Partisan headquarters, and Selvig went to the Partisan Supreme Headquarters in December.

The arrival of American liaison officers at Tito's and Mihailović's headquarters was of greatest importance to both the Partisan leader and the Četnik general: For the first time since Yugoslavia's capitulation in 1941, the U.S. was actively involved in Yugoslav affairs. Both guerrilla leaders set about attempting to influence the American liaison officers. Benson was immediately invited to Tito's headquarters for dinner and was most cordially received. The points made by the Partisans forthwith concerned the pro-Mihailović propaganda in the U.S., which they felt had to be countered, and Četnik-Axis collaboration, which they said had to be exposed in America. Mihailović, on the other hand, did not have a problem with publicity in the U.S. But he wanted to call attention to his more and more unsatisfactory relationship with the British in the hope that the U.S. could be induced to persuade London to be more tolerant of his movement.

Mansfield was attached to Bailey's British mission with Mihailović and Benson to Deakin's British mission with Tito. This pattern was not changed when higher-level British missions were established, headed by Brigadier Maclean, who parachuted with Major Linn M. Farish of the U.S. Army into Partisan territory on September 19 and by Brigadier C. D. Armstrong, who parachuted with Lieutenant Colonel Albert B. Seitz, also of the U.S. Army, into Četnik territory on September 24.

Reference has been made to the relationship between SOE and OSS. Within Yugoslavia, the extent of contact between the two organizations varied, not only by command but also individually. Generally, the situation was much more harmonious in the Partisan area. The policies of the two organizations were more alike there, thus reducing the possibilities of friction.

From the very beginning it was clear, however, that the British were the senior partners in this enterprise. They controlled the communications facilities; it was not until the spring of 1944 that the OSS officers obtained their own radio transmitters. Until then all American messages went over the British network. But things worked out very well between Deakin and Benson as well as between Bailey and Mansfield. All four— Deakin, Benson, Bailey and Mansfield—have in separate conversations confirmed this. Deakin has told the author that Tito had asked him whether he knew of any American plans to send liaison officers, at the same time clearly indicating that such a move would be welcomed by the Partisans. Deakin reported this to Cairo in early July, though at that time OSS had already decided to send one or two American liaison officers to the Partisans. Benson has said that while dependence on British radio links and their operators was not entirely satisfactory, it would nevertheless have been impractical to have had separate communications systems. Both Bailey and Mansfield have expressed their complete satisfaction with their working arrangements in Četnik territory. When Maclean and Armstrong took over the British missions in their respective territories, matters became somewhat more difficult. Maclean and Farish got along very well personally, even though Maclean made certain that access to Tito was possible only with his approval. Armstrong did the same thing but, whereas Farish did not mind. Seitz was furious. In addition Armstrong had an infinitely more complicated task in his relations with Mihailović than Maclean with Tito.

Maclean recalls [35] how he was told one day in Cairo that an American officer was to be attached to his mission. Farish, "a large rugged man like a bear, with an amiable grin," was the American officer slated to join him.[36] "Call me Slim," he said, and Maclean adds, "the name was singularly inappropriate for one so robust. We asked him what he could do. He said he could build aerodromes . . . It was, we told him, the one thing that we needed most. The sooner he put an end to the present uncomfortable mode of entry into Yugoslavia the better, especially as it was confined to one-way traffic."

The Maclean and Armstrong missions assembled in the middle of September at Tocra airfield, which was located east of Benghazi. (Tocra had replaced Derna as the take-off point for SOE Yugoslav operations.) While Maclean's plane had no difficulty finding the prearranged landing spot in Partisan-held territory, Armstrong's flight ran into several problems. First, on two successive days his plane failed to find the correct signal fires and drop zones, then contact could not be established, and on the fourth flight the plane's radio went dead. Finally, on the fifth day (September 24), Armstrong and Seitz landed in Četnik-held territory.[37]

Maclean [38] describes their flight in a Halifax bomber:

Inside the aircraft it was cold and dark and stuffy, and there was hardly room to move . . . every spare inch of space was filled with long, cylindrical containers which were to be dropped with us . . . the aircraft was losing height rapidly. We readjusted our parachute harness . . . I was to go first and Vivian [Lieutenant Colonel Street] was to follow. Slim Farish and [Sergeant] Duncan were to go after that. . . . With a jerk the parachute opened. . . . Then . . . there was a jolt and I was lying in a field of wet grass.

The Maclean mission landed near Jajce, where Tito's headquarters had been established.

Seitz relates that in his group Armstrong jumped first and Seitz followed with Armstrong's batman, Green, last. They landed at a prearranged spot in southern Serbia on Mt. Tornik near the Uvac River not far from Mihailović's headquarters. They were soon greeted by Hudson, "affectionately known as Marko," Bailey and Mansfield, "the young American Marine who had preceded me by about a month." [39] Seitz, who obviously had no use for Armstrong, describes him as "the rare type of Englishman who sneers at everything American and dislikes having Americans close to him."

Seitz says that when Armstrong delivered certain letters to Mihailović from General Wilson, he was not permitted to see or hear the contents of these letters, although Mihailović later showed him Wilson's messages. He adds that he was an American with a British mission and knew full well that this was a British show.

Seitz also notes [40] that he and Mansfield were there only to give "an Allied illusion" to the Yugoslavs. Mansfield was not allowed near headquarters, and when Seitz wanted to see Mihailović he had to obtain Armstrong's approval. Bailey would then go along, the conversation was in Serbo-Croatian, and Seitz says that he was not allowed to speak in French.

Seitz further writes that messages he wanted to send to OSS Cairo were subject to Armstrong's censorship. After some argument, Armstrong was ordered by Cairo to send Seitz's messages through unchanged, although he was permitted to read them before dispatch.

Fotić reports [41] that late in August 1943, Mihailović put into operation a short-wave radio station strong enough to be picked up in the United States. On August 26 Fotić received a message from Mihailović which had been picked up by a U.S. Navy station. The message gave only the

Lieutenant Colonel Seitz, Brigadier Armstrong, General Mihailović and Major Hudson in Serbia, 1943. From *Mihailović—Hoax or Hero*

call sign and the wave length of this station and asked for acknowledgment. Fotić says that through the courtesy of the State and Navy Departments he was able to answer the message, and very soon regular contact was established with the Mihailović station, known as "Woods and Mountains." This contact lasted until the middle of September 1944. Fotić writes that the authenticity of this radio station was challenged by the Partisans, but he says that the State, War and Navy Departments had carefully checked out the identity of the Mihailović station. And Seitz says that upon his arrival in Četnik territory he visited Mihailović's communications center, where he was told of a "hidden transmission station" in the Šumadija which "received and sent messages from and to America." (Šumadija—"Woodlands"—is the area south of Belgrade between the Danube and Western Morava Rivers.)

EFFECTS OF ITALY'S SURRENDER

On September 8, 1943, Italy surrendered, and this event had a profound influence on Yugoslav affairs. The several contending military forces were irregularly disposed throughout the country on that date.

The Partisans had survived the Fifth Offensive and gained the mountains of northeastern Bosnia in July. In August, they actually drove the Germans from some Bosnian strongholds, such as Jajce. On the eve of Italy's surrender, they claimed control of about one-fifth of the territory of Yugoslavia.

The Četniks, who had transferred their main headquarters from Montenegro to Serbia in May, re-established themselves in Montenegro after the Partisans' departure in June and July. They controlled large stretches of mountain areas in both Serbia and Montenegro. Mihailović himself did not, however, return to Montenegro.

Fourteen Italian divisions comprising approximately 308,000 men [42] occupied parts of Slovenia, Dalmatia and Montenegro. The Germans were primed to occupy Italian-held territory and to disarm the Italian troops. So were the Partisans and the Četniks. Everybody knew that an Italian surrender was a high probability, but nobody knew the exact timing of it.

As the news of Italy's capitulation reached the Germans, Partisans and Četniks, all vied desperately with one another to obtain the greatest benefits from that surrender by extending their territory and acquiring arms and men. Both Tito and Mihailović expressed their bitter disappointment to the respective British mission chiefs at not having been advised in time of Italy's impending decision.

Neither Deakin nor Bailey had been told in advance by their principals in Cairo of the forthcoming capitulation. They heard this important news only when it was broadcast world-wide and Wilson issued an appeal to all Italian troops in the Balkans to regard themselves as subordinate to him, not to give up their arms to the Germans and to fight together with the Balkan peoples against Germany. Thereupon, both Deakin and Bailey were ordered by Cairo to negotiate an armistice with the nearest Italian commanders—as if the British missions, not Tito and Mihailović, were in operational charge of the Partisans and Četniks. Tito, in particular, was highly indignant at this proposal, asking Deakin how he thought he was going to disarm the Italian divisions with the Germans racing toward the Dalmatian coast.[43]

In any case Deakin (who was accompanied by Benson) witnessed in Split the disarming of the Bergamo Division by General Koča Popović and the Partisans, and Bailey was present when Major Voja Lukačević and the Četniks accepted the surrender of the Venezia Division in Berane. Hudson and Mansfield were in Priboj when the Italian garrison there capitulated to the Četniks.

It soon turned out that the Italians fell into three distinct groups: the majority who did not wish to continue the war in anyone's behalf and who surrendered, mostly to the Germans but also to the Partisans and Četniks; a minority who sided with Germany; and a minority who joined the Allies, which meant the Četniks and Partisans.

In the ensuing struggle for territory, the Partisans at first gained the upper hand by acting fast and efficiently. Within a few days they occupied practically the whole of the Dalmatian coast, including the larger islands. They even entered Italy on September 15, seizing the province of Istria and the mountains between Trieste and Austria. At the beginning of October they surrounded Zagreb and threatened the rail line between Zagreb and Belgrade.[44]

While the Partisans battled the Germans for control of Slovenia and Dalmatia, they also fought the Četniks, who once again tried to bar them from Montenegro. In the middle of October 1943, the Partisans surprised and killed two important Četnik commanders, Djukanović and Stanišić, and wiped out their garrison not far from the Montenegrin town of Nikšić.

In the aftermath of the Italian surrender, the Partisans seized enormous quantities of arms, equipment and supplies which enabled them to shore up their own poorly supplied forces and to equip the recruits who were flocking in as large areas came under Partisan control. The Četniks, too, inherited Italian arms and equipment, but their haul was smaller by far than that of the Partisans.

Meanwhile, the Germans, who had increased their troop strength in Yugoslavia after Mussolini's fall, rushed even more units into the area, though by no means enough to make up the losses resulting from the Italian surrender.[45] Indeed, immediately upon the Italian capitulation, the Germans launched a series of operations [46] which lasted until the end of February 1944. Their objective was to regain territory that the Italians had surrendered, particularly the Adriatic coast and the islands lying off it. The Partisans called these operations the Sixth Offensive.

Churchill, who visited Washington after the Quebec Conference, became intensely interested in the possibilities that the Italian surrender opened up for operations along the Dalmatian coast. In a memorandum to Roosevelt drafted on the day after Italy's capitulation, Churchill said, ". . . it should be possible to open quite soon one or more good ports . . . enabling munitions and supplies to be sent in by ship. . . . For the moment the utmost efforts should be put forth to organize the attack upon the Germans throughout the Balkan peninsula and to supply agents, arms, and good direction." [47]

On November 20, Churchill circulated a memorandum to the British Chiefs of Staff which included this suggestion:

Seize a port or ports and establish bridgeheads on the Dalmatian coast, and carry a regular flow of airborne supplies to the Partisans. Use the British 1st Airborne Division and all the Commandos available in the Mediterranean, together with the "Plough" force [a force especially equipped and trained for mountain warfare] to aid and animate the resistance in Yugoslavia and Albania. . . . Establish air domination of the Southern Adriatic, and maintain sea superiority there.[48]

Ehrman defends Churchill as a strategist; though he admits that Churchill had dreams, "when faced with the realities he saw well enough the impossibility of a Balkan campaign." [49] Ehrman says that in the memorandum of November 20, Churchill relegated his proposals for Yugoslavia to fourth place and had included them initially only after the British Chiefs of Staff had made similar suggestions ("If necessary, we might form a limited bridgehead on the Dalmatian and Albanian Coasts"). This sentence, however, was dropped by the Chiefs of Staff after Alexander objected, probably because the Germans had meanwhile made heavy territorial gains in their Sixth Offensive. Thereupon, Churchill accepted the Chiefs of Staff's final recommendation, which excluded operations in the Balkans.

Expressing his feeling long after the Cairo and Tehran Conferences had turned down all plans for larger actions across the Adriatic, Churchill said at the Conference of Dominions' Prime Ministers in London on May 3, 1944, a month before the cross-channel invasion, that he was bound to admit that if he had had his own way, the lay-out of the war would have been different. He would have been in favor of rolling up Europe from the southeast and joining hands with the Russians. However, Churchill noted, it had proved impossible to persuade the U.S. to accept this approach. Washington had been set at every stage on the invasion in northwest Europe. He himself had opposed the opening of this campaign in 1942 and 1943, but now he was in favor of it. Russian pressure, too, had been very severe.

Later in the same meeting, however, Churchill said that

. . . there had never been any question of major action in the Balkans. It was merely a question of assistance by Commandos and air action . . . the Americans had all along said that we were leading them up the garden in the Mediterranean. His reply had been that, in return, we had provided them in the garden with nourishing vegetables and refreshing fruits. Nevertheless, the Americans had remained very suspicious, and thought that he was entertaining designs for dragging them into the Balkans. This he had never contemplated doing. He had merely hoped to be able to give adequate help to Tito, and he had viewed the whole Mediterranean problem from a purely military point of view.[50]

It should be pointed out that the possibility of Allied landings troubled the Partisan leaders. Unlike Mihailović, who would have welcomed landings, the Partisans were afraid of them. In the minds of the Partisans, the presence of British and American troops on Yugoslav soil could have made it impossible for them to gain political hegemony after the war.

Dedijer's *Diary* recalls a speech by Milovan Djilas on November 6, 1943, in which he said that a second front in the Balkans should not be established, since the Partisans could take care of the situation for themselves as well as for the Allies.[51]

THE OSS ORGANIZES A TRANSADRIATIC OPERATION

Soon after Italy's surrender, a bizarre event occurred that was to have a great impact upon American-Yugoslav relations. It had a distinctly Balkan flavor.

Two OSS officers in Cairo, Captain Hans Tofte and Lieutenant Robert Thompson, conceived a plan for a sea-borne operation from Italy into Yugoslavia across the Adriatic. Their chief, Major Huot, liked the idea and sent Tofte and Thompson to Algiers to see General Donovan, who was then visiting Allied Force Headquarters (AFHQ). The general approved the plan, and Huot was ordered "to proceed to southern Italy to see what could be done about establishing advance bases from which future operations in Yugoslavia could be launched and controlled." [52]

Both SOE and OSS had for some weeks been thinking of setting up advance bases on the Adriatic at Bari or nearby for the great operational advantages they would offer. There were many problems, however. Yugoslavia was under the jurisdiction of the British Commander in Chief, Middle East, General Wilson. Italy, on the other hand, came under the jurisdiction of General Eisenhower, the Allied Commander in Chief of the North African Theater of Operations. The middle of the Adriatic was the line of demarcation between the two commands. In North Africa, the western part of Libya (Tripolitania) came under Eisenhower, and the eastern part (Cyrenaica) under Wilson.

Huot describes how Eisenhower's consent had to be obtained in order to establish Italian bases for operations in Yugoslavia. For this purpose he and Thompson [53] flew to the general's headquarters in Algiers on Octo-

ber 4, 1943. There they met two Yugoslavs, an encounter which was to
have innumerable consequences.

On October 3, 1943, the *Bakar*, an armed vessel of the Yugoslav Partisan Navy, sailed into the port of Bari. Sergije Makiedo describes [54] how
he and several other Partisan officers, both men and women, had been
ordered to take the vessel from Yugoslavia across the Adriatic to Italy—
"the first time during our struggle that members of the Army of National
Liberation set foot on Allied territory."

The purpose of the *Bakar* operation was to secure a naval base in Italy
for the Yugoslav ships which had left the harbor of Split before the
Germans occupied the town on September 26. For eighteen days after
Italy's surrender, Split had been in Partisan hands. With a number of
wounded Partisans, Jewish refugees and several Italians, Makiedo set out
for Bari without proper credentials and on a slow ship, fearful not only
of German planes but also of Allied mines.

After landing in Bari and meeting the British general commanding
the town, Makiedo and his assistant, Jože Poduje, were sent to Brindisi
to see General F. N. Mason Macfarlane, chief of the Allied military mission with the Italian Government. Macfarlane, in turn, sent the two
Yugoslavs on to Algiers. It was there that on October 6 Makiedo and
Poduje met Huot and Thompson. It soon turned out that the two American OSS officers and the two Yugoslavs had similar ideas: to establish a
supply line between Italy and the Adriatic islands, which were then in
Partisan hands.

Huot's and Makiedo's books complement and supplement each other
in telling the fantastic tale of how the operation was launched with General Eisenhower's personal approval. Four hundred tons of essential supplies were gathered, loaded on HMS *Britannia* and sent to Bari for transfer to the *Bakar* and other Yugoslav ships which had meanwhile arrived
or been "freed" from Italian detention. Huot, Makiedo, Poduje and
Thompson went to Bari by plane and obtained coal and other supplies
there. Huot writes [55] that a British naval vessel "literally built for the
task to which she was now assigned" took them to the island of Vis, which
they sought to reconnoiter in order to find out whether it was still in
Partisan hands. They were greeted by the fire of shore batteries until they
could establish their identity. On Vis, arrangements were made for the
future transfer of materials and supplies, which were to come from Italy.

On October 15, the *Bakar* sailed from Bari to Vis, starting a supply
channel which by the end of 1943 had transported seventy shiploads of
materials to the Partisans. Makiedo relates that he was promoted by
Tito to the position of acting head of the Army of National Liberation

in Italy—welcome news since he had been sent only by Partisan coastal command for a specific purpose and had undoubtedly overstepped his authority by going to Eisenhower's Algiers headquarters.

Huot fails to mention in his book that his orders did not authorize him to go to Yugoslavia, which, nevertheless, he proceeded to do. He actually saw Tito at Jajce, where Benson, the first American to land in Partisan territory, joined them for lunch. Huot states that he called on Maclean's mission before returning to the coast. Maclean was absent, but Deakin was there. On his return trip, Huot went through Livno because he had heard that Maclean and Farish were there, but he found only Farish, Maclean having left a couple of hours before. It was then that Huot asked Farish: "How would you like to make a flying trip back to Washington and deliver your reports orally to the White House and the State Department?" [56] "It's the only way I can hope ever to get my story told," Farish answered, adding: "Bill Deakin and I have talked about it a hundred times. We have both tried to write an account of our experiences here in terms that would explain these people, but it's no use. The story is too big, too complicated. It must be told. It can't be written." Huot told him that he must do both. It was decided then and there that Farish would accompany Huot back to Bari.

After their arrival in Bari on October 26, they found Tofte there, who, with Thompson, had conceived the idea of a trans-Adriatic shipping operation. Others in the Bari office were Sterling Hayden, the film actor,[57] and British SOE officers who had come from Cairo. Maclean arrived a few days later also by ship via Vis. Conferences were held with him for the purpose of coordinating the shipping operation with his mission in Yugoslavia. Thereafter Maclean left for Cairo to meet Eden, who was on his way back from Moscow, where he, Secretary Hull and Foreign Minister Molotov had conferred. Huot flew to AFHQ Algiers, where he was promised captured Italian matériel for transport to the Partisans.

On the next day—it was now early November—Huot left Algiers for Cairo to report in person to Colonel John E. Toulmin, the new OSS chief, who had succeeded Guenther. Toulmin told Huot that he had been transferred out of the theater. There is evidence that Huot's transfer was the result both of OSS's annoyance over his trip to Yugoslavia without orders and Maclean's protest to Middle East headquarters. Huot had seen Tito without reference to Maclean, who was the head of the mission, and all contacts with Tito were supposed to go through him.

There is no doubt, however, that national jealousies played some role, too. Off and on for months British aircraft had been parachuting supplies to the Partisans. Then within a few days and almost single-handedly, two or three Americans had sent more supplies to the Partisans by ship than a hundred airplanes could carry.

It was a highly organized operation with Tofte in charge in Bari, Thompson acting as executive officer of the shipping operation, Lieutenant W. Ellen in charge of the maintenance of vessels and Lieutenant J. Hamilton (Sterling Hayden) in charge of loading and dispatching of ships. Benson was the liaison officer at Vis and Hvar from November 10 until December 22, when he left Yugoslavia.

Even today, the most pro-American British observers appear to have a mental block about this operation. One highly placed British officer finally recalled that perhaps a boatload of Italian arms was landed in Dalmatia, although he must have known that more than seventy crossings were accomplished under American command and more than 6,000 tons of supplies were ferried across. During the same period only 125 tons were dropped into Yugoslavia by air.[58]

The Yugoslavs, however, have an excellent recollection of this enterprising and highly successful effort, and Huot, Tofte, Thompson and Benson are well remembered. They were all decorated by the Government of Yugoslavia shortly after the war.

As early as January 1, 1944, Josip Smodlaka, who was then the "Commissar for Foreign Affairs" of the National Committee of Liberation, thanked Tofte in writing for organizing the shipping base:

I have ascertained that this base has been able—thanks to you and your colleagues of the U.S. Army—to continue with complete success the dispatch of war materials and food to Yugoslavia—a task started under the alert direction of Major L. Huot. In the hope that nothing will be able to disturb the perfect collaboration now in actual existence between the delegates of our army and the representatives of our great ally, the United States of America, I express the hope that you and your valiant assistants, Captain Benson and Lts. Thompson, Greer and Ellen, will continue to be able to bring to a fine conclusion your efforts toward a final victory of the United Nations over the common enemy.[59]

These supply operations in the autumn of 1943 had two important by-products. First, thousands of wounded and sick Partisans were evacuated on the return trips and treated in Allied hospitals in Italy (over 12,000 by the end of the war). Second, for the first time in the war, the Partisans came in contact with Western newsmen. AP's Daniel De Luce slipped aboard one of the vessels which sailed from Italy to Yugoslavia, and *Time* carried a report in its October 18, 1943, issue about his daring venture and his highly positive impressions of the Partisans.

THE FARISH REPORT

After "Slim" Farish arrived in Bari from Yugoslavia, he set down on paper observations which were to achieve a certain fame as the "Farish Report." [60] This report was flown to OSS Washington and delivered to Roosevelt before he boarded the USS *Iowa* on his way to the Tehran Conference with Churchill and Stalin. (Copies were also given by OSS to Hull and the Joint Chiefs of Staff.) There is no doubt that Farish's report, coupled with the British attitude, dramatically changed FDR's view of the Yugoslav situation.

Dated Bari, Italy, October 29, 1943, the report was addressed to Major Louis Huot, OSS Advance Base, Bari. It was entitled: "Preliminary Report on a Visit to the National Army of Liberation, Yugoslavia."

Farish began his report by stating that the Partisan movement

is of far greater military and political importance than is commonly realized in the outside world. . . . The Communist Party is in theory only one element within the Partisan movement, but it is a very active one, and there is every evidence that strongly indoctrinated Party members are working hard to shape the structure of this newly born state according to their social, political, and economic beliefs.

Farish wrote that, as an American, he was enthusiastically received by the Partisans.

There could be no doubt, Farish said, "that the Partisan forces dedicated themselves to the fight against the Axis from the beginning; that they have always fought them; that they are fighting them at this time, and will fight them to the end." Farish then commented on the Četniks and Mihailović, saying that the latter "feared Communism more than he feared the common enemy." He added: ". . . that the Četniks are now fighting the Partisans is a fact to which the observer [Farish] can personally testify."

Farish then sketched the military picture existing at the time: The Partisans had 180,000 men under arms; they controlled one large mountainous area extending from the Montenegro-Serbia border northwest through Hercegovina to western Bosnia. Other mountainous portions of Croatia, Slovenia, Slavonia and the Istrian peninsula were also in their hands. All the Adriatic coast with the exception of the principal seaports was controlled by the Partisans as were almost all coastal islands.

Farish pleaded for immediate delivery of Allied supplies by sea and air and limited air support along the Dalmatian coast. He believed that air support would be particularly important from a morale point of view. With regard to supplies, he felt that air deliveries could never be efficient and that a sea channel across the Adriatic must be opened. (At the time Farish wrote his report such a channel was already in use.)

Farish ended his report by thanking the other members of the military mission—all British but one (Benson)—headed by Maclean for their comradeship and complete courtesy and consideration.

It should be noted that Farish wrote a second report eight months later, after further extended duty in Yugoslavia. It showed that his opinions of the Partisan movement had changed substantially in certain respects, for by then he realized that the Partisans, too, placed less emphasis on the fight against the Germans than on preparing for the political struggle at the end of the war.

MIHAILOVIĆ CONSENTS TO UNDERTAKE TWO
SABOTAGE OPERATIONS

Soon after Armstrong arrived in Mihailović's territory, the Četnik general allowed himself to be pressed by the British into conducting two sabotage operations against the Germans, in all probability the only major ones since the autumn of 1941. They are described by Seitz and Rootham, who witnessed them.

Seitz reports [61] that he was present during an attack by the Četniks on Višegrad on October 2, 1943. This operation was indeed a significant one. It involved not only an important railway bridge over the Drina which was defended by one German and two Ustaše companies but also several minor bridges on the Užice-Višegrad rail line.

What happened thereafter sheds a great deal of light on the situation in Yugoslavia at the time. Having struck their targets, the Četniks drove on toward Sarajevo and crossed over into Partisan territory, and immediately a worthwhile anti-German operation was converted into the pursuit of civil war. The Partisans counterattacked, drove the Četniks back and captured Višegrad. Then Radio Free Yugoslavia announced that the Partisans had destroyed the bridges on the Užice-Višegrad-Sarajevo railroad. The BBC repeated this version, to the consternation of Mihailović and the Četniks.

Rootham describes [62] an action in eastern Serbia which the British proposed and the Četniks agreed to. It was an attack on Danube shipping and took place on October 26, 1943. One German was killed and, Rootham says, fifty Serbs were executed in reprisal.[63]

These actions made Mihailović an even more "wanted man," and he was forced to move his headquarters frequently. As Armstrong wrote: "If he had remained static, he would in time have been accurately pinpointed by the Germans who would have taken appropriate steps to liquidate him and his headquarters." [64]

As the autumn wore on, British supply drops to the Četniks, which had been augmented at the time Armstrong arrived, became less frequent and finally ceased altogether. The meager contents of one of the last shipments, on October 19, 1943, are described by Martin.[65]

At the same time, relations between Mihailović and the British-led mission grew cooler. The general, however, singled out the American members for favorable attention. Seitz, who became doubtful about what he considered the negative British policy vis-à-vis Mihailović, requested Cairo's permission "to spot-check the military strength, potentialities and morale of the Četnik forces and proceed immediately to Washington upon completion thereof to present our findings and recommendations . . ." [66] Not having received an answer, he nevertheless set out on November 6,

Seitz, Hudson and Mansfield with Četnik Major Dušan Smiljanić in Serbia, 1943. *Courtesy of W. R. Mansfield*

1943, to tour Četnik territory. He was accompanied by Hudson, Mansfield, a Yugoslav officer, Captain Borislav Todorović, who had come to Mihailović from Cairo in September 1943, and four Yugoslav aides. In his book, Seitz describes the trip in great detail. Wherever he went, he was assured by Četnik commanders that their sole aim was to fight the Germans, but they protested that they had no arms and moreover were constantly attacked by either Partisans or other anti-Četnik Yugoslav elements, such as the *Ustaše*.

Meanwhile, a third American was dropped into Četnik territory. He was Lieutenant Musulin, who had been selected to go into Yugoslavia several months before. He joined Seitz and Mansfield on November 25, 1943, at Konjuša near Gornji Milanovac for Thanksgiving dinner. Seitz describes [67] how Mihailović honored the Americans on that day by arranging to have eleven fiery A's blazing from mountaintops around their campsite.

Ten days earlier Mihailović had addressed a message to the commander of the U.S. 15th Air Force in Italy in which he spoke of his intention to celebrate Thanksgiving Day in an appropriate way. He invited the 15th Air Force to fly over certain Četnik-controlled areas of Yugoslavia in a show of comradeship. Somehow, this message did not get through until the morning of the 25th, and then it was too late to organize an overflight. Mihailović and his supporters, who did not know that the message had failed to arrive in time, were disappointed.[68]

In December, the Seitz group moved south to the Sandžak, while Mihailović, Armstrong, Bailey and Musulin remained north of the Western Morava River. At Christmas 1943, Seitz decided to join a British party which was about to cross over to Partisan-held territory, hoping to be evacuated to Italy from there. He had not yet received certain letters which Mihailović wanted him to transmit to American authorities, and so he asked Mansfield to stay behind until the letters arrived. Seitz writes that he sent Mihailović a letter of explanation and adds that "it was my duty and also possibly to his [Mihailović's] advantage to be on my way." [69]

Accompanied by Hudson, Seitz joined the British group, consisting of two British liaison officers as well as two escaped British POWs. This party left Četnik territory at the end of December and crossed into Partisan-held territory. They were well received, although Seitz was unhappy that the Partisans, having alleged that they had captured Četniks who had attacked them, refused to produce the prisoners. Seitz clearly implies that he doubted that there were any such prisoners. At the Kolašin headquarters of General Peko Dapčević, one of the Partisan commanders in

Montenegro, he and Hudson were entertained at a dinner attended also by a British major and an American naval officer attached to Dapčević's staff.

After being held up for six weeks because of communications problems, Seitz finally departed by Allied plane from an airfield in Partisan-held Berane on March 15, 1944, together with Hudson, who by that time had spent exactly two and a half years in occupied Yugoslavia.

Meanwhile, Mansfield and Todorović, who had waited in vain for three weeks for Mihailović's letters, had also gone south. So had Bailey, who had left Mihailović's headquarters on January 5 with the aim of reaching the coast for evacuation to Italy. He was soon joined by Major Lukačević.

The two groups walked separately toward the coast, avoiding both Germans and Partisans. In Priboj, Mansfield finally received the Mihailović letters from Ostojić and soon thereafter the Mansfield-Todorović group joined the Bailey-Lukačević party. Together they reached Cavtat near Dubrovnik on January 29. Bailey's radio transmitter was put back in operation, and contact with Cairo was reestablished by Captain Lofts, the signals officer who had dropped to Mihailović and Hudson back in September 1942 and who was now accompanying Bailey. Arrangements were made for a British gunboat to pick up the entire group, but bad weather prevented their departure for two weeks. On February 15 they were finally ferried across to Bari, and on March 3 they arrived in Cairo, thus actually preceding Seitz and Hudson by a couple of weeks, even though the latter had set out earlier.

On November 29, Middle East headquarters had sent a message to the British mission with Mihailović asking what the reaction of the local commanders might be if Mihailović were replaced and whether any of them had received orders from Mihailović to collaborate with the Axis.[70] Rootham writes that he and his British colleagues were shocked, since "no suggestion of collaboration with the Axis or thought of his removal had ever occurred to us." This is a surprising statement, for talk of Mihailović's collaboration, at least with the Italians, was quite common in SOE circles in Cairo at the time of Rootham's departure for Yugoslavia in May 1943. On the other hand, it is no doubt true that Rootham did not observe any collaboration because he served in eastern Serbia, which was occupied by the Germans and where, up to November 1943, no accommodation had been reached.

The antecedents of Četnik arrangements with the Germans can be traced directly to the German "Special Envoy for Southeastern Europe," Hermann Neubacher, who exercised a major influence upon the Yugoslav situation after his appointment in August 1943. On October 29, he reported to Hitler personally about the growing threat posed by Tito, and on the next day he received instructions from the German Foreign Office "to start negotiations with the national insurgents if an opportunity arises." [71] Thus in the autumn of 1943 the German leadership agreed for the first time to attempt some arrangement with the Četniks.

The Germans realized that the Partisan danger was increasing every day and that the Četniks were equally perturbed by Tito's growing strength. Pointing to the unnecessary burden of trying to take on the Partisans and the Četniks at the same time, those Germans who believed that some sort of German-Četnik arrangement was advantageous for Germany finally prevailed, even though they were aware that Mihailović was as anti-German as ever and that he hoped for and believed in an Allied victory.

Several proposals for arrangements with Četnik units, though not with Mihailović, were worked out in the first two weeks of November and on November 19 the first nonaggression agreement was concluded between the German commander in Serbia and Četnik Staff 148.[72] This was followed by other similar pacts with individual Četnik commanders, so that by the end of November three important Četnik leaders, Nikola Kalabić, Dragutin Keserović and Voja Lukačević had been "neutralized" by the Germans.[73] (Lukačević was the same Četnik officer who went south with Bailey in January 1944.) The agreements also called for cessation of all Četnik action against the Nedić regime.

Neither the British nor the American liaison officers had any inkling of these understandings between local Četnik commanders and the German authorities.

There is little doubt that Mihailović knew about these arrangements, that he regarded them as the lesser of two evils and that he stayed in the background in order openly to maintain his anti-German attitude while tacitly hoping to gain an advantage in his primary aim of defeating the Partisans.

There is reason to believe that the passage of the Bailey group to the coast through German-held territory was facilitated by Lukačević's understanding with the Germans—in one town he was even invited to dinner by the German commander, though he did not accept.[74] He told Bailey, Mansfield and Todorović that he had posed as a Nedić follower.

THE MOSCOW FOREIGN MINISTERS' CONFERENCE

Before the Moscow Conference of the Foreign Ministers of the U.S., Britain, and USSR (October 19–30), the American delegation met with Roosevelt on October 5, 1943, to discuss questions likely to arise at the conference. During that meeting, the President declared that he was not sure that Yugoslavia could be restored after the war as a whole country. Croatia might have to be set up separately from Serbia, the President thought.[75]

Thus in October 1943, Roosevelt was still leaning toward the restoration of Serbia as an independent entity. Croatia, he apparently felt, had nothing in common with Serbia and because of its dubious record, particularly since 1941, should be put under a trusteeship after the war.

On October 2, Tito sent a message to Moscow which read:

In connection with the preparations for a conference between the representatives of the U.S.S.R., Britain, America, it is probable that the question of Yugoslavia will be raised.

In this connection, I beg you to inform the Soviet Government of the following:

The Anti-Fascist Council of Yugoslavia and Supreme Headquarters of the National Liberation Army and Partisan detachments of Yugoslavia have empowered me to declare:

First, we acknowledge neither the Yugoslav Government nor the King abroad because for two and a half years they have supported the enemy collaborationist, the traitor Draža Mihailović, and thus bear complete responsibility for this treason to the peoples of Yugoslavia.

Second, we shall not allow them to return to Yugoslavia because that would mean civil war.

Third, we speak in the name of the overwhelming majority of the people, who want a democratic republic based on National Liberation Committees.

Fourth, the only legal government of the people at the present time are the National Liberation Committees headed by the Anti-Fascist Councils.

We shall give a statement to this effect to the British Mission attached to our headquarters.

The British General [Maclean] has already informed us that the British Government will not insist on supporting the King and the Yugoslav Government-in-Exile.[76]

Maclean states [77] that he had told Tito that the British Government had no intention of trying to impose any government on the Yugoslav people against its will; the future form of government was a matter that they would have to decide for themselves.

Dedijer reports that the Soviet Government did not place Tito's statement on the agenda of the Moscow Foreign Ministers' Conference.

On his way to Moscow, Eden stopped in Cairo and had a talk with King Peter and the Yugoslav Prime Minister, Purić. King Peter quotes

Eden as saying that the British aims were "a completely free Yugoslavia and to return him [the King] to the throne." [78] At the same time, according to King Peter, Eden spoke of Mihailović's "passive resistance," which had begun "to look like collaboration with the enemy." King Peter also mentions that, during that talk with Eden, the Yugoslav Government learned for the first time of Maclean's mission with Tito, and apparently both Eden and Purić became quite agitated in the course of the conversation.

Yugoslavia was mentioned at least twice during the Moscow Conference. On the first occasion Lieutenant General Ismay, chief of staff of the British Minister of Defense, said that "operations in the Balkan area will be limited to the supply of patriot armies by air and sea transport, to minor commando forces and to the bombing of strategic objectives." He was reporting decisions reached at the Quebec Conference.

Yugoslavia also came up on October 23 when Eden read a statement in regard to the British attitude toward the resistance movement in Yugoslavia. He said that the long-term desire of the British Government was to see Yugoslavia restored to her former freedom and independence. He added that the British had been in touch with both resistance groups in Yugoslavia—Mihailović and the Partisans. When he had passed through Cairo on his way to Moscow he had discussed with King Peter and the Yugoslav Government the British attitude toward Mihailović and had said that the British Government's chief desire was to have him actively engage in operations against the common enemies, Germany and Bulgaria. He had outlined to the King two operations which the British would like to see Mihailović carry out—the destruction of the Bor copper mines near Zaječar and the cutting of the strategic rail line between Belgrade and Niš. King Peter had promised that if a common policy in regard to Yugoslavia could be agreed upon at the Moscow Conference, he would send immediate orders to Mihailović to carry out those operations, for which it was believed he had adequate forces.

Eden went on to say that it had been made quite plain to the King that if these orders were not carried out, the British Government would have to reconsider its attitude toward Mihailović and the question of sending him further supplies. Eden added that the British were continuing to supply the Partisans by air, and it was hoped in the near future that more ample supplies could be sent by ship across the Adriatic. He then outlined proposals to unite the two factions in the common struggle against Germany and to stop them from fighting each other in the future. He said that he thought this would be possible, since they were operating in different geographical areas.

Hull said that he had nothing to add to Eden's statement and Molotov suggested that the item be deferred.[79]

Eden insisted that the British aim was to assist guerrilla bands in their struggle against the German occupying forces and, whenever possible, to prevent these bands from fighting each other.

At that point, Hull turned to General John R. Deane, chief of the U.S. military mission to the Soviet Union, who said that the U.S. Chiefs of Staff considered that there was a great opportunity in the Balkans, particularly during the winter months, to intensify sabotage and disruptive work in order to undermine German military strength. He said that the OSS had the equipment and trained personnel to carry on these activities and was prepared to penetrate the area by air or other means. He added that the American military authorities hoped that this would be agreeable to the Soviet Government, and he wished to assure them that the purpose of these operations was purely military.

Molotov inquired whether it would be possible to get a clearer picture of the operations envisaged. Deane answered that it was somewhat difficult, since all such operations were of necessity subject to opportunity, but that the OSS had done very valuable work in other countries. That concluded discussion of Yugoslavia at the Moscow Conference.

The Soviet position on Yugoslavia was never made clear, although the Soviet Government did submit a statement on "The Future of Poland and Danubian and Balkan Countries, Including the Question of Federations," in which it warned against making premature political decisions regarding all these countries. In particular, it expressed the opinion that "neither the existing émigré governments nor even the governments which will be set up immediately after the conclusion of peace under conditions still not sufficiently normal will be able fully to ensure the expression of the real will and permanent aspirations of their people." [80]

Churchill says that at the meeting of October 23, Eden "made a frank and fair statement of our attitude in the hope of securing a common Allied policy towards Yugoslavia, but the Russians displayed no wish either to pool information or to discuss a plan of action." [81]

Eden writes [82] that he "hoped that as a result of the Conference the two movements could be advised to avoid conflict with each other. Mr. Molotov had no immediate comment to make and Mr. Hull did not support me. I decided to raise the question again with Molotov later."

Eden also mentions a private talk with Molotov, "with Hull's agreement," in which he told the Soviet Foreign Minister that the British were pressing the Četniks not to take action against the Partisans, and asked him to advise the Partisans not to take action against the Četniks.

"Molotov said his Government had little contact with the Partisans and would like to send a Mission to them," Eden writes, adding: "It would be in contact with the British Mission and might operate from British controlled territory. I welcomed this idea thinking it better that a Russian Mission should work in contact with our own people rather than operate on its own." Eden interrupted his return journey from Moscow again in Cairo where, according to King Peter,[83] he told the Yugoslavs that the Russians had proposed sending a mission to Tito.

Eden also saw Maclean, who had arrived in Cairo from Yugoslavia to deliver a written report for the Foreign Office. Maclean was told by Eden that following the Moscow Foreign Ministers' Conference, another meeting at the chiefs-of-government level would take place soon and that his report was being forwarded to Churchill in anticipation of that conference.

Verbally [Maclean writes], I repeated my main conclusions: that the Partisan Movement was of infinitely greater importance than was generally realized outside Yugoslavia; that it was very definitely under Communist leadership and firmly oriented towards Moscow; that as a resistance movement it was highly effective and that its effectiveness could be considerably increased by Allied help; but that, whether we gave such assistance or not, Tito and his followers would exercise decisive influence in Yugoslavia after the liberation.[84]

After Hull's return to Washington, he saw the Yugoslav Ambassador, on November 19, and, according to Fotić,[85] said that all agreements reached in Moscow were based on the principles of the Atlantic Charter, which assured the sovereignty of every state, great and small. He also told Fotić that the creation of zones of influence had never been raised in Moscow and that he would have opposed it strongly because it would unavoidably lead to new frictions and new conflicts.

8

THE FIRST PARTISAN MILITARY MISSION TO THE
WEST—THE CONGRESS AT JAJCE

Before Maclean left Yugoslavia on his first outbound journey at the end
of October 1943, Tito had expressed the wish to send a Partisan military
mission under Ivo Lola Ribar (son of Dr. Ivan Ribar) to Wilson's headquarters. When Maclean talked to Wilson about it in November the latter agreed. An airstrip in Glamoč in Bosnia was ready, and a captured
German aircraft was available to fly out the mission. The German Sixth
Offensive was in full swing, however, and a bombing attack killed Ribar
and destroyed the plane. Two British officers, Major Robin Whetherly
and Captain Donald Knight, were killed in the same attack. It was thereupon decided to send in a British plane with Maclean aboard. It became
the first Allied aircraft to land in war-torn Yugoslavia. On December 3,
1943, it arrived to pick up Vladimir Velebit, the newly appointed head
of the Partisan military mission; Bill Deakin; Anthony Hunter, who had
parachuted to Croatia in May; two wounded Partisan leaders, Miloje
Milojević and Milentije Popović, and a captured German military intelligence officer. Maclean also returned to North Africa on the same plane.
After a stop in Brindisi, the group proceeded to Alexandria. According
to Wilson, Velebit's mission was not brought to Cairo because King Peter
and the Royal Yugoslav Government were there.

Vladimir Dedijer, who had sustained a head wound which later became
infected, had left Partisan headquarters on November 10 accompanied by
two British officers. They had a perilous journey, first to the island of
Hvar and then by British torpedo boat to Bari. From there he went by
air to Cairo, where he arrived on November 26 and was immediately
operated on in a British hospital.[1] After his recuperation he became a
member of Velebit's mission.

Just before Velebit's departure for Middle East headquarters, a political event of the first magnitude took place at Jajce in Bosnia, on November 29, 1943. Even while the Partisans were engaged by the German Sixth Offensive, the future political order of Yugoslavia was uppermost in the minds of Tito and the other leaders of the movement. As a follow-up to the Bihać Assembly, which a year earlier had founded AVNOJ (the Anti-Fascist Council of National Liberation of Yugoslavia, with Dr. Ribar as president), this second session of AVNOJ was a more elaborate gathering. One hundred and forty-two delegates attended and so did Deakin, representing the British mission (Maclean and Farish were out of the country, and Benson was on Vis). In a long speech, Tito reviewed the Partisan struggle and declared that the time had come for the transformation of AVNOJ from a general political body into the highest legislative body and for the setting up of a "National Committee of Liberation of Yugoslavia" as a provisional government.

Although Tito's relations with the Soviet Union had not been completely smooth during 1943, his speech [2] revealed nothing of the frictions between them or the lack of Soviet responsiveness. On the contrary, it contained the most unreserved praise for the Soviet Union. Tito credited the improved war situation entirely to the Red Army: "As a result of events outside our country, that is as a result of the victories of the Red Army . . . conditions were created for the victories of the other Allies, the British and Americans in Africa, conditions were created for the Allied landings . . . in Italy, and for the capitulation of Hitler's chief partner, Fascist Italy."

The Partisan leader acknowledged the material aid provided by the British and Americans, although he deplored the "hospitality" offered the Royal Yugoslav Government-in-Exile by "Allied countries." He welcomed the presence of British and American liaison officers at his headquarters and reported that "plans are being made for representatives of the Soviet Union to come here." He said it was "the desire of all our people . . . that contact be established as soon as possible with this great fraternal state, in which the peoples of Yugoslavia have the greatest confidence, regarding it as their greatest protector." Tito ended his speech with a call for a free and truly democratic federal Yugoslavia.

The second AVNOJ session decreed the transfer of power from the Royal Yugoslav Government-in-Exile to a seventeen-member National Committee of Liberation [3] in which Tito held the posts of Prime Minister and Defense Minister; the exclusion of King Peter from Yugoslavia until such time as the Yugoslav people were able freely to decide for themselves what form of government they wanted; and the appointment of Tito as Marshal of Yugoslavia. This was the first time that Tito's real name was revealed by the Partisans as Josip Broz. AVNOJ also decided to send an appeal to the U.S. Government to freeze Yugoslavia's gold reserves in the United States, which had remained at the disposal of the Government-in-Exile.⁴ All this took place on the same day that the question of Yugoslavia was being discussed by the American, British and Soviet heads of government in Tehran.

THE TEHRAN CONFERENCE

While Roosevelt was on the USS *Iowa* steaming toward Oran he approved, on November 15, 1943, a U.S. Joint Chiefs of Staff paper regarding Allied strategy in the Balkans and eastern Mediterranean area. This paper, which was to be submitted to the Combined (American and British) Chiefs of Staff, was based on the Quebec Conference decisions of August 1943 and once again called for limiting Allied activities in that area to the supply by air and sea of Balkan guerrillas, to minor action by commando forces and to the bombing of vital strategic targets. The reason given for this limitation was that "the Balkan-Eastern Mediterranean approach to the European Fortress is unsuitable, due to terrain and communication difficulties, for large-scale military operations" and that the "implementation of our agreed strategy for the defeat of Germany will require all available means." ⁵

Still on the USS *Iowa,* the President discussed with the Joint Chiefs of Staff on November 19, 1943, the agenda for his forthcoming conference with Stalin and Churchill. In this connection the question arose of "U.S. policy of non-participation in operations of the eastern Mediterranean-Balkan area." The President said that the U.S. had to pay heed to the Soviet attitude in this matter.⁶ General Marshall, obviously impatient with the British, declared, "We must see the question of this Balkan matter settled." He added: "We do not believe that the Balkans are necessary. To undertake operations in this region would result in prolonging the war and also lengthening the war in the Pacific. We have now over a million tons of supplies in England for 'Overlord' [the code name for the cross-channel invasion]. It would be going into reverse to undertake the Balkans and prolong the war materially." Marshall suspected that the British might like to drop the cross-channel invasion at this time "in order to undertake operations in a country with practically no communications."

After the President's arrival in Cairo, the Joint Chiefs of Staff invited the American Ambassador to Britain, Winant, to give them his latest assessment of British strategic plans. Winant said that he thought the British were very eager to employ fully the resistance which could be developed among the "unorganized forces" in the Balkans.[7]

In Cairo, also, the American Ambassador to the Soviet Union, W. Averell Harriman, and Soviet Deputy Foreign Minister Vyshinsky had a discussion on November 23 in which Harriman asked Vyshinsky whether he had any recent information about Mihailović. Vyshinsky replied in the negative. Harriman said he had none either but thought it was time to tell Mihailović "that he should fish, cut bait, or go ashore." [8] Vyshinsky agreed and added that, from his point of view, Mihailović had so far not only not been helpful in the prosecution of the war but had even been harmful.

On the following day, November 24, the Combined Chiefs of Staff met with Roosevelt and Churchill. The minutes [9] record that Churchill said "it was a lamentable fact that virtually no supplies had been conveyed by sea to the 222,000 followers of Tito." (Churchill was obviously unaware of the OSS trans-Adriatic shipping operation.)

The Prime Minister pointed out that

these stalwarts were holding as many Germans in Yugoslavia as the combined Anglo-American forces were holding in Italy south of Rome. The Germans had been thrown into some confusion after the collapse of Italy and the Patriots had gained control of large stretches of the coast. We had not, however, seized our opportunity. The Germans had recovered and were driving the Partisans out bit by bit. The main reason for this was the artificial line of responsibility which ran through the Balkans. On the one hand, the responsibility for operations here lay with the Middle East Command but they had not the forces. On the other hand, General Eisenhower had the forces but not the responsibility. Considering that the Partisans and Patriots [10] had given us such a generous measure of assistance at almost no cost to ourselves, it was of high importance to insure that their resistance was maintained and not allowed to flag.

The minutes show Churchill's view that

no regular formations were to be sent to Yugoslavia. All that was needed there was a generous packet of supplies, air support and, possibly, a few Commandos. This stepping-up of our help to the Patriots would not involve us in a large additional commitment. Finally, when we had reached our objectives in Italy, the time would come to take the decision whether we should move to the left or to the right.

What Churchill had in mind was a campaign through southern France or through northern Yugoslavia.

Roosevelt replied, the minutes of the meeting say, by pointing out that the Russians would reach the boundaries of Rumania shortly and at Tehran they might ask "what we intended to do in this event. They might suggest a junction of our right with their left. We should be ready to answer this question. The Russians might suggest that we stage an operation at the top of the Adriatic with a view to assisting Tito." (This is the first recorded reference by the President to Tito.) Such a suggestion, as will be seen, was never on the Soviets' minds; Roosevelt's question indicates his misinterpretation of Russian aims.

On the same afternoon, Roosevelt received King Peter and Prime Minister Purić. There is no American record of this discussion, but King Peter recounts that after he thanked the President for providing the B-24s to Yugoslavia, the conversation turned to Mihailović and Tito and the part Yugoslavia should play in the war.

Roosevelt told Purić and me [he writes] that he had been successful in bringing about peace between de Gaulle and Giraud and hoped to be able to bring peace between Mihailović and Tito. Purić pointed out that it might be easier to reconcile two generals of one army than the heads of a national force and a Communist revolution. Roosevelt suggested that since the capitulation of Italy the best way of consolidating the two opposing resistance forces in Yugoslavia was to divide the country into two different operation zones—west and east. He proposed that Tito should control the west and Mihailović the east, but that the whole should be under an Allied Supreme Commander in Italy, General Alexander or General Wilson.[11]

The King then relates that he suggested an Allied landing on the Dalmatian coast.

Roosevelt, however, did not agree with me at all and thought that it would be better to attack the enemy where he was strongest, i.e., in France. . . . Roosevelt was very enthusiastic about the resistance movement in Yugoslavia and said he was going to send Marine officers to Mihailović and a "mission" to Tito. [This is not quite understandable, since at that time American officers were already with both Mihailović and Tito.] In spite of the fact that we differed on several points, Roosevelt declared his full support of my Government and assured me that I could always count on him as a personal friend and ally. He promised to see us on our return [probably Roosevelt's return from Tehran].

Roosevelt also received Wilson and discussed with him the resistance movements in Greece and Yugoslavia, which the President described as "problem children." [12]

On November 26 the Combined Chiefs of Staff met in Cairo with Eisenhower, who said that on the assumption that he would advance in Italy to the Po line, he would propose action to establish small garrisons on the islands off the eastern coast of the Adriatic. From there thrusts as far north as possible could be made into Yugoslavia and the "Patriots" furnished with arms and equipment. If only the Rome line was reached it would not be possible to thrust as far up the Adriatic as he would have liked.[13]

With regard to the supply of equipment to the Yugoslav guerrillas, Eisenhower continued, one officer (Brigadier Miles) had now been placed in charge of these operations, and arms captured in North Africa and Sicily were being shipped in. He believed that all possible equipment should be sent to Tito since Mihailović's forces were of relatively little value. Admiral Sir John Cunningham (Commander in Chief, Allied Fleet in the Mediterranean) agreed that everything should be done to support Tito, who had some hundred thousand men under his control. The Germans would have serious problems in operating against the guerrillas since lateral communications were immensely difficult and there was only one inadequate rail line. They would have to supply their forces largely by sea. It would therefore be impossible for them to bring a concentrated force to bear against Tito. He believed that sea communication could be cut by air and naval action and, in fact, he hoped shortly to be operating destroyers in the Venice-Trieste-Pola area. He questioned whether it would be possible to continue to supply Italian equipment, since this was rapidly running short. Air Chief Marshal Sir Arthur Tedder (Air Commander in Chief, Mediterranean Air Command) said that the present system of air operations into the Balkans worked reasonably well. The tactical commander in Italy was given his targets from Middle East headquarters. He agreed with Sir Charles Portal (Chief of the British Air Staff) that coordination of effort would be more satisfactory if a special commander were to be named and a joint staff responsible for operations in the Balkans set up.

It is clear from the above that there was not complete agreement between Britain and the United States on what to do in the Mediterranean in general and the Balkans in particular. The British (supported by Eisenhower) seemed to favor greater support of the Partisans, while Roosevelt and Marshall wished to concentrate on the invasion of France without any diversionary commitments.

However, when Roosevelt met with the American Joint Chiefs of Staff on November 28 in Tehran, Marshall had apparently softened his stand somewhat, declaring that certainly more could be done along the east coast of the Adriatic by opening up small ports and transporting supplies to the Tito forces. Marshall pointed out that communications inland from the coast were very bad, but he believed that it would not be difficult to get in munitions, foodstuffs and other material aid for the guerrillas. He said that it had been agreed with the British that the Adriatic should be made a separate command under one officer, and he added that the U.S. Chiefs of Staff had also agreed to a unified command in the Mediterranean, subject to the President's approval. (Eisenhower's title was to be changed on December 9, 1943, to Allied Commander in Chief, Mediterranean Theater, with jurisdiction extended to include the Balkans, the Aegean and Turkey.) Marshall believed that the Allies could land ships along the eastern Adriatic coast and thus assist in supporting Tito.

Admiral Leahy, chief of staff to President Roosevelt, said that Eisenhower felt that if he could get far enough north in Italy he could push northeast toward Austria. Marshall added that he could also advance west toward southern France. Those two movements, together with the limited operations on the Adriatic coast, would hold several German divisions.[14]

Roosevelt, also relenting in his opposition to operations in the Adriatic, felt that small groups of commandos operating in support of Tito along the Adriatic coast had great possibilities. Another suggestion was for a small force to penetrate northward from Trieste and Fiume (Rijeka). He said he was much more inclined toward operations from the Adriatic than from the vicinity of the Dodecanese islands. Later, the President thought that commando operations in the Adriatic could be mounted by January 1944, but Marshall questioned whether it would be feasible to undertake very many commando raids, since they might conflict with planned operations in Italy. Thereupon the President said that he was thinking of raids on a small scale, about 2,000 men to a group. They would not require so many landing craft as larger operations.

The first plenary meeting of the three chiefs of government and their advisers took place on the afternoon of the same day, and Roosevelt attempted to ascertain from Stalin how the Allied forces in the Mediterranean could best help the Red Army—through operations in Italy, the Adriatic, the Aegean Sea, or Turkey.[15] Stalin showed no interest in Mediterranean operations; he asked when the cross-channel invasion would take place. Churchill reverted to the Mediterranean, pointing out that the operations of the Partisans in Yugoslavia, which had been more extensive and more effective than those of Mihailović, opened up the prospect of sending them additional help. There was, he added, no plan to send a large army to the Balkans, although more might be done in that area through commandos and small expeditions. Roosevelt said that he

Marshal Stalin, President Roosevelt, and Prime Minister Churchill at Tehran, November 1943. Behind them: Harry Hopkins, Foreign Minister Molotov, Ambassador Harriman, Ambassador Clark Kerr, and Foreign Secretary Eden. *U.S. Army photo*

had thought of a possible operation at the head of the Adriatic to meet up with the Partisans under Tito and then to operate northeast into Rumania in conjunction with the Soviet advance from the region of Odessa.[16]

This statement surprised and disturbed Harry Hopkins, who accompanied Roosevelt as his special assistant. He scribbled a note to the Chief of U.S. Naval Operations, Admiral Ernest J. King: "Who's promoting that Adriatic business that the President continually returns to?" To which Admiral King replied, "As far as I know it is his own idea." [17] Churchill was quick to associate himself with Roosevelt's suggestion and, as we shall see later, quoted it back to him repeatedly.

On the next day, November 29, the Combined Chiefs of Staff met with Marshal K. E. Voroshilov, military adviser to Stalin. General Sir Alan Brooke, Chief of the British Imperial General Staff, noted that since the withdrawal of Italian forces from Yugoslavia the Germans had found it difficult to maintain their communications in that country. Therefore, full advantage ought to be taken of all opportunities to increase the German difficulties in Yugoslavia by assisting the Partisans.[18] A system must be organized for supplying them with arms, and air assistance should be rendered as well. Brooke said that there were now some twenty-one German divisions in all of Yugoslavia. Replying to an indication from Voroshilov that he did not quite agree with these figures, he stated that this was his information and that he would ask British Intelligence to check its accuracy. He said there were also eight Bulgarian divisions in the Yugoslav area in addition to the German divisions.

When Roosevelt met Stalin alone on the afternoon of November 29, he lent him Major Farish's report, calling it "a most interesting report from an American Army officer who had spent six months [actually six weeks] in Yugoslavia in close contact with Tito." [19]

Churchill, Roosevelt and Stalin held their second plenary meeting on November 29, and Brooke reported [20] that the military committee had earlier in the day briefly reviewed the question of providing the Partisans in Yugoslavia with supplies to assist them in containing German forces. Voroshilov pointed out that the question of Yugoslavia had not been considered in detail. Churchill felt that this question was more political than military and he also referred to the number of German and Bulgarian divisions in the Balkans. He said he did not suggest that the Anglo-American forces put divisions into the Balkans, but he did propose that there be a continuous flow of supplies, frequent commando raids and air support furnished as and when needed. He felt it was shortsighted to let the Germans crush the Yugoslavs without giving these brave people now fighting under Tito the weapons for which they might ask. Churchill added that the British had no interests in the Balkans that were exceptional and ambitious in nature, and all they wanted to do was to nail down the twenty-one German divisions in that area and destroy them. He suggested that the British Foreign Secretary, the Soviet Foreign Minister, and a U.S. representative designated by the President (Secretary Hull did not attend the Tehran Conference) hold discussions to see if the proposed activities in the Balkans presented any political difficulties.

Stalin replied that there was no difference of opinion as to the importance of helping the Partisans but that he had to state that from the Russian point of view such questions as Turkey, the Partisans and even the occupation of Rome were really secondary. He was for an invasion of southern France supporting a cross-channel operation.

Roosevelt said that all possible aid should be sent to Tito without making any commitment that would interfere with the cross-channel invasion of France. He added that he thought the Allies should consider the value of the many divisions the Germans had in the Balkans; if the Allies could carry out certain operations with a minimum effort, these German divisions might be placed in a position where they would no longer have the same value. He thought commando raids should be undertaken and that all possible supplies should be sent to Tito in order to force Germany to keep its divisions there.

Stalin said that in Yugoslavia the Germans had eight divisions and that the figures given by Churchill were wrong. We now know that the figures given by Churchill and Brooke were indeed overestimates. Whether due to excellent intelligence or to uncanny guesswork, the figure for the number of German divisions mentioned by Stalin was substantially accurate. The last German order of battle before the Tehran Conference, which was dated October 4, 1943, and was still valid at the time the three heads of government met, shows that the Germans had throughout the Balkans, including Greece, fourteen divisions, several under strength, and in Yugoslavia not more than eight. According to the best estimates, there were approximately 100,000 German troops in all of Yugoslavia. There were only five Bulgarian divisions in the area with most of those troops, however, in Greece.[21]

On several earlier occasions, the British had believed that Axis strength in Yugoslavia was considerably higher than was actually the case. It can only be assumed that the inflated figures advanced first by the Yugoslav Government-in-Exile and later by the Partisans influenced the British estimates.

On November 30, Eden, Molotov and Harry Hopkins (sitting in for Hull) lunched together, at which time Eden raised again the question of a Soviet mission to the Partisans (he had discussed such a move with Molotov at the Moscow Conference) and suggested that the Soviets might want to have an air base in North Africa.[22] He added that the British were ready to provide a base. Molotov thanked Eden, who then explained that the British air base supplying Tito was located at Cairo and asked Molotov where he would like to have a base. Molotov answered that he would leave that to Eden's discretion; since Eden had suggested Cairo, he thought that would be a good location for the Russians, too. Molotov added that the Soviet General Staff planned to send a mission to Yugoslavia and that on his return to Moscow he would be able to say who would be taking part in the mission. Eden said that he would try to have preliminary arrangements made and a place ready for an air base for the Russians at Cairo.

Molotov then completely surprised his luncheon partners by asking whether it would not be better to have a Soviet mission with Mihailović rather than Tito in order to get "better information." (It will be recalled that in 1942 the Soviets had discussed with the Yugoslav Government-in-Exile the possibility of a mission to Mihailović.)

Eden commented that, judging from reports he had received from British officers, it would not be useful to deal with Mihailović. He added, however, that maybe it would be good for the Russians to send some of their people to Mihailović.

In the third plenary meeting on November 30, the question of Yugoslavia was referred to only when Churchill expressed the hope that, in the future course of the war, the Yugoslavs would continue to hold down German divisions.[23] The Yugoslav problem was not raised again in Tehran. The secret "military conclusions" of the conference stressed among other things "that the Partisans in Yugoslavia should be supported by supplies and equipment to the greatest possible extent, and also by commando operations." [24] These "conclusions" were initialed on the evening of December 1, 1943.[25]

Elliott Roosevelt, who accompanied his father to the Tehran Conference, reports [26] that the President told him that Churchill was pushing for an invasion through the Balkans and "it was quite obvious to everyone in the room what he really meant. That he was above all else anxious to knife up into central Europe, in order to keep the Red Army out of Austria and Rumania, even Hungary, if possible." With regard to Stalin, the President said: "And Uncle Joe, when he argued the military advantages of invasion from the west, and the inadvisability of splitting our forces in two parts, he was always conscious of the political implications, too." Then Elliott quotes his father at length to the effect that the American Chiefs of Staff were convinced that the fastest way to victory with the least loss of American lives was through a second front in Western Europe.

AFTER TEHRAN

Roosevelt returned to Cairo on December 2 and had further meetings with Churchill in the Egyptian capital. During that conference it was decided to enlarge the responsibilities of the Commander in Chief, Allied Forces, North Africa (Eisenhower), by adding to his command the Balkan area up to and including Turkey and to call it henceforth the Supreme Allied Command, Mediterranean Theater. With regard to the Balkans, Eisenhower was told by the Combined Chiefs of Staff that it was agreed at Tehran "that our support of the Patriots in the Balkans, which now falls within the area in which you are responsible for Allied operations, should be intensified in order to increase their effectiveness." [27] Their directive continued:

You will be responsible for supporting them to the greatest practicable extent by increasing the supply of arms and equipment, clothing, medical stores, food and such other supplies as they may require. You should also support them by commando operations and by furnishing such air support as you may consider advisable in the light of the general situation. You should examine the possibility of continuing to supply the Patriots with Italian equipment, in the use of which they are already experienced, making good deficiencies in Italian formations to such extent as may be necessary with available British or American equipment. We consider that this mission is of such importance that it would best be controlled on a regular basis by a special commander and joint staff.

As it turned out, Eisenhower was soon to be named Supreme Commander, Allied Expeditionary Forces, based in London, and was succeeded, effective January 8, 1944, by Wilson, who thus once again assumed responsibility for Balkan affairs. (Wilson was succeeded as Commander in Chief, British Forces, Middle East, by General Sir Bernard Paget.)

As far as the recommendation of the Combined Chiefs of Staff was concerned, that a special commander and a joint staff be appointed to support the Partisans, it was not until six months later that Wilson was able to act. On June 1 he created the Balkan Air Force with Air Vice Marshal William Elliot as commander.

The Combined Chiefs of Staff directive to the new commander in the Mediterranean had been held up for a few days because several matters had to be ironed out, two of them in connection with the Yugoslav situation. Perhaps more than anything else, developments in Yugoslavia were the reason for the establishment of the new command.[28]

One problem concerned the status of SOE vis-à-vis the military and diplomatic authorities in the Mediterranean. Maclean had never regarded himself as the head of an SOE mission. His contacts were the Prime Minister, the Foreign Secretary, the British Ambassador to Yugoslavia, the Commander in Chief, Middle East, and only last his principals in SOE London and Cairo.

This problem was compounded by the status of OSS in Cairo, its relationship to SOE and to the Commander in Chief, Middle East, to Maclean, and to other existing authorities. In fact, the British Ambassador to the Yugoslav Government-in-Exile, Ralph Stevenson (who had succeeded Rendel in August 1943), suggested that the matter of coordination between SOE and OSS be raised at the "Sextant" conference.

What worried Stevenson was that Donovan had demanded a considerably increased share in special operations in the Balkans, and that the

OSS was answerable only to the U.S. Joint Chiefs of Staff and not to the
State Department, while SOE carried out a policy agreed upon by the
British Chiefs of Staff and the Foreign Office. Stevenson saw a danger that
OSS would not necessarily pursue the same policy as SOE. He suggested
that Balkan policy be concerted and that special operations be integrated.
To this end, he recommended that the American Ambassador to the
Yugoslav Government-in-Exile in Cairo be included on such committees
as the Special Operations Committee at Middle East headquarters, where
the OSS was already represented, and the Middle East Defense Committee. He also proposed that control of all special operations remain in the
hands of the Commander in Chief, Middle East, who would be advised
as before by the Special Operations Committee, and when necessary the
Middle East Defense Committee. Ambassador Stevenson's suggestions
were, however, not discussed at the Sextant conference.

King Peter regretfully writes that he asked to see Roosevelt on the
latter's return from Tehran, "but was told that he was very ill and not
receiving anybody. . . . I knew that he received many other people and
felt that perhaps he was ashamed to talk to me after the way he had let
me down at the Teheran Conference." [29]

After Roosevelt and his party left for home, the British discussed
among themselves and with King Peter and his Government the problems which arose out of the Tehran and Cairo conferences. Maclean,
Deakin, Velebit and his Partisan military mission, who had meanwhile
arrived in Egypt, were included in some of the conversations.

It was in the course of those talks that Churchill and Maclean had a
discussion during which Maclean opined that Yugoslavia would inevitably be established along Soviet lines. Churchill thereupon asked, "Do
you intend to make Yugoslavia your home after the war?" "No, Sir," Maclean replied. "Neither do I," Churchill said. "And, that being the case,
the less you and I worry about the form of Government they set up, the
better. That is for them to decide. What interests us is, which of them
[Mihailović or Tito] is doing most harm to the Germans?" [30]

Deakin writes [31] that on December 9 in the evening and again on December 10 in the morning, Churchill questioned Maclean and Deakin
closely regarding the Yugoslav situation, not only concerning Tito but
also Mihailović, even though neither Maclean nor Deakin had served in
the Četnik area. "For nearly two hours the Prime Minister interrogated
me as the officer mainly concerned with interpreting the evidence de-
rived from captured German and Četnik documents concerning the links
between Mihailović and his commanders with the Italians and the Germans," Deakin writes, adding: "It was a miserable task." This debriefing

made a deep impression on the Prime Minister, as his subsequent conversations with King Peter and Prime Minister Purić were to show.

Meanwhile, the Partisan military mission in Cairo actively lobbied. Wilson reports [32] that he had dinner with Velebit, who requested the delivery of equipment for the Partisans and the training of a certain number of tank crews and truck drivers. The talks which Velebit conducted with officers at Middle East headquarters concerned chiefly the supplying of the Partisans with arms and the evacuation of wounded Partisans to Allied hospitals in Italy.

Dedijer writes: [33]

. . . the Partisan Military Mission was besieged by correspondents of the big newspapers and agencies in America and Great Britain. . . . Almost nothing had been known in these countries about the struggle of the Partisans. All credit for the resistance against the Germans in Yugoslavia had been given to Draža Mihailović. There were wildly impossible versions of the person of Tito.

It was at that time that C. L. Sulzberger filed from Cairo the first substantially accurate biography of Tito. It appeared in *The New York Times Magazine* of December 5, 1943. And on December 11, *The New York Times* carried a photograph of Tito with the following caption: "Marshal Josip Broz (Tito) at his headquarters 'somewhere in the Balkans' where he is directing operations against the Nazis. This is the first photograph of the leader to reach this country."

BRITISH, AMERICAN AND SOVIET REACTIONS TO THE JAJCE DECLARATION

On December 8, 1943, the British Government was asked in the House of Commons to define its attitude toward the Yugoslav Government in Cairo as a result of the creation of the National Committee of Liberation by the Partisans at Jajce. The Minister of State, Richard Law, answered [34] that he had no information beyond that appearing in the press that such a Committee "with the status of temporary Government" had been set up in Yugoslavia "under the auspices of General Tito, the leader of Partisan forces." (This was the first official and public British reference to Tito.) He added that he was not yet in a position to say what the relationship of that Committee might be "with King Peter and his Government, recognised by his Majesty's Government as the legitimate Yugoslav Government, and now established in Cairo." Asked if the British Government "still" supported Mihailović, Law said: "Our policy is to support all forces in Yugoslavia which are resisting the Germans." He added: "As things are, we are giving the Partisan forces more support than those of Mihailović, for the simple reason that the resistance of the Partisan forces to the Germans is very much greater."

On the following day, at Secretary Hull's press conference in the State Department, a correspondent asked about the U.S. attitude toward a broadcast by the Partisan radio to the effect that the Partisans were going to ask for U.S. lend-lease assistance. The correspondent added that British Minister of State Law had told the Parliament that the British were giving more aid to the Partisans than to Mihailović. In reply, the Secretary said that it was the policy of the Allied nations to furnish supplies to "each or any group" in Yugoslavia that was effectively fighting the Germans, and that the British had affirmed that policy as recently as yesterday. He added that the U.S. had not come to the question of mechanics as far as lend-lease was concerned, but that was not important.[35] There was no reference to either Mihailović or Tito in the Hull statement.

Later the same day (December 9), the State Department made available to the press a background statement: [36]

The Yugoslav people have demonstrated to the whole world their determination to regain their independence and to drive the Axis forces from their country. With inhuman cunning the Nazis strove to divide this people against itself, by partitioning its territory, by establishing conflicting authorities maintained by violence and terror, and by incitement to the lowest passions of civil strife.

It is natural that in repelling an enemy operating with every method of violence and deception, the organizers of Yugoslav resistance should also seek to utilize every regional advantage, every social group, and every skillful and daring leader. Whatever their differences may be, their ultimate purpose is to drive out the enemy and to restore the institutions of free government.

The King and the Government of Yugoslavia, now temporarily established at Cairo, are recognized by all the United Nations as the authority conducting Yugoslavia's participation in the general conduct of the war. Within the country resistance movements under diverse leadership have grown into forces of undoubted military value. In the circumstances it is natural that political factors should also play a part. It is our intention to assist in every possible way the resistance of the Yugoslav people, and to deal with the resistance forces from the point of view of their military effectiveness, without, during the fighting, entering into discussions of political differences which may have arisen among them, and which tend to divert the national energies from the main objective of expelling the Nazis from their country. In line with our consistent policy we consider that political arrangements are primarily a matter for the future choice of the Yugoslav people.

Meanwhile every means is being utilized to obtain factual and objective information on all aspects of the situation in Yugoslavia, for use in the prosecution of the war.

Even in this statement, neither Tito nor Mihailović was mentioned. (The first official and public American reference to Tito did not occur until January 1945.) The clear implication of the statement was that the U.S. Government did not wish to endorse the British position of giving more credit for resistance to the Partisans than to Mihailović. The State Department felt that the British were thus taking steps which would have political ramifications after the war, something the U.S. was not prepared to do.

At the same time, the State Department advised the OWI, which proposed referring to the National Committee of Liberation as a "government" and to the Partisans as the "Yugoslav Army of National Liberation," not to use the word "government" in this connection and not to mention the Partisans, but only "patriot activities throughout Yugoslavia." [37]

In Moscow the reaction to the November decisions of AVNOJ was at first completely negative. Stalin was quoted as saying, when he heard about them after his return from the meeting with Churchill and Roosevelt, that they were "a stab in the back of the Soviet Union and the Tehran decisions." [38] The Soviets went so far as to forbid Radio Free Yugoslavia to broadcast the resolution prohibiting King Peter's return. After Moscow saw, however, that the British and American Governments did not appear to be shocked by the Jajce resolutions, the Soviet Government distributed an announcement on December 14 which referred to the Jajce Congress and, for the first time, officially mentioned Tito's name. The announcement said in part:

The events in Yugoslavia which have already met with a sympathetic response in England and the United States are regarded by the Government of the USSR as favorable facts which will facilitate the further successful struggle of the peoples of Yugoslavia against Hitlerite Germany. They testify also to the real success of the new leaders of Yugoslavia in the manner of the unification of all the national forces of Yugoslavia.

The announcement then referred specifically to "the Četniks of General Mihailović" in the following terms:

[Their] activity, according to available information, up to the present has not facilitated but has rather brought harm to the cause of the struggle of the Yugoslav people against the German invaders and therefore could not fail to be received unfavorably in the USSR.

. . . the Soviet Government, considering it essential to receive more detailed information in regard to all Yugoslav events and concerning the Partisan organizations, has decided to send to Yugoslavia a Soviet Military Mission as the British Government has done previously.[39]

This carefully phrased statement only inched toward the Partisans and in so doing cited the British example. Clearly, the Soviets were not eager in December 1943 openly to embrace the Partisans and thus break with the Government-in-Exile.

A CLASH BETWEEN THE BRITISH AND YUGOSLAV GOVERNMENTS

On December 7, Eden had his first talk with Prime Minister Purić since the Tehran Conference. Purić subsequently told the American Ambassador, McVeagh, that Eden had said that the British would continue to recognize the Yugoslav Government, but at the same time they would support the Partisans. MacVeagh reported to the State Department that Purić was extremely bitter at the British refusal to allow his Government to have direct communications with its people and at what he called the British failure to cooperate and consult with his Government.[40] Purić had added that Allied military support to Communist bands would result in driving the conservative elements of the population into the arms of the Germans for protection. This was an unfortunate remark, because it only confirmed suspicions of Četnik collaboration with the Germans, even though Purić most likely had no knowledge of the first nonaggression pacts concluded between Četnik commanders and German units a few weeks earlier.

On the morning of December 10, after Maclean and Deakin had briefed him, Churchill received King Peter. During the conversation Churchill said that he was greatly impressed by the Partisan movement's strength and significance.[41] He added that his Government possessed irrefutable evidence of Mihailović's collaboration with the enemy and that therefore the desirability of eliminating Mihailović from the Cabinet might be suggested by the British Government in the rather near future.[42]

This represented a change in British policy, which in November had favored Mihailović's replacement as commander of the Yugoslav Army in the Homeland but not his removal from the Cabinet. At that time, the Foreign Office had in mind the possibility of suggesting to King Peter that he summon Mihailović to Cairo and replace him by a commander who would cooperate with the Partisans. Actually, a query was sent on November 29 to the British mission with Mihailović regarding local reaction if Mihailović were to be replaced. But this plan was discarded (and never discussed with the U.S.) when the details of the second AVNOJ session of November 29 became known in London, in particular the denunciation of the King and the monarchy.

After meeting with King Peter, the Prime Minister saw Purić and told him of the British intention to continue, and even increase as much as possible, British military support to the Partisan movement. Purić strongly protested, but Churchill said that, though Mihailović's reasons for inaction might seem good to him, it was obviously to the advantage of the common cause that available assistance be withheld from the forces that were not fighting and given to those that were.

Upon Churchill's suggestion to King Peter that he see Maclean and Deakin, who were then in Cairo, the King arranged meetings with both of them. In each conversation, he was advised to dismiss Mihailović and to order his troops to join Tito; only thus could Peter regain the trust of the Yugoslav people.[43]

When the Royalist Yugoslavs in Cairo saw that little could be expected from the British and not much more from the Americans, they proposed to the Soviet Government on December 10 the conclusion of a treaty of friendship and cooperation. Soviet Ambassador N. V. Novikov replied, however, that his Government did not see the possibility of starting negotiations at that time since it considered the situation in Yugoslavia uncertain.[44]

On December 8, Wilson asked Mihailović to blow up two bridges across the Ibar and the Morava Rivers by December 29. The aim was to paralyze all north-south rail traffic in Yugoslavia. When Mihailović promised Armstrong to carry out these operations the British gave him a few weeks' additional grace.

Rootham reports on how Mihailović followed up his agreement: Rootham's group was to blow up the bridge over the Morava and Armstrong himself the one over the Ibar—but the go-ahead had to come from Mihailović himself.[45] Rootham writes:

There was, afterwards, . . . some considerable question whether this was a "test operation" or not—that is to say, whether it was represented to Mihailović as being his last chance to regain British confidence. . . . Whether or not Mihailović himself understood that it was meant to be his final opportunity to redeem himself is one of the things that we shall probably never know. However that may be, neither operation was ever carried out. . . . Mihailović never gave the order to attack.

Yet there is some indication that Mihailović might have been more cooperative with the Allies if his views had been given greater weight. Whether he was merely temporizing it is impossible to say. But when he met Lieutenant Musulin, the junior American officer who had arrived to assist Seitz and Mansfield, he bitterly complained that the attitude of the British had made it impossible for him to work with them. The meeting with Musulin took place on December 18, 1943, near Bajina Bašta.[46] Mihailović assured Musulin that he was willing to carry out any reasonable assignment under Allied direction. He also expressed the hope that the Americans would play a more independent role than previously. Mihailović and Musulin worked out a plan to attack an important anti- mony mine but, according to Martin,[47] Cairo radioed back that the project was to be dropped. It may be assumed that Middle East head- quarters wanted Mihailović to get on with the bridge attacks and not suggest other projects.

It has also been reported that on December 23, 1943, Mihailović told Armstrong and Bailey: "I wish to do all I can to prevent civil war. I pro- pose that my, and Tito's delegates, meet somewhere in the Sandžak. Hav- ing had a sad experience relative to the word of honor of the Partisan Command, I wish these negotiations to be conducted by the British mili- tary mission." [48]

However, Mihailović's suggestions were not regarded as serious by Cairo which, by that time, was most distrustful of ideas proposed by the Četnik leader.[49]

BRITISH POLICY EVOLVES

Churchill fell gravely ill with pneumonia in Tunis, but Eden flew home and on December 14 reported to the House of Commons on the Cairo and Tehran Conferences. Concerning Yugoslavia, he said that the British were doing all they could to supply the Partisans with munitions and "to support them in every possible way." He also referred to the decision taken at Jajce at the second session of AVNOJ to set up a National Com- mittee of Liberation:

So far as I am aware, this National Committee does not claim authority outside the borders of the area in which it operates. It has certainly not claimed any form of recognition from His Majesty's Government . . . all, including the

Government in Cairo, have declared that the moment their country is liberated they will lay down their offices and it will be for the country to choose its Government. That is a point on which all are agreed—the King, General Tito and the Yugoslav Government.[50]

Messages regarding future action were exchanged between the Foreign Office and the British Ambassador to the Yugoslav Government in Cairo, Stevenson. He in turn appeared to have kept MacVeagh well informed of his proposals to the Foreign Office and of the Foreign Office's thinking. In particular, Stevenson advised the American of the Ibar-Morava bridge sabotage operations which the Commander in Chief, Middle East, had asked Mihailović to undertake.

On December 18 the Yugoslav Prime Minister called in MacVeagh and asked him to intervene urgently with the State Department in view of what he had been told by the British Ambassador, namely, that he should shortly expect joint pressure from the British and American Governments to remove Mihailović from the Cabinet. Purić said that he had told Stevenson that the American position—recognition of the Yugoslav Government and military support for all elements engaged in fighting the enemy—was acceptable but that the British position was "fantastic and dangerous in the extreme." MacVeagh's report to the State Department said: [51]

Aside from the question as to whether the British Ambassador has not gone rather far at this juncture in mentioning the United States, the Department may well wish to consider very carefully any proposals involving a change in our attitude at the present time although doubtless a straddling policy covering the military and political situations may be difficult to maintain indefinitely.

The State Department reacted with concern, instructing the Ambassador to find out more, particularly since no British-American discussions regarding this matter had taken place either in Washington or in London.

Meanwhile, the Foreign Office switched to a new tack, mainly to find out whether Tito rejected the monarchy unequivocally. Ambassador Winant cabled the State Department that the Foreign Office did not think that the AVNOJ declaration "is a final closing of the door on King Peter." [52] And the British Government informed the Soviet Government on December 13 of its hope that, in the interest of Yugoslav unity, it might be possible for Tito, on the one hand, and the King and the Yugoslav Government, on the other, to find common ground.

On December 20 the Soviet Ambassador to Britain, F. T. Gusev, gave Eden a Soviet note in reply. Eden says [53] that it gave hope that the Russians would exert their influence on Tito, since it declared that the Soviet Government agreed with the British that the Partisans and the King ought to work together. The note further said that the Soviets were ready to do everything possible to find a compromise between the two sides.[54] Eden told Gusev that his Government could help by telling Tito to stop polemical pronouncements. The Ambassador answered that the Soviets might well favor this, but he did not know how much influence they had with Tito. Eden countered that the Soviet Government had radio contact with Tito.

On December 23, Eden informed the Soviet Foreign Minister that Maclean had been instructed to go back to Tito "with a view to ascertaining what basis there was for unifying all forces of resistance both in and outside Yugoslavia and of bringing together contending parties." Eden's telegram to Molotov concluded by saying that the British would be glad to receive Soviet suggestions concerning how this objective might be achieved.[55]

Eden writes [56] that on December 23 he suggested to Churchill that the Prime Minister might have a meeting with Tito "to try to bring him to a better frame of mind." He even proposed that there might be a meeting between Tito and the King in Churchill's presence. He mentions, however, that Stevenson and Maclean thought it unwise to bring up the issue of the monarchy with the Partisans.

In a telegram from Cairo to the Foreign Office, Stevenson wrote:

Our policy must be based on three new factors:
The Partisans will be the rulers of Yugoslavia. They are of such value to us militarily that we must back them to the full, subordinating political considerations to military. It is extremely doubtful whether we can any longer regard the Monarchy as a unifying element in Yugoslavia.[57]

When Maclean arrived in Bari from Cairo he learned that the German Sixth Offensive had made such gains that he could return to Yugoslavia only by parachute. Vis was the only Adriatic island still in Partisan hands, and while waiting for his flight, Maclean decided to make a trip there. Velebit, who had also come from Cairo, accompanied Maclean to Vis.

During the preceding weeks, two Americans who had long been slated for service in Yugoslavia had arrived in Partisan territory: Lieutenant Wuchinich joined Major Jones in Slovenia on November 26, and Captain Selvig went to Partisan Supreme Headquarters on December 3. Captain Benson, the first American to land in a Partisan area, left Yugoslavia on December 22 after four months of service there.

In Washington, Fotić called on Hull on December 16, 1943. He reports that the Secretary repeated his press conference statement of December 9, that the United States would furnish supplies to "each or any group" in Yugoslavia that was effectively fighting the Germans. According to Fotić, Hull said that helping the guerrillas in Yugoslavia was a purely military question. Fotić adds: "The Secretary of State, far from endorsing the policy outlined four days [actually, only two days] before by the British Foreign Secretary, let me understand that he would be no party to any pressure which might be brought on the Yugoslav Government to abandon Mihailović and shift its support to Tito." [58]

Fotić further refers to a conversation on December 23, 1943, with James C. Dunn, the State Department's Director of the Office of European Affairs, during which Dunn said that the British policy, as announced by Eden, was not understandable and that the State Department was surprised at the pressure that was being placed upon the King and the Government-in-Exile to abandon Mihailović.

THE SITUATION AT THE END OF 1943

The Allied grand strategy for winning the war evolved clearly in 1943. The U.S. idea of a second front—which was, of course, also a Soviet aim —was accepted at Quebec by Churchill, who originally had doubts about the military feasibility of an invasion of Western Europe and had therefore toyed with the notion of "rolling up Europe" from the southeast. Even after the Quebec decision to launch a second front, the British—and particularly Churchill—continued to believe in the importance of Mediterranean and Balkan operations. In this they were guided, above all, by strategic military considerations, although as 1943 drew to a close, the political aspects of reaching Central Europe ahead of the Red Army began to influence British thinking.

The British decision to support the Partisans in Yugoslavia and to stop supplying the Četniks was entirely a military one. The Partisans were fighting, and the Četniks were not. That was all that counted as far as Churchill was concerned, even though he was aware that the Partisans were resolved to set up a Communist regime in postwar Yugoslavia. But first things came first. The future form of government in Yugoslavia was something to worry about later. And conceivably it might not be so unpalatable, after all, particularly if the British helped the Partisans now.

A further consequence of these considerations was a pronounced deterioration of Britain's relations with the Royal Yugoslav Government, despite the fact that there was certainly greater affinity between them than between the British and the Partisans.

The United States had only military and strategic considerations in mind in the Balkans. It believed that if Tito was fighting and Mihailović was not, then Tito should be supported; but this support should be modest and in no way detract from the pursuit of a grand strategy in which Balkan affairs did not figure. Hence U.S. interest in the Balkans was limited. In the U.S. view, to aid Tito militarily did not mean that the political support of the Yugoslav Government-in-Exile should not continue.

The Russians appear to have been motivated primarily by military considerations. They were convinced that only an invasion of Western Europe would result in real relief to the Red Army. Mediterranean and Balkan operations, the Russians felt, were sideshows and of no help to them. Since these military considerations happened to coincide with the Soviet political design of keeping Western troops out of Eastern Europe, it was easy for Stalin to stress solely the military aspects of his aims.

Even though the Partisans were ideologically their brethren, the Soviets did not send them arms because the Balkans, in 1943, were not central to the Soviet strategic pattern. There is some irony in this if one considers that it was the British who, because they considered the Balkans militarily important, sent arms to the Communist Partisans. The Soviets maintained correct relations with the Yugoslav Government-in-Exile even though they were constantly pushed by the Partisans to break off those ties.

All this changed later, but at the end of 1943, the attitudes of the three major Allies toward Yugoslav affairs were above all guided by military considerations.

Within Yugoslavia, the situation had evolved decisively in the Partisans' favor. They had beaten back, albeit with frightful losses, two further Axis offensives. They had shown a net gain in the size and strength of their forces, particularly after British and American (though not Russian) liaison officers had arrived with the first outside arms help. The Italian surrender was an enormous boon to the Partisans and so were the Big Three decisions at Tehran which recognized the Partisans as an Allied force.

Politically, the establishment of a National Committee of Liberation as a quasi-government was of fundamental importance as a counterweight to the Government-in-Exile in Cairo, which the Congress at Jajce denounced as illegitimate. It was resolved at Jajce, as at Bihać before, that Yugoslavia would be organized on democratic federalist principles, with

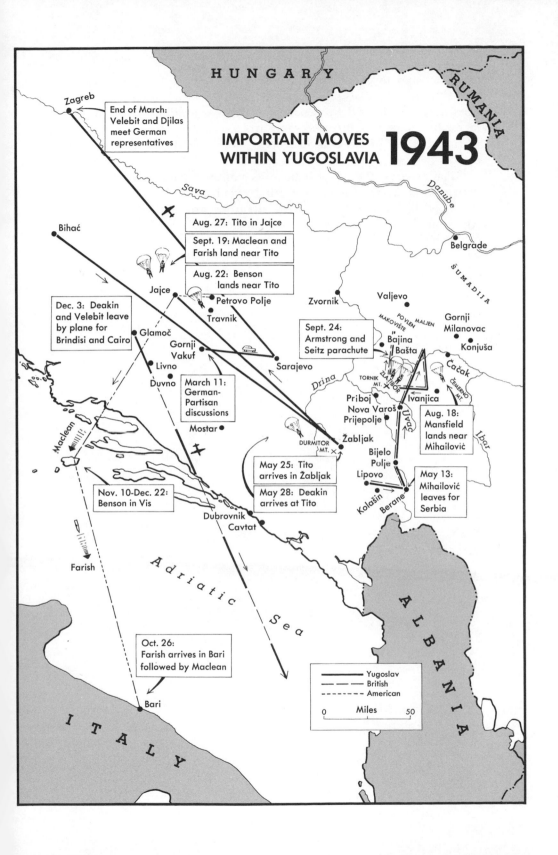

IMPORTANT MOVES
WITHIN YUGOSLAVIA **1943**

HUNGARY

RUMANIA

Zagreb

End of March:
Velebit and Djilas
meet German
representatives

Sava

Danube

Belgrade

Bihać

Aug. 27: Tito in Jajce

Sept. 19: Maclean and
Farish land near Tito

ŠUMADIJA

Aug. 22: Benson
lands near Tito

Jajce

Petrovo Polje

Zvornik

Valjevo

Gornji
Milanovac

Dec. 3: Deakin
and Velebit leave
by plane for
Brindisi and Cairo

Travnik

POVLEN MALJEN

MAKOVIŠTE

Sept. 24:
Armstrong and
Seitz parachute

Bajina
Bašta

Konjuša

Glamoč

Gornji
Vakuf

TORNIK
MT. ✕

ZLATIBOR

Čačak

Livno

March 11:
German-
Partisan
discussions

Drina

ČEMERNO
MT.

Maclean

Duvno

Sarajevo

Priboj

Ivanjica

Aug. 18:
Mansfield
lands near
Mihailović

Mostar

Nova Varoš

Uvac

Prijepolje

Ibar

DURMITOR
MT. ✕

Žabljak

May 25: Tito
arrives in Žabljak

Bijelo
Polje

May 13:
Mihailović
leaves for
Serbia

Nov. 10-Dec. 22:
Benson in Vis

May 28: Deakin
arrives at Tito

Lipovo

Farish

Kolašin

Berane

Dubrovnik

Cavtat

A d r i a t i c

S e a

A L B A N I A

Oct. 26:
Farish arrives in Bari
followed by Maclean

Bari

I T A L Y

Yugoslav
British
American

0   Miles   50

all regions having equal status. Nothing was said or done that would indicate that the future regime would be established along Communist
lines, except perhaps the designation of Tito as head of the quasi-government. But Tito's identity was established as an effective Yugoslav guerrilla leader, not as General Secretary of the Communist Party of Yugoslavia.

Mihailović, on the other hand, was militarily and politically on the
defensive. Whatever armed strength he had, his operations against the
Partisans during the Axis Fourth Offensive proved to be his undoing.
After the Italian capitulation and at German initiative, some of his
commanders concluded armistice agreements with German units. The
AVNOJ decisions at Jajce were a blow from which he was not to recover.

PART IV: 1944

Tito–Allied Hero

NINETEEN FORTY-FOUR was the year in which Germany's defeat became inevitable. In June the Allies landed in Normandy, and by the end of the year Allied forces had driven into Germany from both west and east. In Yugoslavia, too, the Germans were retreating, the civil war had been practically won by the Partisans, and the Allies' views of Yugoslav events evolved further. Having abandoned Mihailović for military reasons, the British allowed political considerations to dominate their Yugoslav policy for the first time. And so did the Russians, who had sent a mission to Tito in February. Yet the U.S. remained unwilling to act in the political sphere.

9

CHURCHILL'S LETTER TO TITO

While Churchill was recuperating in North Africa from his bout with pneumonia, he received a message from Tito wishing him speedy recovery. Since "the crisis in Yugoslav affairs pressed on me," he says,[1] he decided to use the occasion to get directly in touch with Tito. On December 30 he cabled Eden requesting the Foreign Secretary's advice as to whether he should send Tito a substantive message which he had already drafted or ". . . merely give a friendly acknowledgment, in which latter case I fear we shall have lost a good opportunity of my establishing a personal relationship with this important man."

In this cable Churchill said that there was at that stage no possibility of getting Tito to accept King Peter as a *quid pro quo* for repudiating Mihailović.

Once Mihailović is gone the King's chances will be greatly improved and we can plead his case at Tito's Headquarters. . . . I thought we were all agreed in Cairo to advise Peter to dismiss Mihailović before the end of the year. Everything Deakin and Maclean said and all the reports received showed that he had been in active collaboration with the Germans. We shall never bring the parties together till he has been disowned, not only by us, but by the King.

Churchill ended his message to Eden by saying that he did not wish "to hawk this private message [Churchill to Tito] around to the United States and Stalin, with the inevitable delays involved."

Eden replied on January 1, 1944, advising Churchill not to say anything about Mihailović in his message to Tito. He thought Tito would look upon this as a sign of weakness. The King, moreover, might not dismiss Mihailović. Eden concluded: "If we have a public and spectacular

breach with Mihailović, our case against him for treachery must be un-
answerable. I am still without evidence of this. . . . I hope therefore
that we may keep the Mihailović issue open a little longer until we have
got our proofs. . . ." [2]

Churchill was not impressed. On January 2 he cabled [3] Eden: "I have
been convinced by the arguments of men I know and trust, that Mihailović is a millstone tied around the neck of the little King, and he has no
chance till he gets rid of him."

There followed some further correspondence between Churchill and
Eden until the proposed letter was in final form. It was dated Africa,
January 8, 1944.[4] After thanking Tito for his get-well message, Churchill
wrote that he had heard from Deakin about the Partisans' valiant efforts
and that it was his desire to give Tito all aid in human power. He told
Tito that Maclean was a friend of his and that his own son, Randolph,
would soon be in Yugoslavia too; that the British had no desire to dictate
the future government of Yugoslavia; that they would give no further
military support to Mihailović, and that they would be glad if the
Yugoslav Government would dismiss him. Churchill added that the
British could not cast King Peter aside and that they would therefore
continue official relations with him, ". . . while at the same time giving
you all possible military support."

He pleaded for an end to polemics on both sides, and he assured Tito
that he would work "in the closest contact with my friends Marshal
Stalin and President Roosevelt." He expressed the hope that the Soviet
military mission would work in harmony with Maclean's mission.

Churchill's letter originally included the sentence: "I hope that there
may be an end to the polemics on either side once Mihailović has been
turned out, as he has richly deserved to be." After considerable persuasion
by Eden, the Prime Minister agreed to change this sentence. Some toning
down was also suggested by Wilson, who was opposed to a complete
breach with the general, believing that the Četniks were at least holding
down two Bulgarian divisions.[5]

Churchill handed the letter to Maclean who, with Randolph Churchill,
had come to Marrakech where the Prime Minister was convalescing.
Maclean and Randolph returned to Bari to await their parachute drop
to Tito's headquarters. In Bari they were joined by Farish, who had just
come back from a visit to the United States during which he had reported
personally to Roosevelt and other U.S. leaders, both military and civilian,
his impressions of the situation in Yugoslavia.

Although Churchill had not wished to consult his Allies in advance, he promptly sent Roosevelt and Stalin copies of his letter to Tito. Within two days Stalin commented: "Your message to Tito, whom you are encouraging so much with your support, will be of great importance." Roosevelt, however, simply noted on the cable, "I do not think that calls for an answer." Having received no word from Roosevelt, Churchill wrote in a cable to him dated January 18: "I hope you like my letter to Tito. Brigadier Maclean and Randolph hope to jump with it tomorrow." [6]

On January 12, the British Embassy in Washington gave the State Department an *aide-mémoire* regarding British efforts to find "a compromise between the contending groups in Yugoslavia" and reporting that Maclean "has been examining the whole situation with Marshal Tito." Churchill's letter to Tito was not mentioned. The *aide-mémoire* solicited U.S. views on a solution to the Yugoslav problem and expressed "hope that if they concur in His Majesty's Government's appreciation and in the action which is being undertaken, the United States Government will lend His Majesty's Government their support."

Meanwhile, Ambassador MacVeagh sent the State Department a summary of the Churchill letter as given him by the British Ambassador to the Yugoslav Government, and on January 19 the British Embassy in Washington informed the State Department of the letter and of the British inclination to advise King Peter to dismiss Mihailović from his ministerial post and as commander in Yugoslavia, but not before receipt of an answer from Tito.

The U.S. Government did not commit itself one way or the other on the Churchill letter, preferring to await Tito's reply. Fotić, however, reports [7] that on January 28 when he pursued his efforts to get action on Roosevelt's statement at Bolling Field on October 6, 1943, regarding food, ammunition and medical supplies for the Četniks, he was told by John J. McCloy, Assistant Secretary of War, that "the instructions from the President are to direct all assistance to Tito." This is the first indication that Roosevelt's own views regarding the situation inside Yugoslavia had shifted radically after reading Farish's report and as a result of the Tehran Conference. The State Department's attitude, however, was more conservative.

The airstrip from which the Partisan military mission had departed only a few weeks before was no longer available due to the German advances during the Sixth Offensive, during which Partisan headquarters at Jajce had to be abandoned. Hence, Maclean, Randolph Churchill and Farish parachuted into Yugoslavia on January 20 near Tito's temporary headquarters in the Bosnian mountains above Bosanski Petrovac. As

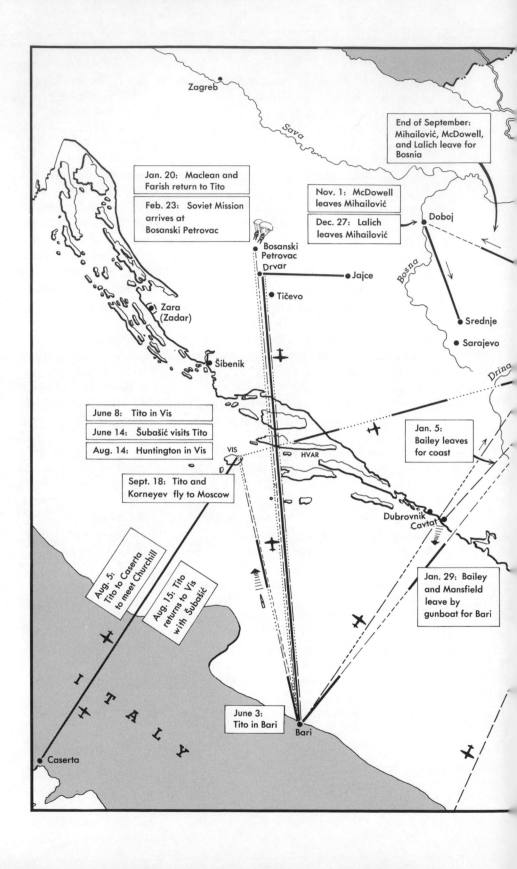

Zagreb

Sava

End of September:
Mihailović, McDowell,
and Lalich leave for
Bosnia

Jan. 20: Maclean and
Farish return to Tito

Feb. 23: Soviet Mission
arrives at
Bosanski Petrovac

Nov. 1: McDowell
leaves Mihailović

Dec. 27: Lalich
leaves Mihailović

Doboj

Bosanski
Petrovac
Drvar

Jajce

Tičevo

Bosna

Zara
(Zadar)

Srednje

Sarajevo

Šibenik

Drina

June 8:   Tito in Vis

June 14: Šubašić visits Tito

Aug. 14: Huntington in Vis

Jan. 5:
Bailey leaves
for coast

VIS

HVAR

Sept. 18: Tito and
Korneyev fly to Moscow

Aug. 5:
Tito to Caserta
to meet Churchill

Aug. 15: Tito
returns to Vis
with Šubašić

Dubrovnik
Cavtat

Jan. 29: Bailey
and Mansfield
leave by
gunboat for Bari

I
T
A
L
Y

June 3:
Tito in Bari

Bari

Caserta

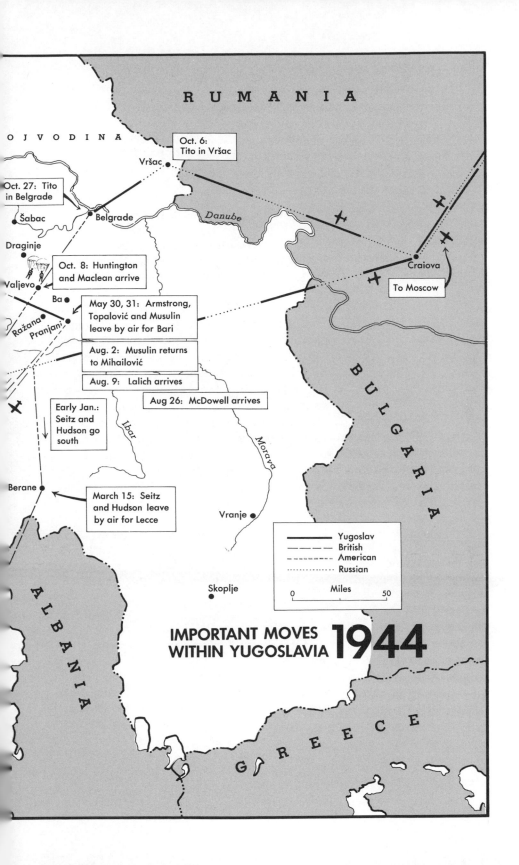

RUMANIA

OJVODINA

Oct. 6:
Tito in Vršac

Vršac

Oct. 27: Tito
in Belgrade

Šabac

Belgrade

Danube

Draginje

Craiova

Oct. 8: Huntington
and Maclean arrive

Valjevo

To Moscow

Ba

May 30, 31: Armstrong,
Topalović and Musulin
leave by air for Bari

Ražana

Pranjani

Aug. 2: Musulin returns
to Mihailović

Aug. 9: Lalich arrives

Aug 26: McDowell arrives

B U L G A R I A

Early Jan.:
Seitz and
Hudson go
south

Ibar

Morava

Berane

March 15: Seitz
and Hudson leave
by air for Lecce

Vranje

———— Yugoslav
— · — · — British
– – – – – American
················ Russian

Skoplje

0   Miles   50

A L B A N I A

IMPORTANT MOVES
WITHIN YUGOSLAVIA **1944**

G R E E C E

soon as Maclean saw Tito, who now wore a marshal's uniform, he handed him Churchill's letter, "He was clearly very much pleased," Maclean says.[8]

Churchill writes [9] that "[it] took nearly a month to get an answer," but considering that Maclean did not deliver the letter until January 20, that Churchill had a reply by February 3 does not seem to indicate excessive delay. Tito's answer began:

Your message is valuable proof that our people have in their superhuman struggle for freedom and independence a true friend and ally at their side, who deeply comprehends our needs and our aspirations. . . . Your Excellency may be sure that we will endeavor to keep your friendship won in a most difficult hour of our people's history and which is extremely dear to us.

Tito then spoke of "our great Allies" (in the plural) and of his wish "to fulfill to the utmost our duty as an Ally," adding: "Aid tendered to us by our Allies very much contributes to ease our situation on the battlefield." Thereupon Tito addressed himself to the main problem raised by Churchill, namely, the British relationship with King Peter, saying that he understood that relationship and promised "as far as the interests of our people permit, to avoid unnecessary politics and not cause inconvenience to our Allies in this matter. . . ." He concluded his letter by affirming that all Partisan efforts were bent against the invader and aimed at creating conditions for a truly democratic Yugoslavia.

Having heard from Ambassador Stevenson the gist of Tito's reply, Ambassador MacVeagh cabled a summary of it to the State Department. On February 5 he received the following message from Washington:

The whole question of our attitude toward the resistance forces within Yugoslavia and their relations to the Government-in-Exile is under review. Certain information essential to the Department in its study of this question has not yet become available, and recent reports through British channels have not been received here.[10]

Clearly, the U.S. was reluctant to follow Churchill's initiative.

As soon as Churchill received Tito's reply he answered, on February 5, again without consulting the U.S.: [11]

I can understand the position of reserve which you adopt towards King Peter. I have for several months past been in favour of advising him to dismiss Mihailović and to face the consequent resignation of all his present advisers. I should be obliged if you would let me know whether his dismissal of Mihailović would pave the way for friendly relations with you and your Movement, and, later on, for his joining you in the field, it being understood that the future question of the Monarchy is reserved until Yugoslavia has been entirely liberated. . . . There is no doubt that a working arrangement between you and the King would consolidate many forces, especially Serbian elements, now estranged. . . . Yugoslavia would then be able to speak with a united voice in the councils of the Allies. . . .

Churchill then took up the military situation, informing Tito that he had asked Wilson to take measures to clear the Germans from the Adriatic islands and to establish a sea line of communication with the Partisans.

On February 7, Ambassador MacVeagh reported to the State Department the content of the second Churchill-Tito letter. He added that concerning the political implications of the letter, the British Ambassador had commented: "We shall burn our fingers." Stevenson had recommended to the Foreign Office an alternative proposal: that the King appoint a new government of national resistance, without Mihailović, recognizing all guerrilla movements on a purely patriotic basis.

MacVeagh, associating himself somewhat with Stevenson's thought, suggested that "the Department may possibly feel that the public sacrifice of Mihailović individually, and the consequent perhaps final antagonizing of the 'Serbian elements now estranged,' are things to be avoided if they are unnecessary." With regard to the military part of the Churchill message, MacVeagh reported that he understood "from our OSS that the British Army authorities are exercised over the Prime Minister's projection of his authority into the strategic picture for diplomatic ends." [12]

Tito answered Churchill on February 9, stating that first, the Yugoslav Government and Mihailović must be "suppressed"; second, the National Committee of Liberation of Yugoslavia should be acknowledged by the Allies as the only government of Yugoslavia, and King Peter should submit to the laws of the Anti-Fascist Council of National Liberation; third, if King Peter accepted all these conditions, the Partisans would not refuse to cooperate with him provided the question of the monarchy be left open until after the liberation of Yugoslavia; finally, King Peter should issue a declaration to that effect.[13]

Through the courtesy of the British Ambassador, on February 15 MacVeagh reported the substance of Tito's reply, adding: "Ambassador Stevenson and I will both be obliged if the Department will be careful not to indicate to the British that he may have let me see the text. Should this happen it is highly likely that I would no longer enjoy the advantages of a source of information hitherto usefully cultivated." [14]

Stevenson told MacVeagh that in his opinion the British Government would be assuming a "grave responsibility if it should advise the King to cast aside all his present support merely to secure an opportunity for further discussions." It was the British Ambassador's view that "such discussions should precede rather than follow action on the King's part."

On February 22, 1944, before he replied once more to Tito, Churchill spoke to Parliament and praised the Partisans in the highest terms:

[The] Communist element had the honour of being the beginners, but as the Movement increased in strength and numbers, a modifying and unifying process has taken place and national conceptions have supervened. In Marshal Tito the partisans have found an outstanding leader, glorious in the fight for freedom. Unhappily, perhaps inevitably, these new forces came into collision with those under General Mihailović. Their activities upset his commanders' accommodations with the enemy.

(The warm praise which Churchill also gave to "a young friend of mine . . . Lieutenant Colonel Deakin" underlined the influence in Yugoslav matters of "men I know and trust," foremost among them his former literary collaborator, Deakin, and his friend Maclean.)

Before delivering the statement, Churchill showed it to Eden, who suggested that he should be less strong in his praise of Tito, for otherwise Tito might think that the British Government was so pleased with him that he need make no concessions with regard to cooperation with King Peter.[15]

Three days later, on February 25, Churchill once again wrote Tito, telling him that orders had been issued to withdraw the British liaison officers from Mihailović and asking whether Tito could not assure him that if King Peter freed himself from Mihailović "and other bad advisers," he "will be invited by you to join his countrymen in the field." He added: "I cannot press him to dismiss Mihailović, throw over his Government, and cut off all contact with Serbia before knowing whether he can count on your support and cooperation." He then told Tito that he had suggested to King Peter that he come to London to discuss these matters with him.

The Foreign Office was not happy with Churchill's direct correspondence with Tito. It felt that, by increasing Tito's stature, the Prime Minister had not made a solution of the Četnik-Partisan problem any easier.

THE BRITISH DECISION TO WITHDRAW THEIR
LIAISON OFFICERS WITH MIHAILOVIĆ

On January 10, 1944, Prime Minister Purić asked Ambassadors Stevenson and MacVeagh whether the Liberators presented to Yugoslavia by Roosevelt—of the four only two remained—could finally be used for the primary and chief task of supplying war material to Mihailović and dropping personnel to him and whether a direct radio link with the general could at last be established. Stevenson was told by London that he should put off answering Purić's query until "further clarification of the political situation."

Meanwhile, in view of Mihailović's failure to blow up the bridges over the Morava and Ibar Rivers, the British Government decided to withdraw its remaining liaison officers. This decision was hastened after the Foreign Office received on January 12, 1944, a full report from SOE Cairo on the evidence against Mihailović. The report said that some of the general's commanders had collaborated with the Germans or Italians—or both—and that Mihailović had condoned and in certain cases approved their actions. In particular it alleged that in March 1943 he had directed operations in the Neretva valley against the Partisans in collaboration with the Axis during the Fourth Offensive, a charge which, as was noted previously, was true as far as cooperation with the Italians went but false regarding the Germans.

At the time the British decided to withdraw their mission, one American officer, Musulin, was still in Četnik territory. The other two Americans, Seitz and Mansfield, it will be recalled, had left Mihailović's headquarters earlier. Mansfield, who had accompanied Bailey, arrived in Cairo on February 20. According to MacVeagh,[16] he carried letters from Mihailović to Roosevelt and Eisenhower "which the OSS now has in its possession."[17] Seitz, accompanied by Hudson, was at that time still in Yugoslavia—in Partisan territory, whence they departed on March 15 for Italy and Cairo.

Donovan forwarded Mihailović's letter, together with Mansfield's report, to Eisenhower in London. Acknowledging receipt of the two documents, Eisenhower suggested to Donovan that he himself not reply to Mihailović directly but that a message be sent through OSS channels to the effect that Eisenhower appreciated Mihailović's courtesy.[18]

Foreign Office approval of the withdrawal of some thirty British officers attached to Mihailović [19] was reported to the Department of State by MacVeagh on February 21. MacVeagh added that the British

Ambassador would shortly inform the Yugoslav Prime Minister that the British Government had decided to give no further military support to Mihailović, and that therefore the retention of British liaison officers could no longer be justified; there was to be no publicity regarding this matter. The British Embassy in Washington informed the State Department directly of the decision to withdraw liaison officers and expressed the hope that the Department "will agree with the action taken."

As a result of the British move, a problem arose regarding Musulin. At first, OSS Cairo decided that he should remain even after the departure of the British liaison officers. SOE, however, told OSS that it would be inadvisable for the two services not to act together. OSS Cairo thereupon referred the matter to Donovan for instructions. In parallel, Stevenson told MacVeagh that the withdrawal was a military decision taken by Wilson, that Musulin could do nothing anyway, and that for him to stay while the British left would give Mihailović a chance to play the U.S. off against Britain.

Unlike SOE, which had solely liaison and operational functions, OSS also had an intelligence collection responsibility. Thus OSS liaison officers had the dual task of satisfying both OSS (SO) and OSS (SI). The British of course had officers in the field who carried out intelligence collection tasks, but they were not on SOE's staff, though they were attached frequently to SOE missions.

The SI (intelligence) section of OSS wanted its collection functions in Četnik territory to continue even if SOE and OSS (SO) were ready to give up their responsibility for liaison and operations. If Musulin had to be withdrawn, Toulmin, the OSS chief in Cairo, favored sending an intelligence mission having only collection functions. In a telegram to the State Department dated February 21, MacVeagh commented that perhaps "this would be a solution whereby we could attain our aims without conflicting with those of our allies or bringing political matters to the fore." [20]

On March 2, 1944, after having authorized the withdrawal of Musulin from Yugoslavia, the OSS suggested to the Joint Chiefs of Staff the replacement of the joint (operations and intelligence) mission by an independent, solely intelligence mission to be carried out by a single American officer. The State Department was informed of this proposal in a letter from Donovan to Hull, also dated March 2.[21]

Mihailović, deeply disturbed by the Partisan political actions taken by the Bihać and Jajce assemblies, decided on a political move of his own. Throughout the war, the Četniks had never matched the political activity of the Partisans with any steps on their part. One conference of Četnik "Intellectual Young People" had been held from November 30 to December 2, 1942, in Montenegro, but the conclusions of the conference, which had a strong Greater-Serbian flavor, were never turned into an action program. Now, after Jajce, Mihailović, who himself had never completely endorsed the radical Greater-Serb views of some of his advisers, decided to call a Četnik "congress" which would attempt to appeal to all Yugoslavs.

The congress took place from January 25 to 28, 1944, at Ba, near Valjevo and was named for Saint Sava, patron of the Serbs. Two hundred and seventy-four delegates gathered and elected as president Dr. Živko Topalović, the leader of the Social-Democratic Party, a small Serbian group. The congress passed resolutions aimed at reorganizing Yugoslavia after the war as a federation of three units—Serbia, Croatia and Slovenia. (The Partisans were thinking of making four states out of what the Ba Congress regarded as Serbia—Serbia proper, Montenegro, Macedonia and Bosnia-Hercegovina.) Until liberation the Central National Committee, the civilian advisory body, set up in 1941 by Mihailović, would assume the political responsibility and cooperate with the Allies and the Royal Government. But the congress came too late to have any impact upon the political situation in Yugoslavia.

It apparently had, however, some limited consequences in the military field in that several of the nonaggression pacts with German units were subsequently denounced either by Četnik commanders or by the Germans, who were wary of the results of the congress.[22]

GENERAL WILSON REORGANIZES THE BRITISH
MISSION TO THE PARTISANS

On January 19, 1944, General Wilson, Allied Supreme Commander in the Mediterranean, asked General Donovan to meet with him and Harold Macmillan, British Minister-Resident, at Allied Force Headquarters in Algiers. Wilson revealed that he proposed to establish a regular military, as distinct from SOE, mission at Tito's headquarters, to be responsible to General Alexander, Commander in Chief, Allied Forces, Italy. He invited the OSS to assign officers to this mission. Maclean was to head it.

Donovan declined this invitation because the mission, though nominally military, was in fact political in character, and he did not want to send American military officers to serve in a junior capacity with a British political mission.

Inasmuch as the Russians had announced that they proposed to send a mission to Tito's headquarters and the British were organizing a new mission, the State Department, the Joint Chiefs of Staff and the OSS considered the possibility of establishing a similar, separate American mission. Clearly, the United States did not wish any longer to be merely part of the British mission, sharing responsibility but having no power to act independently.

In reporting these developments to Secretary of State Hull and Under Secretary Edward R. Stettinius,[23] Assistant Secretary Berle on January 26, said:

If we plan to have any part in the Yugoslav picture to the extent that Tito (Marshal Broz) dominates it, we should have to have independent representation. . . .

A mission could be arranged, presumably through AFHQ in Italy and reporting to the War Department and to the State Department through our mission in Italy or in Algiers. The OSS is in a position to facilitate such a mission; and probably arrangements could be worked out, if desired, to either put men into uniform or use capable men presently connected with OSS. In either case, approval of the Joint Chiefs of Staff would have to be obtained, but it is assumed that this could be got easily, should we wish it. My recommendation would be that we make up such a mission and send it. . . . This would be without prejudice, of course, to our having a similar mission with General Mihailović should that be considered desirable.[24]

James Dunn, who then headed the State Department's Office of European Affairs, commented that the Department should favor a purely military mission and beware of a political mission. Stettinius noted: "I am inclined to agree with the position of the Office of European Affairs." (An independent American military mission was established later in the year.)

Wilson's proposal to establish a military mission to the Partisans and his invitation to OSS to join it were of course connected with the role which SOE and OSS had played in Cairo when Wilson was commander in chief there. Even then he would have liked to have had these organizations under his complete control.

Now that he was Mediterranean commander and, in the aftermath of the Tehran and Cairo Conferences, had received a far-reaching directive from the Combined Chiefs of Staff regarding Yugoslav matters, Wilson went ahead with his plan. Recent events aided him in putting it into effect.

SOE's role in Yugoslav affairs had diminished considerably after the appointment of Maclean, who never regarded SOE as his source of authority but dealt directly with Churchill on political and Wilson on military matters. In addition, the availability of Italian bases had reduced Cairo's importance. The air operations serving Yugoslavia, for instance, were transferred from Tocra in North Africa to Brindisi.

As a first step, Wilson asked SOE and OSS to relocate their Yugoslav sections from Cairo to Italy. While SOE concurred, OSS decided to keep its headquarters in Cairo, although an advance base had already been established in Bari subordinate to OSS Cairo.

The transfer of the SOE Yugoslav section from Cairo to Bari ran into a technical difficulty.[25] All radio transmitters with the liaison missions in Yugoslavia were tuned for Cairo and there was doubt that they could be heard in Bari. In the end, a solution to the problem was found. All messages from Yugoslavia were first received in Cairo and then forwarded to Bari, where they were decoded.

There were political obstacles, too, since the British Ambassador to the Yugoslav Government-in-Exile was stationed in Cairo. However, Wilson's determination to bring Yugoslav operations under his control prevailed and SOE's Yugoslav section moved to Bari in February 1944. That base was then code-named "Force 266" (Cairo's code-name was "Force 133") and came under the command of Viscount (Bill) Harcourt. Deakin, the last head of the Yugoslav section in Cairo, moved over to the staff of Minister-Resident Macmillan.

Concurrently, General Wilson established a joint headquarters in Bari to control all special operations east of Italy. He writes [26] that this was necessary to "solve the adjustment between the Naval and Air forces on the one side and the SOE/OSS on the other, at the same time having to ensure that all activities fitted into the operational picture." Major General W. A. M. Stawell, who was then head of SOE Cairo, was appointed commander of special operations east of Italy. An American officer, Brigadier General W. Caffey, was named head of a special operations section in Algiers with responsibility for all such operations in countries under Wilson's jurisdiction. Maclean, incidentally, did not work long under Stawell. When his mission became the British military mission in March, it was placed directly under Wilson.

With regard to American operations in Yugoslavia, it was undoubtedly a disappointment to Wilson that Donovan did not accept his invitation to attach American officers to the British mission. American operational responsibility for Yugoslavia remained in OSS Cairo under Colonel Toulmin, with Lieutenant Colonel Paul West, successor to Major Huot, as head of special operations and Lieutenant Colonel Valerian Lada-

Mocarski in charge of secret intelligence. Wilson had some leverage of course, inasmuch as the advance OSS base in Bari was within his jurisdiction.

This base, first under the command of Major Robert Koch and, from February 1944, of Lieutenant Commander Edward J. Green, also had SO and SI sections. Operations matters were handled by Lieutenant Robert Thompson, and intelligence by Robert P. Joyce, a Foreign Service officer on loan to OSS.[27] The head of the SI Yugoslav section was Major Frank Arnoldi, who, according to Joyce, was highly pro-Partisan and whose female office staff wore Partisan uniforms with red stars. Joyce appealed to Whitney Shepardson, head of OSS (SI) Washington, and Arnoldi was removed.[28]

In April 1944, Wilson succeeded in having all Yugoslav matters, including the American OSS operations, transferred from Cairo to AFHQ Algiers. At that time, AFHQ established an advance headquarters in Caserta, Italy. Colonel Edward J. F. Glavin supervised OSS operations from there, and the OSS Bari base which had reported to Cairo passed under his jurisdiction. (AFHQ moved its entire headquarters from Algiers to Caserta on July 21, 1944.)

A decision to fortify the island of Vis had been taken early in January in Marrakech, where Churchill was convalescing, at a conference the Prime Minister held with Wilson, the theater commander, and Alexander, Allied commander in Italy. Immediately thereafter, an operational and supply base was established on the island, an airstrip was built, and Allied commandos began to use it as a starting point for coastal raids. The interception of German coastal shipping, raids on German garrisons on the islands which they had occupied during the Sixth Offensive and continued infiltration of supplies by small fishing craft annoyed the Germans considerably. Yet they never attacked Vis, mainly because of the offensive capabilities of the Allied naval forces in the island area, which became, in Wilson's words,[29] "a happy hunting ground" for destroyers and motor torpedo boats. The Partisan garrison at Vis was reinforced by two British Commando forces and a number of SOE and OSS officers. After the visit of a senior British officer, Major General G. W. Templer, the island was further strengthened with a British battalion and a battery of artillery. Vis was put under the direct control of Wilson, because Alexander was deeply involved in the big battles of Anzio and Cassino in Italy.

In the United States, Louis Adamic, who knew President and Mrs. Roosevelt well and occasionally offered his advice on Yugoslav matters, wrote a letter to the President dated February 12 in which he made several suggestions regarding possible means of supplying the Partisans, including the creation of an Allied enclave on the Adriatic. FDR replied noncommittally saying that the problem "has been and is now a matter of interest to the Allied Chiefs of Staff." He added that pressure of work made it impossible for him to see Adamic within the next few weeks.[30]

THE SOVIETS SEND A MISSION TO TITO

A Soviet military mission, consisting of two generals, several colonels and one representative of the NKVD (Secret Police), arrived in Yugoslavia on February 23, 1944. It was not a very high-powered mission despite the rank of its chief, Lieutenant General N. V. Korneyev, whom Stalin called a "poor man . . . not stupid, but . . . an incurable drunkard." [31] Although Korneyev's appointment had been announced in Moscow several weeks earlier, his arrival was delayed because the mission refused to parachute in.

Since there were no airfields in operation in Partisan territory at that time, the Soviet mission was brought in near Bosanski Petrovac by two Horsa gliders borrowed from the Allied airborne forces. Velebit, who was in Bari, was supposed to go along, but for some reason he was left behind, much to his distress.

On their way to Italy, the Soviet mission visited Cairo, where they were briefed by Deakin, and Algiers, where they had dinner with Wilson. To those who came in contact with them, it became evident that they had no clear idea what they were supposed to do once they got to Yugoslavia. Indeed, they were prepared to visit not only Tito but also Mihailović. (It will be recalled that Molotov had suggested at the Tehran Conference that perhaps the Russians should send a mission to the Četniks.)

Maclean describes [32] the arrival of the Soviet mission in Yugoslavia and the exuberance that this event aroused among the Partisans. Tito gave a gala reception in their honor on February 24 at his new headquarters at Drvar in Bosnia, which was attended by Maclean and Farish.

In early March, Alexander Bogomolov, previously Ambassador to the Yugoslav and other exile governments in London and now Soviet member of the Allied Advisory Council for Italy, requested that the Allied and Italian authorities provide facilities for eight transport aircraft in Bari so that the Soviet mission in Yugoslavia could be supplied. Bogomolov explained in his request that his Government desired to maintain its own communications with Tito. This was agreed to with the proviso that the planes function under the control of the Allied

Lieutenant General Korneyev and Marshal Tito in Drvar, 1944. *Courtesy of V. Kljaković*

Mediterranean Command. At the same time, the Partisans requested the Allied military authorities to effect the release of Partisans allegedly imprisoned in Italy and exchange certain German prisoners in Allied hands in order to obtain the release from the Germans of some dozen Partisans. The Soviets in Italy, undoubtedly in coordination with the Partisans, added a request of their own—the transfer of thousands of Italian soldiers of Slav origin to Tito's army.

Identical telegrams which Stalin sent to Churchill and Roosevelt on March 23 regarding Poland provided incidental evidence of the shift in the Soviet position away from tolerance of the Yugoslav Government-in-Exile as Soviet political support for the Partisans increased. He wrote:

I . . . find it hard to tell the difference between Poland's émigré Government and the Yugoslav émigré Government, which is akin to it, or between certain generals of the Polish émigré Government and the Serb General Mihailović.[33]

The relations between the Soviet mission and the Partisans, enthusiastic at first, became less so as time went by. Tito soon found out that the

Soviets were mainly eager to give advice. He wanted supplies, which the Soviets were unable to deliver. And so the Soviet mission began to lose its original attraction for the Partisans. For his part, General Korneyev told Maclean that he would have preferred a post in Washington.

THE STATUS OF U.S. OFFICERS IN YUGOSLAVIA

While SOE and Maclean were now solely and completely under Wilson's Mediterranean Command, the same could not be said of OSS and the American officers with the Partisans. As of January 1944, when Maclean's mission was reconstituted, and until August 1944, when Colonel Ellery Huntington arrived in Vis as head of an independent American mission, the status of the American OSS officers in Partisan territory was not very well defined. While they operated "in conjunction with the British," as the State Department said in March 1944, they reported first to OSS in Cairo and after April, to OSS Caserta via the OSS advance base in Bari.

When Farish returned to Yugoslavia in January 1944, he was still attached to Maclean's mission. Major Richard Weil, Jr., who was with Partisan headquarters in Drvar from February 27 to March 20, was the first American officer to have independent status.

After the decision to withdraw the British mission with the Četniks the British proposed to send a new mission into Serbia, but this time to the Partisans. Major John Henniker-Major was selected to head it. He had been with Maclean at Tito's headquarters, and it was first thought that he should join Partisan General Peko Dapčević, who was about to move overland from Bosnia into Serbia. This turned out to be impossible, and it was decided that Henniker-Major and Farish, who was to accompany him, should first go to Bari, where they arrived on March 19.

On April 16 the two officers parachuted to the east of Vranje near the headquarters of the Macedonian Partisans, who were led by General Mihailo Apostolski. Vukmanović-Tempo, who had been Tito's personal representative in Serbia and Macedonia since late 1942, was also there, as well as Petar Stambolić, the commander of the Serbian Partisans, at that time few and largely inactive.

The Macedonian Partisans were not very numerous or active either. The majority of Macedonians apparently did not consider themselves ethnically Serbs but Bulgarians and, whether Communist or not, wished to be united with their brothers across the border in a Bulgarian state. The minority who preferred to remain within Yugoslavia was divided into those who followed the Četniks and those who adhered to the

Partisans. By proclaiming a Macedonian nationality within Yugoslavia, first referred to at Bihać in November 1942 and stressed at Jajce a year later, the CPY began to take the wind out of the sails of those who wished to join Bulgaria, since the alternative was no longer submersion within a Greater Serbia. By April 1944, Vukmanović-Tempo had succeeded somewhat in his efforts to rally Macedonians to the Partisans' cause, but much work still lay before him and his associates.[34]

Shortly after the arrival of Henniker-Major and Farish, the Macedonian Partisans moved southward accompanied by one British officer, while Henniker-Major and Farish went into central Serbia in the area of the Radan Mountains.[35] There was very close cooperation between the two officers, but they reported separately. Farish was no longer part of the British mission. He was a one-man American mission with the task of reporting on the situation in Serbia, where the Partisans were building up a force to drive out the Četniks. Farish also had the job of locating and trying to evacuate some American airmen who had been wandering about Serbia with the Partisans after their plane had been

Lieutenant Colonel Farish flanked by Vukmanović-Tempo, an unidentified Partisan on his left, and Major Djurić on his right, in Serbia, 1944. From *Ally Betrayed*

shot down on a bombing raid on the Ploesti oil fields in Rumania. Farish found the air crew, arranged for their evacuation by plane and left Serbia on the same aircraft in the middle of June.

After he departed, there was no American in Serbia until an independent American military mission under Colonel Huntington arrived in October. The British mission remained, watching the build-up of Partisan military strength after Koča Popović was sent in to take over from Stambolić, who had little military experience. Popović was accompanied by Major General A. P. Gorshkov, deputy chief of the Soviet military mission to Partisan Supreme Headquarters.

THE UNITED STATES DISSOCIATES ITSELF
FROM BRITISH PRESSURE ON KING PETER

At the end of February, King Peter and Prime Minister Purić were "invited" to London, arriving there on March 10. Eden called on the King on March 15, and requested that he reorganize his Government and dismiss Mihailović. This request was repeated on March 17 by Ambassador Stevenson, who had also come to London. According to Fotić,[36] Stevenson informed King Peter that His Majesty's Government considered that the Government-in-Exile was a body no longer necessary: It should be replaced by a committee of three members acting as constables, whose sole duty would be to take care of the officials in exile while the King awaited the development of events in Yugoslavia and the determination of the future organization of his country.

On March 18, King Peter lunched with Churchill. He describes [37] how he and Churchill disagreed on the role of Mihailović. He quotes Churchill as saying that Mihailović was conserving his forces to fight the Partisans, and his own reply that the only course for Mihailović was to avoid provoking unnecessary reprisals against civilians and to conserve his limited arms for really vital action. "Mr. Churchill wants me to make Tito King of Yugoslavia," Peter told a Foreign Office official after the lunch.

Two days later, on March 20, King Peter married Princess Alexandra of Greece. Fotić called on Hull and said that King Peter desired that President Roosevelt be informed specially in regard to his wedding in view of the genuine interest the President had shown in the King's marriage. Roosevelt thereupon sent King Peter a telegram in which he expressed "both my most sincere felicitations and my best wishes for your health and happiness." [38]

On March 31, Eden sent a memorandum to Churchill suggesting that the best thing "we can do for King Peter is to try to ensure that he puts himself on as good a wicket as possible internationally." To this end, Eden recommended that King Peter form a new government "not as part of a bargain with Tito but in order to improve his own position during the next phase. . . ." Eden writes [39] that he had much sympathy with King Peter.

On April 1, Churchill replied [40] to Eden's memorandum urging that King Peter "be pressed to the utmost limit to get rid of his present fatal millstone advisers."

. . . As you know, I thought this would have been accomplished before the end of last year. I do not know what has been gained by all the spinning out that has gone on. . . . My idea throughout has been that the King should dissociate himself from Mihailović, that he should accept the resignation of the Purić Government or dismiss them. . . .

Churchill then referred to the arrival of "a grandiose Russian Mission to Tito's Headquarters, and there is little doubt that the Russians will drive straight ahead for a Communist Tito-governed Yugoslavia." He ended by asking Eden to act quickly to see that King Peter formed a stopgap government "not obnoxious to Tito." Churchill thought that the Četniks could be made thereby to join the Partisans against the Germans, which they were not now doing "because of the complexities of Serbian politics."

On April 6, Eden called on King Peter again, suggesting that he replace the Government by one composed of three persons favorable to Tito. On April 13, Churchill put renewed pressure on the King to get rid of the Purić Government.[41]

Fotić in Washington perceived a "reserve toward the British policy" on the part of the State Department.[42] He quotes Dunn as telling him on March 17 "that the State Department had been considering a statement which would clarify the American position in regard to the Yugoslav problem." Fotić says:

The State Department was anxious to make it clear that the U.S. Government did not associate itself with the policy expressed by Mr. Churchill and did not wish to take any part in the internal problems of Yugoslavia arising from the struggle between Tito and Mihailović. But the idea of a statement, said Mr. Dunn, had been abandoned to avoid presenting the enemy with the spectacle of disunity among the Allies.

Dunn told Fotić of a forthcoming meeting in London between Under Secretary Stettinius and members of the British Government at which the Yugoslav question would be discussed. He suggested that Fotić give him a memorandum, which Fotić did on March 24.

The State Department also prepared a memorandum for Stettinius which said:

"The important factor in the Yugoslav situation today is not so much the Tito-Mihailović-Cairo conflict, as the interplay of Soviet and British policy in the question." [43] It described Soviet policy: anti-Government-in-Exile, no personal attacks on the King; a very high-ranking mission to Tito; so far no military aid but possibly funds. It also pointed out that the Yugoslav Ambassador in Moscow (Simić) had resigned, switching to Tito and staying on in Moscow. "The Russians profess that their policy is parallel to ours—being designed to get on with the war, leaving politics to the Yugoslav people themselves," the memorandum continued.

It turned next to British policy: from exaggerated praise for Mihailović at first to complete opposition to him and to the Yugoslav Government-in-Exile; the immense personal prestige of Churchill brought into play by direct correspondence with Tito and the appointment of Randolph Churchill to the British mission with the Partisans; publicity for other members of the mission such as Maclean and Deakin. "All this may have been designed to achieve by flattery a position at least parallel to what the Russians had gained by indoctrination," the memorandum added. It also referred to Tito's astuteness in not giving assurances of cooperation with the King despite British blandishments. "London is admittedly unhappy about this deadlock, having already promised a great deal and got nothing in return."

The U.S. policy was then outlined:

1. The U.S. is committed to give military aid where it will do the most good, thus helping Tito in the military sense without political relations with him.

2. The U.S. maintains correct relations with the Government-in-Exile, without illusions as to its weaknesses, and has resisted British pressure to have Mr. Fotić withdrawn.

3. The President has approved a plan to send into Mihailović territory an American intelligence group, though the U.S. liaison officers with Mihailović were withdrawn along with the British Mission.

4. The U.S. has liaison officers with Tito in conjunction with the British.

5. The Tito organization is trying to get its hands on official Yugoslav funds in the U.S. This could be achieved, however, only after political recognition.

6. Secretary Hull's statement of December 9, 1943, is in all respects still applicable. Under the policy therein outlined—to furnish supplies to each or any group in Yugoslavia that is actively fighting the Germans—the United States

could continue to deal with any Yugoslav Government established by orderly processes.

The London conference lasted from April 7 to 29. Stettinius was accompanied by H. Freeman Matthews, Deputy Director of the Office of European Affairs and former Deputy Chief of Mission in London. Matthews had a long discussion regarding Yugoslavia with Sir Orme Sargent, the Deputy Under Secretary, on April 20.[44] Ambassador Stevenson also participated in the discussion.

The British spokesmen declared that they had lost all hope of bringing about a reconciliation between King Peter and Tito inasmuch as Tito did not want the King to return to Yugoslavia. In the British view, therefore, a new Prime Minister would have to be found to minimize Tito's opposition to the King. Such a man might well be Ivan Šubašić, Governor of Croatia at the time of the German invasion, who had been in the United States since 1941.

King Peter writes that Šubašić was first mentioned to him by Churchill on April 12.[45] At that time the Prime Minister said that Šubašić had been recommended to him by Roosevelt through Donovan. Churchill had agreed, even though his first choice had been General Mirković, the man chiefly responsible for the revolt of March 27, 1941.

In a letter of April 17 to Roosevelt, King Peter did not refer to the Šubašić suggestion. Fotić does not mention it either, although elsewhere he calls Šubašić a man who had made a favorable impression "on the OSS branch in charge of political problems in Central Europe and the Balkans."

At the April 20 meeting at the Foreign Office, the British told Matthews that they understood that King Peter had asked Šubašić to come to London. King Peter denies that he ever did this. He states that Šubašić told him on May 9 that he "had been approached by the American Government on behalf of the British Government and informed that I wished to see him." That was in fact what happened. On April 26 Churchill sent the following cable to Roosevelt: [46]

King Peter is very anxious to have the Ban [Governor] of Croatia over here as soon as possible. I am most anxious he should form a government which will not tie him to Mihailović, a weight which cannot well be borne. The Ban is essential to his plans for forming a broad-based administration not obnoxious to the Partisans. Could you find the gentleman and put him on an airplane as early as possible? He may need a little encouragement. Halifax will do this if the Ban is directed to the British Embassy.

King Peter writes that when he saw General Donovan in May, Donovan "was very keen that I should make Šubašić my Prime Minister."

Matthews also learned that the Foreign Office, at least, continued to feel that while Mihailović should be dismissed as minister, he should be retained as commander in Yugoslavia. The telegram summarizing Matthews' talks said: "However much they dislike the collaboration that some of Mihailović's officers have given the Germans (they admit that he himself has never cooperated with the Germans) they recognize how strong his popular support in Serbia is and its probable lasting nature."

Matthews told the British that the United States had no intention of recognizing the Tito regime as a government. He added that the U.S. would not bring pressure upon King Peter to make the changes desired by the British. In his telegram to the State Department Matthews pointed out that the British did not ask for American support.

Thus the Yugoslav problem was aired, but the U.S.-British differences were not resolved, and the U.S. continued to follow a more cautious line. When Fotić gave Hull a copy of King Peter's April 17 letter to Roosevelt, Hull, according to Fotić, said that the U.S. Government was in no way associated with British policy.[47]

King Peter's letter was a touching plea for help and counsel: ". . . being fatherless, I address myself to you, Mr. President, as to a trusted friend." He recounted the whole series of British pressures, said that Tito represented but a small minority of Yugoslavs and expressed the hope that the future of Yugoslavia would be decided with the participation of the U.S.

Within the British Government there was clearly a lack of consensus regarding Yugoslavia. The Prime Minister was most aggressively pro-Tito and anti-Mihailović; the Foreign Office, on the other hand, was inclined to more caution. On April 17, for instance, Churchill circulated to the War Cabinet a dispatch from Maclean on the military situation in Yugoslavia. The Foreign Office, while agreeing that Brigadier Maclean was providing valuable information, did not think this report altogether convincing. Maclean anticipated the ultimate success of the Partisans and assumed that it would be consistent with British interests—that it would lead to the establishment of a strong, democratic and independent Yugoslavia. The British Ambassador, in forwarding the dispatch, pointed out that Maclean did not mention Serbia, where opposition to the Partisans was "solid and uncompromising." Eden thought it desirable to let the War Cabinet see also a report from Hudson received at about the same time. Hudson and, in another report, Bailey mentioned the anti-Communist feeling of the people of Serbia.[48] Both had just returned to England.

Bailey in particular tempered official British thinking. Having spent more than a year in Četnik territory and nine months as British mission chief, he convinced his superiors that Mihailović had not personally collaborated with the enemy, even though his commanders might have, and that in Serbia at least the loyalty to Mihailović was certainly greater than the British had believed.

A meeting was held in the Foreign Office on May 2, attended by Ambassador Stevenson, Maclean, Bailey and Hudson and the same group was invited to Chequers by Churchill on May 6, on which occasion Bailey told the Prime Minister that just as Mihailović underestimated the strength of the Partisans, so Tito underestimated Mihailović's strength in Serbia.

This was the first time that Churchill had been exposed to a direct and first-hand report by a British officer who had observed the Yugoslav situation from the Četnik side; up to then the only direct reports had come from British officers who had been with the Partisans and whom Churchill had known well from before. Maclean had reached Bari as early as November 1943, and he and Deakin talked to Churchill in December, while Bailey had come out only in the middle of February 1944. On the American side, too, Farish had arrived in Italy from Partisan-held territory as early as October 1943, and he had seen high officials in Washington, including Roosevelt, while Mansfield did not come out of the Četnik area until February 1944.

MAJOR WEIL'S MISSION TO THE PARTISANS

On February 27, 1944, Major Richard (Bob) Weil, Jr., an OSS officer, was sent into Partisan territory, where he stayed for about three weeks and apparently got along very well with Tito. As noted earlier, this was the first American mission independent of the British. Tito grasped its significance and gave Weil a letter to Roosevelt:

Sir:

The departure of Lt. Colonel [49] Richard Weil, Jr. AUS, offers me the opportunity of expressing my gratitude to you for the assistance in material and in the cooperation of your Air Force, tendered to our Army of National Liberation by you and the people of America.

The superhuman struggle which has been waged by the people of Yugoslavia for the last three years, aims, not only at clearing our country of the criminal occupiers, but also at the creation of a better and more righteous order, which would guarantee true democracy, equal rights and social justice to all nations of Yugoslavia. These aspirations and perspectives have given our nations the strength to endure all the difficulties and sufferings of this unequal struggle. For the fulfillment of their strivings the people of Yugoslavia expect the aid of your great democratic country, of the people of the U.S.A. and of yourself.

The achievement of the ideals of our nations is arduous. The enemy is still strong. The struggle with the occupier is still tough and extremely bloody. The home traitors Nedić, Pavelić, Rupnik [Slovenian Fascist] and Draža Mihailović, unite their efforts with the occupier to prevent the nations of Yugoslavia from attaining these great and progressive aims. But no sacrifices or difficulties frighten us, for we are convinced in the victory of our righteous cause, as we are certain in the victory of all the Allies over the German Fascist aggressors.

Perhaps no other country is so terribly devastated and ravaged as Yugoslavia. This war will leave painful wounds which will require a long time to heal. And this will be possible only if the nations of Yugoslavia receive full economic and political support in the creation of a new, truly democratic, federative Yugoslavia, in which all nations will have their national rights.

Lt. Colonel Weil will be able to expose to you our needs and wishes. I am convinced that they will be granted your support.

Tito
Marshal of Yugoslavia

15 March 1944 [50]

Weil, in civilian life a New York lawyer, wrote of Tito in his report to OSS dated April 4: "In spite of his known affiliation with Russian Communism, most of the population seem to regard him first as a patriot and the liberator of his country and secondarily as a Communist." He added prophetically: "For whatever it may be worth, my own guess is that if he is convinced that there is a clearcut choice between the two, on any issue, his country will come first." [51]

After his trip to Tito's headquarters, Weil went to Cairo and talked to Ambassador MacVeagh, who reported to the State Department on March 28:

On the political side . . . he [Weil] does provide information from Tito's own mouth of a desire for wider political contacts with the Allies. . . . Weil is personally in favor of our establishing such contact along with the British and Russians basing himself on his belief that Partisan success would surely follow throughout the whole of Yugoslavia and on the desirability of our earning the gratitude and friendship of the Yugoslav people.

MacVeagh added that while Weil was a shrewd observer, his knowledge did not extend beyond the limits of the Partisan picture, and therefore his interpretations might lack the authority of his facts.[52]

On April 7, OSS director Donovan suggested the creation of an independent American military mission to the Partisans, and the Secretary of State concurred on May 18, with the understanding that the mission would be so organized as to operate independently of, but parallel to, the British and Russian missions in Partisan territory.[53] The Secretary pointed out, however, that despite the purely military nature of the mission, a political character would inevitably be attributed to it after its arrival in Yugoslavia. He therefore suggested that once the new head of mission was designated, some detailed discussion of the political questions likely to arise should take place in order to incorporate appropriate instructions in the directive to the mission. The OSS initiative followed Donovan's earlier rejection of the British suggestion of attaching U.S. officers to the new Maclean mission.

The functions of the mission were to be military intelligence, special operations, establishment of supply lines, technical air force intelligence, and psychological operations against the enemy. After the creation of such a mission was approved by the State Department and concurred in by the Joint Chiefs of Staff, Colonel Huntington, long connected with Yugoslav affairs, was appointed by Donovan to head it.[54]

On Orthodox Easter Sunday, April 16, 1944, the U.S. Air Force bombed Belgrade, inflicting heavy civilian casualties. This was a particularly unfortunate coincidence because almost exactly three years earlier, also on a Sunday, the Luftwaffe had attacked Belgrade. Fotić reports [55] that he told Hull about the raid on April 18. "The Secretary showed deep concern and promised that he would use his influence to avoid repetition of the incident," Fotić writes, but adds that "the city continued to be bombed."

VELEBIT'S MISSION TO LONDON—DJILAS' MISSION TO MOSCOW

Late in March, Tito suggested to Maclean that the latter and Velebit, who had just parachuted back into Yugoslavia, visit Wilson's headquarters to discuss arrangements for supplies and for concerted operations.[56] Maclean forwarded this suggestion to Wilson, who agreed. This coincided with a call from the British Government for Maclean to come to London. An airfield was again in operation at Bosanski Petrovac (the German Sixth Offensive had ended late in February), and Maclean and Velebit departed by British aircraft for Algiers. After a few days there they flew on to London arriving on May 1.

Before Velebit left Yugoslavia he was appointed head of a Partisan military mission to London. Somewhat earlier, Milovan Djilas had been assigned to a mission to Moscow, where he, General Velimir Terzić and other mission members spent two months, from early April until early June 1944.[57]

Dedijer writes [58] that Velebit was to have gone on to Washington, but did not because "the official attitude of the United States in the spring of 1944 had strangely begun to alter on Yugoslav matters." He adds that British and American policy had coincided until that time, with Britain having taken the initiative. But then the U.S. "began an independent policy . . . towards events in Yugoslavia." Far from stopping further assistance to Mihailović, "they sent him a military mission headed by a Colonel." Later events "proved Washington's political shortsightedness," Dedijer concludes. (The military mission to which Dedijer refers was undoubtedly the intelligence mission which arrived in Četnik territory on August 26, 1944.) Velebit has told the author that he was never asked to go to Washington. On May 16, Velebit called on Eisenhower and gave him a graphic description of the needs of the Partisans. In a message to Marshall, Eisenhower said that he had suggested to Velebit that he confine his requests to noncombat aircraft.[59] Eisenhower told Marshall that some seventy-five to one hundred obsolete aircraft might be very usefully employed in a supply operation across the Adriatic. It is clear from Eisenhower's message that Velebit made an excellent impression on the Allied Supreme Commander.

Marshall replied to Eisenhower [60] that General Ira C. Eaker, Allied Air Commander in the Mediterranean,[61] had temporarily assigned for Yugoslav operations an additional troop-carrier group from southern Italy and in addition had seven B-25s, thirty heavy bombers of the RAF and forty Italian bombers already engaged in delivering supplies.

With regard to the Partisan mission to Moscow, the State Department cabled a statement of the U.S. position vis-à-vis the Partisans to Ambassador Harriman on April 15 in case General Deane, Chief of the U.S. military mission in the Soviet Union, should come in contact with the Yugoslavs.[62] After explaining U.S. policy—that relations with the Partisans were to be kept on a purely military basis, while official contact should be only with the recognized authorities—the Department authorized Deane to meet with the mission for the exchange of military information. He was told, however, to avoid as far as possible intercourse of a ceremonial or official character.

In the same telegram, the State Department mentioned that Partisan representatives in Cairo (actually the Partisan mission itself) had met with former Governor Herbert H. Lehman, Director General of the United Nations Relief and Rehabilitation Administration (UNRRA).

The Soviet Ambassador to Yugoslavia, Novikov, had called on Lehman, and the Yugoslavs had accompanied Novikov.

In Moscow, Djilas saw Stalin twice; the second conversation was by far the more interesting. It occurred after Tito's headquarters had been over-run, at the end of May, and on the eve of the Normandy invasion early in June. Stalin said he thought that Tito should find more secure head-quarters—an idea obviously transmitted to the Soviet mission with Tito as will be seen presently—and then gave Djilas his views on Soviet-British and Soviet-American relations: "Perhaps you think that just because we are the allies of the English that we have forgotten who they are and who Churchill is. . . . Churchill is the kind who, if you don't watch him, will slip a kopeck out of your pocket. . . . Roosevelt is not like that. He dips in his hand only for bigger coins. . . ." [63]

With regard to the Yugoslav Government-in-Exile, Stalin urged a compromise with the newly designated Prime Minister, Šubašić. Tito no doubt took Stalin's views into account when he met Šubašić later in June.

"As I sum up that evening today," Djilas writes,[64] "it seems to me that I might conclude that Stalin was deliberately frightening the Yugoslav leaders in order to decrease their ties with the West, and at the same time he tried to subordinate their policy to his interests and to his relations with the Western states, primarily with Great Britain."

10

U.S. POLICY EVOLVES

Unhappy with the trend of Yugoslav developments and distrustful of the information emanating from Yugoslavia, the U.S. decided in March to strengthen the American political element at Wilson's headquarters in Algiers. Robert Murphy was the U.S. political adviser there, equal in rank to Harold Macmillan on the British side. Carl F. Norden, the State Department's Yugoslav desk officer, was dispatched to Murphy's staff to provide additional expertise on Yugoslavia. Eventually, he and another Foreign Service officer, Peter Constan, were the first American diplomats to return to Belgrade in January 1945. (It will be recalled that Constan was one of the Foreign Service officers who had finally closed the doors of the American Legation in occupied Belgrade on July 15, 1941.)

Captain Mansfield had returned to the U.S. in the latter part of March 1944, and Colonel Seitz followed him in early April. Both submitted reports to their superiors in OSS in which they declared that they had not seen any collaboration with the enemy by the Četniks. This was not surprising. As far as Četnik collaboration with the Italians is concerned, it should be recalled that Mansfield arrived in Četnik territory only a few days before Italy's capitulation, and Seitz did not go in until after the surrender. With regard to Četnik-German collaboration, neither Seitz nor Mansfield could have seen much either, since the German High Command continued to prohibit any accommodation during most of their stay in Četnik territory. Moreover, what occurred after the ban was lifted was not active collaboration but the secret conclusion of several local non-aggression pacts.

Fotić reports [1] that he talked to Mansfield on March 21, 1944, and with Seitz two weeks later. He writes that the reports of those two officers made a deep impression on American officials and that a decision was taken to send Mihailović immediate help in the form of armaments and other war material. This decision, Fotić adds, was confirmed by the President. Fotić further says that he had several meetings with two high-ranking officers of the OSS, General Miller and Colonel Goodfellow, to discuss priorities for the material to be sent to Mihailović. "A friend of mine in the State Department who was in charge of Yugoslav affairs," Fotić writes, "told me that, because of the reports of Seitz and Mansfield, the road was now clear for the shipment of supplies to Mihailović, entirely in conformity with the policy expressed by the Secretary of State on December 10 [Dec. 9], 1943." [2]

Fotić says that after several days of feverish activity, the discussions were discontinued, "and I was told by another friend high in the government offices that the President's order had been countermanded at the personal request of Mr. Churchill."

Nothing has been found in American files to substantiate Fotić's statements, though there seems to be little doubt that the reports of Seitz and Mansfield made an impression on U.S. officials concerned with Yugoslav affairs and that plans were formulated to resume help to Mihailović. However, this occurred at a time when OSS was making arrangements to send a U.S. intelligence group back into Četnik territory. Churchill's dismay over such a plan and Roosevelt's decision not to send a mission may well have had a negative effect on the idea of resuming help to Mihailović.

Roosevelt's reply to King Peter's letter of April 17 was drafted in the State Department. In a memorandum to the Secretary of State, the President had said: "Will you try your hand at preparing a nice personal letter from me to the King of Yugoslavia? It can start off, 'Dear Peter,' as I have always treated him as a sort of ward." [3] The reply is reprinted in *Foreign Relations of the U.S.* with the notation that no indication can be found of the date on which this letter may have been dispatched.[4]

In his memorandum to Roosevelt of May 17 forwarding the draft reply, Hull said: "Although we have not been associated with the British in their initiative in trying to work out the Yugoslav problem, this seemed to be a good occasion to let the Yugoslavs know the trend of our thinking." At the same time, Hull also enclosed a draft reply to Tito's letter of March 15 to Roosevelt brought out by Major Weil. These two State Department drafts present the best picture of U.S. policy with regard to Yugoslavia as of May 1944.

The draft of Roosevelt's letter to King Peter reads:

Dear Peter:
I have read your letter with most careful attention and have given much thought to the several questions you raise. I shall reply with complete candor

and in simple terms, and I am sure you will see how deeply and sympathetically we in America realize the problems facing the Yugoslav people.

You remember the burst of admiration with which we greeted your country's defiance of Germany three years ago. Believe me, our sentiments have not changed. We are pledged to the liberation of Yugoslavia and we hope again to see the union of its national elements under a common government, democratic in form and fact, as the purposes for which this war is being fought require.

It is one of the misfortunes of the war that your country, battered and dismembered by the enemy, has suffered also from internal conflicts, which in turn have revived other older antagonisms. You try, I know, impartially to defend the interests of Serbs, Croats and Slovenes, and to bind them together in loyalty to the common interest. Let me frankly say that I think your advisers and your officials have not always shown the wisdom necessary to achieve this end. I mention this because you speak of the Government's popularity with the people at home. I wish I could say that our reports from within Yugoslavia confirm this. On the contrary, they indicate that the people in Yugoslavia have sought, and still are seeking, a leadership which would have vision for dealing with the new social forces at work in the world today, and energy for undertaking the vast tasks ahead.

It is characteristic of you that you should find it hard to agree to a proposal which would affect the status of General Mihailovich. Let us not forget that the Mihailovich question has become more political than military. He did not mean it to be so, I am sure, and I really think it would be to the best interest of your country, and only fair to him as well, to use his excellent talents in the field but relieve him of government responsibility. It always seemed to me that this fine soldier should not have been expected to share the administrative burdens and the responsibilities of a member of the Cabinet, or of successive Cabinets, with which he has only intermittent contact, and of whose political decisions he can be kept only very imperfectly informed. In view of the important events ahead, a decision which would emphasize his service as a soldier in the field would be something which military men everywhere would understand. As a loyal officer he too would acknowledge the necessity for such action.

The suggestion that you might reorganize your Government by forming what one may call a "streamlined" administration, was doubtless one of several alternatives advanced in the search for a settlement of some of the troubles in Yugoslavia and some of the unhappy disputes among Yugoslav groups abroad. This is a question on which you will now have the wise counsel of Ban [Governor] Subasic. I was pleased to learn of your decision to call him to London. Some of our officials here saw him before his departure, and he will tell you what our people have been thinking on Yugoslav matters in general and will assure you of our abiding interest in the welfare of your country.

He will report also on our attitude toward the Partisans, which is precisely what Mr. Hull and others have publicly stated—military aid where it can be got through most effectively for resistance forces in operations against the enemy. While our relations with the Partisan leaders are of a military character, we are fully aware of the political implications of the Partisan movement, and of the desire of its leaders for representation or recognition, also in the field of foreign affairs. We contemplate no change in our present relationships, but you, better than anyone else, will realize how useful it would be to us in carrying out this policy if the public generally were sure that an earnest effort is being made to resolve certain basic difficulties. One of them is that the Partisan movement is stronger, and has far greater popular support, and sympathy for it extends into larger areas, than your Government has been willing to acknowledge.

I can assure you that our reports prepared by expert and impartial observers who have been able to evaluate and recheck the intelligence on the spot, as regards both the Mihailovich and the Tito forces, leave no doubt of this. Any fundamental approach to a solution of the unhappy civil strife in Yugoslavia must take this reality into account.

It is indeed our plan to work together with the British and the Soviet Governments in questions relating to Yugoslavia. I want you to know that, though we may be considered to have a less direct interest in Southeastern Europe, we treasure the friendship of your people, and are counting upon their cooperation both for expelling and defeating the enemy and for wholehearted association with us in a long-range program of general security and prosperity. These are the main objectives of us all, and we can speak frankly to the British and Soviet Governments on these things, and you may be sure I shall not forget the points you bring out in your letter.

If some of my observations seem disappointing, it is because my warm friendship for you prompts me to give you in this personal and direct way my thoughts on the several questions you ask.

Do not think I underrate your own admirable efforts on behalf of your country and people. These are times that strain to the limit the energies and wisdom of the most experienced statesmen, and I know with what earnestness and energy you are devoting your young years to your country's service.

I send you from my heart every good wish for your welfare and happiness.

Very sincerely yours,
Franklin D. Roosevelt

From this letter it is evident that Roosevelt had inched closer to the British attitude without, however, adopting it completely. He now shared the British view that Mihailović should leave his government post, but his positive attitude toward Mihailović as a military leader was sharply different from Churchill's rejection of the general. His belief that the Yugoslav Government should be reorganized because it did not handle its affairs with "wisdom" approached the British position. The British of course were considerably more dissatisfied with that Government.

The letter to Tito, which was drafted on May 13 and approved by the President on May 23, was turned over to the OSS on June 14 to be sent forward. In his memorandum to the President of May 17, the Secretary of State urged that the letter be signed by the head of the proposed American military mission to the Partisans. This indirect method of acknowledging Tito's letter was suggested on the grounds that "there has been no abatement in the conflict between Tito and the Government which we continue to recognize," as Hull said in his note to the President. Actually, the letter was neither signed by Colonel Huntington nor delivered to Tito. Exhaustive research has failed to disclose what happened to the draft letter after it was turned over to OSS. It is quite likely that the lack of response from Roosevelt to Tito contributed to the cooling of Tito's attitude toward the United States.

As drafted, the letter to Marshal Tito read:

My Dear Marshal Tito:

The President has directed me to thank you for your attentive reception of the American officers who were sent into Yugoslavia, and for the friendly letter which you handed to Major Weil for delivery to him.

The people and government of the United States do not underrate the valiant contribution which the Yugoslav people have already made to our common cause. We Americans know to what degree the people of Yugoslavia have suffered because they chose the hard but nobler way when the enemy came down upon them, and we realize both the urgent need for help of many kinds, while the war continues, and the tremendous tasks ahead for repairing the ravages of war and rebuilding the institutions necessary to a free people.

I have been particularly directed to say that the information which our officers have already obtained within Yugoslavia will be most useful to our military authorities and to the Allied command in working out the plans for rendering more effective assistance in strengthening resistance in Yugoslavia to the Germans, for contriving improved service of supply, and for fitting the operations in Yugoslavia into the general scheme for the conduct of the war.

It is now our business actively to carry forward this work under arrangements which will be taken up with you separately. The President has directed me to say that he knows that we shall have your unreserved and energetic help.[5]

The chances are that even had that letter been delivered by Huntington it would only have emphasized the different attitudes of Churchill and Roosevelt toward Tito. Churchill had been in correspondence with the Partisan leader for months, while Roosevelt chose an indirect way of answering a letter from Tito. Churchill and Tito exchanged substantive notes, while Roosevelt's reply did not go beyond vague generalities even though the Partisans' military contribution in the fight against the Germans was recognized, indeed, applauded.

Another factor clouding American-Partisan relations was undoubtedly the cool reaction of American authorities to Partisan feelers regarding the dispatch of a military mission to Washington. In a letter to Donovan dated May 18, the Secretary of State set forth his reasons for disapproving such a mission:

I feel sure that its major activity would be political, and the effect would be detrimental to the effort now being made to resolve some of the controversies between the Partisans and the Yugoslav Government. . . . I have in mind also the controversies among groups of Yugoslav-Americans, which have not been helpful to our national unity, and which would doubtless be sharpened by the attendant publicity if a new Yugoslav mission should come here while the general Yugoslav question is in its present fluid state.[6]

Therefore, Hull said, he did not think it advisable for the United States Government to agree to receive a Partisan military mission.

In his memorandum to Roosevelt regarding replies to the letters of King Peter and Tito, the Secretary of State noted: "In this connection, I should say for the record that there is pending also a letter addressed to you by General Mihailović to which it may or may not be advisable to send an acknowledgment, depending on the results of the Yugoslav talks still in progress. In any event, there is at this moment no means of communication with him."

The Mihailović letter referred to was undoubtedly the one which Mansfield had brought out. Contrary to what Hull said about communication, Musulin was at that time still in Četnik territory, and the British mission there had radio contact with Bari.

United States policy with regard to Yugoslavia was summarized on May 19, 1944, in a State Department memorandum prepared by the assistant chief of the Division of Southern European Affairs, Cavendish Cannon.[7] It stated that the United States did not intend to intercede in the internal political affairs of Yugoslavia; it had no special interests to promote and sought no special privileges. It wished to strengthen the resistance forces in whatever way the military situation might permit. The United States would like to see the leaders within Yugoslavia concentrate on the military task ahead and did not feel that either of the leading resistance groups operating in the country could lay solid claim to representing, in the political sense, the sentiments of the country as a whole.

The memorandum said that Great Britain and the Soviet Union had interests in the area which the United States would prefer not to support.

It added that it was important to maintain independence of action, to obtain military and political intelligence and to avoid becoming associated with political transactions "purporting to be on a joint basis, in which the undoubted American prestige in Yugoslavia would be exploited and American responsibility engaged, unless we really know what is going on."

The memorandum also declared that the United States had no engagements to King Peter or to any Yugoslav Government and would not find it difficult to enter into relations with a reconstituted Government.

A NEW YUGOSLAV GOVERNMENT UNDER ŠUBAŠIĆ

On May 17, Churchill informed Tito: "This morning, as a result of British advice, King Peter II dismissed M. Purić's administration, which included General Mihailović as Minister of War." [8] He added that King Peter was about to form an administration under Dr. Ivan Šubašić. "This of course has the strong approval of His Britannic Majesty's Government." Churchill asked Tito "to forebear from any utterances adverse to this new event [the impending replacement of Purić by Šubašić]."

Churchill sent a copy of this telegram to Roosevelt, who replied on May 19:

I am delighted with your telegram to Marshal Tito and I wish you would tell King Peter that I am heartily in favor of it. I sent him yesterday a letter in reply to a very nice letter I had from him.

Incidentally, do you remember my telling you over a year ago of my talk with Peter in which I discussed the possibility of three nations in place of the one, he to be the head of a reconstituted Serbia. . . . [This could only refer to the President's talks with King Peter and Purić in Cairo prior to the Tehran Conference.]

The King with real fire in his eyes, remarked that he was a Serb. I think you and I should bear some such possibility in mind in case the new Government does not work out. Personally, I would rather have a Yugoslavia but three separate States with separate Governments in a Balkan Confederation might solve many problems.

As soon as Churchill received this reply he radioed Tito of the President's "warm approval" and also said that he had forwarded Roosevelt's reply to Stalin.

Churchill had also informed Stalin of his telegram to Tito, sending him a copy of it through diplomatic channels. It "will show you exactly where we stand," he told Stalin in a telegram on May 19.

"My son Randolph, whom you met at Teheran," Churchill continued, "is with Marshal Tito, and writes about the very excellent relations which exist between the Soviet Mission and ours. So may it continue."

Stalin replied on May 22: "I have read your telegram to Marshal Tito. I, too, welcome the good relations between our Missions in Yugoslavia, and I hope they will continue so." [9]

According to Fotić,[10] Churchill told King Peter that he would address Parliament on May 24 and that he therefore expected Purić's resignation to be made known before noon of that day. "Purić having refused to hand in his resignation, and the King having failed to dismiss his Prime Minister, Mr. Churchill simply made the announcement as if the resignation of Purić had already been tendered," Fotić adds.

In his speech, Churchill told the House of Commons of "further positions which have been reached in Yugoslavia as the result of the unremitting exertions of our foreign policy." He reported having "received a message from King Peter that he has accepted the resignation of M. Purić." Churchill continued:

I understand . . . that the Ban of Croatia [Šubašić] is an important factor in the new political arrangements around whom, or beside whom certain other elements might group themselves for the purpose of beating the enemy and uniting Yugoslavia. . . . The reason why we have ceased to supply Mihailović with arms and support is a simple one. He has not been fighting the enemy and, moreover, some of his subordinates have made accommodations with the enemy . . .[11]

Also on May 24, Churchill radioed Tito again and repeated what he had told him one week earlier: "The King has sacked Purić and Company, and I think the Ban of Croatia will rally a certain force round him. . . . I am keeping the Russians and Americans informed of all that goes on between us. . . . Maclean will be coming back soon [to Yugoslavia]. I wish I could come myself, but I am too old and heavy to jump out on a parachute." [12]

As in the matter of who actually summoned Šubašić to London, there are differences of opinion regarding the date of Purić's dismissal. While Churchill cabled Tito as early as May 17 that King Peter had dismissed Purić, King Peter says that he did not dismiss the Government until after Churchill's speech.[13]

Šubašić had been in the United States since 1941. As Fotić says, he was favorably known to the OSS, and it was Donovan who first mentioned his name to Churchill. Whatever brought him there, he was in fact in London during the events which led to his appointment as Prime Minister on June 1, 1944.

THE BRITISH MISSION LEAVES MIHAILOVIĆ

In April 1944, a month before the withdrawal of the British mission to the Četniks, Armstrong, its head, reported:

From the operational point of view Mihailović's orders for inactivity are known and followed almost without exception. Numerous ambushes and acts of sabotage could have been carried out during the last 6–8 months virtually without loss; whether there would have been reprisals or not, is a question which will never be answered. We were constantly assured that there is a plan which will swing into operation when "The Day" is ordered by Mihailović, and that, when that happens, all communications will be interrupted if not blocked entirely. We were never able to find out what the plan is and we don't believe that it exists, except in vague words, though one or two commanders . . . might have scheduled definite personnel for definite operations.

The main pre-occupation . . . ever since the end of October, has been propaganda. This has never wavered from the line that Serbia is hitched, for better or for worse, to the Anglo-American star and that no compromise is possible with the occupying powers. Equally strong is the propaganda against the Partisans who have, in the minds of the people, taken the place of the Germans as Enemy No. 1.[14]

The report added that the mission had no evidence of collaboration with the enemy, but "it seemed fairly clear from the desperate attempts of the local commanders to avoid any action in that region, that a sort of non-aggression pact existed which conduced to the comfort of all concerned."

Armstrong's conclusions were:

1. As a military organisation, the Mihailović set-up could never do more, now that it has reached its present stage of military ill-preparedness and moral defeatism, than accelerate by a few days the already inevitable German withdrawal or collapse.

2. The organisation will continue to fight the Partisans with such weapons as it has, either until it is finally beaten or until there is a Partisan representation in the Yugoslav Government.

In the spring of 1944, the Partisans were on the move in an effort to return to Serbia. The Četniks resisted them; so did the Germans and the followers of Nedić. Once again the Četniks found themselves fighting the same enemy as the Germans and once again charges of collaboration were in the air.

Mihailović's thoughts were revealed in a letter to his commander for central and southeast Serbia, Major Radoslav Djurić, dated May 8, 1944:

In the actions against Tito's bands on the Drina the Germans did not touch us. On the contrary, many of our commanders were helped and enabled to avoid attacks made by the Communists. . . . As we have not sufficient munitions and forces, we cannot carry on fighting on two fronts. At present our most dangerous enemies are the Communists. Therefore, I order that every kind of armed action against the occupier's forces cease but the occupier will be attacked in propaganda. Every commander will be personally responsible to me for the above being carried out.[15]

Thus, what happened in the spring of 1944 was not collaboration on the pattern of the earlier Italian-Četnik arrangements. The Italians and the Četniks helped each other. The Germans and Četniks arranged not to hurt each other. They were and remained enemies, but they deferred reciprocal hostilities until such time as their joint main adversary, the Partisan movement, might be liquidated. Actually, as we shall see, within a few months and even though the Partisans were very much alive, Mihailović called on his followers to rise against the German occupiers.

British planes evacuated the last members of the British mission, landing at an airstrip at Pranjani northwest of Čačak in Serbia on May 29, 30 and 31. Included in the evacuation were Armstrong, more than sixty British officers and men, the last remaining American liaison officer, Lieutenant Musulin, and some forty American airmen whose planes had been disabled over Rumania and who had bailed out over Serbia. Dr. Živko Topalović, the president of the Četnik congress at Ba, who had been designated as Mihailović's emissary to Allied Force Headquarters in Italy, also joined the exodus. His mission was still-born, since AFHQ's policy was to break for good all relations with Mihailović.

The evacuation did not go off altogether smoothly. Mihailović had agreed to it provided that Major Lukačević and another officer then in Cairo be returned to Četnik territory. Wilson writes [16] that when the two officers arrived at Bari they attracted the suspicions of Allied security officers, who searched them and found in their possession one hundred uncensored letters as well as gold sovereigns, jewels and watches which were identified as having been stolen from a safe of the Yugoslav Government in Cairo a short time previously.[17] Wilson recounts that these officers were sent on "minus their ill-gotten gains which caused our liaison officer with the rear party to experience difficulty in getting away." Armstrong and

Topalović left Yugoslavia a day late on the plane that had brought the two Yugoslav officers to Serbia.

Rootham, one of the British officers evacuated at the end of May, reports [18] that the leavetaking was a deeply moving occasion. Mihailović said that whatever anybody might say or think, he and those who thought as he did regarded themselves as the friends and allies of the Western democracies. For that reason if for no other, he considered it his duty by all means in his power to ensure that, since the British mission had been ordered to leave, the evacuation was successfully carried out. Rootham says: "We, as representatives of a large nation, were given by representatives of a small nation a lesson in manners and how to conduct oneself with dignity in adversity." [19]

TITO EVACUATED FROM YUGOSLAVIA

The first Allied correspondents to arrive in Partisan territory with the official blessing of the Allied Mediterranean Command were Stoyan Pribichevich of *Time,* John Talbot of Reuters, and two photographers, Gene Fowler, an American, and an Englishman by the name of Slade. They landed at a British-operated airfield near Bosanski Petrovac on May 4 and were met by Randolph Churchill. After a dinner with Tito on May 9 in Drvar, Pribichevich's first story appeared in several American newspapers, including *PM* of May 15, and a more comprehensive account followed in the May 22 issue of *Time.*

Before Pribichevich and his colleagues arrived in Partisan territory, Sergeant Walter Bernstein, a correspondent for the American Army publication, *Yank,* who had established a close relationship with Partisan representatives in Bari, went to Drvar apparently without the knowledge of the Mediterranean Command. When the British mission became aware of Bernstein's presence in Yugoslavia, he was escorted out of the country on the same plane that brought in Pribichevich and the other correspondents. Bernstein later wrote a series of three articles for the *New Yorker* (April 1945) in which he described his visit with the Partisans.

At the time of Bernstein's sojourn in Yugoslavia, at the end of April, the Associated Press, again through the cooperation of Partisan representatives in Bari, sent written questions to Tito to which he replied. Publication of this long-distance interview was held up, however, by the censors of the Allied Mediterranean Command. Only after strong protests by the AP, including an appeal to President Roosevelt, was the story released under a Bari dateline on April 30 and published in many papers. *The New York Times* carried it on May 21. In the interview, Tito requested material help from the Allies and recognition of his National Committee as the government of Yugoslavia.

On May 25 the Germans launched their Seventh Offensive, an operation involving paratroops and code-named *"Rösselsprung"* ("Knight's Move"). It was the most dangerous of them all in terms of Tito's personal safety. He barely escaped capture by climbing up a dry run cut by a mountain waterfall. As soon as the Allies realized the scope of the German offensive they provided massive air support for the hard-pressed Partisans. Nearly 300 medium bombers and 200 fighters were engaged in those operations over Yugoslavia.[20]

Although there was no American liaison officer at Tito's headquarters when the Germans launched their offensive,[21] there were some Americans at Drvar. The U.S. Army Air Force maintained a weather station there, manned by a captain and three men. Also at Drvar were Lieutenant Colonel L. A. Neveleff of the U.S. 15th Air Force on a special assignment, and Colonel George Kraigher, on a mission for General Eaker, Allied Air Commander in the Mediterranean. Kraigher had dinner with Tito the night before the attack. Lieutenant Robert W. Crawford, who had accompanied Kraigher to Yugoslavia, was killed in the German assault.

The head of the Soviet military mission, General Korneyev, who had for some time urged Tito to leave Yugoslavia by air, renewed his suggestion in view of the narrow escape. Tito at first hesitated but in the end agreed. Once he had decided to leave, he asked the British mission, temporarily headed by Colonel Vivian Street (Maclean was in London), to arrange for his evacuation, and a DC-3 was sent to take him to Bari on June 3. When Street entered the plane he was surprised to find that it had a Russian crew. It turned out that the plane had been supplied under lend-lease and was operated by the Russians from Bari. Maclean says,[22] "Somehow the pilot had managed to obtain this particular assignment for his plane, thereby enabling his Government to claim that they had rescued Tito."

Tito reached Bari only a few days after the arrival there of the last members of the British mission to Mihailović and Topalović, the Četnik leader's representative. Tito was whisked away by members of the Soviet mission, much to the distress of the welcoming British and U.S. delegations at the airport. He was established in a suburban villa, and once there he decided to go to Vis, which was securely held by Allied and Partisan forces. He discussed this with Maclean, who had meanwhile arrived from London, and it was arranged that the Bitish destroyer *Blackmore* would transport him. This was accomplished within a few days, and on

June 9, Murphy cabled the State Department from Algiers: "Marshal Tito and British and Soviet Missions are now established on Vis." [23]

On the same day the BBC announced that Tito, with Allied aid, had shifted his headquarters from one part of Yugoslavia to another.[24] On June 18, C. L. Sulzberger reported in *The New York Times* that Marshal Tito "flew to Italy because there was no airfield available in Yugoslavia. The Marshal is now back in Yugoslavia." Sulzberger was not told, or not permitted to say, that Tito was on an island in the Adriatic.

Meanwhile Pribichevich, Talbot and the two photographers fell into German hands. Pribichevich alone escaped, and *Time* of June 26 carried the story of his adventures. Together with some members of the British and Soviet missions, and the American captain who headed the weather station, Pribichevich was evacuated from an airfield at Tičevo, near Drvar, on June 9. Colonel Kraigher left with a British flight officer in a small plane on May 28 and Lieutenant Colonel Neveleff made his way to the coast, where he obtained transportation to Vis. The Germans were so pleased with their success in the Seventh Offensive that they exhibited Tito's uniform in Vienna. Little did they suspect that Tito had escaped!

GENERAL WILSON CREATES THE BALKAN AIR FORCE

Following up on the Combined Chiefs of Staff directive of December 1943, that a special commander be appointed to support the Partisans, General Wilson proposed that a new headquarters be set up in Bari. Since the Air Force would play the major role in such an understaking, he suggested that it be commanded by an Air Force officer. Wilson says that although the Navy did not like the idea, he nevertheless went ahead.[25]

The Combined Chiefs of Staff approved this arrangement, and on June 1, 1944, the Balkan Air Force (BAF) was established under the command of Air Vice-Marshal William Elliot. Its task was to coordinate, subject to the concurrence of the respective commanders in chief, the planning and execution of "all operations, Air, Sea, Land and Special, on and across the Dalmatian Coast." [26] Liaison with Maclean's mission in Yugoslavia was effected through a subordinate command known as Land Forces, Adriatic. Elliot's command received diplomatic advice from and offered military advice to a representative of Macmillan, British political adviser at AFHQ.

The Balkan Air Force consisted of two offensive fighter wings, a light bomber wing and a special operations wing. The units were mostly British but included several American elements and even a number of Italian

Air Force units, a Yugoslav squadron, a Greek squadron and a Polish flight.[27] They brought with them a wide assortment of planes.

The BAF took over all supply activities across the Adriatic formerly carried out by Eaker's Mediterranean Allied Air Force. In July 1944 almost 2,400 sorties were flown. These included not only the dropping of supplies to the Partisans and the evacuation of wounded, but also the bombing of rail lines, Adriatic and Danube shipping and chrome and steel works in Yugoslavia.

The Allies were thus organized to support Partisan operations within Yugoslavia. The Partisans in turn were helping the Allied war effort: They were not only tying down enemy troops but also carrying out operations at Wilson's request that directly aided the Allied advance in Italy. One such action was the destruction of a railroad bridge in Slovenia which interrupted traffic to Trieste.[28]

U.S. REPRESENTATION TO THE YUGOSLAV GOVERNMENT—ŠUBAŠIĆ MEETS TITO

With the departure of King Peter and Prime Minister Purić from Cairo early in March, American representation to the Yugoslav Government reverted to London, where Rudolf E. Schoenfeld became the U.S. Counselor of Embassy to the Yugoslav Goverment-in-Exile. Šubašić, designated Prime Minister on June 1, requested that the American Embassy be moved from Cairo to London.[29]

On June 20 the Secretary of State recommended to Roosevelt that Mac-Veagh remain in Cairo, since in the foreseeable future all principal matters in U.S. relations with Yugoslavia would be handled in the Mediterranean area and "these questions, from our point of view, are much more important than the matter of formal relations with a Government which more and more is being obliged to conform to British plans." [30]

The State Department cabled MacVeagh on July 1 that Schoenfeld was being accredited to the Yugoslav Government at London as Chargé d'Affaires. While the telegram added that MacVeagh was relieved of his Yugoslav mission, it assigned to him major responsibilities with regard to Yugoslavia. "It is believed that those Yugoslav matters most important to us in the conduct of the war, and as a basis for our long-term relations with Yugoslavia such as the coordination of political, military, economic, relief, refugee and propaganda activities, will be handled in your area and through organizations with which you already are or will be working," the cable said.[31]

Šubašić started out as a one-man government because the Serbs refused to participate. In a proclamation, the King appealed to all Yugoslavs "to lay aside their differences and to postpone all internal political issues until after the liberation of the country, when they will be free to express their will regarding the regime under which they desire to live in the future." He declared that, as evidence of his sincerity, he had decided to form a new government which would "consecrate itself to the high purpose of working with all those elements in our country who are actively resisting the enemy." Since the new government could function effectively only if it received the cooperation of all resistance forces, the King directed Šubašić to establish contact with them before naming the new government.[32] It was therefore decided that Šubašić should go to Bari and Vis.

Late in the evening of June 10, King Peter and Šubašić left London, accompanied by Ambassador Stevenson and Colonel Bailey, in Churchill's private plane. They first stopped in Algiers, where they talked with Wilson and Macmillan. Murphy reported that the plan developed in London included a proposal that under the King's authority, Tito would assume the military command of all Yugoslav forces and Šubašić the political and civil direction. "In other words, a Clémenceau-Foch relationship," Murphy commented.[33]

The party then went on to Malta, and while the King and Bailey remained there, Šubašić and Stevenson proceeded on June 12 to Bari, where Šubašić talked to Topalović, Milhailović's representative, and apparently offered him the possibility of joining the new Government-in-Exile. On June 13, Šubašić and Stevenson continued on a British destroyer to Vis, arriving on the following day. Churchill had previously sent a letter to Tito, emphasizing the importance the British Government attached to the reaching of an agreement between the Partisan leader, on the one hand, and the Yugoslav Government and King Peter on the other.[34]

On June 16, Šubašić and Tito reached agreement that the Šubašić Government should include no elements hostile to the Partisans and that its main task should be to organize aid for them. Šubašić recognized the decisions of the second AVNOJ Congress in November 1943 and the institutions which it had set up, and he undertook to appeal publicly to the people of Yugoslavia to support the Partisans. It was agreed that the question of the monarchy should be left for the Yugoslav people to decide after the war and that a united Yugoslav Government be formed, composed jointly of elements of the Government-in-Exile and of the National Committee of Liberation.[35]

On June 18, King Peter went from Malta to Caserta, where Wilson had his advance headquarters. On the following day, Šubašić returned to

Bari from Vis. Wilson had invited Tito to come, too, and he accepted at first but then declined when he sensed that Wilson might attempt to bring him together with King Peter. Šubašić again talked to Topalović but, after his exposure to Tito, no longer had him in mind for a cabinet position. On June 20, Šubašić went to Caserta, and within a few days, on June 25, the King and Šubašić were back in London. Velebit, who had participated in the Vis talks and whose principal task now was to keep an eye on Šubašić, went along.

Maclean and Randolph Churchill, who had been brought out of Yugoslavia after Tito's headquarters in Drvar was overrun, were in London in the latter part of June, and Macmillan, who also was there, reports [36] that both "strongly supported the view that Britain and King Peter must put their whole weight behind Tito's movement."

The Foreign Office, on the other hand, was clearly unenthusiastic regarding this first Tito-Šubašić arrangement. There was no reference in it to a possible return of the King, and although Tito had assured Šubašić

General Wilson, King Peter and Prime Minister Šubašić, Caserta, June 1944. From *Eight Years Overseas*

that he did not intend to impose Communism on the Yugoslavs after the war, the renunciation of "compulsory Communism" remained only a verbal promise.

Bailey's report of June 30 on the Šubašić visit to Vis said that "Tito has allowed Šubašić to win outside the country in order to consolidate and strengthen his own position inside the country. . . . The strength and the solidity of the Royalist Movement in Serbia, under Mihailović, has, most dangerously, been either grossly underrated or deliberately ignored." [37]

Commenting on Colonel Bailey's report, a Foreign Office memorandum of July 25 underlined the far-reaching questions posed by it—the future Soviet influence in Yugoslavia, and British interest in the unity of the country. It said:

We shall soon have to decide whether or not our present short-term policy—directed towards obtaining military advantages—is calculated to achieve our political objectives in the post-war world. This must depend to a very large extent upon the attitude which we believe Tito will adopt after the war and whether we consider a Yugoslavia united under his aegis would be more likely to become a sphere of Soviet influence than if the country were to split up into its component parts.

After Šubašić's return to London, he devoted his attention to the Yugoslav Government's relations with the Soviet Union, which had been interrupted for several months. The Soviet Ambassador to the Government-in-Exile, Novikov, had not, like his British colleague Stevenson, followed King Peter and Prime Minister Purić from Cairo to London, and unlike the Americans, the Soviets had not appointed a London-based diplomat as envoy. The Yugoslav Ambassador in Moscow, Simić, had resigned but stayed on in Moscow, his sympathies clearly with the Partisans.

In view of this situation, Šubašić sent a telegram to Molotov on July 9 asking him whether the Soviet Government, now that Šubašić and Tito had met in Vis, considered the time appropriate to exchange ambassadors again. The Soviets replied in the affirmative and reaccredited Ambassador Novikov, who transferred his seat from Cairo to London. The Yugoslavs in turn reappointed Simić as Ambassador.[38]

The U.S. attitude toward these developments was one of caution and reserve. As early as the end of May, Murphy in Algiers had alerted the Department of State to the difficulty he perceived in giving U.S. propaganda support to the objective of uniting all forces in Yugoslavia "under Tito's military direction," as Churchill had defined it in Parliament on May 24. This was "not the American objective," Murphy said, and he cited that particular sticking point as "an example of numerous problems that can be expected to come up more frequently in the future" in joint psychological warfare operations.[39]

The U.S.-British differences were revealed even more sharply at the end of June when Murphy, with the subsequent full support of the Department of State, took exception to a directive prepared by the policy committee of the Balkan Air Force. That directive declared:

The general policy is that all possible military support should be accorded to those elements willing and able to resist the enemy. . . . This means in Yugoslavia that we should provide the fullest aid to Tito's Partisans. We should encourage the union of all the fighting units in Yugoslavia with the National Army of Liberation in a single front in accord with the provisions of the Tito-Šubašić agreement. No support will be furnished the Mihailovich forces.

Murphy's objection to the "blanket statement" that no support would be given Mihailović was upheld by the Department of State in a telegram for Murphy on July 8 which endorsed his view that the BAF directive was "inconsistent with our stated policy to aid whatever forces may be fighting the Germans."

The telegram also indicated serious reservations about the Šubašić-Tito agreement:

Available information indicates that the accord is not a compromise between Yugoslav political groups but essentially an arrangement between the British and Tito, representing an almost unconditional acceptance of the Partisan demands.

The telegram said that it appeared that "the exclusion of Serbian interests" in the negotiations following Šubašić's appointment as Prime Minister and "the insistence on giving Tito politically and militarily a free hand for all Yugoslavia have jeopardized the advantages which might have been gained" in the period after the constitution of the Šubašić Government. In any case, "the Department would not approve a directive setting forth an irrevocable decision to withhold supplies from Serbian forces and giving support to a forcible penetration of Tito into Serbia."

U.S.-BRITISH MILITARY POLICY DIFFERENCES
IN THE MEDITERRANEAN

The Seventh and final German Offensive, of which the primary aim seems to have been the overrunning of Tito's headquarters, petered out in June, and although Tito had originally intended to stay only two or three weeks in Vis, he decided to prolong his stay there.

At that time, Alexander's armies were steadily driving north of Rome toward the "Gothic Line" between Pisa and Rimini. Yugoslavia came significantly into the picture when American and British statesmen and military strategists had to decide whether to breach the Gothic Line with all available forces or to withdraw troops for possible landings elsewhere. Two places in particular were under consideration: the south of France, to relieve Eisenhower's cross-channel invasion, and the head of the Adriatic, to turn the Germans' flank in Italy and to aid the Partisans in Yugoslavia.

Alexander felt that he should be given the opportunity to breach the Gothic Line and thereafter to swing either west or east—toward France or through Yugoslavia into Austria. He believed that the eastern alternative, a move through the Ljubljana gap, might prove easier.

On June 14, however, the Combined Chiefs of Staff decided against Alexander and ordered him to halt at the Pisa-Rimini line and to make three divisions available for landings either in the south of France or at the head of the Adriatic.[40] On June 17, General Marshall visited the Mediterranean and argued for "Anvil" (a landing in the south of France), stressing the importance of obtaining a large port like Marseilles through which the divisions waiting in the U.S. could pass. Wilson was unimpressed. On June 19 he told the Combined Chiefs of Staff that he thought his best contribution would be to press forward into the Po valley.[41] With the help of an amphibious operation against the Istrian peninsula at the head of the Adriatic, an advance through the Ljubljana gap might then be possible.

The Allies had landed in Normandy on June 6, and the final decision to invade the south of France was reached mainly because the cross-channel invasion was stalled by bad weather and stiffening German resistance and needed support on the southern flank. The Anvil plan was only adopted, however, after the most outspoken disagreement between the United States and Britain. The U.S. Joint Chiefs of Staff favored the invasion of southern France and were against the "commitment of Mediterranean resources to large-scale operations in Northern Italy and into the Balkans," a view with which the British Chiefs of Staff did not agree.

Churchill appealed to Roosevelt on June 28:

The deadlock between our Chiefs of Staff raises most serious issues. Our first wish is to help General Eisenhower. . . . But we do not think this necessarily involves the complete ruin of all our great affairs in the Mediterranean. . . .

Please remember how you spoke to me at Teheran about Istria. . . . This has sunk very deeply into my mind . . .[42]

Roosevelt replied that Eisenhower needed the southern French ports and that there was enough Allied strength left in Italy to give Alexander ground superiority. As for Istria, the President said that those who proposed such a campaign seemed to disregard the grand strategy as well as "the time factor as involved in the probable duration of a campaign to debouch from Ljubljana Gap into Slovenia and Hungary . . . I cannot agree to the employment of United States troops against Istria and into the Balkans." The President pointed out that thirty-five U.S. divisions could be put into France, while not more than six could be put beyond the Ljubljana gap.[43]

Churchill answered on July 1 that the splitting up of the Mediterranean campaign into two operations (France and Italy) "is, in my humble and respectful opinion, the first major strategic and political error." He reminded Roosevelt again that the idea of a move eastward into Istria came from the President at Tehran. "No one involved in these discussions has ever thought of moving armies into the Balkans; but Istria and Trieste . . . are strategic and political positions, which . . . might exercise profound and widespread reactions, especially now after the Russian advances." [44]

Churchill also commented on Roosevelt's suggestion that the issue be submitted to Stalin for his views. Churchill believed it was "better to settle the matter for ourselves and between ourselves." He thought Stalin might for military reasons prefer an eastward march by the Allies, but for political reasons he might prefer the landing in southern France, so that "East, Middle and Southern Europe should fall naturally under his control."

On the next day, the President answered that a directive to Wilson to land in southern France should no longer be delayed. "At Tehran what I was thinking of was a series of raids in force in Istria if the Germans started a general retirement from the Dodecanese and Greece. But it has not happened yet, and Tito appears to be in a less strong position than he was then. On the same lines, the country in Istria is bad combat terrain in the winter time, worse than Southern France."

Churchill was deeply unhappy. He composed, but did not send, several sharp protests to Washington; privately he said "an intense impression must be made upon the Americans that we have been ill-treated and are furious." [45] His anger was not lessened when it was pointed out to him that the U.S. had often given way to the British over the Mediterranean on earlier occasions. He watched with unconcealed regret the slowing down of the Italian campaign necessitated by the withdrawal of divisions for the landings in southern France.

After the Allies had won important battles in Normandy, Churchill tried once more, by sending a telegram to Roosevelt on August 4. Upon hearing that the President had departed for the Pearl Harbor conference with General Douglas MacArthur and Admiral Chester W. Nimitz, Churchill sent a telegram on August 6 to Harry Hopkins. Roosevelt, however, was convinced that the plans under way were sound. The Allies landed in southern France on August 15, but Churchill makes the point [46] that the first major operation in which these troops participated in conjunction with Eisenhower's army did not take place until mid-November.

FOTIĆ LEAVES AS YUGOSLAV ENVOY IN WASHINGTON

After Šubašić's appointment, Fotić was relieved on June 9 of his post as Yugoslav Ambassador to the United States and instructed to turn the Embassy over to Ivan Frangeš, Counselor of Embassy.[47] Fotić refused to accept the instruction, however, saying that since Šubašić was only "designated," he could not, according to Yugoslav law, take such a step. Fotić so informed H. Freeman Matthews, Deputy Director of European Affairs in the State Department.

On July 7, the Šubašić Government was sworn in. On the following day, Fotić visited Under Secretary Stettinius and told him that he was obliged to refuse to recognize the new Government because it was not representative of the people and interests of Yugoslavia.[48] Stettinius said that he regretted very much that Fotić would no longer represent Yugoslavia in Washington. From that day on, the Embassy's affairs were conducted by Ivan Frangeš, the Counselor, as Chargé. (The new Ambassador, Stanoje Simić, did not arrive in the United States until April 1945.) Fotić stayed on in Washington as a private citizen and continued to use whatever influence he had upon U.S. attitudes toward Yugoslavia.

The Šubašić Government included Dr. Sava Kosanović (a Serb) and Dr. Izidor Cankar (a Slovene) who had come to London from the U.S., and Dr. Juraj Šutej (a Croat). Two supporters of the National Liberation Movement, Sreten Vukosavljević (a Serb) and Dr. Drago Marušić (a Slovene), were also appointed. Tito made it plain on July 9, however, that those two officials were not the representatives of the National Committee of Liberation but only men whom he regarded as "honest patriots." [49] Mihailović of course was excluded from the Government, and Šubašić himself took the post of Minister of the Army, Navy and Air Force.

FARISH'S SECOND REPORT

On June 16, Lieutenant Colonel Farish left Yugoslavia for the last time. (He was killed a few months later in an air crash in Greece.) Farish had spent more time in war-torn Yugoslavia than any other American. After six weeks there in September and October 1943, he had written a report which had directly influenced U.S. policy at the Tehran and Cairo conferences.

By the time of his departure he understood Yugoslavia better, and in his final report,[50] dated Bari, June 28, 1944, he took a more objective view of conditions than in his initial observations. He wrote:

In the case of the forces of Marshal Tito and General Mihailović both sides tell exactly the same stories of incidents which occurred at certain places on the same dates, the only difference being that each side places the blame on the other. . . . Both sides attributed to the other the lack of effective resistance to the Germans. . . . Both sides claim they have been attacked by the other in collaboration with the Germans and will cite time and places as evidence. . . . Both sides believe that the first enemy is the other, with the Germans and Bulgarians second.

Thus Farish had become persuaded that the Četnik-Partisan problem was not a black-and-white proposition, as he had first seemed to believe. Considering that he had spent so many months with the Partisans, the following sentence in his report is revealing: "It appears to me that there are indications in the past few months that there has been less emphasis placed on the fight against the enemy and more preparation for the political struggle to follow the ending of the war." In conclusion he urged that the United States take a greater interest in Yugoslav affairs since there was an enormous amount of good will toward the United States—"the United States of America is mentioned in the same breath with God in Yugoslavia."

The U.S. Government, however, maintained its detachment. Murphy tells [51] that when he accompanied Roosevelt to Cairo in November 1943, he attempted to explain to the President the Tito-Mihailović situation in the hope of getting some definite policy guidance. But Roosevelt was not interested. "We should build a wall around those two fellows and let them fight it out," Murphy quotes Roosevelt as saying. "Then we could do business with the winner." Murphy declares that neither then nor later did Roosevelt have any consistent policy toward Yugoslavia. With regard to military matters, Wilson describes [52] the U.S.' attitude as one of avoiding the Balkans "as if it was a pesthouse."

Indeed, the U.S. Joint Chiefs of Staff, in answer to a British inquiry, declared on May 28, 1944, that no U.S. forces would be employed "as occupational forces in southern Europe, including Austria, or southeast Europe, including the Balkans," and that any U.S. forces located in the area at the end of the war would be withdrawn as soon as practicable. (This was amended later to provide for U.S. occupation troops in Austria.) Concerning U.S. administration of relief, it would be limited, the Joint Chiefs said, to "procurement and shipment of supplies to Albania, Yugoslavia, and Greece," for which the U.S. would supply a few military officers until UNRRA took over.[53]

After Tito's move to Vis, the office of U.S. political adviser at AFHQ, Murphy, assumed broader responsibilities with regard to the Partisans. Two Foreign Service officers, Carl Norden and Frederick T. Merrill, were assigned to Bari to report through Murphy not only what they gathered directly from the Yugoslavs but also what the British told them. Philip Broad was Macmillan's representative in Bari, and on his staff were old Yugoslav hands such as Deakin.

TITO REFUSES TO MEET ŠUBAŠIĆ AGAIN

Ambassador Winant in London cabled the State Department on July 12 that Šubašić had gone on July 10 to Caserta to be General Wilson's guest. There he would meet Tito to discuss such questions as were not resolved when they previously met in Vis. The meeting scheduled for July 12 did not take place, however, for Tito reneged at the last minute. He had discussed plans for his trip with Maclean as late as July 9, but on July 11 he told Maclean that his advisers had urged him not to go since the Šubašić-Tito agreement had made an unfavorable impression in Slovenia and Croatia; if he were to go to Caserta to meet Šubašić again it would have an even more unsettling effect on public opinion.[54]

This was the second time Tito had refused an invitation from Wilson, and the general was irritated. He asked Maclean to tell Tito that under the circumstances it was necessary "to survey Tito's requests for military equipment." Maclean himself was summoned immediately to Caserta.

Churchill wrote a note to Eden on July 15: "If I have been ready to telegraph reproachfully to Tito, it is not because I have in any way changed my view about him and his forces, but because he has given nothing in return for what we have done for him and while he lies under our protection on the island of Vis is the best time to bring the consciousness of this home to him." [55]

The Foreign Office was likewise "extremely annoyed at Tito." One of its officials told Winant: "Tito might have had the grace to have taken this decision 24 hours earlier so that Šubašić would not have gone to Bari and thus would not be placed in the present extremely awkward position." [56] It is quite evident that Tito did not wish to be associated too closely with the Šubašić Government and resented the British efforts to push him in that direction.[57]

The Foreign Office was also disconcerted to find that Maclean appeared to have told Tito that Britain wished him to extend the scope of his movement in Serbia, and that Tito had sent two "extreme" Communist members of the National Committee (Ranković and Kardelj) into Serbia. Eden wired Maclean that British policy was not to help impose the Partisans on Serbia, but to promote cooperation between them and the Serbs.[58]

While in Caserta, Šubašić had a short and inconsequential conversation with Topalović before returning to London on July 18 accompanied by the two supporters of the Partisan movement who had joined his cabinet and by Velebit, the chief of the military mission of the National Liberation Army in London. The U.S. Chargé to the Yugoslav Government-in-Exile, Schoenfeld, had a talk with Šubašić and found him in a pessimistic mood, undoubtedly due to Tito's failure to come to Caserta. Šubašić told Schoenfeld that his only desire was to bring about a united war effort and the avoidance of fratricidal war. He wished above all to see Yugoslavia follow a policy that coincided with that of its three great Allies.[59]

SPHERES OF INFLUENCE?

Earlier in the year, Churchill had come to the conclusion that with the advance of the Red Army into Eastern Europe, some sort of understanding with the Russians regarding the area was imperative. On May 4, 1944, he sent a note to Eden in which he said that "broadly speaking the issue is: are we going to acquiesce in the Communisation of the Balkans and perhaps of Italy? . . . if our conclusion is that we resist the Communist infusion and invasion we should put it to them pretty plainly at the best moment that military events permit. We should of course have to consult the United States first." And again to Eden on the same day: "Evidently we are approaching a showdown with the Russians about their Communist intrigues in Italy, Yugoslavia, and Greece. I think that their attitude becomes more difficult every day." [60]

On the following day, Eden suggested to the Soviet Ambassador that the USSR should temporarily regard Rumanian affairs as mainly their concern under war conditions, while leaving Greece to the British.[61] Yugoslavia was not mentioned in this context, though we shall see later that Churchill's idea was first to add Yugoslavia to the British area and later to split the responsibility evenly between the USSR and Britain.

On May 18, the Soviet Ambassador called at the Foreign Office to inquire whether the United States agreed to the Rumania-Greece proposal. If so, the Soviets would concur.

In Washington, the British Ambassador, Lord Halifax, raised this matter with the Secretary of State on May 30. Mr. Hull, however, considered it would not be a good idea "to abandon the fixed rules and policies which are in accord with our broad basic declarations of policy, principles and practice." In other words, he objected because such a course implied accepting the notion of spheres of influence.[62] Thereupon, Churchill sent a telegram to Roosevelt on May 31 outlining the idea. "I hope you may feel able to give this proposal your blessing," he said. "We do not of course wish to carve up the Balkans into spheres of influence, and in agreeing to the arrangement we should make it clear that it applied only to war conditions . . ." [63]

By June 8, in a telegram to Halifax, Churchill had added Bulgaria to the Russian area and Yugoslavia to the British. "There is no question," he insisted, "of spheres of influence. We all have to act together, but some one must be playing the hand." He added that "we follow the lead of the United States in South America as far as possible, as long as it is not a question of our beef and mutton."

Hull's opposition to Churchill's idea was reflected in Roosevelt's telegram to Churchill of June 11: "In our opinion, this would certainly result in the persistence of differences between you and the Soviets and in the division of the Balkan region into spheres of influence despite the declared intention to limit the arrangement to military matters." [64]

Churchill replied on the same day that he was much concerned by Roosevelt's message. He spoke again only of Rumania and Greece and suggested a three-month trial period. Roosevelt concurred on the following day (while Hull was away from Washington), admonishing Churchill, however, that "we must be careful to make it clear that we are not establishing any post-war spheres of influence." Hull recalls that Roosevelt sent his message without consulting the State Department. Indeed, on the same day on which Roosevelt concurred, the State Department sent a note to the British Embassy in which it stated that it could not give the approval of the U.S. Government to the proposed arrangement since it "would inevitably result in the persistence rather than the elimination of any divergence in the views of the British and Soviet Governments with regard to the Balkan region . . ." [65]

The British immediately reported to the Russians Roosevelt's concurrence in a three-month trial period. In a message to Churchill on June 22, the President, prompted by the Secretary of State, expressed surprise that the Greece-Rumania proposal had been communicated to the United States only after it had been discussed with the Russians. In reply, Churchill vigorously defended the British action. "It would not be possible for three people in different parts of the world to work together effectively if no one of them may make any suggestion to either of the others without simultaneously keeping the third informed," Churchill cabled on June 23, noting that the President had been in direct touch with Stalin on the Polish question without informing Churchill. On Yugoslavia, Churchill said:

I have also taken action to try to bring together a union of the Tito forces with those in Serbia, and with all adhering to the Royal Yugoslav Government, which we have both recognised. You have been informed at every stage of how we are bearing this heavy burden, which at present rests mainly on us. Here again nothing would be easier than to throw the King and the Royal Yugoslav Government to the wolves and let a civil war break out in Yugoslavia, to the joy of the Germans. I am struggling to bring order out of chaos. . . . I am keeping you constantly informed, and I hope to have your confidence and help within the spheres of action in which initiative is assigned to us.[66]

On June 26, Roosevelt cabled, ". . . it appears that both of us have inadvertently taken unilateral action in a direction that we both now agree to have been expedient for the time being. It is essential that we should always be in agreement in matters bearing on our Allied war effort." [67]

Having heard of U.S. doubts the Russians, however, approached Washington directly regarding the British-Soviet arrangement. On July 1, the Soviet Embassy sent an *aide-mémoire* to the State Department inquiring about the United States' position with regard to it. Yugoslavia was not mentioned—only Greece and Rumania. The Russians apparently wanted to hear directly from the U.S. and not via the British. Meanwhile, Churchill sent a telegram to Stalin on July 12 asking him to consent to the three-month arrangement in view of Roosevelt's concurrence. On July 15, Stalin answered that it would be better to await the American reply to the Soviets' own query before concluding the arrangement regarding Greece and Rumania. On the same day, the State Department answered the Soviet note, confirming that the United States assented to the arrangement for a trial period of three months, "this assent being given in consideration of the present war strategy." It added, however, that the U.S. Government was fearful "lest the proposed arrangement might . . . lead to the division in fact of the Balkan region into spheres of influence."

Churchill writes that "we were then unable to reach any final agreement about dividing responsibilities in the Balkan peninsula." In October, however, when Churchill visited Moscow, a British-Russian understanding was reached, as we shall see later. But, as Churchill says, "much had happened on the Eastern Front," thus implying that the terms were less favorable to the West in view of the progress which the Red Army had made in the meantime. Stalin's temporizing on an arrangement with the British was clearly due, however, to his desire not to antagonize the U.S. rather than to his expectation that he might obtain a better deal at a later time when his military position would be stronger.

TITO IN ITALY

Having twice rejected a meeting with Wilson in Italy, Tito changed his mind after he became aware of the Mediterranean Commander's annoyance, but Wilson now decided to let him wait. At first it was suggested, according to Wilson, that the two meet "at some wild spot on the Adriatic shore . . . but I didn't fall for that." [68] Eventually, it was arranged that Tito would go to Caserta on August 5. Wilson sent his private plane to Vis to fetch him and he was put up at a guest house near the commander's official villa.

Murphy, the senior American in the area, was invited on the day of Tito's arrival to a small luncheon party in the marshal's honor. Much has been written about Tito's visit to Wilson, about the Yugoslav bodyguards who came along and followed Tito everywhere, about Olga Humo, his interpreter, and about the dog, Tiger. Murphy reports [69] that he got along well with Tito, who accepted an invitation to dine with him that same evening. The dinner was pleasant, Murphy and Tito chatting in German, and Tito describing some of his hairbreadth escapes from the Germans.

On the next day, Wilson and his staff began their military discussions with Tito and his associates. The first point on the agenda was the question of supplies to the Partisans. Tito wanted tanks and heavy artillery. Wilson attempted to convince him of the difficulties not only of sending

General Wilson and Marshal Tito in Caserta, August 1944. From *Eight Years Overseas*

him heavy equipment but also of maintaining such equipment. Other points discussed related to the coordination of operations of the Balkan Air Force with those of the Partisan ground forces; the formation of a Partisan air force with the assistance of the Allies; the medical treatment in Italy of Partisan wounded; the establishment of Partisan supply bases in Italy, and the transfer to the Partisans of those Yugoslav ships which had become part of the Allied Mediterranean fleet.

While Wilson writes [70] that Tito impressed him with his bearing, ability, frankness and purpose without ever overstating his achievements, Dedijer reports [71] that the Yugoslavs found Wilson's behavior "somewhat offending."

On August 7, Tito visited Alexander's headquarters near Lake Bolsena. The discussions there centered on those ethnic Croats and Slovenes from Istria and from the Slovenian littoral who had been inducted into the Italian Army and whom Tito wanted to join the Partisans. Tito also requested that Istria and the Slovenian littoral be considered a Partisan area of operation. In the evening, Tito was the guest of General Eaker at a reception at his headquarters. In contrast to his reaction to Wilson, Tito seemed to have been impressed by both Alexander and Eaker.

At the end of July, Churchill advised Wilson that he intended to arrive in Italy around August 6 or 7. He wired: "It would be a pity for me to miss Tito, with whom I am quite prepared to discuss political matters of all kinds. Could you therefore stage your meeting with him so that he will be at Caserta at dates including 8th or 9th?" [72] However, cabinet business—Churchill's last attempt to persuade Roosevelt not to insist on an invasion of southern France—delayed his departure until August 11.

For security reasons, Tito was not told of Churchill's impending visit. Everything was done to keep him busy. He was taken to Rome, to Anzio, to Cassino. He had another meeting with Wilson in Caserta on August 10 during which Wilson declared that an Allied landing in Istria might be necessary to hasten the fall of Trieste and weaken the German defenses in Italy. Tito countered by saying that in such a case the Allies must coordinate their operations with the Partisans and respect the Yugoslav authorities on the spot.

On the following day, Tito went to Capri to call on General Donovan, who was visiting there. Colonel Toulmin, the chief of the OSS mission in Cairo, was also there with Colonel Huntington, the chief of the new American military mission, who was about to go to Tito's headquarters at Vis. By that time, Tito appeared to have guessed why he was being kept in Italy, and Maclean relates [73] that while visiting Donovan Tito caught sight of a large plane and said, "Here comes Mr. Churchill."

On August 12, Tito called on Churchill, who writes: "He wore a magnificent gold and blue uniform which was very tight under the collar and singularly unsuited to the blazing heat. The uniform had been given him by the Russians, and, as I was afterwards informed, the gold lace came from the United States." [74]

Churchill says that after he showed Tito Wilson's war room, he asked where Tito's forces could cooperate in opening up a port in Istria so that supplies could be sent in by sea and not only by air. Tito replied that, though German opposition had increased and accordingly Yugoslav losses had mounted, he would certainly favor an operation against the Istrian peninsula in which Yugoslav forces would join.

The conversation then shifted to politics. Tito said that reconciliation was unlikely between him and Mihailović, whose power, he added, rested on German and Bulgarian help. Churchill declared that the King should not be let down, to which Tito replied that he understood British obli-

Prime Minister Churchill and Marshal Tito in Naples, August 1944. *Foto-Tanjug, Belgrade*

gations toward King Peter but was not able to do anything in that regard until after the war.

Tito assured Churchill that he had no desire to introduce the Communist system into Yugoslavia. The Russian mission with the Partisans, Tito said, had also spoken against the idea. When Churchill asked Tito whether he would make public his statement about communism in Yugoslavia, Tito demurred, saying it might seem to have been forced upon him.

After his first talk with Tito, Churchill sent him a memorandum dated August 12,[75] expressing the British desire to see a united Yugoslav government, in which all Yugoslavs resisting the enemy were represented. He also hoped for a "reconciliation between the Serbian people and the National Liberation Movement," a phrase to which Tito subsequently objected, protesting that the Partisan movement was not divorced from the Serbian people. Churchill also declared that the British would continue and if possible increase the supply of war materials to the Yugoslav forces now that the Yugoslav government and the Partisans had reached an agreement. Referring to the Communist issue, he said that "in return" the British expected Tito to announce that he would not impose Communism on the country or use his army to influence the free expression of the will of the people regarding the future regime of the country. He then suggested that Tito meet King Peter in Yugoslavia, to which Tito later replied that the moment had not yet come. Churchill further warned Tito not to use Allied supplies for fratricidal strife.

Earlier in the day, Wilson's chief of staff, General Sir James Gammell, raised with Tito certain strategic plans regarding Istria, and Tito "grumbled at these proposals" in a letter to Churchill dated August 13. What was involved was more than strategy: Tito was anxious to be associated with the future administration of Istria. In their meeting on August 13, Churchill told Tito that the U.S. Government was against territorial changes in time of war and suggested that the best solution might be an Allied military government for the area. In the evening, Churchill entertained Tito at dinner. Šubašić, who had preceded Churchill to Italy, took part in the Churchill-Tito conversations of August 13, though not in the initial one on August 12.

Churchill reported on his talks in identical telegrams to Roosevelt and Stalin on August 14. He said in part:

I told both the Yugoslav leaders that we had no thought but that they should combine their resources so as to weld the Yugoslav people into one instrument in the struggle against the Germans. Our aim was to promote the establishment of a stable and independent Yugoslavia, and the creation of a united Yugoslav Government was a step towards this end.

The two leaders reached a satisfactory agreement on a number of practical questions.

Roosevelt replied on the same day, congratulating Churchill on the prospects of success "in bringing together the opposing factions in Yugoslavia which could bring to an end the civil war in that country and be of assistance to us in the rapidly approaching defeat of the Nazis." Stalin's reply was a mere acknowledgment: "I have received your communication about the meeting with Marshal Tito and Prime Minister Šubašić. Thank you for the information." [76]

Eden says [77] that Churchill was "somewhat disenchanted by his meeting with Tito." In a memorandum to Eden on August 31 Churchill said that a great responsibility would rest on England after the war when all the arms in Yugoslavia—supplied by the West—would be in Tito's possession and could be used by him to subjugate the country. Eden noted on the memorandum that the Foreign Office hardly needed a reminder of this danger and that, in spite of its warnings, the Prime Minister himself had persistently "pushed Tito."

Replying to Churchill, Eden wrote that British policy had been dictated on grounds of short-term military expediency rather than long-term political interest. "It was for this reason," he said, "that we for so long deprecated the policy of forcing the King to break with Mihailović before we had secured the position of the anti-communist Serbs in post-war Yugoslavia, and that we have for some time past been trying to bridge the gulf between the King and the Yugoslav Government-in-Exile on the one hand and the Partisans on the other, in the hope that by securing a united front we could prevent the arms we are giving to Tito from being used against his opponents when the day of liberation comes."

Murphy, on the other hand, reported to the State Department that Churchill had expressed to him satisfaction with his talks with Tito. Murphy said that while he did not participate in British-Yugoslav military and political discussions, he had had several conversations with Tito and his deputy commander in chief, General Sreten Žujović. "Tito was enthusiastic in his reference to United States and the part Americans could play in the reconstruction of Yugoslavia," Murphy said. "I found him direct and able. . . . He spoke of democracy and the Four Freedoms. He welcomed members of American Mission now assigned to his headquarters. He gives every indication of a desire to cooperate." [78]

Tito together with Šubašić, Stevenson and Maclean returned to Vis by plane on August 15. There, Tito and Šubašić continued their talks.

The State Department had strong reservations regarding the Churchill-Tito conversations. Its doubts were expressed in a memorandum that Matthews, deputy director of the Office of European Affairs, sent to Hull on August 18.[79] What troubled the Department most were reports that American arms were being used by Tito's forces "to kill the Serbs," and it cabled Murphy that the United States disapproved of any plan for building up Tito's forces at the expense of the Serbs. Murphy replied that reports of Tito's actions against the Serbs were exaggerated, in the view of "competent American officers" at Caserta. (Reading Maclean's *Eastern Approaches,* in which he described the Partisan campaign against the Četniks in Serbia, one wonders how well informed the "competent American officers" at AFHQ were.)

In this connection, it should be noted that in the late spring of 1944, Allied Force Headquarters and Middle East Headquarters each published a survey on Yugoslavia for official use. Both had a decidedly anti-Četnik and pro-Partisan character. The AFHQ survey was entitled *The Četniks,* and the other, *The National Liberation Movement of Yugo-*

slavia. The antecedents of these handbooks and their subsequent use are not completely clear, but it is likely that any unwitting reader would have found it difficult to remain uninfluenced by them.

On August 20, Šubašić returned from Vis, spending a few hours in Bari with the British before flying on to London. Norden, who saw him only for several minutes, reported to the State Department that the conversations at Vis and at Bari were conducted by the British and the Yugoslavs alone and that no invitation to participate had been extended to U.S. representatives.[80] He relayed the information given him by Ambassador Stevenson that during the Šubašić-Tito discussions at Vis, Tito had agreed to present to the National Committee of Liberation a draft plan for a "single Yugoslav state authority": a merger of Šubašić's Government-in-Exile and Tito's National Committee of Liberation. This, it will be recalled, had already been agreed upon during Šubašić's previous visit to Vis exactly two months earlier. Most other questions at the August meeting at Vis were raised by the Partisans and aimed at obtaining international recognition of the Partisans as the sole Yugoslav military and political force at the expense of the Royal Government and the Četniks.

Norden added in his telegram to the Department that Ministers Kosanović and Cankar, who had accompanied Šubašić to Vis, expressed regret that there had been so little contact with American officials during the last days. "Cankar remarked that everything would have been different in such a case but he hedged when I pressed him for his meaning. . . . Kosanović expressed a desire to be named Ambassador to the United States." (He succeeded in getting this job eventually.) Norden found Šubašić "tired and distraught." The British expressed considerable optimism concerning the trend of events, Norden reported. They felt that the negotiation between Šubašić and Tito of a tentative agreement on a "single Yugoslav state authority" was a definite step forward. Šubašić, on the other hand, was pessimistic after his arduous meetings with the Partisans. At the Bari stopover, Šubašić met with Adam Pribičević, who had arrived a week earlier from Mihailović's headquarters and was thus able to inform the Prime Minister of conditions in the area controlled by the Četniks.

Still another aspect of Churchill's discussions with Tito troubled the State Department deeply. The Partisans appeared to take it for granted that the Italian province of Venezia Giulia would be ceded to Yugoslavia.[81] Murphy was advised by the Department on August 26 that "it is not the position of this Government, nor of the British Government so far as we know, that the Yugoslav claim to a part or all of this region should be acknowledged at this stage." [82] Earlier (August 9), Murphy had been told that the United States believed that Allied military government should be extended to all metropolitan Italian territory within the 1939 frontiers. Any other procedure would prejudice the final disposition of territories and settlement of the frontiers.

HUNTINGTON, NORDEN AND MURPHY IN VIS— PATTERSON APPOINTED AMBASSADOR

In the middle of July, an advance party headed by Lieutenant Timothy Pfeiffer, USN, left Bari by ship for Vis. Its task was to prepare a base for the American military mission. Pfeiffer found a villa which was to be the headquarters of Colonel Ellery Huntington, who arrived on August 14 accompanied by Major Stafford Reid. There the Americans took their

The American military mission with Tito and his dog at Vis in August 1944. Standing, left to right: Henry Lichtenberger, Temple Fielding, Ellery Huntington, Alex Vuchinich. Seated, left to right: Tim Pfeiffer and Stafford Reid. *Courtesy of T. A. Pfeiffer*

place alongside Maclean's British mission and Korneyev's Soviet mission. The three major Allies now had separate representation at Partisan headquarters.

At the end of August, Tito received two American Foreign Service officers in Vis, first Norden, then, a few days later, Murphy. Norden learned from Tito that the Partisans would soon launch an attack in Serbia which, Tito implied, would be directed at both Germans and Četniks.[83] Tito also told Norden that the plan for "a single Yugoslav state authority" was premature. He expressed a strong wish for American economic and especially technical aid. At the same time, Tito declared that the attitude hitherto shown toward his movement had been a great disappointment, and he warned that the Western powers should proceed carefully lest the Yugoslav people turn against them, which he said was already the case with respect to the British (a puzzling remark after all the British had done for him).

Murphy, who had been reassigned to Eisenhower's staff in London and had been invited by Tito to visit him, asked and received the State Department's permission to go to Vis. He writes [84] that the "American Government did not want to give even the appearance of official relations with Tito and his Provisional Government, so I was instructed to make this a personal visit and to go unaccompanied by anyone on my staff; but a B-26 plane was assigned for my trip."

Murphy went to Vis on August 31 and received red-carpet treatment. He had lunch with Tito, some of his associates and members of the Soviet military mission. Aboard a yacht after lunch without the Russians, Tito talked at length about several matters. He said that Soviet forces would not enter Yugoslavia but would leave it to the Partisans to deal with Serbia; that Yugoslavia would insist on having not only Istria but also parts of Greece, trusting that the Allies could afford to be liberal in view of Yugoslavia's sacrifices; that he stood for a liberal and democratic regime; and that he hoped for economic support from the United States.

Murphy writes that he got the impression that Tito "was more a national patriot than an international Communist. He dryly mentioned that the Russian pilot who had 'rescued' him when Tito left his mountain headquarters to go to Vis was flying an American plane from an American-controlled airfield in Italy according to arrangements set up by British officers."

Murphy says that he did not discuss any definite political matters with Tito because "the American Government still had no Yugoslav policy."

Although this may have been true, it was also a fact that, in the spring of 1944 the U.S. role in Yugoslav affairs had increased greatly. The U.S.

15th Air Force based in Bari had become a powerful striking force in the Balkans, and aerial resupply was increasingly handled by the Americans. Tito and the Partisans were well aware of this.

Close Allied-Partisan cooperation was also demonstrated by the response to Tito's request in August that the Allied command evacuate some 900 wounded Partisans who were surrounded by German forces on Mount Durmitor. Twenty-five DC-3s with fighter escort landed on very difficult terrain and airlifted the wounded Partisans to Italy.[85]

The military operation in Serbia which Tito had mentioned to Norden was code-named "Ratweek." It was based on a plan conceived by the British military mission for the harassment of the German retreat through coordinated attacks on communications by the Partisans and the Balkan Air Force. The plan was approved by Wilson and thereafter also by Tito. The operation began on September 1. Yugoslavia was divided into sections, each under a Partisan commander accompanied by a British officer who would specify the targets and arrange for the necessary air and sea support.[86]

From the point of view of Allied policy, this offensive against the Germans was troublesome because the Partisans used it simultaneously to attack the Četniks in Serbia. The Partisan strategy aimed at liquidating the Četniks or at least evicting them from Serbia so that Partisan and not Četnik troops would welcome the Red Army at the Rumanian border. Control of Serbia, moreover, had been the Partisans' goal for some time because they knew that Serbia and Belgrade were indispensable to control over the whole of Yugoslavia. Now, with the deterioration of the German position, the weakening of the Četniks and the approach of the Russians, the Partisans' objective seemed within reach and they struck for it.

Meanwhile, Tito stalled on his agreement with Šubašić. At the end of August, Šubašić had cabled Tito that the time had come to form a government of national unity. Tito evaded the question, referring to it as "unimportant" at a time when the Partisans were fighting "exceptionally hard battles" against the Germans.[87] Eden supported Šubašić's request for the formation of a coalition. In the absence of Churchill, who was in Quebec, he cabled Tito on September 11 that he could not agree that the matter was not of immediate importance. On the contrary, inasmuch as the occupying armies might be forced to evacuate the greater part if not the whole of Yugoslavia in the near future, it was "of the utmost importance that immediate steps should be taken to form a united government."

Eden followed this up with instructions to the British Ambassador in

Moscow to discuss the situation with Molotov and to ask the Soviet Government to use its influence with Tito in the same sense. "Tito, however, had no liking for the growing pressure," Eden writes. There is no doubt that Tito wanted to wait until he was in Belgrade and in a commanding position.

By late summer 1944, the United States had not only a military mission at Partisan headquarters in Vis, but also approximately ten OSS missions in Partisan territory on the mainland, most of which Colonel Huntington visited either before or after his arrival at Vis. On September 5, Alexander C. Kirk suceeded Murphy as political adviser on the staff of the Supreme Allied Commander, Mediterranean Theater, in Caserta.

The American diplomatic representation to the Yugoslav Government-in-Exile was confused. Schoenfeld was Chargé in London; in Cairo, Ambassador MacVeagh, assisted by Counselor Harold Shantz, continued to exercise certain responsibilities with regard to Yugoslavia even though the Yugoslav Government-in-Exile was no longer there. The British Government strongly believed that the United States and other Allied governments should regularize their position by appointing an official representative to the Yugoslav Government in London in order to "strengthen the position" of that government internationally. It approached the United States Government on that subject on September 15. [88] The U.S. itself had already felt that changes were necessary, and on September 20, Richard C. Patterson was designated Ambassador to the Yugoslav Government in London. Eventually, Shantz, the Counselor in Cairo, was transferred to London to be Patterson's deputy, and Schoenfeld was shifted to other duties.

11

THE U.S. SENDS AN AIR CREW RESCUE UNIT
TO ČETNIK TERRITORY

In Četnik territory, devoid of Allied liaison officers since the end of May, a number of American airmen were waiting to be evacuated. Allied air raids had increased sharply in the spring of 1944, and the Ploesti oil fields in Rumania were a frequent target. Many American fliers returning from missions had to bail out of their disabled aircraft. By early July, more than one hundred of these airmen were in the area under Mihailović's control.

According to Fotić,[1] Mihailović had advised Allied Force Headquarters, Caserta, of this fact, but had received no reply. Since he was no longer in contact with his own Government, which had just been recast, he radioed Fotić on July 12 (after Fotić was no longer Ambassador) that these American airmen who had been rescued by the Četniks would like to be evacuated to rejoin their units. "I am of the opinion," Mihailović said, "that the American Air Ministry should take the necessary steps, and it would be still better if the Americans alone took charge of the evacuation, which may easily be performed by planes landing at our airdrome during the night." Fotić recounts that he gave this information to Colonel Goodfellow of the OSS.

These messages, which Mihailović sent to General Wilson's headquarters in Caserta and to former Ambassador Fotić in Washington, aroused a great deal of debate. The command of the U.S. 15th Air Force wanted to rescue the airmen but the British thought it would be a mistake to send any kind of a mission back to Mihailović.

As a solution, agreed to by Wilson, a new organization was created called the Air Crew Rescue Unit, also known as the "Halyard Team." It was not to be a "mission"; its sole task was the evacuation of airmen.

Allied communications with Mihailović's headquarters had been one-sided since the end of May—he transmitted but nobody replied. The military situation in Yugoslavia was fluid, and, although Mihailović spoke of an airfield, it was decided first to determine the exact location of the stranded American airmen in order to plan their evacuation.

Lieutenant Musulin, who only a few weeks earlier had left Mihailović's headquarters with the last of the British mission, was selected to head the rescue unit and to parachute into an area approximately fifty miles southwest of Belgrade. He was accompanied by two other Americans, Master Sergeant Mike Rayachich and a radio operator, Arthur Jibilian. They dropped into Četnik territory on August 2.[2]

The Halyard Team soon established contact with Allied Force Head-quarters in Italy and was able to report that the Pranjani airstrip, from which the British mission had departed at the end of May, was operational. The first American planes arrived on August 9. One of them brought in Captain Nicholas Lalich, who was to take over the Air Crew Rescue Unit upon Musulin's departure from Yugoslavia at the end of August.

On August 10, fourteen American transport planes escorted by six Spitfires evacuated about 250 airmen, among them several British fliers. Evacuated also were a few Frenchmen and Russians freed by Četnik troops near the mines at Bor in northeast Serbia, and twenty to thirty Italians who had joined the Četniks after Italy's surrender. The whole operation lasted ten hours. Several Yugoslavs went along too, to join Dr. Topalović, who had departed for Italy with the British mission at the end of May. They were Adam Pribičević, leader of the Independent Democratic Party; Vladimir Belajčić, a Supreme Court judge before the war; Ivan Kovač, and Captain Zvonimir Vučković. Together with Topalović, this mission had the task of gaining political and military support for Mihailović's movement. It was unsuccessful in reversing Allied policy, which had permanently shifted to supplying only the Partisans. By ironic coincidence, this Četnik mission arrived in Italy while Tito was there, about to begin his discussions with Churchill.

A U.S. INTELLIGENCE MISSION JOINS
MIHAILOVIĆ'S HEADQUARTERS

It has been noted earlier that after the British decided to withdraw all liaison officers from Četnik territory, the OSS proposed on March 2, 1944, to send an American intelligence mission to Mihailović. A briefing paper prepared for Under Secretary Stettinius before he went to London in April stated: "The President has approved a plan to send into Mihailović territory an American intelligence group, though our liaison officers with Mihailović were withdrawn with the British Mission." [3]

Martin reports [4] that OSS in Italy planned a substantial mission—forty men divided into six teams of six with four auxiliary members. These men were apparently selected and subsequently briefed in a villa near Brindisi. Donovan wrote Eisenhower on March 31 that the OSS was placing intelligence officers with Mihailović for the purpose of "infiltrating agents into Austria and Germany." [5] Later in the year, as it will be seen, the chief of the smaller U.S. intelligence group that eventually joined the Četniks met with German authorities in Yugoslavia twice and attempted to arrange for the early surrender of German forces in the Balkans. Thus, the evidence suggests that this was solely an intelligence mission aimed at the German war effort, although former Partisan leaders to this day bitterly consider that it was intended rather as support tendered to Mihailović *in extremis*. When Churchill heard of the U.S. decision, he was sufficiently perturbed to cable the President on April 6, pointing out that the British were in the process of withdrawing their missions from Mihailović and had been "pressing King Peter to clear himself of this millstone which is dragging him down in his own country and works only to the assistance of the enemy." He continued:

If, at this very time, an American Mission arrives at Mihailović's headquarters it will show throughout the Balkans a complete contrariety of action between Britain and the United States. The Russians will certainly draw all their weight on Tito's side which we are backing to the full. Thus we shall get altogether out of step. I hope and trust this may be avoided. [6]

Roosevelt replied on April 8:

My thought in authorizing an O.S.S. Mission to the Mihailović Area was to obtain intelligence and the mission was to have no political functions whatever. In view however of your expressed opinion that there might be misunderstanding by our Allies and others, I have directed that the contemplated mission be not sent.

The men assembled in Italy were thereupon disbanded, yet preparation for a mission on a smaller scale proceeded.

Lieutenant Colonel Robert H. McDowell, the Army intelligence officer in Cairo selected to head the reduced mission, was placed on temporary duty with OSS Bari.

It took several weeks to get his group under way, however. Only on its seventh flight over Serbia was the mission, which included Captain John Milodragovich, Lieutenant Ellsworth Kramer and a radio operator, able to establish contact with Mihailović's headquarters. It landed on August 26 at Pranjani.

Churchill, who had been assured by Roosevelt in April that the intelligence mission would not be sent, learned indirectly of the arrival of American officers in Mihailović's territory. On September 1 he sent Roosevelt a sharply worded message in which he referred to the President's previous commitment:

We are endeavoring to give Tito the support and, of course, if the United States backed Mihailović complete chaos will ensue. I was rather hoping things were going to get a bit smoother in these parts but if we each back different sides we lay the scene for a fine civil war. General Donovan is running a strong Mihailović lobby just when we have persuaded King Peter to break decisively with him and when many of the Četniks are being rallied under Tito's National Army of Liberation. The only chance of saving the King is the unity between the Prime Minister, the Ban of Croatia, and Tito . . . .[7]

On September 3, Roosevelt replied:

The mission of OSS is my mistake. I did not check with my previous action of last April 8. I am directing Donovan to withdraw his mission.

The mission, however, did not leave Yugoslavia until November 1.

McDowell had arrived in Četnik territory at a momentous time. The Red Army was nearing the Yugoslav-Rumanian border, and reached it on September 6. Only Četnik units were there to make contact with the Soviet forces. The Partisans, however, were poised to evict the Četniks from all of Serbia.

Mihailović's arms supply was extremely limited. No Allied help had reached him for almost a year. There was a fleeting possibility of obtaining arms when Nedić, the puppet Serbian Prime Minister, seeing Germany's power diminish, made contact with Mihailović through intermediaries in August.

A meeting between the two took place in Ražana near Užice on August 20.[8] According to Clissold,[9] the initiative came from Nedić, and Mihailović was most reluctant, but Kalabić, one of the Četnik commanders, arranged for them to meet. Mihailović was at first very condescending but showed more interest as Nedić played up to him.

The German special envoy, Neubacher, also speaks of a Mihailović-

Nedić meeting, saying that the two met in a dark room so that neither could prove to the other that they had met. Clissold and Neubacher agree that the question of arms for 50,000 Četniks was discussed. Neubacher says that Nedić reported the request to the Germans without saying that he had met Mihailović. Having heard about the meeting, Neubacher asked Nedić whether it had taken place. Nedić replied that he thought that it was Mihailović whom he had met but that he "could be wrong." [10]

Nedić's unhappy role deserves a word. That he collaborated with the Germans is of course a fact. Yet to compare him with Quisling in Norway, who paved the way for German occupation by conniving with the Germans even before their attack, is inaccurate; he did no such thing. An analogy with General Pétain would be more apt. There is even some evidence that in 1943 Nedić secretly sent a declaration of loyalty to King Peter.[11]

KING PETER DROPS MIHAILOVIĆ, WHO ORDERS MOBILIZATION

Ever since the Šubašić Government had been formed early in July—with Šubašić himself Minister of the Army, Navy and Air Force—it had been wrestling with the problem of what to do with Mihailović in his remaining capacity as chief of staff of the Supreme Command, Yugoslav Army of the Homeland.

In the view of Šubašić, Mihailović's usefulness, whatever it may have been, had come to an end. Several schemes were advanced to remove him from his command, including the appointment of a successor who might be able to work things out with Tito. Two Royalist generals, Glišić and Ristić, were under consideration.[12] But this solution was discarded when it became clear that the Četnik-Partisan conflict transcended the matter of personalities and that no new leader of the Četniks could bring them and the Partisans together. For if a new general were amenable to the Četniks he would be anathema to the Partisans, and if he were sympathetic to the Partisans he would not be accepted by the Četniks.

It was therefore decided to try another tack. Upon the recommendation of the Šubašić Government, a royal decree of August 29 dissolved the Supreme Command, thereby abolishing the post Mihailović occupied, and designated Tito as the sole leader of the resistance forces in Yugoslavia. In addition, Mihailović was put on the retired list.

Mihailović, however, had already taken a step in another direction. Knowing that time was running out for him, and in view of the Red Army's approach to the Yugoslav border, he issued an order for general mobilization to take effect on September 1. It read: "In the name of Peter II, in accordance with our great coalition, and on the basis of the authority vested in me, I proclaim as of zero hour September 1, 1944, total mobilization of the whole nation against all enemies. . . ."

Mihailović had always hoped for an uprising that would coincide with the landing of British and American forces in Yugoslavia. While the situation was different now, he thought that the Russians would appreciate his help in driving the Germans out. After all, neither he nor the Government-in-Exile had ever taken an anti-Soviet position. He had fought the Communists internally, but as late as January 1944, during the Saint Sava congress, a message of solidarity had been sent by the Četniks to the Soviet Union and Stalin.

Colonel McDowell stated later to the Commission of Inquiry in the Case of Draža Mihailović: [13]

When the undersigned reached Mihailović headquarters in August 1944, a general Nationalist mobilization had already been ordered. The undersigned was shown the plans and orders issued for an all-out attack on Axis forces and, along with the other U.S. officers, personally witnessed the troop dispositions made for this offensive. The evidence was unmistakable that General Mihailović had disposed his forces properly for a major effort against the German garrisons, depots, and lines of communication, but in doing this had been obliged to leave his rear and left flank exposed to attack on the part of major Partisan concentrations which only recently had been attacking the Nationalists. Insofar as the small group of American officers were able to cover the front and make observations, during September the Nationalist forces engaged German and Bulgarian forces to the extent of their capability and equipment. Axis movements were thoroughly disrupted and considerable quantities of munitions and prisoners were taken.[14]

Whether or not these statements were somewhat exaggerated—it must be taken into account that McDowell gave his deposition at the time Mihailović was being tried for treason by the Partisans—there is evidence that certain Četnik actions against the Germans and Bulgarians took place early in September 1944.

Also early in September, the Partisans launched their attack against the Četniks in western Serbia. What had happened to the Partisans in previous years—that they found themselves fighting the Germans and the internal enemy at the same time—now happened to the Četniks. While engaged with the Germans and Bulgarians they were the target of a furious Partisan attack.

Another blow fell on September 12, when King Peter, in a broadcast

from London, gave the people of Yugoslavia the gist of the royal decree
of August 29 dissolving Mihailović's command. The King did not mention Mihailović directly, but he called on "all Serbs, Croats and Slovenes
to unite and join the National Liberation Army under the leadership of
Marshal Tito." He told his people that the Šubašić Government had "with
my full knowledge and approval concluded a substantial and advantageous agreement with this our national army, which is unanimously recognized, supported, and assisted by our great Allies—Great Britain, the
Soviet Union, and the United States." [15] He also proclaimed:

> None . . . who remain deaf to this appeal shall escape the brand of traitor
> before his people and before history. By this message I strongly condemn the
> misuse of the name of the King and the authority of the Crown by which an
> attempt has been made to justify collaboration with the enemy and to provoke
> discord amongst our fighting people in the very gravest days of their history,
> thus solely profiting the enemy.

Although the King did not refer to Mihailović by name, it was clear
whom he meant. He writes [16] that both the British and Yugoslav Governments had insisted that Tito's name be stressed; after three meetings with
Churchill, all he could do was "to tone down the presentation of Tito
as a lone hero, and say not a word against Mihailović, and to shorten the
original draft."

The speech had an immediate and devastating effect on the morale of
Mihailović and the Četniks. For more than three years they had fought
for one thing above all: to save the monarchy and to return their King to
a liberated country. They felt they had done no wrong, that their goal
justified the means they had chosen. Now the King, in so many words,
branded them traitors. Many left Mihailović after that broadcast. Those
who stayed on with him continued to fight less for the monarchy than
to save the country from Communism, but above all out of loyalty to
Mihailović.

In these circumstances, the Četniks were forced to abandon all anti-
German actions in order to defend themselves against the Partisans. In
the middle of September, the Partisans overran Mihailović's headquarters
near Pranjani and although the general escaped with a few hundred
Četniks to northeastern Bosnia, his documents apparently fell into Partisan hands. The British liaison officer who accompanied the Partisans
was asked by AFHQ Caserta to submit a full report immediately. He was
warned that it was an essential element of Allied policy that arms sent
to Tito were not for the purpose of fighting Četniks unless the latter

were actively preventing Partisan forces from reaching legitimate military objectives or were actively collaborating with the enemy.[17]

Two Partisan forces, under Koča Popović and Peko Dapčević, controlled considerable areas of Serbia and Macedonia by the end of September even before the Red Army entered Yugoslavia. Popović was advancing through southern and eastern Serbia and Dapčevic through western Serbia toward Belgrade.

After the Red Army crossed over into Yugoslavia on October 1, some Četnik units—Partisan units had not yet reached the border area—offered to collaborate with the Russians. While there was a very limited fraternization in early October, this practice soon ended, and Četniks were handed over by the Russians to the Partisans. One of Mihailović's commanders, Dragutin Keserović, barely escaped being turned over on October 14. In the same action, Lieutenant Kramer of McDowell's mission was arrested and sent to Bulgaria, where he was later released.

TITO RESTRICTS BRITISH AND
AMERICAN LIAISON OFFICERS

In the midst of Allied-Partisan cooperation during operation Ratweek, relations suddenly deteriorated between the British and Americans on the one hand, and the Partisans on the other. Liaison officers with various units noticed that early in September, almost from one day to the next, the atmosphere between them and their Partisan counterparts became colder and more businesslike. An OSS report from Bari dated September 20 conjectured that "the motive behind Tito's move is his desire to curtail and control American and British military representation in the country now that he believes the civil war is all but in the bag and now that British and American supplies are no longer needed." [18]

On September 23 an order was issued by Tito declaring that members of the British and American military missions accredited to Tito's headquarters would not be permitted to circulate beyond corps headquarters. Kirk at AFHQ told the State Department that the general interpretation in Caserta was that the order was issued to exclude any British or American witnesses to the civil war in Yugoslavia.[19] American military authorities took strong exception to Tito's order and retaliated by canceling supply drops and the flights evacuating wounded Partisans. Donovan informed the Secretary of State of these measures on September 24.

To complicate the situation, differences arose between the British and the Americans. Lieutenant Colonel Živan Knežević, military attaché, and Captain Borislav Todorović,[20] assistant military attaché at the Yugoslav Embassy in Washington, had followed Ambassador Fotić in refusing to recognize the Šubašić Government in July. They requested the U.S. War Department to transport them to Mihailović territory if possible. Inasmuch as Mihailović had given particular assistance to downed American airmen, the United States attached considerable importance to acceding to the request. After General Wilson's consent had been obtained, the two Yugoslavs left the United States in the latter part of August and went to Bari, where Allied Supreme Headquarters was to arrange their transport to Yugoslavia.

It appears that Wilson's headquarters had second thoughts on this matter. The British political adviser, Macmillan, in particular, was opposed to sending Knežević and Todorović to Yugoslavia because they allegedly had a long history of political subversion and, in his opinion, were certain to make difficulties once there. Macmillan argued that "the King and Tito would be very suspicious of Allied motives in sending two such people to Mihailović." The British thereupon consulted both Tito and the Yugoslav Government in London, and an agreement was worked out not to return any Yugoslavs to Yugoslavia without the Šubašić Government's prior consent. Kirk countered that these objections should have been raised earlier, while the two men were still in the United States.

What bothered the State Department most was that these consultations had converted a military transaction into a political problem. "It could well have been handled as an arrangement for sending to General Mihailović two Yugoslav officers desiring to fight the enemy in exchange for the 225 Americans who were being returned from Mihailović territory," the State Department said in a telegram to Kirk on September 23. It added:

We have no commitments and are under no obligations requiring clearance with Marshal Tito in matters of this kind. . . . This is another example of the heavy political weighting of all Yugoslav military matters, demonstrating again the advantages, from the point of view of the American policy of keeping out of Yugoslav politics, of restricting military questions to their proper level.[21]

By the time the telegram was sent, the military situation had evolved to such an extent that there was justified doubt in Washington "whether there is now a Mihailović controlled area of sufficient consistency, with facilities for communication."

Knežević and Todorović returned to the United States after having been refused permission to enlist in the United States Army.

TITO "LEVANTS" TO MOSCOW

As the Russian troops neared the Rumanian-Yugoslav border, Tito told General Korneyev, the Soviet mission chief, early in September that he would like to visit Moscow for the purpose of coordinating Partisan operations with those of the Red Army. On the one hand, he wanted the Soviets, as he himself said later,[22] to enter Yugoslavia "to help our units liberate Serbia and Belgrade." On the other, he wanted the Red Army to enter Yugoslavia under agreement with him and only after the expulsion of the Četniks from the frontier area so that the Soviets would find Partisan and not Četnik troops at the border. However, Tito did not breathe a word about his plans to the British and American mission chiefs in Vis.

Wilson writes[23] that he had anticipated Tito's wish to be closer to Belgrade now that the Russians were about to enter Yugoslav territory. He therefore asked Tito to keep him informed of his immediate plans and to take Maclean's mission along in case he moved his headquarters from Vis. "Tito assured me of his cooperation and agreed to keep me informed of his intended movements," Wilson says. However, not until October 13, after his return to Yugoslavia from Moscow, did Tito send a message to Wilson, saying that his departure from Vis had been dictated by military necessity and that previous experience had shown the need to maintain secrecy regarding his movements. Even then he did not tell Wilson where he had gone. His message went on to affirm that his relations with Britain and the United States remained the same as ever.

The Yugoslavs said afterward that the Russians, concurring in Tito's plans, had asked for the greatest secrecy. The Russians in turn said that it was Tito's wish to keep his departure secret from the British and Americans. Whatever the real story was, Tito left Vis late in the evening of September 18 from a British airfield which was occasionally used by Soviet-piloted DC-3s based in Bari. Tito departed in one of these accompanied by two members of his staff (Bakić and Milutinović) and by Korneyev, the Soviet mission chief. A few hours later he landed at Craiova, Rumania. On September 21 he flew from Craiova to Moscow. (Rumania had denounced the Tripartite Pact on August 23 and declared war on Germany two days later.)

The British and American missions in Vis looked for Tito everywhere. They were told he was sick, busy, walking, etc. It soon turned out that he certainly was not in Vis, yet nobody in the West knew where he was. On October 11, during Churchill's and Eden's visit in Moscow, Molotov told Eden that Tito had been in Moscow. Eden says: "The Communist had homed to his lair, which nearly became his cage." [24]

Eden's telegram to the Foreign Office about his talk with Molotov reported that he had told the Soviet Foreign Minister:

We took the strongest objection to Marshal Tito's behavior and to the fact that we had not been told about the visit. If he had had the courtesy to tell us that he was going to Moscow we should have wished him bon voyage. . . . Molotov hurriedly put all the blame on Marshal Tito. He said he was a peasant and did not understand anything about politics. . . . I told Molotov that he must understand the effect that events of this character must have on our relations. There were many people in England who said that the Soviet Government was pursuing its own policy in the Balkans without the slightest regard to us . . . . More explanations about ignorance of Yugoslav peasants followed. . . .

On the following day, Churchill sent a telegram from Moscow to Harry Hopkins in which he said:

Tito, having lived under our protection for three or four months at Vis, suddenly levanted, leaving no address, but keeping sentries over his cave to make out that he was still there. He then proceeded to Moscow, where he conferred, and yesterday M. Molotov confessed this fact to Mr. Eden. The Russians attribute this graceless behaviour to Tito's suspicious peasant upbringing, and say that they did not tell us out of respect for his wish for secrecy.[25]

The American Ambassador in Moscow, Harriman, had reported on September 30 that on the previous day an agreement was reached between the Soviet command and the Yugoslav National Committee of Liberation permitting passage of Soviet troops through Yugoslav territory for the purpose of developing operations against the enemy. Yet Harriman did not then know that Tito himself had headed the Partisan delegation to Moscow. The Soviet-Partisan agreement also included a clause providing that Yugoslav civilian authorities would function in areas freed by the Russians and that the Red Army would leave Yugoslavia upon completion of its military operations against the Germans.[26]

The Šubašić Government knew nothing about the Russian-Partisan agreement; the Soviets did not tell them nor did the Partisans.

Much has been written about Tito's first encounter with Stalin. He had of course been in Moscow before but had never met Stalin. When he left Moscow in 1940 he was the secretary of a relatively unimportant and illegal Communist Party who did not rate a personal interview with the powerful General Secretary of the Communist Party of the Soviet Union.

This time it was different. He now returned as the leader of a most successful movement, a marshal commanding a national army, and as the prospective head of a government. He was put up lavishly and was almost immediately received by Stalin, who embraced him vigorously. The talks went quite well considering the fact that Tito, while treating Stalin with respect, left no doubt that he had come to negotiate, not to take orders. Stalin did not like this, but he raised no objection when Tito insisted that his troops, upon the entry of the Red Army into Yugoslavia, would not come under Soviet command.

It seems also that Stalin favored the restoration of the Yugoslav monarchy, but Tito was uncompromising. As they were talking, Molotov came into the room holding a telegram which supposedly stated that the British had landed in Yugoslavia. "That's impossible," Tito said, and when Stalin asked what he would do if the British really landed, Tito replied: "We shall offer determined resistance." [27]

What were the chances for such a landing? After the Allied advance in Italy had halted at the Pisa-Rimini line in June, a new directive by the Combined Chiefs of Staff dated July 2 gave Alexander the signal to resume operations. By early August his forces reached the Gothic Line. The attack on the line itself began on August 26.

After the successful landings in southern France in the middle of August, the necessity of any move of Alexander's armies westward into France upon breaking the Gothic Line appeared to have been removed. Churchill was therefore eager to pin Roosevelt down on an eastward drive through Yugoslavia. On August 28 he cabled Roosevelt:

I have never forgotten your talks to me at Teheran about Istria, and I am sure that the arrival of a powerful army in Trieste and Istria in four or five weeks would have an effect far outside purely military values. Tito's people will be awaiting us in Istria.[28]

Roosevelt was hesitant in his reply: "It is my thought that we should press the German Army in Italy vigorously . . . and suspend decision of the future use of General Wilson's armies until the results of his campaign are better known. . . . We can renew our Tehran talk about Trieste and Istria at 'Octagon' [second Quebec Conference in September 1944]."

Churchill did not wish to wait. On August 31 he cabled back: "This employment [British 8th and American 5th Army under Alexander] can only take the form of a movement first to Istria and Trieste and ultimately upon Vienna." Roosevelt, however, answered: "It seems to me that

American forces should be used to the westward, but I am completely open-minded about this. . . ."

There is no doubt that, whereas up to the middle of 1944 the British were guided solely by military considerations, political and diplomatic factors now played a major role in Churchill's plans for an eastward drive. The Russian advances, Stalin's failure to support the Warsaw uprising against the Germans and Tito's claims to Istria disturbed him. On the other hand, the United States, more than Britain, had a costly war in the Pacific on its hands and was determined to win in Europe quickly, not to leave too many troops there, and to move on to the Far East to finish the conflict with Japan.

THE SECOND QUEBEC CONFERENCE—
CHURCHILL AND EDEN GO TO MOSCOW

In September 1944, Churchill and Roosevelt met for the first time since the Cairo Conference in December 1943. The meeting took place in Quebec and lasted from September 11 to 16. Yugoslavia was discussed tangentially. Reviewing the military situation, Churchill said he "had always been attracted by a right-handed movement to give Germany a stab in the Adriatic armpit." His account of this review continues:

Our objective should be Vienna. If German resistance collapsed we should of course be able to reach the city more quickly and more easily. If not I had given considerable thought to aiding this movement by capturing Istria and occupying Trieste and Fiume. I had been relieved to learn that the United States Chiefs of Staff were willing to leave in the Mediterranean certain landing-craft now engaged in the attack on the South of France to provide an amphibious lift for such an operation, if this was found desirable and necessary. Another reason for this right-handed movement was the rapid encroachment of the Russians into the Balkan peninsula and the dangerous spread of Soviet influence there.[29]

This time there was no dissent from the President. With the southern France operation safely launched, the American Joint Chiefs of Staff were more sympathetic to a British amphibious landing on the Istrian peninsula. From the American point of view, such a move followed by a drive toward Vienna might have successfully skirted the controversial Balkans and brought additional pressure on Germany.

Upon conclusion of the second Quebec Conference, Roosevelt and Churchill sent Stalin a telegram summarizing military operational decisions reached during the talks. Regarding the Balkans it said: "Operations of our air forces and commando type operations will continue." [30] This was almost identical to the decision of the first Quebec Conference a year earlier.

As soon as Churchill returned to London on September 25 he prepared for a visit to Moscow inasmuch as "everything in Eastern Europe became more intense." [31] The three-month arrangement between Churchill and the Soviets regarding British-Russian responsibilities in the Balkans—never implemented—had run out.

On their way to Moscow, Churchill, Eden, Brooke and Ismay stopped in Naples, on October 6. There they discussed with Wilson and Alexander the progress of the Italian campaign and possible ways to relieve the front there, such as a sea-borne attack on the Istrian peninsula or a landing south of Fiume with a subsequent advance northward.[32]

Churchill and Eden arrived in Moscow on October 9, and Ambassador Harriman was designated by Roosevelt to participate in the British-Soviet discussions. Churchill began the first meeting as follows:

Let us settle about our affairs in the Balkans. Your armies are in Rumania and Bulgaria. We have interests, missions and agents there. Don't let us get at cross-purposes in small ways. So far as Britain and Russia are concerned, how would it do for you to have ninety per cent predominance in Rumania, for us to have ninety per cent of the say in Greece, and go fifty-fifty about Yugoslavia? [33]

Churchill describes how he scribbled the whole suggestion on a piece of paper; Stalin "made a large tick upon it" and returned it to Churchill: "It was all settled in no more time than it takes to set down." Churchill made it clear that he was thinking only of immediate wartime arrangements. The pencilled paper lay in the center of the table. Churchill asked: "Might it not be thought rather cynical if it seemed we had disposed of these issues, so fateful to millions of people, in such an offhand manner? Let us burn the paper." "No, you keep it," said Stalin.

When Tito later learned of the 50-50 agreement he was both annoyed and pleased—annoyed that it was reached behind his back, yet pleased that neither the West nor the East laid sole claim to postwar Yugoslavia.

In a telegram to Roosevelt on October 11, Churchill urged "a common mind about the Balkans, so that we may prevent civil war breaking out in several countries, when probably you and I would be in sympathy with one side and U. J. [Uncle Joe—Stalin] with the other." On the following day he cabled to Harry Hopkins that "the Balkans are in a sad tangle." (It was in that telegram that Churchill also informed Hopkins of Tito's "levanting" to Moscow.)

Churchill explained "the system of percentage" in a cable to London on October 12:

It is not intended to be more than a guide, and of course in no way commits the United States. . . . It may, however, help the United States to see how their two principal Allies feel about these regions when the picture is presented as a whole. . . . Coming to the case of Yugoslavia, the numerical symbol 50-50 is intended to be the foundation of joint action and an agreed policy between the two Powers now closely involved, so as to favour the creation of a united Yugoslavia after all elements there have been joined together to the utmost in driving out the Nazi invaders.[34]

Churchill then pointed out that this policy was intended to forestall civil strife, to produce a joint and friendly policy toward Tito and to assure that weapons furnished him were used solely against the enemy. "Such a policy, pursued in common by Britain and Soviet Russia, without any thought of special advantages to themselves, would be of real benefit," he declared.

Roosevelt cabled Harriman on October 11 that his "active interest at the present time in the Balkan area is that such steps as are practicable should be taken to insure against the Balkans getting us into a future international war." Harriman in turn reported to the President that what the British were after in Yugoslavia was to obtain Russian agreement not to take any independent action but to join with Britain and the United States in bringing the factions together and continue to work with the West "rather than independently as the Russians have in the past." He added: "Eden feels he has made some progress with Molotov." [35]

Harriman further reported that Eden and Molotov had come to an agreement that a meeting between Tito and Šubašić should be arranged at an early date and a joint British-Soviet message sent to both urging that they get together to work out their problems. "Eden hopes that we will agree to participate in this message," Harriman cabled the President, adding: "As soon as I receive it I will send it to Secretary Hull for his consideration." [36]

In a subsequent telegram, Harriman summarized talks between Churchill and Stalin regarding Yugoslavia. Churchill had explained that Britain had no "sordid interests," but wished to see her moral obligations to the Yugoslavs fulfilled, to which Stalin replied that he did not consider Britain's interests in Yugoslavia sordid. "They were very real interests, both in mineral concessions but principally because Yugoslavia had a long stretch of Mediterranean coast," Stalin was quoted as saying.

According to Harriman's report to Roosevelt, Churchill complained to

Stalin (as had Eden before to Molotov) that the latter should have informed him of Tito's trip to Russia. Stalin replied that he had said nothing because Tito had asked him to keep his visit secret. At Tito's request, Stalin had promised to give him arms, principally captured German arms but also some Russian weapons. It was agreed between Stalin and Churchill that they should work jointly in attempting to bring the Yugoslav people together for the establishment of a strong federation but that if it was found that such a federation was impracticable without continued internal strife, Serbia should be established as an independent country. Both agreed that the former solution was far more desirable. This led to a remarkable statement by Stalin on the subject of Pan-Slavism, which he said he considered an unrealistic concept. What the different Slav peoples wanted was their independence. Pan-Slavism, if pursued, meant domination of the Slavic countries by Russia. This was against Russia's interests and would never satisfy the smaller Slavic nations. Stalin said he felt he would have to make a public statement before long to clarify this.[37]

According to Eden,[38] Stalin told Churchill that in Tito's opinion, expressed during the latter's Moscow visit, the Croats and Slovenes would refuse to join any government under King Peter. Stalin thought that the King was ineffectual. Eden called him courageous and intelligent. Churchill said he was young. "How old is he?" asked Stalin. "Twenty-one," Eden answered. "Twenty-one!" Stalin exclaimed. "Peter the Great was ruler of Russia at seventeen." Eden comments that for the moment at least Stalin was more nationalist than Communist.

One other significant Soviet intention was made known during the Churchill visit in Moscow. Stalin told Churchill that after the liberation of Belgrade the Red Army would not advance farther west in Yugoslavia but would concentrate on occupying Hungary. This was reported to Roosevelt by Harriman on October 15.[39]

This time there was no United States protest at the Churchill-Stalin agreement to divide the Balkans as there had been a few months earlier when both Hull and Roosevelt took exception to this approach. The American attitude had not changed, however. While the U.S. acknowledged the usefulness of arrangements for the conduct of the war, it opposed such plans "as would extend beyond the military field and retard the processes of broader international cooperation." [40]

Thus, the U.S. continued to shy away from any political involvement in the Balkans, and it was only Churchill who now felt strongly about projecting British influence on the future political constellation in that area. Stalin's position remained basically unchanged. Even after Tito's visit, or perhaps in view of his discussions with the Partisan leader, Stalin took no political initiative, readily agreed to Churchill's plan, showed understanding for British interests in Yugoslavia and rejected Pan-Slavism. And since Hungary was strategically more important to him than Yugoslavia, he confided to Churchill that the Red Army would not advance in Yugoslavia after the liberation of Belgrade but would move into Hungary.

After Churchill returned to London he spoke in the House of Commons on October 27 and said, regarding Yugoslavia: "We are acting jointly, Russia and Britain, in our relations with both the Royal Yugoslav Government headed by Dr. Šubašić and with Marshal Tito, and we have invited them to come together" to form a united government. He said that "these workaday arrangements" must be looked upon "as a temporary expedient to meet the emergency, and all permanent arrangements await the presence of the United States, who have been kept constantly informed of what was going forward." [41]

THE PARTISANS AND THE RED ARMY TAKE BELGRADE

After Tito's departure from Vis, Huntington returned to Italy, and Maclean, who was in Serbia with Koča Popović's forces, was ordered back to AFHQ by Wilson. On October 8, the chiefs of the American and British military missions left Italy by air for Valjevo in Serbia. Charles W. Thayer, who was deputy head of the American mission, writes [42] that what concerned the British and American mission members most was the whereabouts of Tito, at that time still unknown in the West. Maclean's first question upon landing in Serbia was, "Where is Tito?" The British liaison officer who met him answered that he had no idea.

Tito was in fact back in Yugoslavia by that time. He had left Moscow on October 5 and again stopped at Craiova in Rumania, where he received a Bulgarian delegation with whom he signed an agreement regarding joint action against the Germans. [43] He then went to his new headquarters in Vršac on the Yugoslav-Rumanian border. The British and American missions in Yugoslavia finally learned about Tito's trip to Moscow from their respective Governments.

Following the Tito-Soviet agreement of September 29 regarding the passage of Soviet troops, units of the army group under Marshal Fyodor Tolbukhin's command entered Yugoslav territory on October 1, and drove together with the Partisans toward Belgrade. Niš fell on October 15.

On October 20, the Russians and the Partisans entered Belgrade. King Peter spoke from London, praising the struggle of the National Liberation Army under "Josip Broz Tito, intrepid Marshal of Yugoslavia." A week later, on October 27, the Partisans held a victory parade in Belgrade.

Tito was there with the chiefs of the three Allied missions, Lieutenant General Korneyev, Brigadier Maclean and Major Thayer, who became head of the American military mission after the fall of Belgrade.

In his address on that occasion, Tito said that all during the war he said to himself that in Belgrade the uprising began, and in Belgrade it would end in victory. He paid tribute to the Partisans who had fallen in battle. He expressed his gratitude to the Allies who had made the victory possible. Britain and America, he said, had with the help of their air forces sent the Partisans arms and everything else desired during the past year. The Red Army was now joining in the liberation of Yugoslav territory, and it was the duty of the Yugoslav Army of National Liberation not only to cripple but together with its Allies to wipe out the enemy in Yugoslavia.

As soon as Belgrade was liberated, Huntington returned to Italy. He regarded himself as a "fighting soldier" and felt that with the fighting phase more or less over, the diplomatic chapter, for which his deputy Thayer had been picked, had begun.

Major Thayer, Brigadier Maclean and Marshal Tito in Belgrade, 1944.
Courtesy of V. Kljaković

Maclean reports [44] that only after the victory parade did he have a chance to talk to Tito, for the first time since Vis. He inquired how Tito had enjoyed his visit to Moscow. Slightly put out, Tito asked Maclean how he knew he had been there. He told Maclean that he had gone to Moscow to give the Red Army permission to enter Yugoslav territory. And on his return from Moscow he had gone to the Vojvodina to coordinate operations. Maclean mentioned to Tito that Churchill had been greatly offended by the way in which he had gone off, to which Tito replied: "Only recently Mr. Churchill went to Quebec to see President Roosevelt, and I only heard of this visit after he had returned. And I was not angry."

By the middle of November, the Red Army had veered in the direction of Budapest, and the Partisans established a winter line which divided the country approximately in half. The northwestern part was still in German hands, and within that half Mihailović held an enclave in Bosnia.

TITO AND ŠUBAŠIĆ REACH A NEW AGREEMENT

After Tito's return from Moscow, he invited Šubašić to come to Yugoslavia for new talks. Accompanied by Velebit, Šubašić left London on October 13 and arrived at Tito's headquarters in Vršac on October 23. Both Tito and Šubašić had previously received a joint message from Eden and Molotov in Moscow expressing the hope that the new conversations would result in the formation of a single, unified Yugoslav government. The British-Soviet plan to make the message a tripartite one fell through; the State Department told the British Embassy in Washington that since the U.S. Government "had not been informed of the nature of the proposed solutions of the Yugoslav problem then in discussion," it could hardly undertake to become associated with recommendations regarding the negotiations.[45] Once again the United States refused to become involved in Yugoslav political matters, thus leaving that field entirely to the British and the Russians.

After the liberation of Belgrade the Šubašić-Tito discussions were resumed there on October 28. On November 1, the British and Soviet mission chiefs were called in to witness the initialing of the final draft agreement. Thayer, the new head of the American mission, was not invited. He sent to Caserta a report in which he described the circumstances leading to, and the contents of, the draft agreement, which he said was shown him by Maclean. (The preliminary translation of the complete text was submitted to the State Department from London by the American

Chargé, Schoenfeld, on November 8, and the final translation by Ambassador Patterson on December 16.)

Under the draft agreement, Tito's Anti-Fascist Council (AVNOJ) was to be the supreme legislative body, and a united government was to be made up of twelve members from the National Committee of Liberation and six from the Royal Government. The united government would in due course hold elections to decide the future government of the country. In the meantime, Yugoslavia would in theory continue to be a monarchy, the King remaining abroad and being represented in Yugoslavia by a council of three regents.

It was agreed that Tito and Šubašić would sign the draft only after King Peter had approved it. Maclean took the draft agreement to London to obtain British concurrence. The British, however, showed little enthusiasm for it.

In a telegram to Stalin on November 5, Churchill said that he was "awaiting Dr. Šubašić's return and the result of his report to King Peter." He added: "I was very glad to learn that King Peter was favourably impressed with such accounts as had hitherto reached him. Brigadier Maclean is with me now and tells me how much the atmosphere improved at Partisan headquarters when it was known that Russia and Britain were working together." Stalin replied on November 9: "With regard to Yugoslavia, I have been advised that the trend is favourable to the Allies. Dr. Šubašić plans to come to Moscow to tell us about his latest meetings with Marshal Tito. It appears that we can count on the formation of a united Yugoslav Government before long." [46] Meanwhile, the British representative in Bari pointed out to the Foreign Office that Šubašić would merely be a member of the government while Tito would be prime minister. He added that the full government would in fact consist of twenty-eight and not eighteen members. Of the six to be drawn from the Šubašić Government, two were representatives of the Partisans, and Kosanović had always been pro-Partisan. Tito would thus have a majority of twenty-five to three.

Churchill and King Peter met in London on November 17, at which time Churchill, as related by King Peter to an OSS representative, said that the draft agreement could have been worse and that the monarchy had at least been recognized for the time being. It was at that meeting that King Peter supposedly said to Churchill: "I have been following your advice, Mr. Prime Minister, for the last two years and look where I am today," to which Churchill is said to have replied: "Would you have fared better, Your Majesty, had you followed Mihailović?" King Peter, who wanted to dismiss Šubašić for having agreed to the draft agreement, promised Churchill to wait until Šubašić returned to London.[47]

Churchill also told King Peter that he had asked Stalin not to take any decision on the agreement pending Šubašić's report to the King, and he said Stalin had agreed. Šubašić, however, first went to Moscow to obtain Stalin's agreement, arriving there on November 20, a circumstance which upset the King even more.

Maclean arrived in Caserta on November 28 and told Kirk that Churchill was furious with Šubašić for having gone to Moscow before reporting to the King; nevertheless, he had urged King Peter to accept the agreement and get on as soon as possible with the formation of a government, which would receive British recognition, whereupon Ambassador Stevenson would be sent to Belgrade. Maclean thought that the agreement was not so bad after all, particularly if one considered that Tito was in control of the country and had accepted the regency as a concession.

12

THE U.S. POLICY OF NONINTERFERENCE
IN YUGOSLAV INTERNAL AFFAIRS

Thayer, head of the American military mission in Belgrade, had strict instructions not to get involved in Yugoslav internal affairs in general and the Tito-Šubašić agreement in particular.[1]

In Washington, meanwhile, former Yugoslav Ambassador Fotić sent Roosevelt a letter dated October 14 in which he appealed to the President "to intervene and protect our people in this historic moment." [2]

The President's answer to Fotić, dated November 3, said in part:

You know . . . that the Government of the United States has consistently adhered to a policy of non-interference in the internal affairs of Yugoslavia. It has been our constant wish to see an amicable adjustment of Yugoslav internal difficulties, based on the free will of the people, and with due consideration of the interests of all groups within the country. Our military aid to the resistance forces has been directed against the common enemy, and the allocation of that aid has been determined by military considerations. I earnestly hope that as the enemy is driven from your country there will prevail a spirit of mutual consideration and understanding as a foundation for the new national life to which, we hope, the fine talents of all groups in Yugoslavia will be devoted.[3]

On the preceding day, Roosevelt sent the following answer to a handwritten letter from King Peter:

My dear Peter:
It is good to have your note and I can assure you that I am thinking much of the day when you and your wife will be going back to Belgrade. I think

275

things are shaping up well and I am glad indeed that you see Mr. Churchill and can partake of his great wisdom.

Some day when peace has permanently come to the world you and your wife must come over here and stay with us, either in the White House or at our country place in Hyde Park.

In the meantime, I do hope to see you both one of these days.

My wife and I send you both our warm regards,

Very sincerely yours,

Franklin D. Roosevelt [4]

These two completely noncommittal letters were not based on the factual situation then prevailing. It was most unlikely that King Peter would be able to go back to Belgrade, and it was equally unlikely that after such an intensive and hateful civil war all groups would be willing to unite.

On November 8, Under Secretary Stettinius submitted a memorandum to the President regarding "United States Interests and Policy in Eastern and Southeastern Europe and the Near East." [5] While Yugoslavia was never mentioned, the memorandum took the position that the United States should not identify its interests in the area with those of either Britain or the Soviet Union. It should follow a course of independent interest in favor of equitable arrangements designed to attain general peace and security on a basis of good-neighborly relations. The memorandum enumerated six principles:

1. The right of peoples to choose and maintain for themselves without outside interference the type of political, social, and economic systems they desire, so long as they conduct their affairs in such a way as not to menace the peace and security of others.

2. Equality of opportunity, as against the setting up of a policy of exclusion, in commerce, transit and trade; and freedom to negotiate, either through government agencies or private enterprise, irrespective of the type of economic system in operation.

3. The right of access to all countries on an equal and unrestricted basis of bona fide representatives of the recognized press, radio, newsreel and information agencies of other nations engaged in gathering news and other forms of public information for dissemination to the public in their own countries; and the right to transmit information gathered by them to points outside such territories without hindrance or discrimination.

4. Freedom for American philanthropic and educational organizations to carry on their activities in the respective countries on the basis of most-favored-nation treatment.

5. General protection of American citizens and the protection and further-ance of legitimate American economic rights, existing or potential.

6. Deferment of territorial settlements until the end of the war.

On November 21, the British Embassy submitted an *aide-mémoire* to the State Department inquiring whether the U.S. Government approved the equipping of three or four single-engine fighter squadrons for the Yugoslav armed forces. This was in connection with a proposal for organizing, equipping and training of Yugoslav air and naval forces by Britain, and a similar undertaking by the Soviet Union with respect to Yugoslav land forces.

The State Department replied on December 2 that it was in full agreement that military aid should be extended to Yugoslavia and that coordination of effort should be so planned as to contribute effectively to the conduct of the war against Germany. It pointed out, however, that "presumably for political reasons" there had been some unwillingness in Yugoslavia to coordinate operations with the plans of the Allied forces in the Mediterranean. Therefore it hoped that the Yugoslavs would be required to pledge that they would use Allied aid in coordination to further the conduct of the war.[6]

The State Department then reverted to the "50-50" agreement reached between Stalin and Churchill in Moscow in October, saying that, while it was anxious to support plans of immediate usefulness to the prosecution of the war, "it feels that the contemplated arrangement between the British and Soviet Governments, reaching as it does into the postwar period, involves political questions of considerable importance with regard to the future of Yugoslavia."

THE U.S. WITHDRAWS ITS INTELLIGENCE MISSION
FROM ČETNIK TERRITORY

The fact that the United States had sent an intelligence mission to Mihailović in August became known to Tito, and it annoyed him. Maclean reported that Tito raised this problem with him after the victory parade, declaring that the continued presence of an American (McDowell) with Mihailović was bitterly resented by the Partisans and was certain to affect Partisan relations with the United States and Britain unfavorably.[7] Tito told Maclean that he had proof that McDowell was not limiting his activity to intelligence work but was representing himself, or in any event was permitting himself to be represented, as the official spokesman of the

United States Government sanctioned by Supreme Headquarters, on behalf of which he had promised support to Mihailović. Tito added that there was also evidence that supplies had been sent to the Četniks. This was very disturbing to the Partisans. (In fact, no Allied supplies reached Mihailović after late 1943.)

Tito told Maclean that he had been assured some time ago that instructions had been given for McDowell's immediate withdrawal but that he was still in Yugoslavia, running from one place to another with Mihailović. Tito said he could not understand this aspect of Allied policy, since the fact of Mihailović's collaboration with the Nazis was now generally accepted, and even King Peter had publicly denounced him. According to Tito, so long as there was an American mission with Mihailović it would be difficult to give Colonel Huntington facilities he would otherwise have liked to grant. (Actually Huntington had already left Yugoslavia, turning over his mission to Thayer.) In reporting this conversation to Wilson, Maclean commented that mention of Mihailović made Tito and his followers see even redder than usual and that they were completely baffled as to why there could be any adequate reason for the United States to maintain a mission with Mihailović.

Kirk reported to the State Department the gist of Maclean's conversation with Tito, noting that McDowell had been endeavoring for more than a month to leave Yugoslavia but had met with many difficulties due to the increased tempo of the fighting. OSS Caserta informed Kirk that McDowell and his party were ready to be evacuated but that bad weather had made it impossible for a plane to land at his present headquarters.

There was obviously some confusion at AFHQ between the McDowell mission and the air crew rescue unit. Thus when Tito complained about McDowell, Wilson answered that the mission dealt only with the evacuation of air crews. McDowell's mission, which lasted little more than two months, became the subject of controversy and recrimination and was a major item introduced by the prosecution during the trial of Mihailović in 1946. Charges were then made that McDowell had assured Mihailović that the U.S. Government would support the Četniks exclusively. To this McDowell replied:

I definitely did not tell General Mihailović that "the United States would aid him and his government exclusively." To have done so would have been to convict myself as both liar and fool. It was painfully obvious to all of us around the General that no American nor British aid was available for his cause, while nearly every night we could see or hear American planes coming over to drop supplies and munitions to the Communists.[8]

It is established that McDowell met twice with Rudi Stärker, representing Hermann Neubacher, the senior German Foreign Office official in the Balkans. The first meeting took place early in September in Pranjani, and the second later in the month at Draginje near Šabac while the Četniks were retreating to Bosnia.[9] Mihailović was present at both talks. The subject of the McDowell-Stärker conversations was the possible surrender of German forces in the Balkans. Stärker devoted himself mostly to the plea that the U.S. must save Europe from bolshevism through cooperation between Germany and the U.S.[10] He appeared interested in insuring the surrender of German troops to American and British forces. In a statement after the war before the Commission of Inquiry in the Case of Draža Mihailović, McDowell, defending Mihailović against charges of collaboration, stated:

The undersigned was instructed to listen to and transmit any German offer. General Mihailović was most unwilling to have any contact with Germans but agreed to Stärker's coming, on the invitation of the undersigned. The undersigned had two interviews with Stärker. As the General was with the undersigned, both prior to and after these interviews, there could have been no opportunity for the General to have had private meetings with Stärker.

Neubacher writes[11] that McDowell wanted to follow up his discussions with Stärker by a meeting with Neubacher himself (Martin quotes McDowell as confirming this[12]), but Ribbentrop prohibited it, and Hitler called Neubacher "crazy" for having forwarded McDowell's proposal. Neubacher adds that McDowell passed word that he was authorized by his Government to talk with Neubacher about the German forces in the Balkans, to talk and report about matters going beyond the Balkans, and to transport a duly authorized German representative from Yugoslavia to a neutral country or even to the U.S. The war was coming to an end, and the McDowell-Neubacher connection, which came to nothing, was one of several attempts by both sides to shorten the conflict.

McDowell was evacuated on November 1 from an airfield near Doboj, in Bosnia, accompanied by his assistant, Captain Milodragovich, and his radio operator. It had been suggested that McDowell quit Mihailović's headquarters and seek the nearest Tito force, but eventually a plane was sent in. Wilson writes[13] that he offered to bring Mihailović out at the same time, but the general refused. McDowell confirms this,[14] saying that he was instructed by OSS Bari to offer Mihailović the opportunity to leave with him. The general, however, turned it down emphatically, rejecting the life of an exile or refugee and insisting that he would remain and die in his own country.

THE BRITISH GOVERNMENT PROPOSES
TO EVACUATE MIHAILOVIĆ

On November 15, Macmillan at AFHQ took up with his American opposite number, Kirk, a proposal of the British Government for the evacuation of the Četnik leader. According to Macmillan, "the British Government felt that while Mihailović should not be treated as a national hero
there was considerable feeling that he should be rescued from Yugoslavia
and placed in honorable forced residence abroad," Kirk reported.[15]

The Foreign Office thought that any action in this matter should be
taken jointly with the United States. Macmillan asked whether Kirk
would be willing to request OSS to evacuate Mihailović and arrange for
his early departure for the United States, where he thought that Mihailović would be much happier because there were so many Serbs living
there.

Kirk told Macmillan that he could understand the desire of the British
Government to do something with regard to Mihailović's present situation in view of the fact that he had rendered valuable services to the
British war effort in the past and, as the BBC had so clearly stated during
1941 and 1942, had kept alive opposition to Nazism in Yugoslavia. Kirk
added that, although he had no instructions with regard to this matter,
it was obvious that serious complications would confront the United
States Government if it undertook to evacuate Mihailović or to transport
him to the United States for future residence.

Macmillan replied that he would recommend that if the Foreign Office
felt strongly that Mihailović should be evacuated, preferably with United
States participation, it should take up the matter through Lord Halifax,
the British Ambassador in Washington. He added that he would report
to the Foreign Office Kirk's reactions and "would point out that the
British Government would have to envisage Mihailović's honorable forced
residence in Malta, Egypt, or somewhere else in the British Empire at
British expense."

The Macmillan-Kirk talk was followed by a conversation which the new
American Ambassador to the Yugoslav Government-in-Exile, Richard
Patterson, had on November 24 in London with the Yugoslav acting
Foreign Minister, Kosanović.[16] Kosanović called Patterson in to tell him
that, according to rumors, "Mihailović with American or British help,
and probably American, is on his way to Italy." He added: "The Yugoslav
Government is concerned about this, for among other things Mihailović
would thus escape punishment." He also said that if Mihailović left Yugo-

slavia he might create difficulties for the King with Tito and the Yugoslav people.

Kosanović then referred to the fact that Lieutenant Colonel Knežević had been transported by the Americans to Bari for transfer to Mihailović, and he also asserted that an American aircraft had recently brought out of Četnik territory Adam Pribičević, one of the Serbian leaders. Kosanović said that the Yugoslav Government considered these acts "unfriendly."

Kosanović disclosed that he had already talked to British Ambassador Stevenson, who had reported that Churchill had discussed the problem of Mihailović with Tito (there is no record of this). Churchill had told Tito that if Mihailović fell into British hands he would be interned in British territory, and Britain would not permit him to be extradited. Kosanović said that Stevenson had assured him that the British would not help Mihailović to escape. Kosanović declared that if the United States Government should assist Mihailović, the Yugoslav Government might come to the conclusion that the United States was officially supporting him.

Patterson discussed this problem the same afternoon with his British colleague, Stevenson, who showed him his telegram to Halifax asking the latter to discuss with the State Department the question of the disposition to be made of Mihailović. Stevenson's thought was that the United States and Britain should join in bringing Mihailović out if his life was at stake, but not otherwise.

Over the next few months the British Embassy in Washington repeatedly raised with the State Department the question of what to do about Mihailović, seeking a joint policy for recommendation to General Wilson, preferably for Mihailović's "rescue and honorable detention." But the State Department did not take a definite stand until two months after the war had ended in Europe. On July 5, 1945, the Department cabled Kirk that "it may shortly become necessary to take a position" regarding Mihailović:

We have therefore informed the [British] Embassy (1) that we have never had any information indicating that Mihailović wanted to give himself up for purposes of his own security; (2) that we would not agree to having an American military group, or a joint Anglo-American mission, sent into Yugoslavia to rescue him from the Partisans; (3) that if he joins up with Allied armies we think that he and any followers having the semblance of armed forces should be immobilized, moved to the rear, and held according to the program proposed for any dissident Yugoslavs . . .; (4) that as regards notification, since factors of military security would not now be involved, we see no reason why, if Mihailović enters Allied lines, the fact should not be made public at once by a general announcement rather than a special and separate communication to Marshal Tito.[17]

Thus, the U.S. Government's policy with regard to Mihailović can be summarized as follows: on the one hand, not to make an effort to rescue him; on the other, should he reach Allied territory, not to turn him over to the Partisans, even if they requested his return.

THE LAST AMERICAN LEAVES MIHAILOVIĆ

After McDowell's departure from Yugoslavia, Captain Lalich of the air crew rescue unit stayed on for almost two months. He left Yugoslavia by air on December 27 from the same airstrip near Doboj from which McDowell had departed. Between August 9 and December 27, the rescue unit had evacuated 432 Americans and more than one hundred other Allied personnel from Četnik territory.[18]

It should be noted also that 2,000 Allied airmen who bailed out over Partisan territory, which was then appreciably larger than that of the Četniks, were likewise evacuated. By that time Allied airmen were advised to bail out over Partisan rather than Četnik territory in an emergency. Allied liaison officers who could look after rescued airmen and call for evacuation missions from Italy were stationed permanently with the Partisans.

Lalich, the last American in Četnik territory, said goodbye to Mihailović on December 11 in Srednje, north of Sarajevo. The general was reported to have been in good spirits, telling Lalich that the Allies had made a mistake but that some day they would be back with the Četniks. This was an extraordinary statement in view of the hopeless situation in which Mihailović found himself by then, as Tito consolidated his power in Belgrade.

In November, Mihailović saw Stärker again. The two previous meetings in September were essentially McDowell-Stärker discussions in which Mihailović took no active part. This time the German came to talk to Mihailović and asked whether it was true that he wished his organization to be placed at the service of the Germans. Mihailović replied: "We were and still are enemies. It is a sad coincidence that I am, like you, fighting against the Partisans. This is a sad coincidence which I regret." [19]

During the autumn of 1944, Mihailović maintained regular contact with Topalović in Italy. Much to the annoyance of the British when they discovered this traffic, Topalović used a Polish transmitter in Bari for sending messages to Mihailović. In one of these messages early in October

Captain Lalich and General Mihailović in Bosnia, 1944. From *Ally Betrayed*

he said: "We draw your attention to the fact that in the American mission to the Partisans there is a certain Major Hauer, a diplomat. It would be useful to contact him as soon as he gets to Belgrade. The mission is now at Valjevo and the Chief is Colonel Huntington." ("Hauer" was undoubtedly Thayer.) The British stopped radio traffic to Mihailović in December, but Caserta instructed Bari not to discontinue monitoring Mihailović's transmissions. "As long as no out messages are sent this cannot possibly be described as maintaining contact with Mihailović," the instruction said.

In his radio exchange with Topalović, the Četnik leader made a last-minute attempt to reestablish relations with the Allies. He instructed Topalović to submit a proposal whereby 50,000 Četniks would be placed under Wilson's command. Topalović submitted this proposal on October 21. Having received no reply, he was instructed by Mihailović to submit another proposal in which he suggested on November 13 that the 50,000 Četniks would be available for combat in Yugoslavia or anywhere else. This proposal was also not acknowledged, so Topalović made yet a third *démarche* on November 29, submitting a plan for cutting off German troops then in Albania. No reply was ever given.[20]

NO ALLIED LANDINGS IN YUGOSLAVIA

On his return from Moscow, Churchill stopped once more in Naples, where he again presided at a meeting of the Mediterranean Command on October 21. In the two weeks which had passed since the previous meeting, the military situation had evolved in several respects. In Yugoslavia, the Red Army and the Partisans had entered Belgrade, and the Germans had given up much of the Dalmatian coast. In Italy, however, the Allied advance was grinding to a halt and an early advance upon Vienna through the Ljubljana gap was becoming less likely every day.

Churchill puts the blame for the slow-up in Italy on the withdrawal of Allied divisions for the landings in southern France. He implies that had these troops not been withdrawn, the Gothic Line would have been breached and the "right-handed drive" through Yugoslavia to Vienna been made possible. Instead, he says, "except in Greece, our military power to influence the liberation of Southeastern Europe was gone." [21]

Wilson proposed at the October 21 Mediterranean Command meeting that in light of the current situation, forces might be used more economically along the Dalmatian coast than in a direct assault upon Istria. Churchill liked this idea, although he thought that the emphasis on Yugoslavia might trouble the United States.[22]

The Wilson proposal to land light forces south of Zara (Zadar) and thereafter to pass three or four Allied divisions through Zara, Split and Dubrovnik to advance north was, however, not well received in London and Washington. The British Chiefs of Staff did not like the plan because it would not have achieved anything until February 1945. The U.S. Joint Chiefs of Staff agreed with this analysis on November 17 and questioned whether Wilson would have the capability of carrying out a large-scale operation in the Balkans even by February. They pointed out that development of Dalmatian ports and the mountainous Balkans were obstacles too large to overcome before spring. Again, having the larger military picture in mind, the Joint Chiefs repeated the American argument that the Mediterranean campaign should support the Western front. "It would seem that the transfer of major forces to the Balkans would gravely reduce such containing and attrition power as we now possess in Italy," they said, adding that "the proper action at this time is to introduce light forces into the Dalmatian ports in order to maintain pressure and harass the German forces withdrawing from the Balkans."

While the British and American Chiefs of Staff were considering the Wilson proposal, it became apparent that the Germans had consolidated their military position in the western half of Yugoslavia, making Allied landings risky and in all probability very costly. But there were other reasons why an Allied campaign in the Balkans lost its appeal, even for Wilson.

In the middle of October, Tito had asked the British to supply some field artillery for operations in Montenegro, and on October 20 Wilson instructed Land Forces, Adriatic, to provide sixteen to twenty pieces. Since the Partisans had no experience in handling these weapons, a small British force known as "Floyd Force" (Brigadier Sir Henry Floyd commanding) landed at Dubrovnik on October 28 to operate under the orders of the local Partisan commander. At first, all went well. Floyd Force carried out a successful operation against the Germans early in November, earning the thanks of the Yugoslavs. But in the second half of the month, the atmosphere suddenly changed. The British artillery, which was by then operating inland, was ordered by the Partisan command to withdraw at once to the neighborhood of Dubrovnik on the pretense that the Germans were threatening to attack the town. On November 25, a Partisan broadcast stated that no agreement had been signed authorizing the entry of British and American troops into Yugoslavia "such as had been signed between Yugoslavia and the Soviet High Command." Floyd Force thereafter found itself in an unenviable position. It was not used again and was finally withdrawn in the middle of January 1945.[23]

Wilson was also annoyed because Tito, after his arrival in Belgrade, no longer wanted to discuss the military situation in Bosnia, where the Germans had been slipping through the Partisan net. Wilson had proposed landing some British troops at certain Dalmatian ports to assist the Partisans in bottling up the retreating Germans. He says: "In spite of Tito's procrastination, small detachments of our troops were assisting the Partisans against the Germans in Bosnia, but in order to keep them supplied it was necessary to get the ports working. . . ."[24] Wilson says that he requested Tito to authorize the landing of British naval forces at Split, Zadar and Šibenik for the repair of port facilities. On November 19, Wilson followed this up by asking Tito to permit the landing at Zadar of a British force consisting of one armored and one artillery regiment to help the Partisans, who were in difficulties against the Germans. Tito was not willing to give this order and instead wanted the equipment to be handed over to the Partisans, "an absurd request as the Partisans had not the trained personnel to handle and maintain it," Wilson noted.

Wilson then reports that Tito was anxious to have the Allies open an airfield close to Zadar, but Wilson insisted that if any part of the Balkan Air Force was moved across the Adriatic it would have to be protected by Allied troops. "It was not until well on into November that agreement was given to these requests and then only verbally," he writes, and despite this the British troops found themselves restricted and hampered by local Yugoslav leaders.

These incidents annoyed Churchill, and he sent a strongly worded letter to Tito dated December 2, complaining about Tito's lack of cooperation and the rude attitude of the Partisans toward the British: "I bring all this to your notice because I am sure you will understand that such incidents can scarcely fail to hinder the attainment of our common objective." It was clear that Churchill's enthusiasm for Tito, already diminished after their meeting in Naples, had waned further. On December 7, Maclean, back in Belgrade, delivered Churchill's letter. Tito's immediate response was the explanation to Maclean that he was beginning to feel the strain of so much work and was thus obliged to leave an increasing number of problems to inexperienced subordinates. He answered the letter on December 21, assuring Churchill that the incidents had been cleared up. But he added: "With regard, however, to the basing of Allied forces, you will agree that it is only natural that we should wish to be duly consulted." [25]

On December 2, Wilson received a new directive from the Combined Chiefs of Staff. It said that his first and immediate objective was Bologna and that the introduction of major forces into the Balkans was not favorably considered. But it ordered: "You should continue to introduce light forces through liberated Dalmatian ports in order to harass and exert pressure and attrition on the Germans withdrawing from the Balkans."

On November 25, Wilson had been named head of the Joint Staff mission in Washington, replacing Field Marshal Sir John Dill, who had died on November 4, and General Alexander was appointed Supreme Commander of the Mediterranean Theater. The actual change in command took place on December 12, after Alexander was promoted to field marshal. General Mark Clark succeeded Alexander as commander in chief of the Allied armies in Italy, and U.S. General Joseph T. McNarney became Alexander's deputy, replacing General Jacob L. Devers.

REACTIONS TO THE TITO-ŠUBAŠIĆ AGREEMENT

Tito and Šubašić, upon his return from Moscow, signed two additional agreements on December 7—one regarding "Elections for the Constituent

Assembly and Organization of Public Powers," the other on "Property of H. M. the King and Regency Council." [26]

In his conversation with Tito on that day, Maclean said that if Tito and Šubašić succeeded in forming a convincing government, the British would consider granting recognition. Maclean added that recent events in Yugoslavia did not conform to Western ideas of democracy. The Churchill letter of December 2, which dealt primarily with the British-Partisan incidents, also stressed the desirability of democratic elections in carrying out the Tito-Šubašić agreement.

Thayer, chief of the American military mission, reported to Caserta that he got the feeling from Maclean that Churchill's representations to Tito for real democracy in Yugoslavia were mainly for the record and did not reflect any great conviction that they would materially alter the course of developments.[27] In his answer to Churchill on December 21, Tito gave renewed assurances regarding free elections "in accordance with the principles of true democracy and terms of the Atlantic Charter."

Thayer also reported that he had talked with Šubašić on the latter's return from Moscow. Šubašić related that Stalin had expressed to him abhorrence of any Yugoslav "experiments" in Communism and had insisted on free expression of popular opinion. Stalin appeared to have been shocked to learn that some delegates were "elected" by acclaim, a procedure which he characterized as "undemocratic."

Šubašić told the British, but not Thayer, that the King's return to Yugoslavia was out of the question. To Thayer, he said only that it would cause disorders and riots. He also told Thayer that he was returning to London fully conscious of his "failures," which he was inclined to blame partially on the United States and Britain: "When one is faced with the ultimate decision in a fateful dilemma, friends are not of much use." According to Thayer, Šubašić's exposure to "the way democracy works in Russia" apparently had given him a different conception of the meaning of his agreement with Tito. Nevertheless, Thayer was sure that Šubašić would urge King Peter to accept it as the only way to save the monarchy, at least until the constitutional assembly could be elected.[28]

Ambassador Patterson and his Counselor, Harold Shantz, saw Šubašić on December 11 upon the latter's arrival in London.[29] Šubašić expressed the hope that King Peter would approve the Tito-Šubašić agreement, whereupon he would return to Belgrade, since he felt that he must "strike while the iron is hot."

In a later conversation with Patterson, Šubašić said that he was much disturbed by King Peter's coolness and the fact that Churchill repeatedly postponed seeing him. He gave Patterson copies of his answers to fourteen questions posed by the Foreign Office regarding the Tito-Šubašić agreement. Patterson said that Šubašić evaded the issues; the implication was that he realized his inability to make interpretations with any assurance that Tito would accept them. The only unequivocal statement Šubašić made was that the Partisans would be declared the regular army. Outside this army, there would be no military formation.

Patterson also reported that Šubašić was annoyed at statements made at a press conference by the chief of the Partisan military mission in London, Velebit, to the effect that no decision had been reached as to how the Yugoslavs would choose between the monarchical and republican forms of government. Patterson says that he learned in strict confidence that Šubašić had requested Velebit not to make any more statements to the press.[30]

Among all interested parties, it was really Churchill who championed the Šubašić-Tito agreement. Patterson reported to the State Department on December 18: "Ambassador Stevenson called on me today and said that the personal views of Churchill and Eden were favorable to the Tito-Šubašić agreement . . . which they consider 'the best possible under the circumstances.' " Stevenson told the Ambassador that Stalin had solicited Churchill's views on it and that Eden requested the views of Secretary Stettinius [31] before Churchill met with King Peter and Šubašić later in the week.

On December 21, Churchill, Eden, Stevenson and King Peter met at the latter's request, at which time the King told the British leaders that the agreement was unconstitutional. Churchill, according to King Peter's statement to an OSS representative,[32] said that Tito had done many unconstitutional things and would probably do more but since he had the power, what could be done about it? The King declared that he would sign the agreement only if he could name the regents. Churchill was said to have replied, "You can't accept one part of the agreement and reject another. You should accept it entirely and wholeheartedly. There is no time to change it." Stettinius' views appear not to have been formulated or forwarded to Patterson before Churchill's meeting with the King.

Meanwhile, the British Ambassador in Washington advised the State Department that the agreement seemed to afford a "satisfactory basis on which to build a new federal Yugoslavia," in the view of the British Government. The Ambassador asked that, if the State Department shared this opinion, it instruct Patterson so to inform King Peter. Thereupon the Department sent a telegram instructing Patterson to inform Šubašić and the King that, while the principles of the agreements between Tito and Šubašić appeared acceptable, the question was whether an effective and loyal implementation of those principles could be obtained. The telegram, dated December 23, continued:

You should add, that, as concerns our general attitude, this Government has consistently defended the rights of the various peoples of Yugoslavia to work out their own forms of Government without the exercise of any foreign influence or the imposition of the rule of any one national or political group within the country over other elements.[33]

The instruction further stated that if the King accepted the agreement, the question of "recognition" by the United States Government would not arise; in other words, Patterson would continue as Ambassador to the new Government. If the King rejected it, however, and Tito should repudiate the Government-in-Exile and request recognition of his "organization," the attitude of the United States would depend on a reexamination of the situation within Yugoslavia.

The State Department replied in similar vein to the British Embassy. It declared that it was not prepared to exercise any influence beyond its instructions to Patterson since this "would involve responsibilities which this Government considers it should not take in the circumstances, as regards decisions by which the future of Yugoslavia may be so vitally affected." [34]

The United States thus continued to shy away from taking a position on the political crisis in Yugoslavia, while Britain became ever more deeply involved. Stalin was still unwilling to intervene and he asked Churchill for his views before commenting on the Tito-Šubašić agreement.

ADDITIONAL PROBLEMS BETWEEN
THE WESTERN ALLIES AND TITO

In early October 1944, discussions began in Bari between the Allied command and a delegation from the National Committee of Liberation regarding civilian relief for Yugoslavia before UNNRA could assume relief responsibilities. A draft agreement was finally prepared, but the Partisan representatives who took copies of the agreement to Belgrade never returned to Bari to sign it. Belgrade objected to a paragraph which provided for Allied observers. The Allies insisted on this paragraph to ensure the impartial distribution of supplies and to prevent the use of such supplies as a weapon of political coercion.

As winter set in, the food situation, particularly in Dalmatia, became desperate, and Field Marshal Alexander, the new Supreme Commander, Mediterranean, called a meeting on December 15 which Kirk attended. Alexander was concerned lest a situation develop in which the Allies would be charged with withholding food from starving people because of a technicality.[35]

A directive to Alexander from the Combined Chiefs of Staff had clearly specified the requirement for Allied observers and hence it could not be ignored. Alexander instructed Maclean to take the matter up with Tito. Kirk told the State Department that the Allies were in a difficult situation. They had two choices: They could send food unconditionally, since people were actually starving, or wait for an agreement. But in either case a public relations effort was necessary. If the first course were adopted, the Allies would have to inform the recipients that food was being provided immediately and unconditionally. In the alternative, they would have to give the reasons for withholding the food, which would entail blaming Tito. Kirk proposed the first course, although he said that he resented "the tactics of the Yugoslavs in jockeying the Allies into a position where their humanitarian motives are impugned when the fault lies in Tito refusing the safeguards essential to the achievement of those motives." In reply, the State Department stated that it opposed any relaxation of the Allied stand with respect to observers.

Meanwhile, Maclean took up the problem with Tito,[36] who accused the Allies of not being serious and of trying to impose administrative controls that would infringe on Yugoslav sovereignty. He said that there was no need for observers, since the Partisans were distributing relief and food to supporters and opponents alike. Maclean suggested that if this were true, Tito should have no objection to observers, who might even help to dispel rumors that he was trying to impose a Communist regime by force. He proposed that Tito submit a counterproposal for a fixed number of observers to enter Yugoslavia initially. Finally, Tito agreed to one hundred. Maclean said that he had no authority to negotiate, but would forward Tito's suggestion. In reply, Maclean was told by Caserta [37] not to pursue the matter further pending Alexander's projected visit to Belgrade. (This visit did not take place until February 1945.)

In the meantime, the Partisans launched a propaganda campaign charging that Allied relief was not reaching the starving Yugoslavs because of Anglo-American insistence on sending observers into Yugoslavia in derogation of Yugoslav sovereignty. They contended that the Soviet Union was making available generous quantities of wheat, the only obstacle being Allied failure to furnish shipping from Black Sea ports. Supplementing this propaganda campaign was one initiated by leftist organizations in the United States demanding the release of Yugoslav ships from the Allied shipping pool for the transportation of relief goods to Yugoslavia.[38]

Negotiations for a relief agreement were finally concluded in Belgrade early in 1945 after an Allied delegation headed by two generals arrived from Caserta.[39]

There were other problems, too. The British and American military missions in Yugoslavia—each had several teams in Partisan territory—continued to suffer from restrictions on their movements, a policy which had begun in September 1944. Thayer also reported a welter of unfriendly articles in the Belgrade press, which lost no occasion to enhance the prestige of the Soviet Union while impugning the motives of the Western Allies.

We now know that soon after the liberation of Belgrade serious problems arose between the Red Army and the Yugoslav Communist leadership due mainly to the behavior of the Russian troops. This resulted in a most unpleasant confrontation between Tito and General Korneyev.[40] Moreover, the wheat presented to Belgrade as a Soviet gift turned out to be Yugoslav wheat collected by the retreating Germans and confiscated by the Russians. Worst of all, the Russians belittled the role of the Partisans and exaggerated the contribution of the Red Army in the liberation of Belgrade. Yet Yugoslav Communist propaganda extolled the Soviet Union and attacked the West.

The restriction of movement, the press attacks, the incidents on the Dalmatian coast and the rigid attitude of Tito's emissaries at the relief talks in Bari led Kirk to send a thought-provoking analysis to the State Department. In a telegram dated December 11 he said that these developments reflected a deliberate policy on the part of Tito and his Partisans.[41] He pointed out that while it could be argued that many of the excesses could be ascribed to revolutionary exuberance and inexperience, the United States should not close its eyes to the potentialities of a revolutionary and authoritarian regime. He argued that such a regime owed its existence to one of the most dynamic and courageous of the European resistance movements; that it was supported by a highly political army and an ably controlled press and propaganda; that it was strong in race consciousness, territorial ambition and suspicion of the Western world; and that it was led by an able and ambitious leader who had shown a considerable capacity for cynicism and international blackmail. Kirk added that the West could not rely on the frequently cited "reasonableness" of a leadership whose principal figures were apostles of a faith inspired by envy or made vindictive by repression. He thought that the new Yugoslav leaders were schooled in naked power and ignored the meaning of give and take, fair play and law in the lives of men and nations.

While Yugoslavia might be geographically remote, he said, the United States could not be "indifferent to events in a country whose fate is bound seriously to affect the equilibrium of political and moral forces in Europe, particularly after the withdrawal of United States and British forces from southern Europe." Yugoslavia, Kirk said, was not only situated close to Italy and the eastern Mediterranean, but its complete absorption in the Soviet orbit would have repercussions far beyond its neighbors.

Kirk concluded that the Western Allies were faced with a situation of serious potentialities brought about to a large extent by the bankruptcy of previous regimes. The defects of the past made the new regime more acceptable to the average Yugoslav than might have been expected. Kirk suggested that the United States should seek to hold the Yugoslav rulers to the spirit of the democratic principles they voiced glibly but which doubtless reflected the true aspirations of the great majority of the Yugoslavs after the suffering of the past years. Such an attitude, he thought, would strengthen congenial and deserving elements while maintaining United States prestige and integrity. He also warned that experience so far indicated that the West would be ill advised to press its military or economic aid upon a government which at best showed many symptoms of having been unduly flattered. Even though it accepted assistance, it might not with any certainty be counted among the friends of the West.

On November 26 Kirk had recommended on the basis of reports received from OSS that the State Department send official representatives to Yugoslavia. He pointed out that the British were already taking steps to reestablish their representation in Belgrade. Kirk felt that the value of Bari as a listening post was rapidly diminishing, and he suggested that the staff there be sent to Belgrade to assume the protection of American interests and to reopen an American diplomatic mission.[42]

This recommendation was followed by a message from Thayer pointing out the desirability of sending one or two Foreign Service officers to Belgrade as soon as possible for the protection of American interests and in order to make administrative arrangements for the eventual establishment of the Embassy there.[43]

On December 16, the State Department advised Kirk that it approved the recommendation that Carl Norden and Peter Constan proceed to Belgrade as Kirk's representatives. Norden's assignment, the State Department said, should be regarded as exploratory in nature, and he should be careful not to give the impression that he was reestablishing a regular mission. Until relations between the Government-in-Exile and the National Committee of Liberation were clarified, the State Department considered it necessary that Norden function on this informal basis. Clerical personnel should not be sent in, pending his judgment of the usefulness of his activities, but such personnel would be assigned if he so recommended after investigation on the spot. The State Department contemplated that Norden's primary duties would be to advise and assist the Swiss Consulate, which had handled U.S. interests since July 1941.[44]

The Yugoslav authorities in Belgrade refused to give clearance for Norden and Constan, however, on the grounds that their duties regarding civilian matters would be political and not within the scope of the military mission headed by Thayer, and because the Swiss Consulate was already authorized to protect American interests and property. Tito's *chef de cabinet,* Mitar Bakić, declared that permission for civilian representation would not be granted pending the establishment of regular diplomatic missions.[45]

Thayer, who visited Caserta at the end of the year, was asked by Kirk to take the matter up personally with Tito. On his return to Belgrade, Thayer concluded an agreement with Bakić paving the way for Norden and Constan to proceed to Belgrade.

THE SITUATION AT THE END OF 1944

The war in Europe was coming to a close with the defeat of Germany certain; the only question remaining was, how soon? Allied armies from the west and the east had reached German territory. If Churchill had had his way, the Western Allies might have broken through the German defenses in Italy and also landed in the Balkans. Originally inspired primarily by military and strategic considerations, these British desires were reinforced in the course of 1944 by strong political motivations. As the Red Army advanced westward, Churchill, Eden and others became convinced that the Soviets were intent on replacing the old order in Eastern Europe with regimes amenable to Moscow. It was for these reasons that Churchill had suggested a demarcation line between the British and the Soviets in the Balkans.

The United States continued to be animated entirely by military considerations. Therefore, the British proposal for an Italian-Balkan advance was vetoed in favor of a landing in southern France. Because the State Department suspected political motives in the Churchill plan for a demarcation line in Eastern Europe, it opposed it.

As the Red Army drove the Germans out of Soviet territory in the course of 1944, the leaders in the Kremlin began to focus more on the postwar situation in Eastern Europe than on the immediate destruction of the German armed forces. Soviet behavior before Warsaw, as well as the decision to turn toward Budapest after the fall of Belgrade rather than help the Partisans clear Yugoslav territory, were cases where political motivations won out over purely military considerations. In this context, the attitude of the three major Allies vis-à-vis Yugoslavia can be understood more easily.

As they began to give more weight to political factors, the British leaders, particularly Churchill, reappraised their Yugoslav policy. This reappraisal gained impetus after the Prime Minister met Tito in August 1944 —a disappointing encounter from Churchill's point of view. Whether or not Churchill had secretly hoped that Tito was not that much of a Communist, Tito's reluctance to state publicly that he would not introduce Communism into postwar Yugoslavia disturbed the Prime Minister. Moreover, Tito's claim to non-Yugoslav territory such as Istria contributed to Churchill's annoyance. From then on, the British Government's actions with regard to Yugoslavia assumed an ever more political character. All possible steps were taken in an attempt to retain British influence in Yugoslavia—the 50-50 agreement in Moscow, for instance—and to obtain a Yugoslav coalition government in which Western-oriented members would play at least some role.

The United States did not entertain such considerations. Not having supported Tito in the first place—though for purely military reasons not denying him military aid—American leaders were not greatly surprised to learn of Tito's aims and aspirations. The U.S. supported the Royal Yugoslav Government-in-Exile and saw no reason to deviate from this support even though it was at the same time giving military assistance to Tito because he was resisting the Germans. Since the American military interest in the Balkans was only peripheral, it took the U.S. Government a long time—until late 1944—to become involved in the political situation in Yugoslavia, and then only because of British pressure.

For the Soviet Union the problem was more complicated, precisely because Tito was General Secretary of the Communist Party of Yugoslavia, Moscow-trained and yet so different from the other Communist leaders of Eastern Europe. In the Russian drive to secure the borders of the Soviet Union with adjacent friendly regimes as a matter of first priority, Tito and his Partisans might have been expected to play a useful role in Moscow's plans. But this was not the case for several reasons. First of all, Yugoslavia was more distant, and the Kremlin leaders did not at that time regard that country as falling within the vital security area of the Soviet Union. Second, the Soviets did not wish to antagonize the Western Allies over something that was not so important to Moscow. Finally, Tito did not seem to the Soviets the kind of man with whom the Kremlin might readily do business. His telegrams to Moscow did not show the subservience expected. He even contradicted Stalin in the presence of other Soviet Party officials. He was preferable to Mihailović, but not that much, from the Soviet point of view, at least not in 1944.

Within Yugoslavia, the Partisans—*i.e.* the Communists—had won the civil war. They were installed in Belgrade and, with the help of the Red Army, had thrown out of Serbia not only the Germans but also the Četniks. Half of the country was under their control, and the King and the Royal Government had abandoned Mihailović and switched their support, very half-heartedly in the case of the King, to Tito. Mihailović was somewhere in Bosnia with an ever decreasing number of supporters but determined to struggle to the end in his own country.

Many non-Communists who had joined the Partisans had become aware, particularly in 1944, that those who controlled the movement had no intention whatsoever of abiding by the spirit of the Bihać and Jajce congresses and that there was a fundamental divergence of opinion concerning the real meaning of democracy and freedom. Quite a few Partisans of course had become Communists during the war; compared to a return to the *status quo ante,* others saw in Communism the lesser evil. Still others decided to make the best of a prospect which, deep in their hearts, they hated and feared: the loss of civil liberty, the expropriation of property, the large-scale arrests and the executions of people who had opposed the Partisans.

PART V: 1945

Victory Amid Tragedy

NINETEEN FORTY-FIVE was the year in which World War II ended in victory for the Allied powers. Germany surrendered on May 7. In Yugoslavia, the victorious Partisans consented to a fusion (in name only) with the Yugoslav Government-in-Exile under which the monarchy supposedly was to be preserved. The Yalta Conference in February revealed new alignments. Stalin was now Tito's patron, for political reasons, while Churchill, for the same reasons, had lost all his enthusiasm for the Partisan leader. The British-Russian debate on Yugoslavia at Yalta did not appear to have stirred Roosevelt's interest.

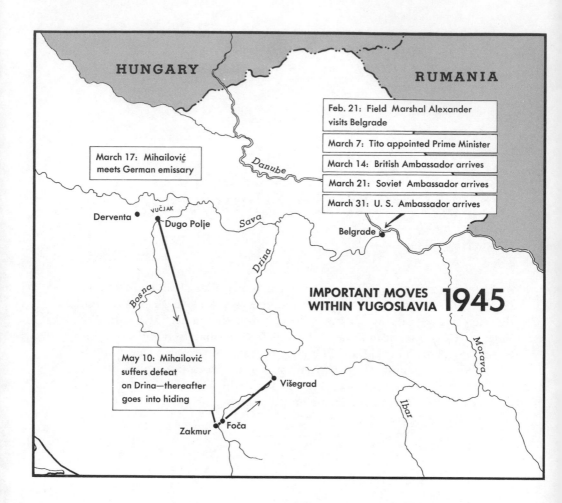

HUNGARY

RUMANIA

Feb. 21: Field Marshal Alexander
visits Belgrade

March 7: Tito appointed Prime Minister

March 14: British Ambassador arrives

March 21: Soviet Ambassador arrives

March 31: U. S. Ambassador arrives

March 17: Mihailović
meets German emissary

Danube

Derventa

VUČJAK

Dugo Polje

Sava

Drina

Belgrade

IMPORTANT MOVES
WITHIN YUGOSLAVIA 1945

Bosna

Morava

May 10: Mihailović
suffers defeat
on Drina—thereafter
goes into hiding

Višegrad

Ibar

Zakmur

Foča

13

KING PETER OBJECTS TO THE TITO-ŠUBAŠIĆ AGREEMENT

In letters dated December 29, 1944, and January 4, 1945, King Peter outlined for Churchill his conclusions that the regency proposed in the Tito-Šubašić agreement was unconstitutional. The legal arguments impressed at least Eden, who writes [1] that in a memorandum dated January 2 he expressed sympathy with the King, "if his argument is that he doesn't want to give the communist dictatorship a cloak of respectability, if royal approval is respectability these days." The British Cabinet, however, decided that Churchill should advise the King to sign the agreement.

On January 6, Ambassador Patterson reported to the State Department that despite British urging, King Peter was reluctant to give his assent to the agreement. He had expressed his hope to Patterson that Roosevelt would support him vis-à-vis Churchill. The State Department felt that the American position was generally well known to the British and to Churchill in particular, and that it could not say whether the President would want to express himself again on this subject. It cabled Patterson on January 7: "As King Peter knows, the President has given much thought to the developments in Yugoslavia, and it is believed that the instructions sent to you and the memorandum already communicated to the British Government reflect his views on the matters in question." [2]

On the same day, Stettinius sent Roosevelt Patterson's telegram of January 6 and the State Department's reply and asked: "Will you please indicate whether you consider that any further messages in this matter would be appropriate?" [3] There is no record of a Presidential reply, and no message was sent by the President to Churchill supporting King Peter.

On January 9, in the presence of Eden and Stevenson, Churchill advised King Peter to sign the Tito-Šubašić agreement, adding: "But I am not a Yugoslav. You know your people best. It is for you to decide." [4] According to Patterson's account of this meeting—which he had from King Peter and later from Stevenson—when King Peter reiterated that he himself wanted to choose his regents, Churchill sharply countered: "You cannot choose them yourself. As a constitutional monarch, you must always take the advice of your Ministers." He then warned: "The three great powers will not lift one finger nor sacrifice one man to put any King back on any throne in Europe." Churchill expressed his belief that if the King signed the agreement he would retain his constitutional position. If he refused he would be by-passed and left "isolated and impotent."

After the conference with Churchill, Eden told King Peter that the latter had too many incompetent advisers living in London on Yugoslav pensions. If they wanted to engage in politics, they should go back to Yugoslavia.

On January 11, without advising his own Prime Minister and against Eden's advice, King Peter issued a declaration in which he rejected the Tito-Šubašić agreement on two grounds: "the suggested form of the regency" and the fact that the "Anti-Fascist Council of National Liberation would wield unrestricted legislative power until a Constituent Assembly had finished its work." King Peter declared that this suggested the transfer of power to a single political group.[5] The Foreign Office told the American Embassy in London that the King had ruined his chances of returning to Yugoslavia, and even the retention of the monarchy seemed doubtful. King Peter himself told Patterson: "I may get my throat cut for this." [6] Šubašić wrote King Peter that the objections raised by the King could be resolved quickly, and he asked for an audience.

Churchill cabled Roosevelt on January 14: "We are now examining the situation to see how we can save the agreements and preserve the title of the Royal Yugoslav Government until the people or peoples of those mountainous regions have a chance of going to the poll." [7]

The Foreign Office informed Tito and the Russians that it considered the King's action as not binding since he had taken it without consulting his Prime Minister.[8] It also instructed its Ambassador in Washington to tell the State Department "politely that it was all very well and good for [the] United States to stall on [the] Yugoslav situation, but that [the] British Government was obliged to take a definite position and could not afford to take [the] same 'waffling' line as the State Department." [9]

Meanwhile, King Peter sent a telegram through Velebit to Tito in which he proposed meeting him at a time and place to be named by Tito to redraft the passage about the regency in such a way as to make it "constitutional." Tito replied to Velebit that he would only receive messages from the King through the Yugoslav Government.

The State Department informed Patterson on January 17 that in its opinion King Peter's declaration need not be considered a rejection of the Tito-Šubašić agreement.[10]

On January 18, Churchill told the House of Commons that if King Peter's assent could not be obtained, it would be presumed. Thereupon, King Peter protested to Churchill by letter, and Churchill in turn instructed Stevenson on January 21 to tell King Peter that if he did not accept the agreement within twenty-four hours, the British Government would ask Šubašić and his Government to go to Belgrade and work out with the National Committee of Liberation a new government under a regency. Ambassador Stevenson would then be accredited to the regency and proceed to Belgrade. King Peter, however, made excuses to delay receiving Stevenson.

The British Embassy in Washington approached the State Department on January 22 orally and subsequently by note, hoping to enlist U.S. support for joint action. The British felt that the Russians might unilaterally recognize the National Committee of Liberation as the Yugoslav government. They also thought that King Peter was acting in the belief that the U.S. would not support the British.

Even before receipt of the British note, Under Secretary Joseph Grew sent Roosevelt a memorandum notifying him of Eden's request for Stettinius' views. The State Department's proposed reply to the expected note was attached to Grew's memorandum, and the President's views were requested. The President had scarcely given his approval when word of a new development arrived: King Peter had dismissed Šubašić for concluding an agreement with Tito without previous consultation with the King.

The British Government informed Šubašić that King Peter's action did not affect its intention to see the Tito-Šubašić agreement carried out. For that purpose the British were ready to transport Šubašić and his Government to Belgrade. They also informed Tito to this effect.

The British Embassy sent an *aide-mémoire* to the State Department on January 23 declaring that "united action by the Three Powers is essential and the quicker and more decisive it is, the less is the likelihood of trouble." [11] The British proposed that Tito be informed jointly by the three powers that if he would "concert with Šubašić" to carry out the agreement, they would accredit ambassadors to the Regency Council. Pending the formation of such a government, no government formed unilaterally either by the King or by Tito would be recognized.

Under Secretary Grew made the following statement to the press on January 23:

This Government has not participated in the discussions concerning the agreement between Prime Minister Šubašić and Marshal Tito for the establishment of a unified government in Yugoslavia. We have been kept informed of recent developments, however, and we approve of the main objective, namely, to enable the Yugoslav Government-in-Exile and the various elements within the country to work together, within Yugoslavia, in the tasks arising from the liberation.[12]

In off-the-record remarks at the same press conference, Grew said that "what this Government most wanted was unification of the various elements within Yugoslavia and also to see eventually a fair and free election in Yugoslavia, so that the people of the country would be able to choose their own government and the form of that government."

The reply of the State Department to the British note of January 22, which had been approved by the President but not sent because of King Peter's dismissal of Šubašić, was redrafted in view of the British aide-mémoire of January 23. It said that while it shared the objective under which the Yugoslav Government would return to the country to work together with the various elements in Yugoslavia, it would be difficult to go beyond a provisional representation to an interim government if the King continued to object to the Tito-Šubašić agreement. Provision for free elections was fundamental, the State Department said, and it implied that if a provisional U.S. mission in Yugoslavia were to be satisfied that free elections had indeed taken place, United States recognition would follow.[13]

The Department informed Patterson of the substance of its note and authorized him to apprise Šubašić and King Peter of its position. It concluded: "The Department is not communicating with Marshal Tito but has no objection if Dr. Šubašić either directly or through General Velebit wishes to inform him of this communication."[14]

In Belgrade, meanwhile, Tito expressed his willingness to have Šubašić join him to carry out the agreement even if the King withheld his concurrence. Thayer reported to Kirk that "Tito was in exceptionally good humor probably because he believes that the London crisis has damaged the King's cause irreparably."[15]

THE KING PETER-ŠUBAŠIĆ "AGREEMENT
WITH RESERVATIONS"

King Peter and Šubašić discussed the situation again and on January 25 agreed on the following solution to the crisis: the King would withdraw Šubašić's dismissal, but Šubašić and his Government would tender their resignations, and immediately thereafter the King would call upon Šubašić to form a new government with wider representation. The task of the new government would be to make the Tito-Šubašić agreement operative, while taking into consideration the two objections made public in King Peter's declaration of January 11.

Patterson, in reporting [16] this development to the State Department, said that at "the eleventh hour General Velebit persuaded Šubašić to do nothing until he [Velebit] wired Tito for his reaction." And Patterson added: "I believe King and Šubašić might have gotten together some days ago if British had taken a less active part. . . ."

Tito did not react to this "agreement with reservations" between Šubašić and King Peter. However, the British Embassy informed the State Department on January 27 that Stalin would like to see the Tito-Šubašić agreement come into force at once "with recognition by the three principal Allies" and "no reservations of any kind." It asked the Department to send immediate instructions to Patterson "to do something helpful" in deciding King Peter to play his part.[17] This was the first indication that Stalin had begun to take an active interest in the political situation in Yugoslavia. By communicating this news, the British were hoping to persuade the U.S. to abandon what the Foreign Office had called its "waffling" line.

At the same time, Cadogan, Permanent Under Secretary of State for Foreign Affairs, told Ambassador Winant in London that both Eden and he very much hoped that the United States would join the British and Soviet Governments in recognition of the Yugoslav Government and that they were troubled by the American suggestion of a "provisional representation" in Belgrade. Cadogan said further that the possibility of a rift between the United States, on the one hand, and the British and Soviet Governments, on the other, was a factor in King Peter's holding out against the agreement.

Later in the afternoon of the same day (January 27), the British Ambassador in Washington, Halifax, telephoned acting Secretary Grew (Stettinius had already left for the conferences at Malta and Yalta) and made the same points that Cadogan had made to Winant in London. Grew replied that the U.S. "must wait and see what happens after the government is set up and what commitments it makes." The Department of State cabled Patterson that since he had already seen to it that both King Peter and Šubašić had a clear understanding of the United States' attitude and intentions, it was neither necessary nor desirable for him to take the responsibility of trying further to influence decisions on major Yugoslav political questions being discussed between King Peter and Šubašić.

In a telegram to Winant, the State Department said, also on January 27, that the U.S. felt it had gone a long way to meet the British position but that it could not go further in view of its policy toward liberated countries.[18] The telegram reiterated that the U.S. had stated its willingness to send its diplomatic mission to Belgrade on the assumption that the Tito-Šubašić agreement would be carried out, and that Patterson had received orders to be ready to proceed to Belgrade upon the transfer of the Government there.[19]

King Peter announced on January 29 that he had accepted the resignation of his cabinet. He then immediately commissioned Šubašić to form a new and enlarged cabinet, which was sworn in the same day. Šubašić telegraphed Tito and asked if he consented to the changes and if he would agree to the extension of AVNOJ by the inclusion of former members of the Yugoslav Parliament to form a "temporary" parliament. While waiting for a reply, the Government arranged with the British that it would leave for Belgrade on February 7 regardless of Tito's answer.

On the day the new cabinet was formed, Winant informed the State Department that the British Government had completed arrangements for the transfer of the Yugoslav Government to Belgrade. He added that the Foreign Office was happy that U.S. representatives would go to Belgrade along with the British and that it assumed that Patterson and his staff would proceed to Belgrade even if a split between King Peter and the Yugoslav Government should occur at the last minute.[20]

Difficulties arose immediately regarding the composition of the Regency Council. King Peter had nominated former Prime Minister Simović, who had been involved in the coup d'état of March 1941; Dr. Juraj Šutej, a Croat member of the Šubašić Government, and Dušan Sernec, a Slovene and a member of Tito's National Committee of Liberation.

On February 5, Tito told Thayer in Belgrade that he would not accept Šutej. He suggested Ante Mandić, a Croat member of AVNOJ, instead. He said he was agreeable to Simović and Sernec. On February 6, Patterson learned that Šubašić now opposed Simović. King Peter gives[21] as

Šubašić's reason that Simović had not consulted the other members of the Government when he gave the order to capitulate in 1941. Whether Šubašić was acting on instructions from Tito, who apparently had changed his mind about Simović, is not quite clear. Šubašić requested that Simović be replaced by Sreten Vukosavljević, who had joined the Šubašić Government after the negotiations in Vis in June 1944.

The King insisted on retaining Šutej despite Tito's opposition. Although Šubašić and his ministers had been scheduled to leave for Belgrade on February 7, whether or not an agreement was reached, their departure was postponed. Thayer reported from Belgrade that Tito told Maclean on February 9 that the Šubašić Government was greatly concerned over "legitimacy" and was anxious to stay in London until the composition of the regency had been settled.[22] Tito wanted to proceed with "other arrangements" but then decided to await the outcome of the Big Three Conference at Yalta. He told Maclean that he would not take an irrevocable step until Churchill returned to London. Thayer thought that it was significant that Tito expected Churchill to return with a formula favorable to him.

THE FIRST U.S. DIPLOMATIC REPRESENTATIVES
ARRIVE IN BELGRADE

The first two U.S. diplomatic representatives, Foreign Service officers Carl Norden and Peter Constan, arrived in Belgrade on January 16, 1945. (It will be recalled that Constan was in the last group of Americans who left Belgrade, on July 15, 1941.) Both the State Department and the Partisans placed severe limitations on their activities and movements: The State Department was anxious to avoid the impression that the U.S. was re-establishing a regular diplomatic mission, and the Partisans curtailed the scope of their functions since the U.S. had not yet formally installed its diplomatic mission in Belgrade.

Thus, the main official contact continued to be maintained through the American military mission under Thayer. Relations were correct, although Thayer felt that the Partisans showed a lack of cooperation and hospitality to the U.S. mission. There is no doubt that Tito was suspicious of American policies and motives, and he once complained to Thayer that a "majority of Americans were opposed to his regime." [23] Thayer in turn reported to Caserta that it would be unfortunate "if the impression were permitted to gain currency that we might in any way short of military measures alter the present course of events in Yugoslavia . . . [for] there is not the slightest evidence that any form of pressure from the

United States would increase the chances of the population to express itself freely in a genuine election. . . ." [24] From Caserta, Kirk informed the State Department on January 20 that Thayer had reported "his opinion that, despite superficial professions of warmest friendship for United States, we are regarded by Partisan officials with a suspicion which, though far less acute than that directed at British, is so deep rooted that it will require much patient effort to overcome." [25]

Although the Partisans were strongly Soviet-oriented, they were also determined not to depend entirely on Moscow. The idea of keeping a door ajar to the West was influenced to a great extent by economic factors. The Soviet Union, itself ravaged, would be less able to provide Yugoslavia with economic aid than the West, particularly the United States. But political factors played a role too. While the Partisan leaders, as good Marxists, directed most of their political suspicions at the West, some of them were reserved toward the Soviets, who had failed to aid them in their early struggle, who were condescending in their attitude almost throughout the war and whose behavior in liberated territory was resented.

MIHAILOVIĆ ABANDONED

Mihailović and his Četniks continued to hold an enclave in Bosnia within the part of the country still in German hands. Before he left Yugoslavia in November 1944, Colonel McDowell had suggested to Mihailović that he move with his troops toward the Italian border, where U.S. forces would meet him. This was easier said than done. Blocking such a move were the combined German and Croatian forces. At Mihailović's back were the Partisans. Winter was about to set in with all its hardships of inclement weather, difficulty of movement and food and supply shortages.

Nevertheless, Mihailović decided to make the move, but winter soon halted his advance. Having lost many men after King Peter's appeal to join the Partisans, he now lost more to frost and starvation. In addition, a typhus epidemic took many lives in January 1945. In March one of Mihailović's principal lieutenants, Pavle Djurišić, set out for Italy with about 7,000 to 9,000 soldiers and refugees, apparently against the general's advice. They fell into an *Ustaše* trap, and only about a third of them escaped.

On March 17, Stärker, the German emissary who had three times previously seen Mihailović, paid the general a visit at his headquarters, which was then in the Bosnian village of Dugo Polje in the Vučjak Mountain area near Derventa. In the course of the discussion, Stärker requested that Mihailović transmit to Allied headquarters in Italy a secret German offer of capitulation.[26] Mihailović passed on this offer to Caserta. It was one of the last messages sent by him. Soon thereafter, in late March, he decided to attempt a return to Serbia.[27]

By early May, three Četnik columns had reached the Drina close to Foča. However, on May 10 approximately 6,000 Četniks ran into Partisan forces and about half of them were annihilated. The other half broke through but were practically wiped out in another battle two days later. Only 300 to 400 Četniks escaped, among them Mihailović.[28] He was forced to go into hiding and to disperse his decimated organization, hoping to resurrect it one day. Some of his associates went back to Serbia, but Mihailović did not. He stayed first in the Zakmur district near Foča. During the battles in May he had lost his last radio transmitter, and now all communication with the outside world, even with his supporters within Yugoslavia, was cut off.

On March 13, 1946, Mihailović was captured by Tito's men east of Višegrad near the Bosnian-Serbian border. His hiding place, a foxhole, was apparently revealed, wittingly or unwittingly, by Kalabić, one of his chief lieutenants. Whether Kalabić was a party to the elaborate plan devised to capture Mihailović or was himself tricked into believing that those who sought him were attempting to save him has never been clear. Mihailović was tried in June, convicted and executed by the Tito regime on July 17, 1946. Of his immediate family, only his wife visited him in jail. His son and daughter, having denounced him as a traitor, had gone over to the Partisans earlier during the war.

Although those events took place at a time beyond the scope of this study, it should be stressed that the trial was anything but a model of justice, as the stenographic record amply proves.[29] It is clear that Mihailović was not guilty of all, or even many, of the charges brought against him. Yet one wonders what kind of trial Tito would have received, in the aftermath of civil war, had he and not Mihailović been the loser.

THE YALTA CONFERENCE

Bound for the Yalta Conference, which was to be his last encounter with Churchill and Stalin, Roosevelt left Newport News, Virginia, aboard the USS *Quincy* on January 22, 1945, landing in Malta on February 2. Secretary Stettinius, Harry Hopkins and the Joint Chiefs of Staff were already assembled there when the President arrived, and meetings with the British had been in progress for three days.

As it related to the military situation, Yugoslavia was hardly mentioned in these initial British-American sessions. The Combined Chiefs of Staff directive of December 2, 1944—that major Allied forces would not be introduced into the Balkans—still stood and there was no thought of changing it. In the political meetings, however, Yugoslavia was discussed in connection with its future borders with both Austria and Italy.

The United States reiterated its oft-stated policy that revisions of boundaries must await a peace settlement. At a preliminary meeting between Stettinius and Eden on February 1, the latter mentioned that if Tito should wish to occupy the part of Austria he claimed, a problem might arise for British troops responsible for the Yugoslav-Austrian border under the proposed zone agreement. Eden suggested, and Stettinius concurred, that it would help matters if at Yalta the three powers agreed to inform Tito that the borders must remain as they were until the peace treaty.[30]

The Yalta Conference began on February 4, but Yugoslavia was not discussed until the fifth plenary meeting on February 8. This time, in contrast to Tehran, Stalin brought it up. The atmosphere had changed radically, and Stalin was now Tito's protagonist.

Before adjourning for the day, Stalin said that he had "one small matter" that he wished to bring up: He wanted to know what was holding back the formation of a unified government in Yugoslavia. Churchill said that the King had been persuaded, even forced, to agree to a regency. Šubašić was leaving soon for Yugoslavia, if he had not left already (he had not), to appoint the regents and form the government. Churchill said that Eden had told him that there were "two slight amendments" to the agreement reached between Šubašić and Tito which he would take up with Molotov. He added that he had always made it plain, both privately and publicly, that if the King would not agree to a regency, he would be by-passed. He felt that in regard to the two amendments if Stalin said two words to Tito the matter would be settled. Stalin replied that Tito was a proud man and now the popular head of a regime and might resent advice. Churchill thought that Marshal Stalin could risk that. President Roosevelt did not participate in this debate.[31]

The Foreign Ministers met on the following day and again the Russians brought up the Yugoslav question. Molotov said that he could not understand the British desire to supplement the Tito-Šubašić agreement when steps had not even been taken to put the original agreement into force. He proposed that the original agreement be executed and that subsequent questions be discussed later. However, Eden felt that the British amendments were reasonable and provided for a more democratic Yugoslavia. When Molotov persevered, Stettinius suggested that representatives of Eden and Molotov be appointed to draw up a statement on the Yugoslav situation. This was accepted.[32]

What the British recommended was that the new Yugoslav government, when constituted, should declare that the Anti-Fascist Council of National Liberation (AVNOJ) was extended to include members of the last parliament who had not compromised themselves, thus forming a body to be called a "temporary parliament." They recommended that the legislative acts passed by AVNOJ be subject to ratification by a constituent assembly.

Later in the day at a heads-of-government meeting, Molotov raised again the question of the Tito-Šubašić agreement, insisting that it be put into effect. He said that Churchill, in messages to Stalin, had urged this, that there had been a series of delays, and that this conference should put the agreement into effect, irrespective of the wishes of the King.[33]

Churchill asked whether the Soviet Government had agreed to the two British amendments. Molotov replied that amendments meant more delays. It would be better, he thought, to ask Tito and Šubašić about the amendments after the agreement had been put into effect. Churchill inquired whether it was too much to ask that legislative acts of the temporary authorities be subject to confirmation by democratic processes. Stalin replied that delays were very undesirable and that if the British proposed amendments, the Soviets might submit some too. Meanwhile, the Yugoslav government was hanging in the balance. This annoyed Churchill, who said that Tito was a dictator and could do what he wanted. Stalin replied that Tito was not a dictator, but the head of a national committee without any clear government and that this was not a good situation. Eden replied that it was not a question of amendments before the agreement went into force, but merely of requesting that they be adopted.

Stalin finally agreed to the two British amendments, but he thought the government should first be formed and the amendments then proposed to it. Eden felt that once agreement upon the amendments was reached, Tito could be asked, after the principal agreement was in force, to adopt them. Stalin agreed and added that a telegram might be sent stating the desire of the three powers to have the agreement put into effect regardless of the King's wishes.

Churchill and Eden said that the question of the King had been settled and was anyway not important; Šubašić was on his way to Yugoslavia (he was still in London) to put the agreement into effect. Neither Roosevelt nor Stettinius participated in this exchange.

On the next morning, February 10, the Foreign Ministers met, and Eden informed his colleagues that Šubašić had been delayed in London because the question of naming the three regents had not been settled. However, in the British view there was no reason why this should hold up execution of the agreement. After some discussion with Molotov, in which Stettinius did not join, it was agreed that the British would furnish a draft of a telegram to be sent to Tito and Šubašić.[34]

During a heads-of-government meeting in the afternoon, Eden read the text of a proposed telegram, and at that point Roosevelt for the first time intervened in the Yugoslav debate, saying that he was not sure whether the United States would be able to associate itself with the telegram. However, when the text of the telegram was once more read to him, he agreed that it was satisfactory.[35]

There followed some discussion between the British and the Russians as to the exact wording of the message. Molotov wanted to confine it to a statement that the three powers had concurred that the Tito-Šubašić agreement should be put into effect, while Churchill wished to mention also the nature of the British amendments. A compromise was finally reached. The amendments were to be mentioned, but reference to the temporary nature of the new government was left out because Stalin thought it offensive to Yugoslav sensibilities.

The British delegation immediately cabled the Foreign Office to get in touch with Šubašić and Tito and inform them of the agreement. The message said that the Soviets and the Americans were also informing their representatives with Šubašić and Tito, and it directed that "action should be concerted between the representatives of the three Allied Governments." [36] The Yalta communiqué, signed on February 11, stated concerning Yugoslavia:

We have agreed to recommend to Marshal Tito and Dr. Šubašić that the Agreement between them should be put into effect immediately, and that a new Government should be formed on the basis of that Agreement.

We also recommend that as soon as the new Government has been formed, it should declare that:

(i) The Anti-Fascist Assembly [Council] of National Liberation (AVNOJ) should be extended to include members of the last Yugoslav Parliament (Skupschina) who have not compromised themselves by collaboration with the enemy, thus forming a body to be known as a temporary Parliament; and

(ii) legislative acts passed by the Anti-Fascist Assembly of National Liberation . . . will be subject to subsequent ratification by a Constituent Assembly.

There was also a general review of other Balkan question(s).[37]

The last sentence referred to the question of the future Austro-Yugoslav and Italo-Yugoslav borders, which was discussed but not concluded owing to lack of time. Eden also gave Stettinius and Molotov identical notes concerning the interim administration of Venezia Giulia which in substance proposed that a provisional line of demarcation be established between the area to be controlled by Tito and the area to be placed under Allied military government.

A meeting of the Combined Chiefs of Staff with Roosevelt and Churchill on February 9 approved a directive to Field Marshal Alexander, Allied Supreme Commander, Mediterranean, which stated with regard to Yugoslavia:

> Subject to the requirements of the Italian Theater, you should continue to give all possible support to the Yugoslav Army of National Liberation, until the territory of Yugoslavia has been completely cleared. You will carry out such minor operations on the eastern shores of the Adriatic as your resources allow.[38]

DISAGREEMENT ON THE REGENCY

Upon the conclusion of the Yalta Conference, Maclean received a telegram from Eden instructing him to inform Tito of the tripartite recommendations. The telegram added that the American and Soviet mission chiefs would receive similar instructions from their Governments. Thayer, however, heard nothing from the President or the State Department. When Ambassador Kirk inquired about this, he received the following reply from the State Department on February 12:

> The communiqué of the Crimea Conference now being released contains a passage similar to the message of instructions which Maclean thinks Thayer should have received. Neither the OSS nor the Department has any knowledge of instructions to or intended for Thayer on this matter. Unless he receives such direct instructions he ought not to furnish explanations or interpretations of the communiqué.[39]

It turned out that Maclean was the only mission chief to inform Tito of the tripartite recommendations. The Soviet mission chief, Major General A. F. Kiselev, who had replaced Korneyev after the liberation of Belgrade, was still in Moscow, and the acting mission chief did not receive any instructions. Thayer was asked by Tito's personal representative, Bakić, whether he had received any messages from the Yalta Conference; Thayer replied that he had not.

It is evident that the U.S. delegation to the Yalta Conference did not inform either the State Department or the U.S. representatives with Šubašić and Tito of the Yalta decisions regarding Yugoslavia. Whether this failure was intentional cannot be gathered, but that Roosevelt showed little interest in the Yugoslav question at Yalta is clear. This undoubtedly contributed to the lack of concern on the part of Stettinius and the other members of the delegation.

Tito told Maclean that he accepted the Yalta formula without reservation and added that the sooner Šubašić arrived in Belgrade the better. He wondered, however, how the agreement was to be implemented without the participation of the King.[40]

In London, the King and the Šubašić Government agreed to the Yalta recommendations on February 12. On the following day, King Peter signed a statement which he gave to his Government before its departure for Belgrade. It said that the "Royal Government goes to Belgrade with my full accord and is carrying . . . instructions from me."

In the first of three parts of those instructions, the King named to the regency Dr. Milan Grol, Dr. Juraj Šutej and Dr. Dušan Sernec. He expressed the hope that the National Committee of Liberation would respect his choice, "based on careful thought and aimed at representing useful elements to the state and to the smooth functioning of their duties."

When accepted by the National Committee, the regency would be appointed "by my royal decree," sworn in at Belgrade "by the high clergy in the presence of the Royal Government who will also invite to be present the President of the National Committee of Liberation, Marshal J. B. Tito." The section on the regency ended with the assertion that the Government must be held responsible to the Regency Council and must inform the King of all important developments in the country.

The next part of the instructions declared that the united government would not be formed until the regency had been duly appointed and sworn in. "The United Government is to comprise many shades of opinion representing as many political parties and views as is possible," the instructions said. The final section declared that the Yalta recommendations were to be implemented.[41]

Šubašić traveled by way of Caserta, where he expressed optimism regarding the regency situation, and arrived in Belgrade on February 15. Tito, however, had informed Thayer that he would not accept Šutej under any circumstances; Thayer commented that "it may take some time to form the regency." Indeed, after Šubašić's arrival in Belgrade even more difficulties arose. On February 22, Tito told Maclean that he would not accept either Šutej or Grol.

Eden thereupon sent messages to both Šubašić and Tito. To Šubašić he expressed the anxiety of the British Government lest the whole agreement be endangered through Šubašić's insistence on Šutej and Grol, presumably because they were acceptable to the King. He reminded him that the Yalta Conference communiqué made no reference to the King. It was the British intention, Eden said, that while the names of the regents should be submitted for the King's approval, the agreement would nevertheless come into force if this approval was not forthcoming.

Eden told Tito that the British Government was apprehensive because of the disagreement on the regency. He said that he was urging Šubašić to come to an agreement on this point and that he earnestly hoped that Tito would not jeopardize the agreement for which "we have all striven and to which we attach such importance."

Through the British Embassies in Washington and Moscow, Eden suggested that the U.S. and Soviet Governments also send messages to Šubašić and Tito.[42]

On February 25, the State Department handed a note to the Yugoslav Chargé, Ivan Frangeš, referring to the Yalta communiqué declarations regarding Yugoslavia and liberated Europe. In the latter, it pointed out, the heads of government had "declared their mutual agreement to concert the policies of their three Governments to assist liberated peoples to solve by democratic means their pressing political and economic problems." [43] The note continued:

Among the situations in which this assistance would be applicable would be cases where in the judgment of the principal Allies the conditions within a liberated state require that interim governmental authorities be formed which would be broadly representative of all democratic elements in the population and pledged to the earliest possible establishment through free elections of Governments responsible to the will of the people.

Accordingly, the United States Government would like to see Dr. Šubašić and Marshal Tito reach an early agreement, in accordance with these principles and in a spirit of mutual understanding, in the negotiations now taking place in Belgrade.

This was the channel and manner by which the U.S. Government informed the Yugoslav authorities of the President's concurrence in the Yalta declaration on Yugoslavia. The State Department avoided the Thayer-Tito channel because it did not wish to give the National Committee of Liberation in Belgrade implied recognition or suggest that Thayer had diplomatic status.

Marshal Tito, Brigadier Maclean, Field Marshal Alexander and General Velebit in Belgrade, February 1945. *Courtesy of V. Kljaković*

ALEXANDER VISITS TITO

On February 21, Alexander, accompanied by U.S. General Lyman L. Lemnitzer, went to Belgrade to discuss with Tito the Partisans' military plans for the spring. They were very well received, and Alexander was given an outline of the intended operations, which were to begin on March 20. During these meetings in Belgrade, arrangements were completed for the Balkan Air Force and the Partisan army staff to work out a detailed air-support plan for operations on the Yugoslav coast, and Alexander's naval representative began conversations on naval matters with Partisan representatives.

In the discussions, the question of additional supplies was raised by Tito.[44] His forces had received since November increasing quantities of arms and ammunition from the Allies. He now requested 100,000 uniforms and 10,000 trucks. Alexander replied there was some prospect of aid in food, clothing and gasoline but little hope of providing trucks, of which there was a shortage. Tito said that the Russians had furnished 800 trucks, food, ammunition and artillery.

Tito expected the Germans to make a stand in the mountains of

Austria where, he said, his 200,000 troops could be very useful to the
Allies. He also suggested Yugoslav occupation of a part of Austria following Germany's defeat.

An important subject discussed by Alexander was the question of the
control of the Italian province of Venezia Giulia. Before his departure
for Belgrade, Alexander appeared to have been ready for purely military
reasons to make certain concessions to Tito. However, he was prevailed
upon by Kirk to talk about Venezia Giulia only in the most general
military terms.[45]

Alexander told Tito that as a result of preliminary planning, it seemed
essential to establish Allied Military Government (AMG) control in
Venezia Giulia within the 1939 frontiers in order to maintain Allied
forces in Austria. Alexander explained that this would not prejudice
boundary considerations in a final peace settlement. Tito accepted Alexander's plan provided his already established civil administration in
those parts of Venezia Giulia occupied by Partisan troops would remain.
He foresaw chaos unless his authorities were allowed to function; however, he agreed that they would be responsible to AMG. He commented
also that if the object of Allied occupation was to protect lines of communication between Trieste and Austria, he did not consider Allied
occupation of the whole Istrian peninsula necessary, and offered the use
of communications facilities through Slovenia. Alexander pointed out that
his remarks were purely exploratory and that the matter would have to
be referred to the Combined Chiefs of Staff.

At Yalta, it will be recalled, the British had submitted a note to the
U.S. and USSR regarding the interim administration of Venezia Giulia,
suggesting a provisional line of demarcation dividing it between the
AMG and Tito's forces. The State Department replied to this note on
March 14, after Alexander's visit to Tito, expressing little enthusiasm for
the British proposal.[46]

In the end, the British swung around to the American view, that all
of Venezia Giulia should be under AMG, particularly after Tito in April
reneged on his agreement with Alexander concerning AMG administration of Venezia Giulia, saying that "conditions have changed" since their
meeting. (A most unhappy wrangle developed over the future of the area
which was not to be settled until nine years after the end of the war.)

Before returning to Italy, Alexander and Lemnitzer visited Marshal
Tolbukhin's headquarters in Hungary. Thayer gives an amusing account
of that visit.[47] Thayer also reports on a visit by General Eaker, commander of the Mediterranean Air Force, who came to Belgrade on March
10 to receive a decoration from Marshal Tito. The award cited Eaker's

role in dropping supplies to the Partisans and evacuating wounded Partisans during the fighting. Again Tito was a gracious host. Thayer reciprocated by giving a lunch in his headquarters, the "Mission House," which Tito attended.

YUGOSLAV GOVERNMENT FORMED—
THE ALLIED AMBASSADORS ARRIVE IN BELGRADE

On February 26, the Šubašić-Tito negotiations culminated in an agreement, the text of which was given by Šubašić to Norden, one of the two Foreign Service officers dispatched to Belgrade by Kirk. This agreement, between the Royal Government and the National Committee of Liberation, called for the names of Sernec (a Slovene) and Dr. Ante Mandić (a Croat) to be submitted to the King together with the names of four Serbian candidates from whom the King was to choose one. When King Peter did not immediately accept the proposed regents, the British Ambassador was instructed by his Government to put pressure on him. Churchill suggested to Eden that the King should be told that if he continued his obstruction, Britain would ask him to leave the country.[48]

In London, Stevenson told Patterson that "if the King does not agree by this week end, his consent will be presumed and the United Government formed." [49] Stevenson asked Patterson to seek similar instructions, which he did, but the State Department replied on March 3: "You may advise Stevenson that we are not disposed to press the King with respect to his selections for the Regency Council. . . ." [50]

By that time the King had issued a communiqué appointing as regents Mandić and Sernec as well as Srdjan Budisavljević, a former minister in the Government-in-Exile and one of the four Serbs proposed by Šubašić and Tito. He did not reveal his decision in advance to either Šubašić or Ribar, the head of the Anti-Fascist Council of National Liberation, who was in London at that time. Of the three regents, two were Partisans. On March 3, in the presence of Queen Alexandra, King Peter received Ribar and gave him the decree appointing the regents. The decree bore his signature as well as that of Šubašić, who had signed in blank before his departure for Belgrade. Thayer reported that the three regents took the oath on March 5. Tito was not present.

On March 6, the Royal Yugoslav Government submitted its resignation to the regents, and the members of the National Committee of Liberation thereupon submitted their resignations to the Anti-Fascist Council of National Liberation. On March 7, the Regency Council appointed a United Yugoslav Government of twenty-eight ministers under the premiership of Tito, with Šubašić as Foreign Minister. This was the first and last act of the Regency Council.[51]

The new Yugoslav Government consisted of six members of the former Šubašić Government and twenty-two from within the country. Of the latter, twenty were ministers in Tito's National Committee of Liberation, and two were regarded as Tito supporters. Of the six members of the former Šubašić Government, two were appointed after the Šubašić-Tito negotiations at Vis in the summer of 1944, and one, Kosanović, had been the chief Tito protagonist in the U.S. while he was an official of the Yugoslav information center in New York. Thus only three, namely Šubašić, Šutej and Grol, could be regarded as representatives of groups not affiliated with the Partisans. Their power in the Government was practically nil. Grol and Šutej had no portfolios, although the former was Vice Premier. All three left the Government within a few months (Grol on August 18, and Šubašić and Šutej on October 11, 1945).

On March 13, the Yugoslav Chargé in Washington officially notified the State Department of the nomination of the regents and the formation of the new government. On March 21, the State Department informed the Yugoslav Chargé that Ambassador Patterson and his staff had been authorized to proceed to Belgrade to establish the American Embassy there.

As the anniversary of the 1941 coup d'état in Belgrade approached, President Roosevelt sent a curiously insensitive greeting on March 27 to King Peter in London saying that on "this memorable occasion the American people look forward to the day of victory when the valiant people of Yugoslavia will regain complete possession of their country."

Eden reports [52] that on March 10 and 11, Churchill wrote him that he was reaching the conclusion that Britain's role "should become one of increasing detachment" and that "our inclination should be to back Italy against Yugoslavia at the head of the Adriatic." On March 18, Eden replied that a policy of withdrawal would not be wise. He argued that Britain should not withdraw "and leave the whole business to Tito and Moscow."

Ambassador Stevenson arrived in Belgrade on March 14, the new Soviet Ambassador, Ivan V. Sadchikov, a week later and Ambassador Patterson arrived at Belgrade airport from London on March 31. Patterson came to a Yugoslavia vastly different from the one American Minister Lane had left almost four years earlier. Thayer and Harold Shantz, the Counselor, who had arrived a few days before, had made arrangements to take over the old Legation building (called the "Bank Building").

Lieutenant Colonel Thayer, Major General Kiselev and Ambassador Patterson in Belgrade, April 1945. *Courtesy of V. Kljaković*

From a window of the office a gory stain discolored the grey stone wall where a German sniper had been shot and bled to death on the window sill. A small house was rented for the Ambassador's residence.

In conjunction with the American military mission, the Office of War Information had begun operating in Belgrade, and on the day of Patterson's arrival an information center was opened in the presence of many high Partisan officials in the building where the United States Information Service still has its library.

On April 2, Patterson, after a formal call on the regents,[53] had his first talk with Prime Minister Tito during which, according to Patterson, Tito expressed most cordial sentiments toward the U.S. On April 4, Tito gave a large dinner for the British, Soviet and American Ambassadors. On the next day he left for Moscow, where he concluded, on April 11, a "Treaty of Friendship, Mutual Aid and Post War Cooperation" with the Soviet Union.

Two weeks after Patterson's arrival Thayer left Yugoslavia to assume charge of the OSS mission in Austria. His successor was Major Franklin A. Lindsay.[54]

Marshal Tito in Moscow signing Friendship Treaty in the presence of
Marshal Stalin, Foreign Minister Molotov and Deputy Foreign Minister
Vyshinsky. *Foto-Tanjug, Belgrade*

Meanwhile an offensive begun March 20 was in full swing to drive the
Germans out of the rest of the country. Four Partisan armies were on the
move. The 1st Army, under Peko Dapčević, was closing on Zagreb; so
was the 2nd, under Koča Popović. The 3rd, under Kosta Nadj, was aim-
ing at the Austrian border, while the 4th, under Petar Drapšin, advanced
toward the Italian frontier, entering Trieste on May 1, two days before
the Allies. German resistance crumbled as the Allies pounded the Wehrmacht from west, south and east. On May 7, 1945, Germany surrendered [55] and the war in Europe had ended, with far-reaching consequences for the political order on the entire continent.

A new chapter had begun, too, in the turbulent history of the land
of the South Slavs.

Epilogue

A new chapter had indeed begun in the history of Yugoslavia. A Communist regime was legally installed in Belgrade. Although the Partisans received outside military help after the middle of 1943, that material aid did not determine their victory: Tito and his followers won the civil war because they were from the first militarily more active and later politically more astute than the Četniks. Only an Allied landing in Yugoslavia —which Churchill would have welcomed but Roosevelt and Stalin opposed for military reasons—might have altered the outcome of the internal Yugoslav struggle.

Differences in personality, ambition, policies and programs of the respective Yugoslav resistance leaders almost seem in retrospect to have been fated to distinguish the winner from the loser in their tragic contest. It became evident as the war progressed that Tito was by far the stronger personality, whose ambitions framed a larger view of Yugoslavia and even of his own importance on the world scene. As a Serbian patriot, Mihailović's ambitions were far less pretentious. Unlike Tito, who importunately rose to international challenge, Mihailović described himself at his trial as a man who "wanted much . . . began much, but the gale of the world swept away me and my work."

Tito's allegiance was at first unswervingly to the Soviet Union as world leader of Communism even though it failed to support him politically or militarily until the war was virtually over. Progressively he converted his disillusionment and frustration into independence, and in the end it might be said that his allegiance was more to himself than to any external force. Mihailović's allegiance was steadfastly to the King and to the Serbian people. Before his struggle ceased he had been dismissed by the one and abandoned by the other.

A product of the hard school of Communist training and illegal activity in several countries, Tito was a superb organizer, while Mihailović lacked that talent altogether. Discipline was a weapon of the Partisans, but Mihailović found himself unable to control his subordinates, and some Četnik leaders brought early disgrace upon his movement.

Tito's policies were dynamic, Mihailović's basically static, and the programs these policies dictated were contrastingly aggressive and defensive. The original aim of the Mihailović movement—to resist the invaders—withered away as the specter of Communist control of ever larger portions of the country reared its head. Although hostile to the Germans and the Italians, the Četniks allowed themselves to drift into a policy of accommodation with both in the face of what they considered the greater danger.

Mihailović gambled all in the faith of an Allied victory that would deliver the country from the external enemy, and in the meantime he and his followers sought to prevent the spread of an alien ideology threatening their conception of a new postwar Yugoslavia. The Communists, on the other hand, began resistance to the Axis only after the German attack upon the Soviet Union and at first fought solely in support of the Red Army. But Partisan resistance turned into a revolutionary movement, and it spread the cloak of a popular front over its struggle, thus ably serving the new aim of achieving political control of the country at the end of the war.

The evolution of events in Yugoslavia had a direct effect upon British-Yugoslav and Soviet-Yugoslav relations and, to a lesser extent, upon American-Yugoslav relations.

The British originally supported the Yugoslav Government-in-Exile and Mihailović because they were presumed to have significance militarily. But Churchill quickly turned elsewhere after concluding that the Četniks were not fighting the external enemies and had indeed made pacts with them. Military support then went to the Partisans on the strength of firsthand reports to Churchill that they were effectively tying down substantial Axis forces. That the Partisans were under Communist leadership troubled Churchill little. Since Churchill did not intend "to make Yugoslavia his home after the war," he told Maclean at the end of

1943, "the less you and I worry about the form of Government they set up, the better." This view changed later, particularly after Soviet designs in the Balkans became clearer toward the end of the war. Nevertheless, Churchill pushed the Yugoslav Government-in-Exile relentlessly into a one-sided agreement with the Partisans, hoping thereby to retain some British influence in Yugoslavia when the war ended.

The Soviets showed surprisingly little interest in their Communist allies in Yugoslavia, and because they did not wish unnecessarily to disturb relations with the British and U.S. Governments, they supported the Yugoslav Government-in-Exile well into 1943. Radio messages from the Comintern to the Partisans invariably instructed Tito to put Soviet interests first. Since military operations in Yugoslavia were of little importance to Stalin, he sent a Soviet mission to join Tito only in February 1944, almost a year after the British dropped liaison officers to the Partisans. Soviet political interest in Yugoslavia was unfocused until Stalin championed Tito at the Yalta meeting of the Big Three early in 1945.

The United States followed Yugoslav affairs in some detail but failed to evolve a policy toward Yugoslavia and resolutely refused to exert any influence. In the U.S. view, Yugoslavia was not of crucial military importance to the Allied grand strategy. Roosevelt was at first pro-Serb, a mentor to the young King Peter and advocate of a re-established Serbian kingdom. His attitude changed later, after he had read a report from an American liaison officer with the Partisans toward the end of 1943. His change of view, however, did not affect his conviction that events in Yugoslavia were remote from U.S. interests and not central to Allied military operations. Although political considerations rapidly overtook military considerations in the calculations of Churchill and Stalin as the war came to a close, Roosevelt remained interested solely in a rapid end to the European war so that American might could be concentrated on the unfinished war in the Pacific.

Once installed in Belgrade as Prime Minister, Tito began to organize the country strictly along Party lines. Yugoslavia was now a federal state, but that was about the only promise made at the Bihać and Jajce congresses that was kept. Civil rights, inviolability of private property, individual initiative, no radical social changes, free elections after the war—none of these promises was kept. The new power in Belgrade was a tightly authoritarian Communist regime.

At the end of 1945, the few non-Communists in the Government, whose influence had been nil anyway, were eased out, and the monarchy which had continued in name only was abolished. Within days after the end of the war in Europe, Tito's forces had attacked Mihailović and his

Četniks and practically wiped them out. The civil war was finally over, even though Mihailović himself was captured only ten months later, tried and executed in July 1946.

Internationally, the Tito regime was ready to look to Moscow despite the many disappointments which the Partisans had experienced throughout the war at the hands of the Soviet Union. Even before the war in Europe had ended, Tito went to Moscow to sign a "Treaty of Friendship, Mutual Aid and Post War Cooperation" with the Soviet Union, and he and his regime took this pact most seriously. Thus, in the prosecution of the "Cold War," Yugoslavia played initially an important supporting role. Yugoslav delegates at international meetings, most of the time speaking Russian, often outdid the Soviets in their anti-Western rhetoric. Relations with the West grew correspondingly worse. Two American planes flying from Italy over Yugoslavia to Austria were shot down in 1946, and Marshall Plan aid was rejected in 1947, following the Soviet lead.

Stalin, however, never really felt comfortable with Tito, who had argued with Moscow in telegrams to the Comintern and had come to power on his own. Moreover, Tito had gone to Italy to see Churchill before he went to Moscow to meet with Stalin. The Soviets, therefore, soon began a systematic drive to tie Yugoslavia politically and economically closer to the Soviet Union. The Yugoslav leaders had been quite ready for such an association, but they resented the Soviet methods of conniving and intriguing, of interfering in Yugoslav internal affairs and of inciting lower-echelon Party members against their leaders.

On June 28, 1948, the Communist world was shaken by a cataclysmic split between Yugoslavia and the Soviet Union. Completely unexpectedly, except for the main participants, Yugoslavia was expelled from the Cominform (Communist Information Bureau, founded in 1947 and in some respects a successor to the Comintern).

We now know that the conflict was long in coming and that the seeds for this rupture were planted early, during the war, as this narrative has tried to demonstrate.

The telling factor was that Tito did not have Stalin to thank for his victory in the civil war. No foreign Party leader who did not owe his existence to the Soviet Union and who did not show complete subservience to the Communist motherland could be a true and reliable Communist in Stalin's eyes. How different was the behavior of the Yugoslav Communists from that displayed by the leaders of the other fraternal parties in Eastern Europe who were put in power by the Soviets. Stalin's suspicions had only increased when the Yugoslav Communists began to play a leading role with regard to the other Communist movements in the Balkans—in Albania, Bulgaria and particularly in Greece, where the uprising in 1946 against the Greek Government was strongly abetted by the Communist Party of Yugoslavia.

Tito thus was not, in Stalin's opinion, a subordinate and could never become one even if he had wanted to, which he clearly did not. Therefore, he must be replaced by a Yugoslav Communist owing his appointment to Moscow. But Stalin gravely miscalculated. The loyalty to Tito of the Yugoslav Communists who had fought under his leadership during the war was practically unanimous, and although the country experienced a massive military and economic squeeze by the Soviets and their satellites, they stood firm in their support of him.

The U.S. Government quickly understood the importance of the event. In what turned out to be one of the major foreign policy successes since the war, President Truman seized the opportunity and provided Yugoslavia with desperately needed economic and military help. Tito, remembering his cordial relations with the Western liaison officers during the war and the help he had received—military, economic and moral—accepted the outstretched hand of the U.S. Yugoslavia remained free and independent. More than that: The break between Yugoslavia and the USSR had important positive consequences for the West—a non-Communist Greece, the return of Trieste to Italy and the nonparticipation of Yugoslavia in the Warsaw Pact. The roots of these developments lay in the convulsive wartime events which this study has traced.

Notes

CHAPTER 1

1. Hitler's "Barbarossa" directive of December 18, 1940.
2. *Documents on German Foreign Policy, 1918–1945,* Series D, Vol. XII, p. 95.
3. On June 18, four days before the German attack on the Soviet Union, Turkey signed a "Treaty of Friendship and Nonaggression" with Germany.
4. Winston S. Churchill, *The Second World War,* Vol. III, p. 110.
5. *Foreign Relations of the United States (FRUS),* 1941, Vol. II, p. 961.
6. *The Diaries of Sir Alexander Cadogan,* p. 366.
7. Constantin Fotić, *The War We Lost,* p. 85.
8. Churchill, *op. cit.,* Vol. III, p. 168.
9. *Documents on German Foreign Policy, 1918–1945,* Series D, Vol. XII, pp. 451 f.
10. *Ibid.,* p. 395.
11. *FRUS,* 1941, Vol. II, p. 975.
12. Department of State *Bulletin,* April 12, 1941, p. 449.
13. Churchill, *op. cit.,* Vol. III, p. 223.
14. *FRUS,* 1941, Vol. II, p. 979.
15. *Ibid.,* p. 980.
16. *Ibid.,* pp. 980 f.
17. Fotić, *op. cit.,* pp. 114 f.
18. *Ibid.,* p. 115.
19. More on Mihailović in David Martin, *Ally Betrayed,* pp. 19 ff., and Fotić, *op. cit.,* pp. 144 ff.
20. Christie Lawrence, *Irregular Adventure,* pp. 230 ff.
21. Fotić, *op. cit.,* p. 155.
22. Several books have been written about Tito's life, including Vladimir Dedijer's *Josip Broz Tito,* Fitzroy Maclean's *Disputed Barricade* and Phyllis Auty's *Tito.*
23. The Comintern, short for *Comm*unist *Intern*ational, often called the Third International, was founded in 1919 by Lenin to organize revolutions through Communist parties in every country.
24. Dedijer, *Josip Broz Tito,* pp. 274 f.
25. *Hronologija,* p. 44.

327

26. Text of Comintern telegram reprinted in Milorad M. Dratchkovitch, "The Communist Party of Yugoslavia," in *The Comintern: Historical Highlights*, p. 193.

27. The majority, who were for fusion, were called *"Belaši,"* or "Whites."

28. *Documents on German Foreign Policy, 1918–1945*, Series D, Vol. XIII, p. 215.

29. *Ibid.*, p. 308.

30. The German military commander for Serbia was first General Helmuth Förster, then from June to August 1941 General Ludwig Schröder, who was succeeded by General Heinrich Dankelmann.

31. *Documents on German Foreign Policy, 1918–1945*, Series D, Vol. XIII, p. 400.

32. *Ibid.*, pp. 479 f.

33. List was succeeded as Commander, Southeast (commander of 12th Army with headquarters in Salonika), in November 1941 by General Walter Kuntze and in August 1942 by General Alexander Löhr. In November, Böhme was succeeded by General Paul Bader, who in April 1942 became simultaneously military commander for Serbia.

34. *Hronologija*, p. 97.

35. F. W. Deakin, *The Embattled Mountain*, p. 126.

36. John Ehrman, *Grand Strategy*, Vol. V, p. 77.

37. This date supplied by British Foreign Office. Subsequent entry and exit dates of British and American liaison officers are also based on official sources.

38. Tito, *Vojna Djela*, I, p. 105.

39. Deakin, *op. cit.*, pp. 134 ff.

40. On that date a message was sent by Mihailović to Cairo that Hudson had arrived in Ravna Gora. See Vojmir Kljaković, "Velika Britanija, Sovjetski Savez i Ustanak u Jugoslaviji 1941. Godine," in *Vojnoistorijski Glasnik*, Br. 2/1970, p. 77.

41. Jovan Marjanović, *Ustanak*, pp. 304 ff.

42. *Op. cit.*, p. 80.

43. Michael Howard, *Grand Strategy*, Vol. IV, p. 386.

CHAPTER 2

1. Maclean, *op. cit.*, p. 151.

2. *Nazi Conspiracy and Aggression*, Vol. III, pp. 597 f.

3. Directive reprinted in original German in Slavko F. Odić, *Dosije bez Imena*, p. 25.

4. *Documents on German Foreign Policy, 1918–1945*, Series D, Vol. XIII, pp. 708 f., cites a telegram of the Plenipotentiary of the German Foreign Ministry with the military commander in Serbia: "The executions in Kragujevac occurred although there had been no attacks on members of the Wehrmacht in this city, for the reason that not enough hostages could be found elsewhere." Present Yugoslav estimates put the figure of executed males closer to 5,000. See Jozo Tomasevich, "Yugoslavia During the Second World War," in *Contemporary Yugoslavia*, p. 370, note 74.

5. To Phyllis Auty. See Auty, *op. cit.,* p. 191.

6. *The Četniks,* p. 11.

7. Gert Buchheit, *Der Deutsche Geheimdienst,* pp. 353 ff.

8. *The Četniks,* p. 10.

9. The borderline between German-occupied and Italian-occupied territory was approximately the frontier between Old Serbia (prior to 1912) and the Sandžak. The latter derives its name from the Turkish *sanjak,* which means administrative district. The area known now as Sandžak was originally called the "Sandžak of Novi Pazar" and remained within the Ottoman Empire but with Austrian garrisons after Serbia had become totally independent in 1878. In 1913, after the Balkan Wars, the Sandžak was divided between Montenegro and Serbia. During the interwar period, Yugoslavia was partitioned first into *oblasti* (provinces) and after 1929 into *banovine* (districts) an attempt to obliterate the old national dividing lines, but when the country was overrun by Axis forces in 1941, the Germans and Italians agreed on a dividing line which ran slightly south of the frontier between Old Serbia and the Sandžak, *i.e.,* with Priboj and Nova Varoš occupied by the Italians and Novi Pazar by the Germans.

10. Dedijer, *With Tito Through the War,* p. 46.

11. Report by Jakša Djelević, one of Mihailović's closest collaborators, in *Knjiga o Draži,* I, p. 185.

12. *Ibid.,* p. 197.

13. Vučković letter to author.

14. *Documents on German Foreign Policy, 1918–1945,* Series D, Vol. XIII, pp. 944 ff.

15. Major Jezdimir Dangić, an independent Bosnian Četnik leader, who was persuaded by the German Intelligence Service (Captain Matl) to place himself under Nedić, had never acted under Mihailović's orders.

16. C. L. Sulzberger in *The New York Times Magazine,* December 5, 1943.

17. Auty, *op. cit.,* p. 185.

18. *Kriegstagebuch des Oberkommandos der Wehrmacht, 1940–1945,* Vol. I, p. 860.

19. Letter from Vojmir Kljaković to author quoting from the archives of the Vojnoistorijski Institut.

20. *Hronologija,* p. 71.

21. E. L. Woodward, *British Foreign Policy in the Second World War,* p. 334.

22. Fotić, *op. cit.,* p. 170.

23. Dedijer, *Tito,* p. 168.

24. Dedijer, *Josip Broz Tito,* pp. 308 f.

25. Kljaković, *op. cit.,* pp. 90 f.

26. *Ibid.,* p. 94.

27. Churchill, *op. cit.,* Vol. III, p. 836.

28. Kljaković, *op. cit.,* p. 97.

29. *FRUS,* 1941, Vol. II, p. 984.

30. Fotić, *op. cit.,* p. 128.

CHAPTER 3

1. George Rendel, *The Sword and the Olive*, p. 213. Rendel had succeeded R. I. Campbell on July 29, 1941, as British Minister to the Yugoslav Government-in-Exile.

2. Deakin, *op. cit.*, p. 155.

3. The regular troops of the Independent State of Croatia were called *Domobrani* (Home Guard) and were distinct from the paramilitary and highly political *Ustaše*. There were about 34,000 of the former and 10,000 of the latter. See *Kriegstagebuch*, Vol. II, p. 138.

4. Deakin, *op. cit.*, p. 174.

5. *Zbornik*, III, 4, p. 150.

6. Dedijer, *With Tito Through the War*, p. 78.

7. *Zbornik*, II, 3, p. 345.

8. Clissold reprints the whole letter in *Whirlwind*, pp. 86 f., without giving a source.

9. *Zbornik*, II, 3, p. 390.

10. *The Trial of Dragoljub-Draža Mihailović*, p. 386.

11. *Op. cit.*, p. 174.

12. *With Tito Through the War*, p. 120.

13. *Hronologija*, p. 213, mentions the February 8 meeting of the Montenegrin Partisans and the decisions taken but omits the part about joining the Soviet Union.

14. *The Trial of Dragoljub-Draža Mihailović*, p. 284.

15. *Zbornik*, II, 3, p. 98.

16. *The Trial of Dragoljub-Draža Mihailović*, p. 142.

17. Lawrence, *op. cit.*, p. 229.

18. Vučković letter to author citing recollections of Nikola Kordić.

19. *The Trial of Dragoljub-Draža Mihailović*, p. 139.

20. *Ibid.*, p. 122.

21. Dedijer, *Tito*, p. 177.

22. This radiogram and subsequent messages between the Partisans and the Comintern are reprinted in M. Pijade, *About the Legend that the Yugoslav Uprising Owed Its Existence to Soviet Assistance*, pp. 6 ff.

23. *Ibid.*, p. 12.

24. *Op. cit.*, p. 173.

25. *Ibid.*, p. 172.

26. *Ibid.*, p. 166.

27. Author's files.

28. *Op. cit.*, p. 167.

29. Department of State Executive Agreement Series, No. 263.

30. Original in Franklin D. Roosevelt Library, Hyde Park, New York.

31. *FRUS, Conferences at Washington, 1941–1942, and Casablanca, 1943*, p. 445.

32. *FRUS,* 1942, Vol. III, pp. 806 ff. During his call, Fotić left with Welles texts of Mihailović's telegrams to the Yugoslav Government in London.

33. Letter from Sir Llewellyn Woodward to author.

34. *FRUS,* 1942, Vol. III, pp. 814 f.

35. Pijade, *op. cit.,* p. 16.

36. Dedijer, *Tito,* pp. 181 f.

CHAPTER 4

1. *FRUS,* 1942, Vol. III, pp. 821 f.

2. *Ibid.*

3. The text of this and later telegrams can be found in Živan L. Knežević, *Why the Allies Abandoned the Yugoslav Army of General Mihailović,* Part One, pp. 35 ff.

4. Knežević, *op. cit.,* Part One, p. 8.

5. See *Kriegstagebuch,* Vol. II, pp. 991 ff. Thus on December 16, for instance: "In Belgrade 8 arrests, 60 Mihailović supporters shot." Or on December 27: "In Belgrade 11 arrests, 250 Mihailović supporters shot as retaliation. . . ."

6. Knežević, *op. cit.,* Part Three, p. 2.

7. Dušan Plenča, *Le Mouvement,* note 58 enumerates some of the agreements.

8. Martin, *op. cit.,* p. 137, note 3.

9. See Charles Zalar, *Yugoslav Communism,* p. 85.

10. Knežević, *op. cit.,* Part Three, p. 3.

11. *Ibid.,* p. 4.

12. *FRUS,* 1942, Vol. III, pp. 833 f.

13. Date provided by British Ministry of Defence.

14. Knežević, *op. cit.,* Part Three, p. 2.

15. Actually the message was sent by Brigadier C. S. Vale on behalf of the General Staff. Text in Knežević, *op. cit.,* Part Three, p. 3.

16. Foreign Office files.

17. Memorandum of conversation reprinted in *The Trial of Dragoljub-Draža Mihailović,* p. 314. Sir Orme made similar remarks to the American Chargé three months later.

18. Plenča, *Medjunarodni Odnosi,* p. 186.

19. Britain and Yugoslavia had raised their missions to Embassies on May 22, 1942.

20. Foreign Office files.

21. Department of State *Bulletin,* September 5, 1942, p. 729.

22. *FRUS,* 1942, Vol. III, p. 817.

23. Fotić, *op. cit.,* p. 189.

24. *Ibid.,* p. 191.

25. *The Eagle and the Roots,* pp. 479 f.

26. *FRUS,* 1942, Vol. III, p. 840.

27. In a memorandum dated December 19, 1942.

28. *FRUS,* 1942, Vol. III, p. 841.

29. *Neretva-Sutjeska, 1943*, p. 89.

30. Maclean, *Disputed Barricade*, p. 194. After the formation of the First Proletarian Brigade in December 1941, four more were created in March and June 1942.

31. Pijade, *op. cit.*, p. 20.

32. Under the same signature, Tito had sent a congratulatory message to the Soviet Union on the occasion of the twenty-fifth anniversary of the Bolshevik Revolution and Radio Free Yugoslavia, reported this fact on November 7, 1942, thus mentioning Tito's name for the first time. Soviet media, however, did not refer to Tito until a year later.

33. *The Essential Tito*, pp. 10 ff.

34. *Antifašističko Vece Narodnog Oslobodjenja Jugoslavije*.

35. For details of the Bihać Assembly see Maclean, *op. cit.*, pp. 196 ff. Also Drachkovitch, *op. cit.*, pp. 209 ff.

Chapter 5

1. *FRUS*, 1943, Vol. II, p. 969.

2. *Ibid.*, p. 975.

3. Foreign Office files.

4. *Op. cit.*, Vol. IV, p. 708.

5. Deakin, *op. cit.*, p. 195.

6. B. Sweet-Escott, *Baker Street Irregular*, p. 162.

7. Churchill, *op. cit.*, Vol. V, p. 463.

8. Zalar, *op. cit.*, p. 105.

9. Dedijer, *With Tito through the War*, p. 258.

10. Foreign Office files.

11. Howard, *op. cit.*, p. 391.

12. *FRUS*, 1943, Vol. II, p. 976.

13. *Ibid.*, p. 984.

14. *Ibid.*, pp. 987 f.

15. Fotić, *op. cit.*, p. 220. For full text see also Knežević, *op. cit.*, Part Two, pp. 2 f.

16. *Op. cit.*, p. 221.

17. *FRUS*, 1943, Vol. II, p. 988.

18. *Ibid.*, p. 1000.

19. *Ibid.*, p. 1001.

20. *Op. cit.*, pp. 222 f.

21. *FRUS*, 1943, Vol. II, p. 1007.

22. *Ibid.*, p. 1009.

23. Martin, *op. cit.*, p. 216, quoting Knežević, *op. cit.*, Part Two, pp. 9 f., but improving on the English translation.

24. The text of the British order to Mihailović is contained in Mihailović's telegram No. 1598. The quotations are taken from Knežević, *op. cit.*, Part Two, pp. 10 ff.

25. Among other principal branches were the following: secret intelligence (SI), research and analysis (R&A), counterespionage (X-2), morale operations (MO).

26. See Sweet-Escott, *op. cit.*, pp. 129 ff.

27. Ehrman, *op. cit.*, Vol. V, p. 322.

28. Deakin, *op. cit.*, p. 201.

29. Robert E. Sherwood, *Roosevelt and Hopkins*, p. 711.

30. Memorandum of conversation drafted by Assistant Secretary Berle, reprinted in *FRUS*, 1943, Vol. II, p. 985.

31. *FRUS*, 1943, Vol. II, pp. 989 ff.

32. Foreign Office files.

33. No. 279. Franklin D. Roosevelt Library.

34. *The Četniks*, pp. 59 f.

35. See *Kriegstagebuch,* Vol. III, pp. 169, 191, 216.

36. *Neretva-Sutjeska, 1943*, p. 95.

37. *Zbornik*, II, 8, pp. 360 f.

38. *Ibid.*, p. 359.

39. *Kriegstagebuch*, Vol. III, p. 473, where there is also a reference to a Četnik attack on an SS supply depot in Mostar: "Cetniks clearly established as attackers."

40. E. Wiskemann, *The Rome-Berlin Axis*, p. 293.

41. On December 28, 1942, Löhr was promoted (Hitler directive No. 47) from Commander, Southeast (12th Army) to commander of Army Group E with responsibility for the entire Balkan area.

42. Records of the German Foreign Office in National Archives in Washington, Microfilm T 120, Roll 615 (245–266). Some of the text is taken from Italian translation in *Hitler e Mussolini*, pp. 131 ff., where this long Hitler letter is mistaken for three different communications.

43. See Deakin, *The Brutal Friendship*, pp. 187 ff.

44. *Hitler e Mussolini*, pp. 141 f., where the letter is dated March 8; the above-mentioned microfilm indicates the date of March 9.

45. Roatta became Chief of Staff of the Italian Army succeeding General Vittorio Ambrosio who in turn succeeded Cavallero as Chief of the Italian General Staff.

46. Wiskemann, *op. cit.*, p. 298.

47. *Hitler e Mussolini*, pp. 156 f.

48. Several times Mussolini made a distinction between the Četniks and Montenegrin nationalists, implying that the former were bad and the latter good.

49. The commander of the German troops in Croatia was General Rudolf Lüters who like the commander of German troops in Serbia, General Bader, reported to the Commander, Southeast, General Löhr.

50. Dedijer, *On Military Conventions*, p. 111.

51. *Ibid.*, p. 112.

52. *Ibid.*

53. NOKW 1088, Record Group 238, World War II War Crimes.

54. The Kasche-Ribbentrop telegram exchange in author's files through the courtesy of the German Foreign Office.

55. Paul Leverkuehn, *German Military Intelligence,* p. 151.

56. Walter Hagen, *Die Geheime Front,* p. 268.

57. *Dnevnik,* Vol. II, p. 167.

58. In 1952, Tito married Jovanka Budisavljević, a Serb from Croatia.

59. Maclean, *op. cit.,* p. 206, mentions a message which the Partisans received from the Comintern complaining because they had agreed to exchange prisoners. Tito told Maclean later that he answered: "If you cannot . . . help us, then at least do not hinder us."

60. *Conversations with Stalin,* p. 9.

CHAPTER 6

1. *FRUS,* 1942, Vol. III, p. 810.

2. *Borba,* banned in 1929, resumed its publication in Užice in 1941 as the official organ of the CPY, had to stop publication when the Germans overran Užice, but appeared again in 1942 when large parts of Bosnia came under Partisan control.

3. Document in author's files through the courtesy of F. W. Deakin.

4. Knežević, *op. cit.,* Part One, p. 18.

5. *Ibid.,* p. 29.

6. *FRUS,* 1943, Vol. II, p. 996.

7. Dedijer, *Tito,* pp. 199 ff.

8. *FRUS,* 1943, Vol. II, pp. 1026 ff.

9. Basil Davidson, *Partisan Picture,* p. 104 n. Plenča, *Medjunarodni Odnosi,* p. 187, n. 50, says that Pavlović and Erdeljac had reported that they were recruited by a member of the Communist Party of Canada, Phillips, and a British officer named Lesbudge who before the war worked in Yugoslavia in the Trepča mines. (His real name was Lethbridge.)

10. *Zbornik,* II, 9, p. 159.

11. *Ibid.,* p. 176.

12. William Jones, *Twelve Months With Tito's Partisans,* p. 2. The exact date of Jones's arrival obtained through the courtesy of the British Foreign Office. It conforms with a message which Croatian Partisan headquarters sent to Tito on May 20: "A Major Jones arrived on the night of May 18–19. He says that he was sent as liaison officer . . ." (letter from Vojnoistorijski Institut).

13. *Zbornik,* II, 9, p. 264.

14. The "Hoathley I" group reported that it had early in May made contact with Bosnian Partisan headquarters. It eventually teamed up with the first British mission to Tito.

15. Wilson succeeded Alexander on February 17, 1943, when the latter was appointed Eisenhower's deputy at Allied Force Headquarters, North Africa.

16. Deakin, *The Embattled Mountain,* p. 217.

17. Oxford lecture.

18. See the excellent eye-witness account by Deakin in *op. cit.*, pp. 10 ff.

19. Churchill, *op. cit.*, Vol. V, p. 463.

20. Howard, *op. cit.*, p. 482.

21. Ehrman, *op. cit.*, Vol. V, p. 79.

22. By September 1943, 144 tons of supplies had been dropped into Yugoslavia, by far the larger amount to the Partisans.

23. *Op. cit.*, pp. 72 f.

24. *Miss Fire*, p. 49.

25. *Ibid.*, p. 94.

26. *Ibid.*, p. 73.

27. See Martin, *op. cit.*, pp, 39 f., where a photocopy of the offer is reprinted.

28. *Kriegstagebuch*, Vol. III, p. 779.

29. *Ibid.*, p. 812.

30. Heinz letter to author.

31. Memorandum of conversation by the Under Secretary of State, *FRUS*, 1943, Vol. II, p. 1003.

32. Fotić, *op. cit.*, pp. 205 ff.

33. *FRUS*, 1943, Vol. II, p. 1010.

34. *Ibid.*, p. 1007.

35. Memorandum in author's files.

36. Fotić, *op. cit.*, p. 207.

CHAPTER 7

1. Plenča, *Le Mouvement*, p. 20, quoting Prime Minister Jovanović's notes.

2. *FRUS*, 1943, Vol. II, pp. 1012 ff.

3. Plenča, *op. cit.*, p. 21.

4. *FRUS*, 1943, Vol. II, pp. 1016 ff.

5. *Ibid.*, pp. 1015 ff.

6. Churchill, *op. cit.*, Vol. V, pp. 464 f. Howard, *op. cit.*, p. 505.

7. See Order of Battle of July 7, 1943, in *Kriegstagebuch*, Vol. III, p. 735.

8. *Hronologija*, p. 505. Plenča, *Medjunarodni Odnosi*, p. 189.

9. Churchill, *op. cit.*, Vol. V, p. 465. Full text in Foreign Office files.

10. *Op. cit.*, p. 182.

11. *Op. cit.*, p. 204.

12. *Kriegstagebuch*, Vol. III, pp. 853 and 890.

13. Howard, *op. cit.*, pp. 518 ff.

14. Maurice Matloff, *Strategic Planning for Coalition Warfare, 1943–1944*, p. 213.

15. Henry L. Stimson and McGeorge Bundy, *On Active Service*, pp. 436 f.

16. Matloff, *op. cit.*, p. 215.

17. Churchill, *op. cit.*, Vol. V, pp. 82 f.

18. Matloff, *op. cit.*, p. 225.

19. The military conclusions were cabled by Roosevelt and Churchill to Stalin. Telegram in Franklin D. Roosevelt Library.

20. Henry M. Wilson, *Eight Years Overseas,* p. 179.

21. *Ibid,* p. 169.

22. *FRUS,* 1943, Vol. II, p. 1041.

23. The entire correspondence is reprinted in *FRUS,* 1943, Vol. II, pp. 1041–1048.

24. Fotić, *op. cit.,* p. 211.

25. Copy of letter in Franklin D. Roosevelt Library.

26. *Op. cit.,* p. 213.

27. *The Public Papers and Addresses of Franklin D. Roosevelt,* Vol. 12, pp. 422 f.

28. Dedijer reports that the turnover of the four Liberators prompted the Partisans to ask whether such an action was in accord "with the Atlantic Charter." (*With Tito through the War,* p. 385.)

29. Fotić remarks (*op. cit.,* p. 219) that "in spite of the President's solemn promise, they never had an opportunity to fly any supplies to their commander, Draža Mihailović, not even those famous packages of condensed food sent to Cairo as the President's gift to Mihailović more than a year before."

30. *FRUS,* 1943, Vol. II, p. 985.

31. *Ibid.,* p. 1016.

32. King Peter, *op. cit.,* pp. 121 f.

33. *FRUS,* 1943, Vol. II, p. 1023, note 65.

34. Author's files through the courtesy of George Selvig.

35. *Eastern Approaches,* p. 297.

36. Linn (Slim) Farish, an oil field geologist from Texas, who had joined the Canadian Forces early in the war, was in the British Army in the Middle East when Major Huot recruited him for OSS work.

37. Letter from Brigadier Armstrong to author.

38. *Op. cit.,* pp. 214 ff.

39. Albert B. Seitz, *Mihailović, Hoax or Hero,* pp. 33 ff., calls Hudson "Lt. Col. Duane H." (Hudson had been promoted in the meantime). He refers to Bailey as "Col. B." and Mansfield as "Lt. M."

40. *Op. cit.,* p. 13.

41. *Op. cit.,* p. 228.

42. Data supplied by the Historical Department, Office of the Chief of Staff, Italian Army.

43. Tito, *Govori i Članci,* VI, p. 327.

44. Ehrman, *op. cit.,* Vol. V, p. 79.

45. See German orders of battle of July 7, October 4 and December 26, 1943, in *Kriegstagebuch,* Vol. III, pp. 735, 1160, 1402.

46. *Achse* (Axis), *Adler* (Eagle), *Wildsau* (Wild Sow), *Kugelblitz* (Fireball) and others.

47. Churchill, *op. cit.,* Vol. V, p. 136.

48. Ehrman, *op. cit.,* Vol. V, p. 555.

49. *Ibid.,* p. 112.

50. *Ibid.,* p. 555.

51. *Dnevnik,* Vol. II, p. 505.

52. L. Huot, *Guns for Tito,* p. 2.

53. Huot, whose book was written before the war ended, used fictitious names.

54. *Prva Partizanska Misija.*

55. Huot, *op. cit.,* p. 90.

56. *Ibid.,* p. 257.

57. See his book, *Wanderer,* pp. 310 ff. and his change of name to John Hamilton.

58. Ehrman, *op. cit.,* Vol. V, p. 80.

59. Author's files.

60. *See FRUS, Conferences at Cairo and Tehran, 1943,* pp. 606–615.

61. *Op. cit.,* p. 27.

62. *Op. cit.,* pp. 134 ff.

63. The ratio of one hundred hostages to be executed for one German killed which had been in effect since the autumn of 1941 was reduced by the German military commander for Serbia on February 28, 1943, to fifty. Text in *Zbornik,* I, 5, pp. 439 ff.

64. Letter to author.

65. *Op. cit.,* p. 222: "The shipment consisted of 16 canisters of demolitions, 8 British rifles, 1 German Mauser with a broken stock, 1 captured Italian 2-inch mortar. There was no ammunition for either the rifles or the mortar."

66. Seitz, *op. cit.,* p. 40.

67. *Op. cit.,* p. 65.

68. Martin, *op. cit.,* pp. 227 f.

69. *Op. cit.,* p. 87.

70. Rootham, *op. cit.,* p. 171.

71. *Kriegstagebuch,* Vol. III, p. 1233.

72. *Ibid.,* p. 1294. The German commander in Serbia, General H. G. Felber, successor to Bader, had the title of Military Commander, Southeast, and was subordinate to the Commander in Chief, Southeast, Field Marshal von Weichs.

73. Hermann Neubacher, *Sonderauftrag Südost,* p. 166.

74. *Knjiga o Draži,* I, p. 396.

75. *FRUS,* 1943, Vol. I, p. 543.

76. Dedijer, *Tito,* pp. 204 f.

77. *Disputed Barricade,* p. 244.

78. *Op. cit.,* p. 134.

79. *FRUS,* 1943, Vol. I, p. 617.

80. *Ibid.,* pp. 662 f.

81. Churchill, *op. cit.,* Vol. V, p. 466.

82. *The Reckoning,* p. 414.

83. *Op. cit.,* p. 137.

84. *Eastern Approaches,* p. 390.

85. *Op. cit.,* p. 261.

CHAPTER 8

1. Dedijer, *Dnevnik,* Vol. II, p. 602, Vol. III, pp. 12 ff.

2. *The Essential Tito,* pp. 15–32, gives the full text of this speech.

3. *Nacionalni Komitet Oslobodjenja Jugoslavije (NKOJ).*

4. Dedijer, *Tito,* p. 207.

5. *FRUS, Cairo and Tehran,* p. 210.

6. *Ibid.,* p. 259.

7. *Ibid.,* p. 302.

8. *Ibid.,* pp. 309 f.

9. *Ibid.,* pp. 330 ff.

10. It is not quite clear what Churchill meant by that distinction. He certainly was not thinking of the Četniks.

11. *Op. cit.,* p. 135.

12. Wilson, *op. cit.,* p. 187.

13. *FRUS, Cairo and Tehran,* p. 360.

14. *Ibid.,* pp. 478 f.

15. *Ibid.,* p. 489.

16. *Ibid.,* p. 493.

17. Sherwood, *op. cit.,* p. 780.

18. *FRUS, Cairo and Tehran,* p. 516.

19. *Ibid.,* p. 529. No record has been found of the return by Stalin of the copy lent him by Roosevelt.

20. *Ibid.,* p. 534.

21. See German order of battle of October 4, 1943, in *Kriegstagebuch,* Vol. III, p. 1160. According to German estimates, the Partisan strength at that time was 90,000 men, that of the Četniks 30,000 (*Ibid.,* Vol. IV, p. 1552).

22. *FRUS, Cairo and Tehran,* p. 574.

23. *Ibid.,* p. 579.

24. *Ibid.,* p. 652.

25. Churchill, *op. cit.,* Vol. V, p. 404. It was released to the public in 1947 (State Department press release 240).

26. *As He Saw It,* p. 184.

27. *FRUS, Cairo and Tehran,* p. 795.

28. Ehrman, *op. cit.,* Vol. V, p. 196.

29. *Op. cit.,* p. 137. On December 7, the anniversary of Pearl Harbor, King Peter sent FDR a telegram in which he expressed his best wishes for success toward decisive victory. Roosevelt's reply stressed "our close association."

30. Maclean, *Eastern Approaches,* pp. 402 f.

31. *The Embattled Mountain,* p. 262.

32. *Op. cit.,* p. 188.

33. *Tito,* p. 210.

34. See Hansard, *Parliamentary Debates,* 8 December 1943, p. 945.

35. Department of State, Division of Current Information, December 9, 1943.

36. *FRUS,* 1943, Vol. II, pp. 1038 f.

37. *Ibid.,* p. 1024.

38. Dedijer, *Tito,* p. 209.

39. *FRUS,* 1943, Vol. II, pp. 1025 f.

40. *Ibid.,* p. 1023.

41. *Ibid.,* p. 1028.

42. King Peter writes (*op. cit.,* p. 138) that Churchill was in bed and in an extremely bad temper.

43. King Peter, *op. cit.,* pp. 138 ff. Deakin (*op. cit.,* p. 263) and Maclean (*Eastern Approaches,* p. 404) also report on their meetings with the King.

44. Fotić, *op. cit.,* pp. 274 f. Novikov had succeeded Bogomolov as Soviet Ambassador to the Yugoslav Government-in-Exile after it had moved from London to Cairo.

45. *Op. cit.,* p. 193.

46. Date supplied by Musulin.

47. *Op. cit.,* p. 224.

48. *The New York Times,* August 6, 1944, p. 23; written answers to questions submitted by C. L. Sulzberger.

49. Mihailović said during his trial (*op. cit.,* p. 212) that Cairo replied negatively on January 3, 1944.

50. Eden, *Freedom and Order,* pp. 235 f.

51. *FRUS,* 1943, Vol. II, p. 1032.

52. *Ibid.,* p. 1036.

53. *The Reckoning,* p. 432.

54. In Cairo, British Ambassador Stevenson asked Soviet Ambassador Novikov what his Government's attitude was toward the King. He replied: "Its attitude is shown by the fact that I am accredited to him" (*FRUS,* 1943, Vol. II, p. 1025).

55. *FRUS,* 1943, Vol. II, p. 1038.

56. *Op. cit.,* p. 432.

57. Churchill, *op. cit.,* Vol. V, p. 468.

58. Fotić, *op. cit.,* p. 261.

Chapter 9

1. *Op. cit.,* Vol. V, p. 469.

2. Eden, *op. cit.,* p. 433.

3. *Op. cit.,* Vol. V, p. 470.

4. *Ibid.*

5. E. L. Woodward, *British Foreign Policy in the Second World War,* p. 341.

6. Churchill's cables to Roosevelt and Roosevelt's comment in Franklin D. Roosevelt Library; Churchill's cable to Stalin and Stalin's reply in *Stalin's Correspondence,* I, pp. 182 ff.

7. *Op. cit.,* p. 262.

8. Maclean, *Eastern Approaches,* p. 418.

9. *Op. cit.,* Vol. V, p. 471.

10. *FRUS,* 1944, Vol. IV, p. 1343.

11. Churchill, *op. cit.,* Vol. V, p. 473.

12. *FRUS,* 1944, Vol. IV, p. 1346.

13. Churchill, *op. cit.,* Vol. V, p. 474.

14. *FRUS,* 1944, Vol. IV, p. 1347. Only on March 2 did the British Embassy in Washington transmit directly to Roosevelt the Churchill letter of February 5 and Tito's answer of February 9.

15. Woodward, *op. cit.,* p. 343.

16. *FRUS,* 1944, Vol. IV, p. 1349.

17. The author has been unable to locate the texts of these letters.

18. *The Papers of Dwight David Eisenhower,* Vol. III, p. 1815. Its editors have also been unable to locate Mihailović's letter to Eisenhower.

19. At that time there were about sixty British officers with the Partisans (*FRUS,* 1944, Vol. IV, p. 1352).

20. *FRUS,* 1944, Vol. IV, p. 1350.

21. *Ibid.,* p. 1350, note 53. The OSS proposal was subsequently adopted.

22. *Kriegstagebuch,* Vol. IV, p. 640.

23. Stettinius succeeded Welles as Under Secretary on September 25, 1943.

24. *FRUS,* 1944, Vol. IV, p. 1339.

25. Sweet-Escott, *op. cit.,* p. 199.

26. *Op. cit.,* p. 205.

27. Major Walter M. Ross succeeded Green as commander at Bari in October 1944. Major Frank Richardson was the last commander of the Bari base, which was deactivated on March 1, 1945. Thompson was succeeded in late May 1944 by Lieutenant B. Nelson Deranian, USN.

28. Arnoldi was succeeded by Captain Armin Sucker, who in turn was replaced in September 1944 by Arthur M. Cox.

29. *Op. cit.,* p. 204.

30. Originals in Franklin D. Roosevelt Library.

31. Djilas, *op. cit.,* p. 111.

32. *Eastern Approaches,* p. 433.

33. *Stalin's Correspondence,* I, p. 213, and II, p. 134.

34. About the Partisan effort in Macedonia see Palmer and King, *Yugoslav Communism and the Macedonian Question,* pp. 61 ff.

35. Letter from Sir John Henniker-Major to author.

36. *Op. cit.,* p. 245.

37. *Op. cit.,* pp. 144 f.

38. Franklin D. Roosevelt Library.

39. *Op. cit.,* p. 440.

40. Churchill, *op. cit.,* Vol. V, p. 476.

41. *FRUS,* 1944, Vol. IV, p. 1360.

42. *Op. cit.,* p. 262.

43. *FRUS*, 1944, Vol. IV, p. 1353.

44. *Ibid.*, pp. 1362 ff.

45. *Op. cit.*, p. 147. Churchill and King Peter met on April 12 and 13.

46. No. 633, Franklin D. Roosevelt Library.

47. Fotić, *op. cit.*, p. 264.

48. Woodward, *op. cit.*, p. 344.

49. Temporary promotions in the field were frequent and may explain this and other differences in rank.

50. *FRUS*, 1944, Vol. IV, pp. 1356 f.

51. Robert Murphy, *Diplomat Among Warriors*, p. 221.

52. *FRUS*, 1944, Vol. IV, p. 1356.

53. *Ibid.*, pp. 1369 f.

54. Huntington was in charge of all special operations in OSS Washington between April and August 1943. At the time of his appointment as head of the American military mission, he was commander of the OSS detachment of the U.S. 5th Army under General Mark Clark.

55. *Op. cit.*, p. 254.

56. Ehrman, *op. cit.*, Vol. V, p. 276.

57. Djilas, *Conversations with Stalin*, pp. 29 ff.

58. *Tito*, pp. 214 f.

59. *The Papers of Dwight David Eisenhower*, Vol. III, pp. 1869 f.

60. See Harry C. Butcher, *My Three Years With Eisenhower*, p. 549 (entry for May 28).

61. Successor to Marshal Tedder who had gone to London with Eisenhower.

62. *FRUS*, 1944, Vol. IV, p. 1358.

63. Djilas, *op. cit.*, p. 73.

64. *Op. cit.*, p. 82.

CHAPTER 10

1. *Op. cit.*, p. 265.

2. *Ibid.*, p. 267.

3. Franklin D. Roosevelt Library.

4. *FRUS*, 1944, Vol. IV, pp. 1366 ff. From the files of the Franklin D. Roosevelt Library it appears that the letter was signed and forwarded on May 23 to the State Department for transmittal via regular State Department channels.

5. *Ibid.*, pp. 1368 f.

6. *Ibid.*, pp. 1369 f.

7. *Ibid.*, pp. 1370 ff.

8. Churchill, *op. cit.*, Vol. V, p. 477.

9. Roosevelt's telegram in Franklin D. Roosevelt Library; Churchill's telegram to Tito in Foreign Office files; Churchill-Stalin exchange in *Stalin's Correspondence*, I, pp. 219 ff.

10. *Op. cit.*, p. 252.

11. Hansard, *Parliamentary Debates*, 24 May 1944, pp. 775 f.

12. Churchill, *op. cit.,* Vol. V, p. 478.

13. *Op. cit.,* p. 151.

14. *The Četniks,* pp. 21 f.

15. *Ibid.,* p. 26. Soon after, Major Djurić defected to the Partisans, a heavy blow to Mihailović.

16. *Op. cit.,* p. 213.

17. Martin, *op. cit.,* p. 89, carries Lukačević's side of the story, namely that the gold was taken to prevent it from falling into Partisan hands. (Lukačević had accompanied Colonel Bailey out of Yugoslavia and went with him to London, where he attended King Peter's wedding.)

18. *Op. cit.,* p. 218.

19. *Ibid.,* p. 195.

20. Ehrman, *op. cit.,* Vol. V, p. 277. Velebit, returning from London, was in Gibraltar when he heard of the German offensive. He left for Bari immediately.

21. There were American liaison officers in Partisan territory—Selvig in Croatia and Farish in Serbia—but none at Supreme Headquarters.

22. *Disputed Barricade,* pp. 260 f.

23. *FRUS,* 1944, Vol. IV, p. 1377.

24. Martin, *op. cit.,* p. 240.

25. Wilson, *op. cit.,* p. 212.

26. Ehrman, *op. cit.,* Vol. V, p. 274. See also Headquarters MAAF General Order No. 12 which states: "Effective 1 June 1944 Headquarters Balkan Air Force is designated and activated. . . ." (*History of Headquarters Mediterranean Allied Air Forces Dec. 1943 through 1 Sept. 1944,* Vol. II.)

27. *The Army Air Forces in World War II,* Vol. III, p. 399.

28. Maclean, *Disputed Barricade,* p. 255.

29. *FRUS,* 1944, Vol. IV, p. 1379, note 8.

30. *Ibid.,* p. 1383, note 15.

31. *Ibid.,* pp. 1382 f. In reality, MacVeagh had little to do regarding Yugoslavia with all activities now concentrated in London or the Mediterranean Theater. By the second half of August telegrams concerning Yugoslavia were no longer even repeated to Cairo.

32. *Ibid.,* p. 1377, note 5.

33. *Ibid.,* p. 1378.

34. *Ibid.,* p. 1380.

35. Maclean, *Disputed Barricade,* p. 272; also full text in King Peter, *op. cit.,* pp. 156 f.

36. *The Blast of War,* p. 440.

37. Foreign Office files.

38. Plenča, *Medjunarodni Odnosi,* pp. 270 f. Simić stayed on in Moscow until the spring of 1945, when he was transferred to Washington. The first Ambassador of the Tito Government in Moscow was Vladimir Popović, who presented his credentials in May 1945.

39. *FRUS,* 1944, Vol. IV, pp. 1385 ff.

40. Ehrman, *op. cit.,* Vol. V, pp. 346 ff.

41. Churchill, *op. cit.,* Vol. VI, p. 61.

42. *Ibid.,* p. 63.

43. *Ibid.,* pp. 722 f.

44. Ehrman, *op. cit.,* Vol. V, p. 356.

45. *Ibid.,* p. 361.

46. Churchill, *op. cit.,* Vol. VI, p. 68, note 5.

47. In the course of the following months one Yugoslav Ambassador or Minister after another was relieved of his duties, including Bogoljub Jeftić, the Ambassador to Britain. The post in London remained vacant until June 1945, when Ljubo Leontić presented his credentials as Yugoslav Ambassador at a time when Tito was already installed as Prime Minister in Belgrade.

48. *FRUS,* 1944, Vol. IV, p. 1388.

49. Fotić, *op. cit.,* p. 259; Plenča, *Medjunarodni Odnosi,* p. 266.

50. Author's files.

51. *Diplomat Among Warriors,* p. 220.

52. *Op. cit.,* p. 217.

53. Ehrman, *op. cit.,* Vol. V, p. 389; also Matloff, *op. cit.,* pp. 504 f.

54. *FRUS,* 1944, Vol. IV, p. 1390.

55. Foreign Office files.

56. *FRUS,* 1944, Vol. IV, p. 1391, note 30.

57. See letter from Donovan to Dunn reporting on a conversation between Tito and Pribichevich on July 14, 1944, *ibid.,* pp. 1392 f.

58. Woodward, *op. cit.,* p. 345, note 2.

59. *FRUS,* 1944, Vol. IV, p. 1395.

60. Churchill, *op. cit.,* Vol. VI, pp. 72 f.

61. Eden, *op. cit.,* p. 459.

62. *FRUS,* 1944, Vol. V, pp. 112 f; also Cordell Hull, *Memoirs,* Vol. II, pp. 1451 ff, and Herbert Feis, *Churchill-Roosevelt-Stalin,* pp. 338 ff.

63. Churchill, *op. cit.,* Vol. VI, p. 74.

64. *Ibid.,* p. 75.

65. *FRUS,* 1944, Vol. V, p. 120.

66. Churchill *op. cit.,* Vol. VI, p. 78.

67. *FRUS,* 1944, Vol. V, p. 127.

68. Wilson, *op. cit.,* p. 226.

69. *Op. cit.,* p. 222.

70. *Op. cit.,* p. 226.

71. *Tito,* p. 226.

72. Churchill, *op. cit.,* Vol. VI, p. 87.

73. *Disputed Barricade,* p. 275.

74. Churchill, *op. cit.,* Vol. VI, p. 88.

75. *Ibid.,* pp. 91 f.

76. Churchill's telegrams to Roosevelt and Stalin are in Churchill, *op. cit.,* p. 93, and *Stalin's Correspondence,* I, p. 253; Roosevelt's and Stalin's replies in Franklin D. Roosevelt Library and *Stalin's Correspondence,* I, p. 254.

77. *Op. cit.,* p. 470.

78. *FRUS,* 1944, Vol. IV, pp. 1396 f.

79. *Ibid.,* pp. 1397 f.

80. *Ibid.,* pp. 1399 f.

81. Venezia Giulia was created by Italy after World War I and included the cities of Trieste and Gorizia, the Istrian peninsula and Fiume (Rijeka), all of it former Austro-Hungarian territory, though approximately 50 per cent of the population was either of Croatian or Slovenian origin.

82. *FRUS,* 1944, Vol. IV, p. 1401.

83. *Ibid.,* pp. 1402 f.

84. *Op. cit.,* p. 223.

85. Dedijer, *Tito,* p. 225.

86. Ehrman, *op. cit.,* Vol. V, p. 386.

87. Woodward, *op. cit.,* p. 347.

88. *FRUS,* 1944, Vol. IV, p. 1407.

CHAPTER 11

1. *Op. cit.,* p. 268.

2. Martin, *op. cit.,* p. 248. See also Corey Ford, *Donovan of OSS,* pp. 207 ff.

3. *FRUS,* 1944, Vol. IV, p. 1355.

4. Martin, *op. cit.,* p. 229.

5. *The Papers of Dwight David Eisenhower,* Vol. III, p. 1815, note 2.

6. This telegram from Churchill (No. 638) and Roosevelt's reply (No. 515) are in the Franklin D. Roosevelt Library.

7. *Ibid.;* Churchill's No. 776, Roosevelt's No. 617.

8. *Hronologija,* p. 839.

9. *Whirlwind,* pp. 204 ff.

10. Neubacher, *op. cit.,* p. 164.

11. Nedić left Belgrade in September 1944, was arrested in Austria after the war by U.S. authorities and turned over to the Yugoslavs early in February 1946. He fell out of a window at Belgrade secret police headquarters, probably a suicide.

12. *FRUS,* 1944, Vol. IV, pp. 1390, 1399.

13. This commission, composed of four well-known American jurists, was set up by the Committee for a Fair Trial for Draža Mihailović and took evidence from American airmen who had been rescued by the Četniks and from American liaison officers who had served with Mihailović.

14. Martin, *op. cit.,* p. 261.

15. Fotić, *op. cit.,* p. 277.

16. *Op. cit.,* p. 162.

17. *FRUS,* 1944, Vol. IV, pp. 1407 f.

18. *Ibid.,* p. 1412, note 63.

19. *Ibid.,* p. 1412.

20. Knežević was previously secretary of the Yugoslav War Cabinet in London, and Todorović had left Yugoslavia with Bailey and Mansfield in early 1944.

21. *FRUS*, 1944, Vol. IV, p. 1409.

22. Tito, *Govori i Članci*, II, p. 10.

23. *Op. cit.*, p. 234.

24. Eden, *op. cit.*, p. 471.

25. Churchill, *op. cit.*, Vol. VI, p. 230.

26. Plenča, *Medjunarodni Odnosi*, pp. 342 ff.

27. Dedijer, *Tito*, pp. 233 f.

28. Churchill, *op. cit.*, Vol. VI, p. 123.

29. *Ibid.*, p. 151.

30. No. 66, Franklin D. Roosevelt Library.

31. Churchill, *op. cit.*, Vol. VI, p. 208.

32. Ehrman, *op. cit.*, Vol. VI, p. 47.

33. Churchill, *op. cit.*, Vol. VI, p. 227.

34. *Ibid.*, p. 233.

35. *FRUS*, 1944, Vol. IV, p. 1009.

36. *Ibid.*, p. 1011.

37. *Ibid.*, pp. 1012 ff.

38. *Op. cit.*, p. 485.

39. *FRUS, The Conferences at Malta and Yalta, 1945*, p. 365.

40. *Ibid.*, p. 104.

41. Hansard, *Parliamentary Debates*, 27 October 1944, pp. 492 f.

42. *Hands Across the Caviar*, p. 19.

43. After advancing Soviet troops had reached the Bulgarian border, Bulgaria left the Tripartite Pact and declared its neutrality early in September. The Soviets were not satisfied and declared war on Bulgaria on September 5; three days later Bulgaria declared war on Germany.

44. *Eastern Approaches*, p. 519.

45. *FRUS, Malta and Yalta*, p. 257.

46. Churchill-Stalin exchange in *Stalin's Correspondence*, I, pp. 267 and 269.

47. *FRUS*, 1944, Vol. IV, p. 1423.

CHAPTER 12

1. Thayer, *op. cit.*, p. 89.

2. Fotić, *op. cit.*, p. 290.

3. Copy in Franklin D. Roosevelt Library.

4. *FDR: His Personal Letters, 1928–1945*, edited by Elliott Roosevelt, Vol. II, p. 1551. King Peter's letter is dated September 17.

5. *FRUS*, 1944, Vol. IV, pp. 1025 f.

6. *Ibid.*, p. 1426.

7. *Ibid.*, p. 1415.

8. Quoted by Martin, *op. cit.*, p. 347.

9. *The Trial of Dragoljub-Draža Mihailović*, pp. 254 and 265.

10. McDowell to author.

11. *Op. cit.,* pp. 206 ff.

12. *Op. cit.,* p. 349.

13. *Op. cit.,* p. 239.

14. Letter to author.

15. *FRUS,* 1944, Vol. IV, p. 1422.

16. *Ibid.,* p. 1424.

17. *FRUS,* 1945, Vol. V, pp. 1242 f.

18. Martin, *op. cit.,* p. 245.

19. *The Trial of Dragoljub-Draža Mihailović,* p. 268.

20. *Knjiga o Draži,* II, pp. 176 ff.

21. Churchill, *op. cit.,* Vol. VI, p. 126.

22. Ehrman, *op. cit.,* Vol. VI, p. 50.

23. *Ibid.,* p. 54.

24. *Op. cit.,* p. 239.

25. Foreign Office files.

26. Texts reprinted in *FRUS, Malta and Yalta,* pp. 253 f.

27. *FRUS,* 1944, Vol. IV, pp. 1429 f.

28. *Ibid.,* pp. 1428 f.

29. *Ibid.,* pp. 1432 f.

30. *Ibid.,* pp. 1439 f.

31. Stettinius succeeded Hull as Secretary of State on December 1, 1944. At the same time Joseph C. Grew replaced Stettinius as Under Secretary.

32. *FRUS,* 1944, Vol. IV, p. 1443.

33. *Ibid.,* p. 1444.

34. *FRUS, Malta and Yalta,* p. 257.

35. *FRUS,* 1944, Vol. IV, p. 1435.

36. *Ibid.,* p. 1441.

37. *Ibid.,* p. 1445.

38. *FRUS, Malta and Yalta,* p. 265.

39. Thayer, *op. cit.,* p. 91.

40. Djilas, *op. cit.,* p. 88.

41. *FRUS,* 1944, Vol. IV, pp. 1431 f.

42. *Ibid.,* p. 1434, note 7.

43. *Ibid.,* p. 1434.

44. *Ibid.,* p. 1436.

45. *Ibid.,* p. 1446.

CHAPTER 13

1. *Op. cit.,* p. 506.

2. *FRUS,* 1945, Vol. V, p. 1174.

3. Franklin D. Roosevelt Library.

4. *FRUS,* 1945, Vol. V, pp. 1175 f.

5. *FRUS, Malta and Yalta,* p. 258.

6. *FRUS,* 1945, Vol. V, p. 1177, note 12.

7. *Ibid.,* p. 1179, note 21.

8. Woodward, *op. cit.,* p. 349.

9. *FRUS,* 1945, Vol. V, p. 1179.

10. *Ibid.,* p. 1181.

11. *Ibid.,* p. 1186.

12. *Ibid.,* p. 1187.

13. *FRUS, Malta and Yalta,* p. 259.

14. *FRUS,* 1945, Vol. V, p. 1188.

15. *Ibid.,* p. 1189, note 46.

16. *Ibid.,* p. 1189.

17. *Ibid.,* p. 1190.

18. Outlined in Briefing Paper for Yalta Conference. *FRUS, Malta and Yalta,* pp. 102 f.

19. *FRUS,* 1945, Vol. V, p. 1191.

20. *Ibid.,* p. 1194.

21. King Peter, *op. cit.,* p. 181.

22. *FRUS,* 1945, Vol. V, p. 1197.

23. *Ibid.,* p. 1209.

24. *Ibid.,* p. 1209, note 15.

25. *Ibid.*

26. See Clissold, *op. cit.,* p. 216.

27. In reaching this decision he was probably hoodwinked by the Communist secret police. See Tomasevich, in *Contemporary Yugoslavia,* p. 111.

28. *Hronologija,* pp. 1106 f.

29. See *The Trial of Dragoljub-Draža Mihailović, passim.*

30. *FRUS, Malta and Yalta,* p. 505.

31. *Ibid.,* p. 781.

32. *Ibid.,* pp. 810 f.

33. *Ibid.,* pp. 843 ff.

34. *Ibid.,* p. 873.

35. *Ibid.,* p. 900.

36. *Ibid.,* p. 920.

37. *Ibid.,* p. 974.

38. *Ibid.,* p. 833.

39. *FRUS,* 1945, Vol. V, p. 1198, note 78.

40. *Ibid.,* p. 1198.

41. *Ibid.,* pp. 1199 f.

42. *Ibid.,* p. 1203.

43. *Ibid.,* p. 1202.

44. *FRUS,* 1945, Vol. IV, pp. 1106 f.

45. *Ibid.,* pp. 1103 ff.

46. *Ibid.,* pp. 1114 f.

47. *Hands Across the Caviar*, pp. 110 ff.

48. Woodward, *op. cit.*, p. 349.

49. *FRUS*, 1945, Vol. V, p. 1205, note 98.

50. *Ibid.*, p. 1205.

51. On November 29, 1945, a date beyond the scope of this study, the Constituent Assembly unanimously passed a declaration proclaiming the Federative National Republic of Yugoslavia and abolishing the monarchy. Elections for the Constituent Assembly had taken place on November 11—the nature of these elections has been the subject of considerable controversy—with more than 80 per cent of the electorate endorsing the Tito regime.

52. *Op. cit.*, p. 523.

53. Patterson did not need to present new credentials to the Chief of State after his arrival in Belgrade, since the King still nominally held that position.

54. One day after the war in Europe ended, the Yugoslavs requested that the American and British military missions leave the country. The American mission was withdrawn on July 4, 1945.

55. At the time of Germany's surrender, the German Army still held the northern part of Yugoslavia, including large sections of Croatia. Pavelić escaped to Austria, whence he made his way to Argentina. He died in Spain in 1959.

Bibliography

Adamic, Louis. *The Eagle and the Roots*. New York: Doubleday, 1952.

Auty, Phyllis. *Tito*. London: Longmans, 1970.

Buchheit, Gert. *Der Deutsche Geheimdienst*. Munich: List, 1966.

Butcher, Harry C. *My Three Years with Eisenhower*. New York: Simon and Schuster, 1946.

Četniks, The. Allied Force Headquarters, 1944.

Christman, Henry M., ed. *The Essential Tito*. New York: St. Martin's Press, 1970.

Churchill, Winston S. *The Second World War*. 6 vols. Boston: Houghton Mifflin, 1948–1953.

Clissold, Stephen. *Whirlwind*. London: Cresset, 1949.

Craven, W. F., and Cate, J. L., eds. *The Army Air Forces in World War II*, Vol. III. Chicago: U. of Chicago, 1951.

Davidson, Basil. *Partisan Picture*. Bedford: Bedford, 1946.

Deakin, F. W. "Britain and Yugoslavia," Oxford Lecture, 1962.

———. *The Brutal Friendship*. Garden City, N.Y.: Anchor, 1966.

———. *The Embattled Mountain*. New York and London: Oxford, 1971.

Dedijer, Vladimir. *Dnevnik* [*Diary*]. 3 vols. Belgrade: Prosveta, 1970.

———. *With Tito Through the War* [abridged translation of *Dnevnik*]. London: Hamilton, 1951.

———. *On Military Conventions*. Lund: Gleerup, 1961.

———. *Josip Broz Tito—Prilozi za Biografiju*. Belgrade: Kultura, 1953.

———. *Tito* [abridged translation of *Josip Broz Tito . . .*]. New York: Simon and Schuster, 1953.

Dilks, David, ed. *The Diaries of Sir Alexander Cadogan*. New York: Putnam, 1972.

Djilas, Milovan. *Conversations with Stalin*. New York: Harcourt, Brace & World, 1962.

Documents on German Foreign Policy, 1918–1945, Series D, Vols. XII, XIII. Washington: U.S. Govt. Printing Office, 1962–1964.

Drachkovitch, Milorad M., and Lazitch, Branko, eds. *The Comintern: Historical Highlights*. New York: Praeger, 1966.

Dragnich, Alex N. *Tito's Promised Land*. New Brunswick, N.J.: Rutgers, 1954.

Eden, Anthony. *Freedom and Order*. Boston: Houghton Mifflin, 1948.

———. *The Reckoning*. London: Cassell, 1965.

Ehrman, John. *Grand Strategy*, Vols. V, VI. London: H.M. Stationery Office, 1956.

Eisenhower, Dwight David, *The Papers of*. Baltimore and London: Johns Hopkins, 1970.

Feis, Herbert. *Churchill–Roosevelt–Stalin*. Princeton: Princeton, 1957.

Ford, Corey. *Donovan of OSS*. Boston: Little, Brown, 1970.

Foreign Relations of the United States, 1941–1945, including *Conferences at Cairo and Tehran, 1943*, and *Conferences at Malta and Yalta, 1945*. Washington: U.S. Govt. Printing Office.

Fotitch [Fotić], Constantin. *The War We Lost*. New York: Viking, 1948.

Hagen, Walter. *Die Geheime Front*. Stuttgart: Veritas, 1952.

Hitler e Mussolini, Lettere e Documenti. Milan: Rizzoli, 1946.

Hoptner, J. B. *Yugoslavia in Crisis*. New York: Columbia, 1962.

Howard, Michael. *Grand Strategy*, Vol. IV. London: H.M. Stationery Office, 1956.

Hronologija [Chronology], 1941–1945. Belgrade: Vojnoistorijski Institut, 1964.

Hull, Cordell. *Memoirs*. New York: Macmillan, 1948.

Huot, Louis. *Guns for Tito*. New York: Fischer, 1945.

Jones, William. *Twelve Months with Tito's Partisans*. Bedford: Bedford, 1946.

Kljaković, Vojmir. "Velika Britanija, Sovjetski Savez i Ustanak u Jugoslaviji 1941. Godine" [Great Britain, the Soviet Union and the Uprising in Yugoslavia, 1941], in *Vojnoistorijski Glasnik*, Br. 2/1970.

Knežević, Radoje, ed. *Knjiga o Draži [Book About Draža]*. 2 vols. Windsor: Srpska Narodna Odbrana, 1956.

Knežević, Živan L. *Why the Allies Abandoned the Yugoslav Army of General Mihailović*. Washington: n.p., 1945.

Kriegstagebuch des Oberkommandos der Wehrmacht, 1940–1945. Frankfurt am Main: Bernard & Graefe, 1965.

Lawrence, Christie. *Irregular Adventure*. London: Faber, 1947.

Leverkuehn, Paul. *German Military Intelligence*. New York: Praeger, 1954.

Maclean, Fitzroy. *Eastern Approaches*. London: Cape, 1950.

———. *Disputed Barricade*. London: Cape, 1957.

Macmillan, Harold. *The Blast of War*. New York: Harper & Row, 1967.

Makiedo, Sergije. *Prva Partizanska Misija [The First Partisan Mission]*. Belgrade: Sedma Sila, 1963.

Mansfield, Walter R. "Marine with the Chetniks," in *The Marine Corps Gazette*, Jan.–Feb., 1946.

Marjanović, Jovan. *Ustanak i Narodno-Oslobodilački Pokret u Srbiji 1941 [Uprising and the National Liberation Movement in Serbia, 1941]*. Belgrade: IDN, 1963.

Martin, David. *Ally Betrayed*. New York: Prentice-Hall, 1946.

Matloff, Maurice. *Strategic Planning for Coalition Warfare, 1943–1944*. Washington: U.S. Govt. Printing Office, 1959.

Mihailović, Dragoljub-Draža, The Trial of. Belgrade: Union of Journalists Association, 1946.

Murphy, Robert. *Diplomat Among Warriors.* New York: Doubleday, 1964.

National Liberation Movement of Yugoslavia, The. Middle East Headquarters, 1944.

Nazi Conspiracy and Aggression, Vols. I–VIII. Washington: U.S. Govt. Printing Office, 1946.

Neretva-Sutjeska, 1943. Belgrade: Vojnoistorijski Institut, 1969.

Neubacher, Hermann. *Sonderauftrag Südost.* Göttingen: Musterschmidt, 1956.

Odić, Slavko F. *Dosije Bez Imena [The Dossier Without a Name].* Zagreb: Naprijed, 1961.

Palmer, Stephen E., Jr., and King, Robert R. *Yugoslav Communism and the Macedonian Question.* Hamden: Shoe String Press, 1971.

Peter II, King of Yugoslavia. *A King's Heritage.* London: Cassell, 1955.

Pijade, M. *About the Legend That the Yugoslav Uprising Owed Its Existence to Soviet Assistance.* London: n.p., 1950.

Plenča, Dušan. *Medjunarodni Odnosi Jugoslavije u Toku Drugog Svjetskog Rata [The International Relations of Yugoslavia in the Second World War].* Belgrade: IDN, 1962.

———. *Le Mouvement de Libération Nationale en Yougoslavie et les Allies.* Belgrade: IDN, 1961.

Rendel, George. *The Sword and the Olive.* London: Murray, 1957.

Roosevelt, Elliott. *As He Saw It.* New York: Duell, Sloan & Pearce, 1946.

———, ed. *FDR: His Personal Letters, 1928–1945.* New York: Duell, Sloan & Pearce, 1950.

Roosevelt, Franklin D., The Public Papers and Addresses of, Vols. 10–13. New York: Harper and Brothers, 1950.

Rootham, Jasper. *Miss Fire.* London: Chatto & Windus, 1946.

Seitz, Albert B. *Mihailović, Hoax or Hero.* Columbus: Leigh House, 1953.

Seton-Watson, Hugh. *The East European Revolution.* New York: Praeger, 1951.

Sherwood, Robert E. *Roosevelt and Hopkins.* New York: Harper, 1948.

Stalin's Correspondence with Churchill, Attlee, Roosevelt and Truman, 1941–1945. New York: E. P. Dutton and Co., 1958 (originally published in Moscow by the Foreign Language Publishing House, 1957).

Stimson, Henry L., and Bundy, McGeorge. *On Active Service in Peace and War.* New York: Harper, 1948.

Sweet-Escott, Bickham. *Baker Street Irregular.* London: Methuen, 1965.

Thayer, Charles W. *Hands Across the Caviar.* London: Joseph, 1953.

Tito, Josip Broz. *Govori i Članci [Speeches and Articles],* I–XVI. Zagreb: Naprijed, 1959, 1969.

———. *Vojna Djela [Military Works],* I–III (1941–1961). Belgrade: VIZ Vojno Delo, 1961.

Vuchinich, Wayne S., ed. *Contemporary Yugoslavia*. Berkeley and Los Angeles: U. of Calif., 1969.

Wilson, Henry Maitland. *Eight Years Overseas*. London: Hutchinson, 1950.

Wiskemann, Elizabeth. *The Rome-Berlin Axis*. London: Oxford, 1949.

Wolff, Robert Lee. *The Balkans in Our Time*. Cambridge, Mass.: Harvard, 1956.

Woodward, E. L. *British Foreign Policy in the Second World War*. London: H.M. Stationery Office, 1962.

Zalar, Charles. *Yugoslav Communism*. Senate Committee on the Judiciary, 87th Congress, 1961.

Zbornik Dokumenata i Podataka o Narodnooslobodilačkom Ratu Jugoslavenskih Naroda [*Collection of Documents and Facts About the National Liberation Struggle of the Yugoslav Peoples*], I–XIV. Belgrade: 1950–1960.

Abbreviations

AFHQ	Allied Force Headquarters
AVNOJ	Anti-Fascist Council of National Liberation (Yugoslav)
BAF	Balkan Air Force (Allied)
BBC	British Broadcasting Corporation
CPY	Communist Party of Yugoslavia
FRUS	*Foreign Relations of the United States*
JCS	Joint Chiefs of Staff (U.S.)
OSS	Office of Strategic Services (U.S.)
OWI	Office of War Information (U.S.)
SOE	Special Operations Executive (British)
UNRRA	United Nations Relief and Rehabilitation Administration

List of Persons Mentioned

(The identification of the persons in this list is limited to circumstances and positions considered in this study.)

Adamic, Louis, American writer of Slovenian descent, author of *The Eagle and the Roots.*

Alexander, King of the Serbs, Croats and Slovenes; later King of Yugoslavia.

Alexander, Sir Harold, General, Commander in Chief, British Forces, Middle East, later Allied Commander in Italy; later Field Marshal and Supreme Allied Commander, Mediterranean Theater.

Alexandra, wife of King Peter II.

Ambrosio, Vittorio, General, Commander of Italian 2nd Army in Croatia, later Chief of Staff of the Army; later Chief of the General Staff.

Amery, Julian, official of SOE.

Apostolski, Mihailo, Macedonian Partisan leader.

Armstrong, C. D., Brigadier, head of British mission to the Četniks.

Arnold, Henry H., General, USA, Commanding General, U.S. Army Air Forces and Chief of the Air Staff; member of the Joint Chiefs of Staff and of the Combined Chiefs of Staff.

Arnoldi, Frank, OSS officer in Bari.

Atherton, Terence, SOE officer in Yugoslavia.

Auchinleck, Sir Claude, General, Commander in Chief, British Forces, Middle East.

Bader, Paul, German commanding general in Serbia, later also military commander for Serbia.

Bailey, S. W., British liaison officer with the Četniks.

Bakić, Mitar, member of Tito's staff.

Baldwin, Hanson W., military editor of *The New York Times.*

Belajčić, Vladimir, Četnik representative at AFHQ.

Belousova, Pelagea (Polka), Tito's first wife.

Benson, Melvin O., American liaison officer with the Partisans.

Benzler, Felix, Plenipotentiary of the German Foreign Ministry with the military commander for Serbia.

Berle, Adolf A., Jr., U.S. Assistant Secretary of State.

Bernstein, Walter, *Yank* correspondent.

Biddle, Anthony J. Drexel, Jr., U.S. Minister, later Ambassador, to Yugoslav Government-in-Exile in London.

Biroli, *see* Pirzio Biroli

Bogić, Dragomir, Yugoslav Chargé d'Affaires in the Soviet Union.

Bogomolov, A. E., Soviet Minister, later Ambassador, to Yugoslav Government-in-Exile in London; later Soviet member of the Advisory Council for Italy.

Böhme, Franz, German commanding general in Serbia.

Boughey, Peter, official of SOE.

Broad, Philip, British Foreign Service officer assigned to Bari.

Brock, Ray, correspondent of *The New York Times*.

Brooke, Sir Alan, General, Chief of the British Imperial General Staff; member of the Combined Chiefs of Staff; later Field Marshal; later Lord Alanbrook.

Broz, Aleksandar, Tito's younger son.

Broz, Žarko, Tito's elder son.

Budenz, Louis, editor of *The Daily Worker*, New York.

Budisavljević, Jovanka, Tito's present wife.

Budisavljević, Srdjan, Dr., member of Regency Council.

Cadogan, Sir Alexander, British Permanent Under Secretary of State for Foreign Affairs.

Caffey, W., Brigadier General, USA, head of special operations, AFHQ, Algiers.

Campbell, John, member of British mission to Partisans.

Campbell, Ronald Ian, British Minister to Yugoslavia.

Canaris, Wilhelm, Admiral, chief of the German Intelligence Service.

Cankar, Izidor, Dr., Minister in Yugoslav Government-in-Exile.

Cannon, Cavendish, American Foreign Service officer.

Cavallero, Ugo, General, Chief of the Italian General Staff.

Churchill, Randolph F.E.S., British liaison officer with the Partisans, son of Prime Minister Churchill.

Churchill, Winston S., British Prime Minister.

Ciano, Galeazzo, Italian Foreign Minister.

Cincar-Marković, Aleksandar, Yugoslav Foreign Minister.

Clark, Mark, General, USA Commander, U.S. 5th Army, later Allied commander in Italy.

Clark Kerr, see Kerr.

Clissold, Stephen, British liaison officer with the Partisans; author of *Whirlwind*.

Constan, Peter, American Foreign Service officer.

Cox, Arthur M., OSS officer in Bari.

Crawford, Robert W., American officer in Drvar.

Cripps, Sir Stafford, British Ambassador to the Soviet Union.

Cunningham, Sir Andrew, Admiral of the Fleet, R.N., First Sea Lord and Chief of the Naval Staff; member of the Combined Chiefs of Staff.

Cunningham, Sir John, Admiral, R.N., Commander in Chief, Allied Fleet in the Mediterranean.

Cvetković, Dragiša, Yugoslav Prime Minister.

Dalton, Hugh, British Minister of Economic Warfare.

Dapčević, Peko, Partisan commander.

Davidson, Basil, head of Yugoslav section, SOE Cairo; author of *Partisan Picture*.

Davis, Elmer, director, OWI.

Deakin, F. W., British liaison officer with the Partisans; author of *The Embattled Mountain*.

Deane, John R., Major General, USA, chief of the United States military mission to the Soviet Union.

Dedijer, Vladimir, Partisan officer; author of *Dnevnik, Josip Broz Tito*.

De Luce, Daniel, AP correspondent.

Deranian, B. Nelson, OSS officer in Bari.

Devers, Jacob L., Lieutenant General, USA, Deputy Supreme Allied Commander, Mediterranean Theater.

Diklić, George, Yugoslav-Canadian member of "Hoathley I" mission.

Dill, Sir John, Chief of the British Imperial General Staff.

Dimitrov, Georgi, General Secretary of the Comintern.

Dippold, Benignus, German commanding general of 717th Infantry Division.

Djilas, Milovan, Member of Politburo of Central Committee of CPY; later head of Partisan military mission in Moscow.

Djonović, Jovan, Yugoslav representative in Cairo.

Djujić, Momčilo *Pop* (Father), Četnik officer.

Djurić, Radoslav, Četnik officer who switched to Partisans.

Djurišić, Pavle, Četnik officer.

Donovan, William J., Colonel, later Brigadier General, USA, director, OSS.

Dragičević, Veljko, radio operator who accompanied Captain Hudson.

Drapšin, Petar, Partisan commander.

Druzić, Milan, Yugoslav-Canadian member of "Hoathley I" mission.

Dunn, James Clement, American Foreign Service officer, director, Office of European Affairs, Department of State; later Assistant Secretary of State.

Eaker, Ira C., Lieutenant General, USA, Air Commander in Chief, Mediterranean Allied Air Forces.

Eden, Anthony, British Secretary of State for Foreign Affairs.

Eisenhower, Dwight D., General, USA, Commander in Chief, Allied Forces, Northwest Africa; later Supreme Commander, Allied Expeditionary Forces.

Ellen, W., American officer in Bari.

Elliot, Sir William, Air Vice-Marshal, R.A.F., commander, Balkan Air Force.

Erdeljac, Petar, Yugoslav-Canadian member of "Fungus" mission.

Farish, Linn M., American liaison officer with the Partisans.

Felber, H. G., German commanding general in Serbia.

Floyd, Sir Henry, British officer in Partisan territory.

Förtsch, Hermann, General, chief of staff of German Balkan command.

Fotić, Constantin, Yugoslav Minister, later Ambassador, to the United States.

Frangeš, Ivan, Counselor of Yugoslav Embassy in Washington.

Franz Ferdinand, Austrian archduke.

Gammell, Sir James, General, chief of staff of General Wilson.

Gavrilović, Dr. Milan, Yugoslav Minister to the Soviet Union.

George VI, King of England.

Glaise von Horstenau, Edmund, German plenipotentiary general in Croatia.

Glavin, Edward J. F., commander of OSS in Caserta.

Glenconner, Lord, head of SOE Cairo.

Goodfellow, Preston, official of OSS.

Gorshkov, A. P., Major General, deputy head of Soviet mission to Partisans.

Green, Edward J., commander of OSS base in Bari.

Grew, Joseph C., U.S. Under Secretary of State.

Grol, Milan, Dr., member of Yugoslav Government in 1945.

Guenther, Gustav, head of OSS mission in Cairo.

Gusev, F. T., Soviet Ambassador to Britain.

Halifax, Viscount, later Earl of, British Ambassador to the United States.

Harcourt, Viscount, commander of SOE base in Bari.

Harriman, W. Averell, U.S. Ambassador to the Soviet Union.

Harrison, H. D., editor of Yugoslav section of BBC.

Harwood, Sir Henry, Admiral, R.N., Commander, British Fleet, Mediterranean.

Has, Herta, mother of Tito's second son.

Hayden, Sterling (John Hamilton), OSS officer; author of *Wanderer*.

Heinz, Friedrich W., German officer of the Brandenburg Division.

Henniker-Major, John, British liaison officer with the Partisans.

Hitler, Adolf, Chancellor of the German Reich.

Hopkins, Harry L., special assistant to President Franklin D. Roosevelt.

Hudson, D. T. (Bill), British liaison officer with the Četniks.

Hull, Cordell, U.S. Secretary of State.

Humo, Olga, Tito's interpreter.

Hunter, A. D. N., British liaison officer with the Partisans.

Huntington, Ellery C., Jr., official of OSS, later head of American military mission to the Partisans.

Huot, Louis, head of special operations section, OSS Cairo; author of *Guns for Tito.*

Ilić, Bogoljub, General, Yugoslav Minister of the Army and Navy, later only of the Army.

Ismay, Sir Hastings, Lieutenant General, Deputy Secretary to the British War Cabinet and Chief of Staff to the Minister of Defence.

Javorski, Boža, Četnik officer.

Jeftić, Bogoljub, Yugoslav Ambassador to Britain.

Jephson, Ronald, British radio operator.

Jevdjević, Dobrosav, Četnik officer.

Jibilian, Arthur, radio operator of U.S. Air Crew Rescue Unit.

Jones, William D., British liaison officer with the Partisans.

Jovanović, Arso, Chief of Staff of National Liberation Army.

Jovanović, Slobodan, Prime Minister of Yugoslav Government-in-Exile.

Joyce, Robert P., Foreign Service officer on loan to OSS, head of secret intelligence at OSS Bari.

Kalabić, Nikola, Četnik officer.

Kardelj, Edvard, member of Politburo of Central Committee of CPY.

Kasche, Siegfried, German Minister in Croatia.

Keeble, Brigadier, chief of staff, SOE Cairo.

Keitel, Wilhelm, Field Marshal, Chief of the German High Command.

Kerr, Sir Archibald Clark, British Ambassador to the Soviet Union.

Keserović, Dragutin, Četnik officer.

King, Ernest J., Admiral, USN, Commander in Chief of the Fleet and Chief of Naval Operations; member of the Joint Chiefs of Staff and of the Combined Chiefs of Staff.

Kirk, Alexander C., U.S. political adviser to the Supreme Allied Commander, Mediterranean Theater.

Kiselev, A. F., Major General, head of Soviet mission to Partisans.

Klugman, James, official of SOE.

Knežević, Radoje, adviser to King Peter.

Knežević, Živan L., secretary of Yugoslav War Cabinet, later military attaché in Washington; author of *Why the Allies Abandoned the Yugoslav Army of General Mihailović*.

Knight, Donald, British liaison officer with Partisans.

Koch, Robert, commander of OSS base in Bari.

Korneyev, N. V., General, head of Soviet mission to Partisans.

Kosanović, Sava, Dr., Minister in Yugoslav Government-in-Exile.

Kovač, Ivan, Četnik representative at AFHQ.

Kovačević, Blagoje, Četnik guard.

Kraigher, George, Colonel, U.S. Army Air Forces.

Kramer, Ellsworth, American liaison officer with the Četniks.

Krek, Miha, member of Yugoslav Government-in-Exile.

Krnjević, Juraj, member of Yugoslav Government-in-Exile.

Lada-Mocarski, Valerian, OSS officer in Cairo.

Lalatović, Mirko, Četnik officer.

Lalich, Nicholas, American liaison officer with the Četniks.

Lane, Arthur Bliss, U.S. Minister to Yugoslavia.

Law, Richard K., British Minister of State.

Lawrence, Christie, British officer in Yugoslavia, author of *Irregular Adventure*.

Leahy, William D., Admiral, USN, Chief of Staff to the Commander in Chief of the United States Army and Navy, member of the Joint Chiefs of Staff and of the Combined Chiefs of Staff.

Lebedev, Victor Z., Soviet Chargé d'Affaires in Yugoslavia.

Lehman, Herbert H., director general, UNRRA.

Lemnitzer, Lyman L., General, USA.

Leontić, Ljubo, Yugoslav Ambassador to Britain.

Leskošek, Franc, member of Politburo of Central Committee of CPY.

Likić, Slobodan, Četnik radio operator.

Lindsay, Franklin A., American liaison officer with the Partisans, later head of OSS mission in Belgrade.

List, Wilhelm, Field Marshal, Wehrmacht Commander, Southeast.

Litvinov, M. M., Soviet Ambassador to the United States.

Ljotić, Dimitrije, Serbian Fascist leader.

Lofts, P. H. A., Lieutenant, British signals officer.

Löhr, Alexander, General, commander of the 12th Army; later commander of German Army Group E; later commander in chief in the Balkans.

Lozovsky, S. A., Assistant Minister for Foreign Affairs of the Soviet Union.

Lukačević, Voja, Četnik officer.

Lüters, Rudolf, General, commander of German troops in Croatia.

Macfarlane, F. N. Mason, chief, Allied military mission with the Italian Government.

Maclean, Fitzroy H. R., Brigadier, head of British mission to the Partisans; author of *Eastern Approaches, Disputed Barricade.*

Macmillan, Harold, British political adviser to the Supreme Allied Commander, Mediterranean Theater.

MacVeagh, Lincoln, U.S. Ambassador to the Yugoslav Government-in-Exile in Cairo.

McBaine, Turner H., OSS officer in Cairo.

McCloy, John J., U.S. Assistant Secretary of War.

McDowell, Robert H., head of American intelligence mission to Mihailović.

McNarney, Joseph T., Lieutenant General, USA, Deputy Supreme Allied Commander, Mediterranean Theater.

Maisky, I. M., Soviet Ambassador to Britain.

Makiedo, Sergije, Partisan officer; author of *Prva Partizanska Misija.*

Mandić, Ante, member of Regency Council.

Mandić, Nikola, Četnik guard.

Mansfield, Walter R., American liaison officer with the Četniks.

Marshall, George C., General, USA, Chief of Staff of the Army; member of the Joint Chiefs of Staff and of the Combined Chiefs of Staff.

Marušić, Drago, Dr., Partisan sympathizer who joined Yugoslav Government-in-Exile

Masterson, Tom, official of SOE.

Matl, Josef, German intelligence officer.

Matthews, H. Freeman, Counselor of American Embassy in London; later deputy director, Office of European Affairs, Department of State.

Mauran, Frank, official of OSS.

Merrill, Frederick T., American Foreign Service officer.

Mihailović, Dragoljub (Draža), Colonel, later General, Minister of the Army, Navy and Air Force in Yugoslav Government-in-Exile, Chief of Staff of Supreme Command of Yugoslav Army in the Homeland.

Milanović, Vladimir, Yugoslav Assistant Foreign Minister.

Milodragovich, John, American liaison officer with the Četniks.

Milojević, Miloje, Partisan officer.

Milutinović, Ivan, member of Politburo of Central Committee of CPY.

Milutinović, *Pop* (Father), Serbian priest.

Mirković, Borivoje, commander of the Yugoslav Air Force.

Moljević, Stevan, political adviser to Mihailović.

Molotov, V. M., Minister for Foreign Affairs of the Soviet Union.

Murphy, Robert D., U.S. political adviser to the Supreme Allied Commander, Mediterranean Theater.

Mussolini, Benito, Italian Prime Minister.

Musulin, George, American liaison officer with the Četniks.

Nadj, Kosta, Partisan commander.

Nedić, Milan, head of the puppet state of Serbia.

Neubacher, Hermann, German Special Ambassador for Southeastern Europe.

Neveleff, L. A., Lieutenant Colonel, U.S. Army Air Forces.

Ninčić, Momčilo, Yugoslav Foreign Minister.

Norden, Carl F., American Foreign Service officer.

Novikov, N. V., Soviet Ambassador to the Yugoslav Government-in-Exile in Cairo and London.

O'Donovan, Patrick, Atherton's radio operator.

Ostojić, Zaharije, Četnik officer.

Ott, Hans, German engineer.

Paget, General Sir Bernard, Commander in Chief, British Forces, Middle East.

Pantić, Branislav, Četnik officer.

Patterson, Richard C., U.S. Ambassador to Yugoslavia.

Paul, Prince, Regent of Yugoslavia.

Pavelić, Ante, leader of the Fascist state of Croatia.

Pavlović, Dragoslav, Četnik officer.

Pavlović, Pavle, Yugoslav-Canadian member of "Fungus" mission.

Pećanac, Kosta, leader of the Četnik organization.

Perović, Lieutenant, Četnik officer.

Peter I, King of Serbia, later of the Serbs, Croats and Slovenes.

Peter II, King of Yugoslavia.

Pfeiffer, Timothy, American liaison officer with the Partisans.

Pijade, Moše, member of CPY.

Pirzio Biroli, Alessandro, General, Italian military governor of Montenegro.

Plotnikov, V. A., Soviet Minister to Yugoslavia.

Poduje, Jože, assistant to Sergije Makiedo.

Popović, Koča, Partisan commander.

Popović, Milentije, Partisan officer.

Popović, Vladimir, Yugoslav Ambassador to the Soviet Union.

Portal, Sir Charles, Air Chief Marshal, RAF, Chief of the Air Staff, member of the Combined Chiefs of Staff.

Pribičević, Adam, Serbian politician.

Sernec, Dušan, Member of Regency Council.

Shantz, Harold, Counselor of American Embassy to the Yugoslav Government-in-Exile in Cairo, later in London; later assigned to Belgrade.

Shepardson, Whitney, OSS official in Washington.

Simić, Alexander, Yugoslav-Canadian member of "Fungus" mission.

Simić, Stanoje, Yugoslav Minister, later Ambassador, to the Soviet Union; later Ambassador to the United States.

Simović, Dušan, General, commander of the Yugoslav Air Force, later Yugoslav Prime Minister; later also Minister of Navy and Air Force.

Smodlaka, Josip, Partisan officer.

Stalin, I. V., General Secretary of the CP of the USSR, later also Chairman of the Council of People's Commissars of the Soviet Union.

Stambolić, Petar, member of CPY.

Stanišić, Bajo, Četnik officer.

Starčević, Ivan, member of British mission to Partisans.

Stärker, Rudi, official of German Intelligence Service.

Stawell, W. A. M., Major General, head of SOE in Cairo, later commander of special operations east of Italy.

Stettinius, Edward R., Jr., U.S. Under Secretary of State, later Secretary of State.

Stevenson, Ralph C. S., British Ambassador to Yugoslavia.

Stilinović, Marijan, Partisan officer.

Stimson, Henry L., U.S. Secretary of War.

Street, Vivian, British liaison officer with the Partisans.

Stuart, W. F., British liaison officer with the Partisans.

Šubašić, Ivan, Governor (Ban) of Croatia, later Prime Minister of Yugoslav Government-in-Exile in London.

Subbotić, Ivan, Yugoslav Minister to Britain.

Sulzberger, C. L., correspondent of *The New York Times*.

Šutej, Juraj, Dr., Minister in Yugoslav Government-in-Exile.

Sweet-Escott, Bickham, official of SOE, author of *Baker Street Irregular*.

Talbot, John, Reuters correspondent.

Tedder, Sir Arthur, Air Chief Marshal, RAF, Air Commander in Chief, Mediterranean Air Command.

Terzić, Velimir, member of Partisan military mission in Moscow.

Thayer, Charles W., American Foreign Service officer on loan to OSS; deputy head, later head of American mission to the Partisans.

Thompson, Robert, OSS officer.

Tito, Josip Broz, General Secretary of the CPY, Commander in Chief of National Liberation Army, later Yugoslav Prime Minister.

Todorović, Borislav, Četnik officer, later assistant military attaché of Yugoslav Embassy in Washington.

Tofte, Hans, OSS officer.

Tolbukhin, Fyodor, Marshal of the Red Army.

Topalović, Živko, Dr., Serbian politician.

Toulmin, John E., head of OSS mission in Cairo.

Trifunović, Miša, Prime Minister of Yugoslav Government-in-Exile.

Truman, Harry S, President of the United States.

Uzelac, M., Četnik officer.

Vašić, Dragiša, political adviser to Mihailović.

Velebit, Vladimir, Dr., member of CPY, head of Partisan military mission in London.

Vlahović, Veljko, member of CPY.

Voroshilov, K. E., Marshal, military adviser to Stalin.

Vučković, Zvonimir, Četnik officer.

Vukmanović-Tempo, Svetozar, member of CPY.

Vukosavljević, Sreten, Partisan sympathizer who joined Yugoslav Government-in-Exile.

Vyshinsky, A. Y., assistant, later first deputy Minister for Foreign Affairs of the Soviet Union.

Weichs, Maximilian von, Field Marshal, German commander in chief in the Balkans.

Weil, Richard, Jr., American liaison officer with the Partisans.

Welles, Sumner, U.S. Under Secretary of State.

West, Paul, OSS officer in Cairo.

Whetherly, Robin, British liaison officer with the Partisans.

Wilson, General Sir Henry Maitland, Commander in Chief, British Forces, Middle East, later Supreme Allied Commander, Mediterranean Theater.

Winant, John G., U.S. Ambassador to Britain.

Wroughton, Walter, member of British mission to the Partisans.

Wuchinich, George, American liaison officer with the Partisans.

Zečević, Vlada *Pop* (Father), Četnik who switched to the Partisans.

Zujović, Sreten, Deputy Commander in Chief of the National Liberation Army.

Chronological Table

1941	Yugoslavia	General
January		22 Tobruk captured by British forces.
	23–25 Col. Donovan visits Belgrade.	
February		6 Benghazi captured by British forces.
		11 British decide to halt advance in Benghazi and offer help to Greece.
	14 Yugoslav Prime Minister and Foreign Minister meet Hitler.	
		22 Eden and Dill in Athens.
		24 British approve Greek expedition.
		25 Mogadiscio occupied by British forces.
		26 Eden and Dill in Ankara.
March		1 Bulgaria joins Tripartite Pact.
		2 Eden and Dill back in Athens.
	4 Prince Paul visits Hitler in Berchtesgaden.	4 German troops enter Bulgaria.
		4 First British troops leave Egypt for Greece.
		11 Lend-Lease Act becomes law in U.S.
	21 U.S. Minister in Belgrade offers Yugoslavia lend-lease aid.	
	25 Yugoslavia signs Tripartite Pact.	

1941	Yugoslavia	General
March	27 Coup d'état in Belgrade.	
		30 German counteroffensive launched in North Africa.
April	1 Dill in Belgrade.	
	6 Germans invade Yugoslavia.	6 Germans invade Greece.
		6 British enter Addis Ababa.
		8 Salonika occupied.
	14 and 16 King Peter and Yugoslav Government leave country for Athens.	
	17 Yugoslavia capitulates to Germans.	
	21 Yugoslav Government in Jerusalem.	21 British decide to leave Greece.
		23 Greek Government goes to Crete.
		30 Germans decide to postpone attack on USSR.
May	12 Mihailović reaches Ravna Gora.	
	16 U.S. Minister leaves Belgrade.	
		20 Germans attack Crete.
June		18 German-Turkish neutrality pact signed.
		22 Germans invade USSR.
	26 Churchill receives Yugoslav Prime Minister.	
		30 Germans enter Lwow.
July	4 Communist Party of Yugoslavia decides to rise against occupier.	
		5 Germans reach Dnieper line.
		21 Russians evacuate Bessarabia.
August		14 Smolensk evacuated.
	17 Partisans inform Comintern of their military activities.	

1941	Yugoslavia	General
August	29 General Nedić forms puppet government in Serbia.	19 Leningrad attacked.
September	5 U.S. appoints Minister to Yugoslav Government-in-Exile. 13 Mihailović's first radio message to his Government received in London. 19 Mihailović and Tito meet. 20 Capt. Hudson arrives in Yugoslavia.	19 Germans occupy Kiev.
October		2 Germans launch offensive against Moscow. 16 Russians evacuate Odessa. 20 Soviet Government moves to Kuibyshev.
	21 Germans execute many male residents of Kragujevac. 27 Tito and Mihailović meet again. 28 Četnik-Partisan clashes begin.	
November	14 Mihailović meets German officers. 18 Third Četnik-Partisan meeting. End of November: German First Offensive drives Četniks to Ravna Gora and Partisans out of Serbia.	14 Red Army counterattacks on Moscow front. 22 Germans enter Rostov. 28 Red Army recaptures Rostov.
December	7 Mihailović promoted to brigadier general.	7 Japanese bomb Pearl Harbor. 8 U.S. and Britain declare war on Japan. 8 Tobruk relieved. 11 Italy and Germany declare war on U.S.

1941	Yugoslavia	General
December		22 Major Japanese attack on Philippines.
	24 Tito reaches Rogatica in Bosnia.	24 Benghazi recaptured by the British.
		25 Hong Kong surrenders.
January (1942)	11 Jovanović appointed Yugoslav Prime Minister and Mihailović Minister of the Army, Navy and Air Force.	2 Japanese enter Manila. 11 Japanese enter Kuala Lumpur.
	15 (approx.) German Second Offensive against Partisans launched.	
		20 Japanese invade Burma. 21 Rommel counterattacks in North Africa.
February	4 Major Atherton lands in Yugoslavia.	
	8 Partisans set up Soviet Republic in Montenegro.	
		15 Singapore falls. 20 Russian winter offensive halted. 28 Japanese land in Java.
March		8 Japanese land in New Guinea. 17 General MacArthur appointed Commander, Southwest Pacific.
	19 Atherton arrives at Partisan headquarters in Foča. 31 Third Offensive launched against Partisans.	
April	20 Yugoslav Minister in USSR instructed to ask Soviets to persuade Partisans to place themselves under Mihailović.	18 Doolittle air raid on Tokyo.

1942	Yugoslavia	General
May		6 Corregidor falls. 8 Germans launch attack in Crimea. 8–9 U.S. victory in Battle of Coral Sea.
	9 Jovanović asks the British for arms and ammunition. 16 Roosevelt decides to send food to Yugoslavia.	
		26 Rommel attacks in North Africa. 30 1,000 RAF bombers raid Cologne.
June	1 Mihailović arrives in Montenegro.	4–7 Battle of Midway. 18 Churchill arrives in Washington. 21 Tobruk captured by Germans.
	22 King Peter arrives in U.S. 24 Partisans begin long march north.	
July		1 Rommel held at El Alamein. 1 Sevastopol falls.
	6 Radio Free Yugoslavia accuses Mihailović and Četniks of collaboration.	
		23 Rostov captured by Germans.
	24 U.S.-Yugoslav lend-lease agreement signed.	
August	3 Yugoslav démarche in Kuibyshev.	
		7 U.S. landings in Solomon Islands. 19 British raid on Dieppe.
September	9 Mihailović calls for civil disobedience to Nedić regime. 20 Yugoslav Government asks Mihailović to sabotage German communication lines.	

1942	Yugoslavia	General
September		21 Fighting in suburbs of Stalingrad.
October	5–6 Sumner Welles discusses Yugoslav situation with Soviet Ambassador.	20 German attack on Stalingrad fails. 25 German-Italian attack on El Alamein fails.
November	5 Bihać entered by Partisans. 26 Partisan assembly at Bihać.	4 British offensive in Egypt. 6 Rommel races back to Libya with remnants of his army. 8 U.S. armed forces land in North Africa. Algiers falls to Allies. 12 Hitler sends army to Vichy France. 13 Tobruk again in British hands. 19 Russians counterattack at Stalingrad.
December	16 Yugoslav Government issues statement summarizing Mihailović's actions. 25 Col. Bailey arrives at Četnik headquarters. 31 Welles assures Fotić that U.S. Government has full confidence in Mihailović.	12 Germans fail to relieve encircled forces at Stalingrad. 13 Rommel dislodged from Agheila. 22 Eisenhower pushes toward Tunis.
January (1943)	1 Eisenhower sends New Year's greetings to Mihailović.	

1943	Yugoslavia	General
January	17 Radio Free Yugoslavia invites Allied commission to come to Yugoslavia. 20 Axis Fourth Offensive begins.	14–24 Casablanca Conference (Roosevelt, Churchill; also Giraud, DeGaulle). 30 British bomb Berlin. 31 General Paulus captured at Stalingrad.
February	 28 Mihailović's speech attacks British.	14–16 Rostov and Kharkov recaptured by Red Army. 17 Germans attack U.S. forces in Tunisia.
March	3 British decide to send missions to Partisans. Mid-March: Partisans break out of Axis ring. 25 Partisan representatives arrive in Zagreb. 30 British Government protests Mihailović's speech.	4 U.S. victory in Battle of Bismarck Sea. 16 Kharkov retaken by Germans. 23 British break through Axis defenses in Tunisia.
April	6 Yugoslav Government shares British concern about Mihailović's speech. 15 (approx.) OSS mission established in Cairo. 21 Canadians of Yugoslav origin drop "blind" into Partisan territory.	7 U.S. attacks from west in Tunisia. 12 British attack from east in Tunisia.

1943	Yugoslavia	General
April		26 Soviet Union breaks relations with Polish Government-in-Exile.
May		7 U.S. troops take Bizerte; British enter Tunis.
		11 Churchill arrives in Washington.
		12 Battle of North Africa ends.
	15 (approx.) Mihailović returns to Serbia.	
	15 German Fifth Offensive begins.	
	18 First British mission arrives in Partisan territory.	
		21 Comintern disbanded.
	28 British mission arrives at Tito's headquarters.	
June		11 Pantellaria surrenders.
		12 Lampedusa occupied.
	23 British policy changes.	
	26 New Yugoslav Government.	
July	3 Alexander sends message to Tito.	
		10 Sicily invaded.
		25 Mussolini ousted.
	28 Maclean to head British mission to Tito.	
August		1 U.S. bombers attack Ploesti oil fields.
	10 New Yugoslav Government.	
		17–24 First Quebec Conference.
	18 First American liaison officer arrives at Četnik headquarters.	
	22 First American liaison officer arrives at Partisan headquarters.	
		23 Kharkov retaken by Red Army.

1943	Yugoslavia	General
September		8 Italy surrenders.
	9 Partisans, Četniks and Germans all move to take over Italian-occupied territory (start of German Sixth Offensive).	9 Allies land at Salerno.
		10 Germans seize Rome.
		23 Red Army takes Smolensk.
	28 King Peter and Government arrive in Cairo.	
October		1 Allies take Naples.
	2 Četniks attack Višegrad.	
		13 Italy declares war on Germany.
	15 OSS starts trans-Adriatic shipping operation.	
		19 Moscow Foreign Ministers' Conference begins.
		25 Russians cross Dnieper at Dniepropetrovsk.
	29 Farish report.	
November		6 Red Army liberates Kiev.
		20 U.S. troops land on Tarawa and Makin.
		22 First Cairo Conference begins.
		28 Tehran Conference begins.
	29 Partisan Congress at Jajce.	
December	1 Tehran Conference promises supplies and equipment for Partisans.	
	3 Partisan military mission leaves for Cairo.	3 Second Cairo Conference begins.
	8 General Wilson asks Mihailović to undertake two sabotage operations	
	10 Churchill meets King Peter.	
		14 Russians attack around Vitebsk.
		15 Allied attacks halted in Italy.
		24 Russians attack beyond Kiev.

1944	Yugoslavia	General
January	8 Churchill writes Tito. 19 General Wilson to set up military mission to Tito. 25–28 Četnik congress at Ba.	 22 Allies land at Anzio. 27 German siege of Leningrad lifted.
February	 20 (approx.) British decide to withdraw liaison officers from Četniks. 23 Soviet military mission arrives in Partisan-held Yugoslavia.	3 Red Army enters Estonia. 12 Attack on Mt. Cassino. 24 First big combined Anglo-American air attacks by day and night on single German target (Schweinfurt).
March	 10 King Peter and Prime Minister Purić arrive in London. 15 (approx.) U.S. decides to send intelligence mission to Mihailović. 18 Partisans attack both Germans and Četniks.	6 Red Army begins spring offensive in Ukraine. 18 Germans enter Hungary. 30 Russians take Cernauti in Rumania.
April	7 General Donovan proposes establishment of independent American mission to Partisans. 16 U.S. bombs Belgrade. 20 British-U.S. discussions regarding Yugoslavia in London.	 10 Red Army captures Odessa. 15 Red Army takes Tarnopol. 22 U.S. landings in Dutch New Guinea.

1944	Yugoslavia	General
May	1 Velebit arrives in London.	
		9 Russians capture Sevastopol.
		11 Allied attack in Italy.
	12 Roosevelt answers King Peter's letter.	
		18 Mt. Cassino taken.
		23 Allied force in Anzio joins in offensive.
	24 King Peter dismisses Purić.	
	25 Germans launch Seventh Offensive; Tito almost captured.	
	29, 30, 31 British liaison officers leave Mihailović.	
June	1 Šubašić becomes New Yugoslav Prime Minister.	
	1 Balkan Air Force set up.	
	3 Tito evacuated from Yugoslavia to Bari.	
		4 U.S. troops enter Rome.
		6 Allies land in Normandy.
	8 Tito arrives on Vis.	
		13 First V-1 lands in England.
	16 Šubašić and Tito meet.	16 U.S. bombers attack Japan.
		26 U.S. troops enter Cherbourg.
July		3 Red Army enters Minsk.
	7 Šubašić Government sworn in.	
		19 Allies take Leghorn.
		21 U.S. troops land in Guam.
		28 Red Army takes Brest-Litovsk.
August		1 Poles rise in Warsaw; Russians halt advance near Warsaw.
	2 U.S. Air Crew Rescue Unit arrives at Mihailović's headquarters.	
		4 Allies enter Florence.
	5 Tito goes to Caserta.	

1944	Yugoslavia	General
August	12 Tito meets Churchill in Italy.	
	12 225 U.S. airmen flown out of Serbia.	
	14 U.S. military mission arrives on Vis.	
		20 Roosevelt and Churchill appeal to Stalin to help Poles in Warsaw; appeal rejected.
		24 U.S. troops enter Grenoble.
		25 Paris liberated.
		25 Allies attack Gothic Line.
		25 Rumania declares war on Germany.
	26 U.S. intelligence mission arrives at Mihailović's headquarters.	
	31 Murphy visits Tito on Vis.	31 Russians enter Bucharest.
September	1 "Ratweek" begins in Partisan territory.	
	1 Mihailović orders general mobilization.	
		2 Allies enter Pisa.
		3 British enter Brussels.
		5 Russians declare war on Bulgaria.
	6 Russians reach Yugoslav border.	
		8 Bulgaria declares war on Germany.
		10 Finland surrenders.
	12 King Peter broadcasts to Yugoslavia.	11–16 Second Quebec Conference.
		12 U.S. 1st Army enters Germany.
	18 Tito leaves Vis for Moscow.	18 U.S. planes drop supplies to Warsaw.
	20 Patterson designated U.S. Ambassador.	
		21 Allies enter Rimini.
	29 Partisan-Red Army agreement for entry of Soviet	

1944	Yugoslavia	General
September	troops into Yugoslavia. Late in month: Mihailović leaves Serbia for Bosnia.	
October	1 Red Army enters Yugoslavia.	
		3 Warsaw uprising ends. 5 Red Army enters Hungary.
	6 Tito returns to Yugoslavia from Moscow.	
		7 Germans decide to leave Greece.
	8 U.S. and British military missions arrive in Serbia.	
		9 Churchill and Eden in Moscow; agreement on demarcation between British and Soviets in the Balkans.
	15 Red Army and Partisans take Niš.	15 Allied forces enter Greece.
		18 Greek Government returns to Athens. 19 Philippines invaded.
	20 Partisans and Red Army enter Belgrade.	20 East Prussia invaded by Red Army. 20 Aachen taken by U.S. troops.
	23 Šubašić arrives in Yugoslavia. 28 Floyd Force lands in Yugoslavia.	23–26 U.S. victory in battle for Leyte Gulf.
November	1 U.S. intelligence mission leaves Mihailović. 1 New Tito-Šubašić agreement. 2 Roosevelt replies to King Peter.	
		5 U.S. air raid on Manila.
	17 Churchill meets King Peter. 17 Patterson presents credentials. 20 Šubašić in Moscow.	
		22 U.S. troops take Metz.

1944	Yugoslavia	General
December		3 Civil war in Greece.
		3 Russians prepare for attack on Budapest.
	7 Šubašić and Tito sign two additional agreements.	
		16 Germans counterattack in Ardennes.
		20 Germans advance toward Liège.
	21 King Peter tells Churchill that Tito-Šubašić agreement is unconstitutional.	
		25 Churchill and Eden in Athens.
	27 U.S. Air Crew Rescue Unit leaves Mihailović.	
		31 Lublin Committee sets up new Polish regime.
January (1945)		3 Allies attack in Ardennes.
		9 U.S. troops land on Luzon.
	11 King Peter rejects Tito-Šubašić agreement.	
	16 First U.S. diplomatic representatives arrive in Belgrade.	
		17 Red Army takes Warsaw.
		20 Hungarian Government signs armistice.
	22 King Peter dismisses Šubašić.	22 Roosevelt leaves for Yalta Conference.
		22 Burma Road to China opened.
	29 King Peter reappoints Šubašić.	
		30 Malta Conference begins.
February		4 Yalta Conference begins.
		4 U.S. troops enter Manila.
	11 Yalta Conference asks that Tito-Šubašić agreement be put into effect.	
		13 Red Army clears Budapest.
		13–14 Dresden air raid.
	21 Field Marshal Alexander visits Tito.	

1945	Yugoslavia	General
February		26 U.S. troops reach Rhine south of Düsseldorf.
March	3 Regents appointed by King Peter.	
		6 Russians set up government in Rumania.
	7 New Yugoslav Government formed with Tito as Prime Minister.	7 U.S. troops cross Rhine at Remagen.
		8 Negotiations begin for surrender of German troops in Italy.
	14 British Ambassador arrives in Belgrade.	
	17 Mihailović receives German emissary.	
	20 Partisans begin offensive.	
	21 Soviet Ambassador arrives in Belgrade.	
		29 American troops occupy Frankfurt.
		29. Red Army enters Austria.
		30 Red Army takes Danzig.
	31 American Ambassador arrives in Belgrade.	
April		1 U.S. troops land on Okinawa.
	2 Ambassador Patterson talks to Tito.	
	5 Tito leaves for Moscow.	
	6 Partisans take Sarajevo.	
	11 Tito signs treaty with USSR.	
		12 President Roosevelt dies.
		13 Red Army takes Vienna.
		14 Eisenhower halts on Elbe.
		18 U.S. Army reaches Czechoslovak frontier.
		19 U.S. troops take Leipzig.
		21 Bologna taken by American troops.
		22 Allies reach Po River.
	25 Partisans take Fiume (Rijeka).	25 U.S. and Russian troops meet.

1945	Yugoslavia	General
April		25 Russians encircle Berlin.
		25 San Francisco U.N. Conference opens.
		28 Mussolini killed.
		29 Germans surrender in Italy.
	30 Partisans reach outskirts of Trieste.	30 U.S. troops in Munich.
		30 Hitler commits suicide.
May	1 Partisans meet Allied troops at Monfalcone.	1 Japanese leave Rangoon.
	2 Partisans receive German surrender in Trieste.	2 Berlin surrenders.
		5 Russians ask Eisenhower to halt in Czechoslovakia.
		7 Germans sign terms of surrender to Allies.

Index

ABOUT THE AUTHOR

Walter R. Roberts, a graduate of Cambridge University where he was a Rouse Ball Scholar at Trinity College, was doing research at the Harvard Law School when the United States was drawn into the Second World War in 1941. He entered Government service the following year, with the Office of War Information, and now holds the position of Associate Director of the U.S. Information Agency, its highest career post.

His first assignment was broadcasting for the Voice of America to Nazi Germany, and his long years of Government service have included State Department experience as an adviser with the American delegation that met in hundreds of sessions leading to the Austrian State Treaty in 1955. Subsequently he was named Deputy Director of USIA's European area office, and in 1960 he was assigned to Yugoslavia as Counselor of the American Embassy.

It was then that he became aware of the inadequacy of the literature describing wartime events in and concerning Yugoslavia. He began to seek information that would answer the questions raised by the existing accounts and fill the gaps they left. This interest developed into a full-fledged research project which the author continued to pursue after he left Yugoslavia in 1966. With the bulk of the material in hand, a year at Brown University as Diplomat in Residence finally gave him the opportunity to write this book.